The Buddhist Roots of Zhu Xi's Philosophical Thought

The Buddhist Roots of Zhu Xi's Philosophical Thought

Edited by JOHN MAKEHAM

UNIVERSITY PRESS

Oxford University Press is a department of the University of Oxford. It furthers
the University's objective of excellence in research, scholarship, and education
by publishing worldwide. Oxford is a registered trade mark of Oxford University
Press in the UK and certain other countries.

Published in the United States of America by Oxford University Press
198 Madison Avenue, New York, NY 10016, United States of America.

© Oxford University Press 2018

All rights reserved. No part of this publication may be reproduced, stored in
a retrieval system, or transmitted, in any form or by any means, without the
prior permission in writing of Oxford University Press, or as expressly permitted
by law, by license, or under terms agreed with the appropriate reproduction
rights organization. Inquiries concerning reproduction outside the scope of the
above should be sent to the Rights Department, Oxford University Press, at the
address above.

You must not circulate this work in any other form
and you must impose this same condition on any acquirer.

Library of Congress Cataloging-in-Publication Data
Names: Makeham, John, 1955– writer of introduction.
Title: The Buddhist Roots of Zhu Xi's Philosophical Thought / John Makeham.
Description: New York : Oxford University Press, 2018. |
Includes bibliographical references and index.
Identifiers: LCCN 2017053676 (print) | LCCN 2017060682 (ebook) |
ISBN 978–0–19–087856–6 (updf) | ISBN 978–0–19–087857–3 (epub) |
ISBN 978–0–19–087858–0 (online content) | ISBN 978–0–19–087855–9 (hardcover)
Subjects: LCSH: Zhu, Xi, 1130-1200. | Neo-Confucianism. | Buddhist
philosophy. | Buddhism–China–Doctrines.
Classification: LCC B128.C54 (ebook) | LCC B128.C54 B84 2018 (print) |
DDC 181/.112–dc23
LC record available at https://lccn.loc.gov/2017053676

9 8 7 6 5 4 3 2 1

Printed by Sheridan Books, Inc., United States of America

Should you want to examine thoroughly the Buddhist doctrines in order to determine which to accept and which to reject, then you would certainly have already converted to Buddhism even before you've been able to complete your investigations! . . . Although most Confucians sooner or later stray into Buddhism, it is not their intention to do so—and do so, of course, by dint of circumstance. This is because even though they grow mentally and physically exhausted and wish to cease, they nevertheless feel uncomfortable about doing so and are unable to stop. And so, seeing that the Buddhists have a reasoned set of teachings, circumstances conspire to compel them to follow those teachings.

釋氏之說，若欲窮其說而去取之，則其說未能窮，固已化而為佛矣。. . . 儒者其卒多入異教，其志非願也，其勢自然如此。蓋智窮力屈，欲休來，又知得未安穩，休不得，故見人有一道理，其勢須從之。

—CHENG YI 程頤 (1033–1107), *Er Cheng ji* 二程集
(Collected Works of the Cheng Brothers)

CONTENTS

Acknowledgments ix
List of Contributors xi

Introduction 1
John Makeham

CHAPTER 1 The Radiant Mind: Zhu Xi and the Chan Doctrine of *Tathāgatagarbha* 36
John Jorgensen

CHAPTER 2 Zhu Xi's Critique of Buddhism: Selfishness, Salvation, and Self-Cultivation 122
Justin Tiwald

CHAPTER 3 Buddhism and Zhu Xi's Epistemology of Discernment 156
Stephen C. Angle

CHAPTER 4 The *Ti-Yong* 體用 Model and Its Discontents: Models of Ambiguous Priority in Chinese Buddhism and Zhu Xi's Neo-Confucianism 193
Brook A. Ziporyn

CHAPTER 5 Monism and the Problem of the Ignorance and Badness in Chinese Buddhism and Zhu Xi's Neo-Confucianism 277
John Makeham

Index 345

ACKNOWLEDGMENTS

On behalf of the contributors, I wish to thank the Australian Research Council for providing the DORA grant that made it possible to carry out the research and to conduct the workshops that underpin this volume; P. J. Ivanhoe for helping to conceive the project and for hosting the first workshop in 2013 at City University of Hong Kong; Dan Lusthaus for also helping to conceive the project and for contributing to the annual workshops; the Press's readers for their constructive feedback; and the Special Collections Division, National Central Library, Taiwan, for granting permission to reproduce the Dunhuang manuscript version (dating from the Five Dynasties) of the diagram from *Chan yuan zhuquan ji duxu* 禪源諸詮集都序 (Preface to the Collected Writings on the Chan Source) in the Appendix to Chapter 5.

—John Makeham, August 2017

CONTRIBUTORS

Stephen C. Angle is Professor of Philosophy and East Asian Studies, Wesleyan University. A philosophy writer and researcher specializing in Chinese Philosophy, Confucianism, Neo-Confucianism, and comparative philosophy, his research focuses on philosophy's role in human rights, politics, and ethics both in China and globally.

John Jorgensen is Senior Research Associate, China Studies Research Centre at La Trobe University. A specialist in Chinese, Japanese, and Korean Chan Buddhism, he taught at Griffith University in Queensland and was a researcher at the Australian National University before taking up his current role at La Trobe University.

John Makeham is Chair and Director of the China Studies Research Centre at La Trobe University. A specialist in the intellectual history of Chinese philosophy, he has a particular interest in Confucian thought throughout Chinese history and, in more recent years, in the influence of Sinitic Buddhist thought on pre-modern and modern Confucian philosophy. Educated in Australia, China, Taiwan, and Japan, he has held academic positions at Victoria University of Wellington, University of Adelaide, National Taiwan University, Chinese University of Hong Kong, and The Australian National University (ANU).

Justin Tiwald is Professor of Philosophy at San Francisco State University and has taught as a visiting professor at South China Normal University and the University of California Berkeley. He has published widely on Chinese thought, both as an area of historical inquiry and as regards its intersections with issues in contemporary philosophy. These include Confucian, Daoist, and Neo-Confucian accounts of moral psychology, well-being, and political authority, as well as the implications of Confucian views for virtue ethics, individual rights, and moral epistemology.

Brook A. Ziporyn is Professor of Chinese Religion, Philosophy, and Comparative Thought at the Divinity School, University of Chicago. He is a scholar of ancient and medieval Chinese religion and philosophy. Prior to joining the Divinity School faculty, he taught Chinese philosophy and religion at the University of Michigan (Department of East Asian Literature and Cultures), Northwestern University (Department of Religion and Department of Philosophy), Harvard University (Department of East Asian Literature and Civilization), and the National University of Singapore (Department of Philosophy).

The Buddhist Roots of Zhu Xi's Philosophical Thought

| Introduction

JOHN MAKEHAM

"NEO-CONFUCIANISM" REFERS TO an intellectual movement that reinvented Confucian thought during the Song dynasty (960–1279). The term also describes a set of family resemblances discerned across clusters of philosophical ideas, technical terms, arguments, and writings associated with particular figures from the Song to Qing (1644–1911) periods in China. Having become the orthodox ideology of the political and social elite in late imperial China, for seven hundred years it formed the ideological basis of the Chinese civil service examination system and constituted the core of educational training. It was also a theory of how to learn and how to apply learning, and was the arbiter of moral norms.[1] Neo-Confucian philosophy is the most influential body of Chinese philosophical discourse of the past millennium.[2] It not only extended to and was further developed in Japan, Korea, and Vietnam, profoundly shaping intellectual, institutional and social practices,[3] but its intellectual legacy also continues today in Greater China to animate New Confucian philosophy, the most vibrant form of contemporary Chinese philosophy.

One group of eleventh-century Neo-Confucian pioneers began to distinguish themselves from other *ru* 儒 (Confucians) by claiming to have

---

[1] For more detailed discussion of the term Neo-Confucian, see introduction to *Dao Companion to Neo-Confucian Philosophy*, ed. John Makeham (New York: Springer, 2010).
[2] For an authoritative, thematic-based introduction to Neo-Confucian philosophy, see Stephen C. Angle and Justin Tiwald, *Neo-Confucianism: A Philosophical Introduction* (Cambridge, UK: Polity Press, 2017). For a recent monograph on Neo-Confucian metaphysics and philosophy of mind, see JeeLoo Liu, *Neo-Confucianism: Metaphysics, Mind, and Morality* (Hoboken, NJ: Wiley-Blackwell, 2018).
[3] See, for example, the recent study by Philip J. Ivanhoe, *Confucian Reflections on Learning and the Moral Heart-Mind in China, Korea, and Japan* (New York: Oxford University Press, 2016).

rediscovered the Learning of the Way (*daoxue* 道學). Cheng Yi 程頤 (1033–1107) claimed that he had been the first since the classical period to take up the mantle of transmitting the *dao*—the learning of the sages—and to rediscover its significance. Elsewhere, he also included his elder brother, Cheng Hao 程灝 (1032–1085), as a transmitter.[4] Unlike Tang-dynasty Confucian thinker and essayist Han Yu 韓愈 (768–824)—who in his essay "Yuan dao" 原道 (Tracing the Way to its Source)[5] also described how the transmission of the way of the sages had been disrupted after Mencius—Daoxue thinkers emphasized it was the learning of the sages that had been rediscovered. It was the lost teachings of the sages that provided profound insights into the workings of a morally inflected cosmos and the place of humans and human society within that cosmos. This theme of rupture and recovery found in the writings of eleventh-century Daoxue thinkers more generally highlights a self-conscious awareness of new beginnings.[6]

These thinkers saw themselves as engaged in recovering the true and deep-seated roots of Sinitic culture—the teachings of the sages of antiquity as "transmitted" by Confucius and Mencius—which had been eclipsed since the Han dynasty (206 BC–AD 220) by foreign (Buddhist) and subversive (Daoist) ideologies resulting in political chaos and social dislocation. They maintained that reunifications begun in the Sui-Tang (581–907) periods, which suffered violent disruptions, were now to be cemented with the recovery of Confucian stability. They were also critical of traditional commentators for failing to apprehend the intentions behind the sages' words and so breach the profound historical distance separating contemporary students from the learning of the sages. In the Daoxue self-narrative, they were returning to the roots, the sources, not creating something new.

By the late twelfth century, the influence of Daoxue thinkers was such that they "were defining the vocabulary and the issues of intellectual culture to such an extent that men with little interest in moral philosophy chose to argue for their positions within the framework of *Tao-hsueh*."[7] As

---

[4] Hoyt Cleveland Tillman, *Confucian Discourse and Chu Hsi's Ascendancy* (Honolulu: University of Hawaii Press, 1992), 21–22.
[5] Han Yu, "Yuan dao" 原道 (Tracing the Way to Its Source), in *Changli xiansheng ji* 昌黎先生集 (Han Yu's Collected Writings), *Sibu beiyao* 四部備要 (The Essential Collection of the Four Divisions) (Beijing: Zhonghua shuju, 1936), 11.4b.
[6] See, for example, the preface by Zhang Zai's 張載 (1020–1077) disciple Fan Yu 范育 (d.u.) to Zhang's *Zheng meng* 正蒙 (Correcting Youthful Ignorance), *Zhang Zai ji* 張載集 (Zhang Zai's Collected Works) (Beijing: Zhonghua shuju, 2006), 4–5.
[7] Peter K. Bol, *"This Culture of Ours": Intellectual Transmissions in T'ang and Sung China* (Stanford, CA: Stanford University Press, 1992), 329. Although Daoxue thinkers were part of a

a self-styled heir to this movement, Zhu Xi 朱熹 (1130–1200) identified a group of Daoxue thinkers whose authority rested on their claim to have apprehended the intentions behind the sages' words. Zhu's first attempt to write a history of the Daoxue school, *Yi-Luo yuanyuan lu* 伊洛淵源錄 (Records of the Yi-Luo School, 1173), identified himself as heir to a lineage of Five Masters of the (Northern) Song period: Cheng Yi, Cheng Hao, Zhou Dunyi 周敦頤 (1016–1073), Zhang Zai 張載 (1020–1077), and Shao Yong 邵雍 (1011–1077). In affiliating himself with these seminal figures, Zhu was able to appropriate this authority and so identify himself as a knower rather than a seeker.

Zhu Xi is arguably the most important Chinese philosopher of the past millennium, both in terms of his influence and legacy and for the sophistication of the systematic philosophy he developed. Many of the resources he drew upon to do this—the Four Books, the *Book of Change*, the writings of Zhou Dunyi, Zhang Zai, the Cheng brothers, Shao Yong, and thinkers associated with the Daoxue tradition more generally—have been well studied.[8] Despite his importance as a philosopher, the role of Buddhist thought and philosophy in the construction of Zhu's systematic philosophy remains poorly understood.

One widely shared view of the Buddhist influence on Neo-Confucian thought more generally is Charles Wei-hsun Fu's stimulus-response thesis: "[I]t was mainly through the challenge and stimulation of Mahāyāna Buddhist thought . . . that the orthodox Neo-Confucianists began to realize the necessity of rediscovering the metaphysico-religious significance of the fundamental principles existent in early Confucian classics, and reestablished these principles as the chief philosophical weapon to launch forceful attacks against (Mahāyāna) Buddhism in China."[9]

The historian Peter K. Bol regards the closely related view that Neo-Confucians were able to provide a better ethical foundation for their philosophy by borrowing philosophical concepts such as *li* 理 (pattern, principle) from Buddhism and *qi* 氣 (vital stuff) from Daoism, as having been developed in response to the critiques made by Qing scholars "who sought to supplant the intellectual authority of Neo-Confucians by

---

much broader development known as "Song Learning," the legacy and influence of this group has been profound.

[8] For a recent volume, which aims to contribute to our understanding of Zhu Xi as a philosopher in his own right rather than just a "great synthesizer," see David Jones and Jinhe Li, eds., *Returning to Zhu Xi: Emerging Patterns within the Supreme Polarity* (Albany: SUNY Press, 2015).
[9] Charles Wei-hsun Fu, "Chu Hsi on Buddhism," in *Chu Hsi and Neo-Confucianism*, ed. Wing-tsit Chan (Honolulu: University of Hawaii Press, 1986), 378.

arguing that Song and Ming Neo-Confucians did not have a correct understanding of the Classics and antiquity because they had been influenced by Buddhism and Daoism."[10] Similar developments also occurred in Japan. For example, the Ming-dynasty Chan monk Konggu Jinglong 空谷景隆 (1387–1466) blithely asserted—providing no evidence whatsoever—that a key concept introduced in Cheng Yi's preface to his commentary on the *Book of Change* ("*Yi zhuan* xu" 易傳序)[11] was actually derived from Huayan master Chengguan's 澄觀 (557–640) *Huayan jing shu* 華嚴經疏 (Commentary to the Flower Garland Sutra).[12] This view was subsequently propagated by the Edo-period evidential scholar Ōta Kinjō 太田錦城 (1765–1825) in his attempts to discredit "Zhu Xi learning." Ōta also attributes the origin of Zhang Zai's and Zhu Xi's *qizhi zhi xing* 氣質之性 (psychophysical nature) and *tiandi zhi xing* 天地之性 (heaven-and-earth bestowed nature) distinction to the *Śūraṃgama-sūtra* (*Shoulengyan jing* 首楞嚴經).[13]

Given that scholars have long debated the relationship between Buddhism and Neo-Confucianism, just what do we know about Zhu Xi's philosophical engagement with and responses to Buddhism?[14] What aspects of Buddhism did he criticize and why? Was his engagement limited to criticism (informed or otherwise), or did Zhu also appropriate and

---

[10] Peter K. Bol, *Neo-Confucianism in History* (Cambridge, MA: Harvard University Asia Center, 2008), 103. Cf. Yan Yuan's 顏元 (1635–1704) criticisms of Zhu Xi's *renxin* 人心 (human mind) / *daoxin* 道心 (mind of the way) distinction as evidence that Zhu was promoting Buddhism in the guise of Confucianism, cited in P. J. Ivanhoe, *Confucian Moral Self Cultivation* (Indianapolis: Hackett, 2000), 79. Justin Tiwald cites the case of Dai Zhen 戴震 (1724–1777), noting: "Dai used his considerable philological skills to demonstrate (convincingly, for many) that his Neo-Confucian predecessors had read the Confucian classics through Daoist and Buddhist lenses, which he faulted for many of the errors he found in their moral thought." See his "Dai Zhen on Human Nature and Moral Cultivation," in Makeham, *Dao Companion to Neo-Confucian Philosophy*, 399.
[11] "Intrinsic reality and function are a single source; there is no gap between the apparent and the subtle" (體用一源，顯微無間). Cheng Yi, *Zhouyi Cheng shi zhuan* 周易程氏傳 (Cheng Yi's annotation of the *Book of Change*) (Beijing: Zhonghua shuju, 2011), 1. As I show in my chapter in this volume, intrinsic realty and function (*ti yong*) became a cornerstone of Zhu Xi's metaphysics.
[12] Yiyuan Zongben 一元宗本 (*jinshi* 1553), *Gui yuan zhi zhi ji* 歸元直指集 (Directly Pointing to Returning to the Origin: Collected Writings), X61.1156, 460c20-21.
[13] Imai Usaburō 今井宇三郎, "*Isen Ekiden* jijo kō" 伊川易傳自序考 (A Study of Yichuan's "Preface to the *Commentary on the Book of Change*"), *Nippon Chūgoku gakkai hō* 1 (1950), 32–33; Araki Kengo 荒木見悟, *Bukkyō to Jukyō: Chūgoku shisō o keiseisuru mono* 佛教と儒教: 中国思想を形成するもの (Confucianism, Buddhism, and the Formation of Chinese Thought) (Kyoto: Heirakuji shoten, 1963), 299–300n95.
[14] For example, some modern scholars have claimed that the Huayan Buddhist doctrine of the "non-obstruction of Li and phenomena" (*li shi wu ai* 理事無礙) influenced Zhu Xi's understanding of the theory of "one pattern differentiated in particulars" (*li yi fen shu* 理一分殊). See P. J. Ivanhoe, *Confucian Moral Self Cultivation* (Indianapolis: Hackett, 2000), 46–48.

repurpose Buddhist ideas to develop his own thought? If Zhu's philosophical repertoire incorporated 融攝 conceptual structures and problematics that are marked by a distinct Buddhist pedigree, what implications does this have for our understanding of his philosophical project? These were questions that contributors to this volume were asked to consider when they first began to formulate their individual contributions in 2012. The five studies in this volume present a rich and complex portrait of the Buddhist roots of Zhu Xi's philosophical thought. Collectively, they illuminate a greatly expanded range of the intellectual resources Zhu incorporated into his philosophical thought, explaining how and why he did so, to provide new perspectives on what he achieved as a philosopher.

I.1 Chan, Huayan, and Tiantai

Before turning to introduce the content of this volume's five chapters, some account of Buddhist thought in the Song is in order, in particular pertinent aspects of Chan 禪, Huayan 華嚴, and Tiantai 天台. Just as developments in pre-Qin philosophy were traditionally filtered through the prism of Han sources, so too, knowledge of developments in Chan Buddhism during the Tang has largely been shaped by Song sources, with transmission histories playing a key role as a narrative tool and also a legitimizing device for the Chan school. As Peter N. Gregory notes, "the vision of the Ch'an tradition as a multibranched lineage stemming from a common ancestor and linked together by a mind-to-mind transmission did not take hold as the commonly accepted representation of the tradition until the publication of the *Ching-te Record of the Transmission of the Flame* (*Ching-te ch'uan-teng lu*) in the beginning of the eleventh century."[15] For the purposes of this volume on the Buddhist roots of Zhu Xi's philosophical thought, notable

---

[15] Peter N. Gregory, "The Vitality of Buddhism in the Sung," in *Buddhism in the Sung*, eds. Peter N. Gregory and Daniel A. Getz Jr. (Honolulu: University of Hawaii Press, 2002), 4. Gregory also notes that even though Zongmi 宗密 (780–841) had already subsumed the various lineages into a unified vision of the Chan tradition, at the time it was but one of a number of contending claims. Albert Welter identifies *Zutang ji* 祖堂集 (Patriarch Hall's Anthology, 952) as an early example of the standardization of Chan "as a uniform tradition dedicated to common goals and principles.... This new structure proposed that Chan represented a common heritage," albeit one in which lineage was now linked unilaterally to Huineng 慧能 (trad. d. 713), the sixth patriarch. See his *Monks, Rulers, and Literati: The Political Ascendancy of Chan Buddhism* (New York: Oxford University Press, 2006), 69. See also Welter's *Yongming Yanshou's Conception of Chan in the Zongjing Lu* (New York: Oxford, 2011), chap. 4, for a study of how Yongming Yanshou 永明延壽 (904–976) incorporated the patriarchs of Chan factions and their writings into his overarching conception of Chan, in his encyclopedic *Zongjing lu* 宗鏡錄 (Records of the Source-Mirror, ca. 961).

developments in Chan Buddhism during the Song include the growth of Chan as the dominant form of monastic Buddhism with an institutional base; and factional disputes in the twelfth century between the Caodong tradition's (Caodong zong 曹洞宗) promotion of "silent illumination" (*mozhao* 默照) and Dahui Zonggao's 大慧宗杲 (1089–1163; of the Linji tradition) promotion of focusing on the punch-line of a *gong'an*, known as the *huatou* 話頭 or "point of the story."[16]

The proliferation of monasteries with public abbacies in the Northern Song (920–1127) benefitted Chan—in particular, the transmission families associated with the lineages of Linji Yixuan 臨濟義玄 (d. 866) and Yunmen Wenyan 雲門文偃 (862/4–949)—enabling it to develop an independent identity and an institutional base. And because Chan masters needed the support of the elite laity if they were to be able to hold abbacies at public monasteries and thereby perpetuate their own dharma transmission families, this encouraged them to forge close links with the educated elite. This situation prevailed until the transition to the Southern Song in the late eleventh century when public monasteries increasingly became dominated by Huayan and Tiantai schools, and Chan transmission families had to compete with one another to secure the support of the educated elite.[17]

It was against this background that the Caodong lineage re-emerged in the late eleventh century and grew to prominence in the early twelfth century, relying on officials and literati for political and financial support. "Silent illumination" refers to the Caodong school's approach to enlightenment, which Morten Schlütter describes as being "associated with a quiet meditation in which the inherent Buddha-nature that all sentient beings possess naturally shines forth," and traces its development to Furong Daokai 芙蓉道楷 (1043–1118) and his descendants, for whom it served "partly as a teaching that could appeal to educated lay people."[18]

This competition for literati support was also a factor motivating Dahui's attacks on silent illumination Chan. Dahui claimed a lineage

---

[16] See Mario Poceski, *The Records of Mazu and the Making of Classical Chan Literature* (New York: Oxford University Press, 2015), 24; Albert Welter, *The Linji Lu and the Creation of Chan Orthodoxy: The Development of Chan's Records of Sayings Literature* (New York: Oxford University Press, 2008), in particular, chaps. 2, 3, and 4; Morten Schlütter, *How Zen Became Zen: The Dispute over Enlightenment and the Formation of Chan Buddhism in Song-Dynasty China* (Honolulu: University of Hawaii Press, 2008), 16–17. Dahui's method is also known as *kanhua* 看話 (observing the key phrase) Chan. On the late origin of this term, see Schlütter, *How Zen Became Zen*, 215n27.

[17] Schlütter, *How Zen Became Zen*, chaps. 3 and 4.

[18] Schlütter, *How Zen Became Zen*, 3, 11; see also 162–164, 167–168.

back to Mazu Daoyi 馬祖道一 (709–788) via Linji Yixuan. His teachings had strong appeal among the scholar-gentry, to whom he specifically directed some of his teachings. Zhu Xi had become concerned that Dahui was undermining support among the educated elite for Daoxue or more broadly for Confucianism. In particular, he was also concerned that second-generation followers of the Cheng brothers had become vulnerable to Dahui's teachings. Ari Borrell has drawn attention to Zhu's "obsession" with purging the Cheng lineage of Daoxue of the corrupting influence of Zhang Jiucheng 張九成 (1092–1159), second-generation follower of Cheng Yi and leading figure in Southern Song Daoxue, who was also renowned as "the most accomplished lay disciple" of Dahui.[19]

Elsewhere, Borrell contrasts the messages that Zhu and Dahui conveyed to Wang Yingchen 汪應辰 (1118–1176), a cousin of Zhu Xi, and a teacher of Zhu's intellectual and political ally, Lü Zuqian 呂祖謙 (1137–1181)—the leading figure of Daoxue movement from the late 1160s to 1181[20] and also a prominent disciple of Zhang Jiucheng. In addition to Zhang Jiucheng, other first- and second-generation disciples of the Cheng brothers who had also been followers of Dahui include: You Zuo 游酢 (1053–1123), Yang Shi 楊時 (1053–1135), Zhang Shi's 張栻 (1133–1180) father Zhang Jun 張浚 (1097–1164), Lü Zuqian's teacher Wang Yingchen, Zhang Jiucheng's teacher and friend, Lü Benzhong 呂本中 (1084–1145), Zeng Kai 曾開 (*jinshi* 1103), the vice minister of rites who had been a student of You Zuo, Zhu Xi's early teacher Liu Zihui 劉子翬 (1101–1147), and Liu's elder brother Liu Ziyu 劉子羽 (1086–1146).[21]

Take the case of Lü Benzhong, who had held close relations with first-generation Cheng disciples—You Zuo, Yang Shi, Yin Tun 尹焞 (1061–1132) and Wang Pin 王蘋 (1082–1153)—and who also had been given detailed instructions on so-called *kanhua* Chan by Dahui.[22] In his essay, "Zaxue bian" 雜學辨 (Critique of Adulterated Learning, 1166), Zhu sets out a number

---

[19] Ari Borrell, "*Ko-Wu* or *Kung-an*? Practice, Realization, and Teaching in the Thought of Chang Chiu-Ch'eng," in Gregory and Getz, *Buddhism in the Sung*, 63.
[20] Tillman, *Confucian Discourse*, 83.
[21] Ichiki Tsuyuhiko 市來津由彥, "Shushi no 'Zatsugaku ben' to sono shuhen" 朱熹の「雜學弁」とその周邊 (Zhu Xi's "Critique of Adulterated Learning" and its Surrounding Context), in *Sōdai no shakai to shūkyō* 宋代の社會と宗教 (Song Dynasty Society and Religion), ed. Sōdaishi kenkyūkai 宋代史研究會 (Tokyo: Kyūko Shoin, 1985), 14; Koichi Shinohara, "Tahui's Instructions to Tseng K'ai: Buddhist 'Freedom' in the Neo-Confucian Context," in *Meeting of Minds: Intellectual and Religious Interaction in East Asian Traditions of Thought: Essays in Honor of Wing-tsit Chan and William Theodore de Bary*, eds. Irene Bloom and Joshua A. Fogel (New York: Columbia University Press, 1997).
[22] Jiang Yibin 蔣義斌, "Lü Benzhong yu Fojiao" 呂本中與佛教 (Lü Benzhong and Buddhism), *Foxue yanjiu zhongxin xuebao* 佛學研究中心學報 2 (1997): 140–141.

of criticisms of Lü's commentary on the *Great Learning*. These criticisms provide some insight into the kinds of philosophical objections Zhu had to Dahui's Chan. Consider the following two pairs of related examples.

Commenting on the following line from the *Great Learning*, "The extension of knowledge lies in the investigation of things and after things are investigated knowledge is attained" (致知在格物，物格而後知至。), Lü Benzhong writes:

> Extending knowledge and investigating things are the foundation for cultivating one's person. Knowledge means innate knowledge—just like that of Yao and Shun. When principle has been fathomed then naturally knowledge is achieved. Because this is just the same as with Yao and Shun, suddenly it [innate knowledge] appears of itself, and tacitly one discerns it.
>
> 致知格物，脩身之本也。知者，良知也，與堯、舜同者也。理既窮則知自至。與堯、舜同者，忽然自見，默而識之。

In response, Zhu comments:

> Extending knowledge and investigating things are the starting point of the *Great Learning*, and concern the commencement of learning. As one thing is investigated, one thing is known. The benefits of this are gradual and after this gradual accumulation of knowledge has gone on at length one achieves comprehensive interconnection [of patterns]. After this, one intuitively acts decisively and without hesitation, such that one's intentions are sincere and one's mind is set straight. Accordingly, there are certainly varying depths in the extension of knowledge. How could these [varying depths in the extension of knowledge] rashly be taken to be the same [achievement] as that of Yao and Shun and to be perceived so suddenly? This is tantamount to the Buddhists' empty talk of "being completely enlightened upon hearing [the Dharma] just once" or "directly entering the realm of the Buddha in one moment of transcendence." This is not the true undertaking of one [who has entered the] sage's gateway [i.e., Confucianism], which is to elucidate the good and to make one's person sincere.
>
> 致知格物，〈大學〉之端，始學之事也。一物格則一知至，其功有漸，積久貫通，然後胷中判然不疑所行，而意誠心正矣。然則所致之知固有淺深，豈遽以爲與堯、舜同者，一旦忽然而見之也哉。此殆釋氏一聞千悟、一超直入之虛談，非聖門明善誠身之實務也。[23]

---

[23] *Zhu Xi ji* 朱熹集 (Collected Works of Zhu Xi), eds. Guo Qi 郭齊 and Yin Bo 尹波 (Chengdu: Sichuan jiaoyu chubanshe, 1996), *juan* 72, 3791.

In the second example, Lü Benzhong writes:

> The subtle differences between flora and distinctions between implements all come down to the patterns of things. To seek how they function as the patterns of flora and implements one undertakes the investigation of things. If I preserve my mind [i.e., not let it become distracted] to focus on the principles of flora and implements, then suddenly I will know them—this is the investigation of things.
>
> 草木之微、器用之別，皆物之理也。求其所以爲草木器用之理，則爲格物。草木器用之理，吾心存焉，忽然識之， 此爲物格。

In response, Zhu comments that after a sustained process of incremental investigation,

> only then will the comprehensive interconnection resulting from practices applied over a long period gradually reach its end. How could it be possible suddenly to come to know things in the way that Yao and Shun did, with no reason other than that it was achieved merely by preserving the mind [i.e., not letting it be distracted] to focus on a given flora or implement? This again is [nothing other than the Chan] Buddhist teaching of "becoming enlightened by hearing a sound and awakening the mind by seeing a color."[24]
>
> 然後積習貫通，馴致其極，豈以爲直存心於一草木器用之間，而與堯、舜同者無故忽然自識之哉。此又釋氏聞聲悟道見色明心之說。[25]

In both cases, Zhu rejects the claim that genuine knowing can be achieved through a sudden moment of awareness, requiring no sustained practice and discipline. For Zhu, knowing is an incremental, gradual process, the goal of which is to achieve the comprehensive interconnection (*guantong* 貫通) of principles/patterns (*li* 理).

Zhu's criticisms are also prompted by an even more fundamental concern: that the Buddhists took the mind to reveal the nature but what they actually perceive is no more than the capricious, subjective mind. On this point, Zhu may not have had Dahui in mind but rather the Chan tradition associated with the Linji school more generally and with the figure of

---

[24] Dahui frequently cites this phrase as used by Yunmen Wenyan. See, for example, *Yunmen kuangzhen Chanshi guanglu* 雲門匡眞禪師廣錄 (Extensive Record of Chan Master Yunmen Kuangzhen), T47.1988, 554a13.

[25] *Zhu Xi ji, juan* 72, 3791–3792.

Mazu more specifically.[26] For Mazu, the mind is the buddha-nature—and so there is no need for cultivation or gradual practice:

> The present seeing, hearing, listening, and sensing have always been your inherent nature, which is also called inherent mind. There is no separate buddha [=buddha-nature] apart from this mind. This mind has always existed and exists right now, without depending on having to be created. It has always been pure and is pure right now, and does not need to be wiped clean. One's inherent nature is nirvana; one's inherent nature is pure.
>
> 今見聞覺知。元是汝本性。亦名本心。更不離此心別有佛。此心本有，今有。不假造作。本淨今淨。不待瑩拭。自性涅槃。自性清淨。[27]

For Zhu Xi, these antinomian views had dire ethical implications because they threaten to remove the need for moral discipline and effectively validate any sort of behavior on the grounds that it is an expression of our inherent buddha-nature.

Zhu expressed similar concerns about another closely related teaching—typically identified with Mazu's Hongzhou school—that "function is the nature" (作用為性), specifically linking it with views expressed by Dahui.[28] His attack on Mazu Chan was clearly echoing criticisms made much earlier by Huayan and Chan master, Zongmi 宗密 (780–841):

> The idea of Hongzhou is that giving rise to mind [thoughts], snapping fingers and moving eyeballs, what is done and what is acted on, are in their entirety the function of the buddha-nature, and there is no other function.

---

[26] There remains some disagreement among modern scholars as to whether certain teachings attributed to the historical Mazu—such as the encounter dialogue—were in fact taught by him. Mario Poceski, *Ordinary Mind as the Way: The Hongzhou School and the Growth of Chan Buddhism* (New York: Oxford University Press, 2007), 10–11, argues that such dialogues cannot be traced back to the Tang period, whereas Jinhua Jia insists that Mazu and his disciples "actually performed a new kind of religious practice—encounter dialogue." Jinhua Jia, *The Hongzhou School of Chan Buddhism in Eighth-through Tenth-century China* (Albany: State University of New York Press, 2006), 80. For our purposes, when discussing Daoxue thinkers such as Zhu Xi, it is important to bear in mind that the traditional iconoclastic image of Mazu and Linji as enlightened eccentrics was very much informed by Song accounts of their practices and doctrines. In other words, what is germane is the reception of their image in the Song.

[27] *Zongjing lu*, T48.2016, 492a22-25.

[28] *Zhuzi yulei*, juan 126, 3022, citing *Dahui yulu*, T47.1998A, 829c24-27. See also Yanagida Seizan 柳田聖山, "Bukkyō to Shushi no shūhen" 佛教と朱子の周邊 (On Buddhism and Zhu Xi), *Zen bunka kenkyūjo kiyō* 禪文化研究所紀要 8 (1976): 20–26.

The entirety of craving, anger, and stupidity, of doing good and doing evil, experiencing pleasure and experiencing pain, these are all buddha-nature.

洪州意者，起心動念、彈指動目、所作所為，皆是佛性全體之用，更無別用。全體貪、嗔、癡、造善、造惡、受樂、受苦：此皆是佛性。²⁹

As John Jorgensen notes in his chapter in this volume, this doctrine was completely antithetical to Zhu's stress on the principles/patterns (*li*) that had to be sought and preserved so that humans did not descend to the level of animals. "For Mazu, the activities or functions themselves when performed naturally are the nature. It is not about finding principles, it is about performing them. The Hongzhou school with which Mazu is affiliated, saw the actions of searching and investigating to be intentional and thus misleading. For Zhu Xi, this was an alarming proposition not least because it dismissed the need to practice, including moral practice."

Theoretical resources developed over centuries in Huayan and Tiantai are also crucial to understanding Zhu Xi's engagement with, and appropriation of, Buddhist thought for his own philosophical ends. The following survey combines an account of both schools so as to convey not only how, already in the Tang, Tiantai theorists drew heavily on Huayan doctrine, but also to show how philosophical issues internal to Huayan became replicated in Tiantai circles during the Northern Song. The significance of the late-sixth-century Buddhist text, the *Treatise on Giving Rise to Faith in the Great Vehicle* (*Dasheng qixin lun* 大乘起信論), is also introduced. The *Dasheng qixin lun* played a seminal role in the development of Sinitic Buddhist traditions such as Chan, Huayan, and Tiantai, to become one of the most influential texts in the history of East Asian Buddhism.

Tiantai came into existence and flourished during the Sui dynasty (581–618) but declined in the early Tang (618–907), enjoying only a brief period of revival in the eighth century. After this, core texts became lost or were transmitted only outside China. By the eleventh century, however, it once again began a revival, but as key texts were recovered, Tiantai masters had to confront the problem of different versions of those texts written by earlier theorists, such as the school's de facto founder, Zhiyi 智顗 (538–597). Many of the ensuing debates at the time concerned divergent Northern Song interpretations of the teachings of Zhiyi and Zhanran 湛然

---

²⁹ Zongmi, *Zhonghua chuan xindi Chanmen shizi chengxi tu* 中華傳心地禪門師資承襲圖 (Chart of the Master-Disciple Succession of the Chan Gate that Transmits the Mind-Ground in China), X63.1225, 33a22.

(711–782), often involving scholiastic issues of textual corruption and divergent glossing of key terms. Zhanran wrote extensive commentaries on the writings of Zhiyi, and as the key figure in the attempt to revive Tiantai in the eighth century, Zhanran was subsequently identified with Tiantai orthodoxy.

One of Zhiyi's key innovations was to develop the doctrine of the Three Truths, creatively transforming the Madhyamaka idea of the Two Truths,[30] as posited by the celebrated Mādhyamikan, Nāgārjuna (second through third centuries). The Three Truths are Emptiness, Provisional Positing, and the Middle/Center. Any dharma (any entity or phenomenon, mental or physical) is empty (*kong* 空) because it is causally determined through multiple networks of causes and conditions and has no self-nature. At the same time, because *this* dharma can be referred to—even negatively, in the sense of its not being *that* dharma—it can also be said to be provisionally posited (*jia* 假). Thus any dharma is both empty and provisionally posited, with neither emptiness nor provisional positing being privileged over the other. The realization that emptiness is provisional positing (emptiness can be provisionally posited) and that provisional positing is emptiness (the provisional posited is empty of self-nature) is the third of the Three Truths and is known as the center (*zhong* 中). In the hands of Tiantai theorists such as Zhiyi, however, the relationship between these Three Truths becomes one of mutual identity such the middle/center is both emptiness and provisional positing, just as emptiness is both provisional positing and the center, and provisional positing is both emptiness and the center.[31] Any one of the three necessarily entails the other two. And unlike the view attributed to the so-called Separate Teaching (*biejiao* 別教), the center is not ontologically privileged. This became a pivotal issue in Tiantai debates during the Northern Song. Zhiyi used the term Separate Teaching to refer to Tathāgatagarbha thought[32]—with which the *Dasheng qixin lun* is paradigmatically identified by later Huayan and Tiantai thinkers—but later Tiantai theorists used it to refer to Huayan thinkers.

---

[30] Conventional truth (statements and their referents) and ultimate truth (the emptiness, lack of self-nature, of statement and their referents).

[31] On this point, see comments by Andō Toshio 安藤俊雄, cited in Brook A. Ziporyn, *Evil and/or/as The Good: Omnicentrism, Intersubjectivity, and Value Paradox in Tiantai Buddhist Thought* (Cambridge, MA: Harvard University Asia Center, 2000), 119 and the broader analysis by Ziporyn, 118–122.

[32] *Tathāgatagarbha* (*rulaizang* 如來藏) means the repository of a buddha, the potential to achieve buddhahood, and in China the *tathāgatagarbha* doctrine is particularly associated with the idea that buddha-nature (*foxing* 佛性) exists within all sentient beings. The Tathāgatagarbha

Peter N. Gregory identifies Zhanran's incorporation of the Huayan theory of mind in the eighth century as central to subsequent doctrinal controversies in the Song.[33] In this connection, he identifies the *Dasheng qixin lun*'s Tathāgatagarbha-influenced doctrine of One Mind—in which suchness qua *tathāgatagarbha* is presented as the basis and source of all defiled and undefiled dharmas—to have enabled the Huayan doctrine of nature origination (*xingqi* 性起) to be developed.[34] For early Huayan theorists such as Zhiyan 智儼 (602–668), nature origination is the idea that the nature (here to be understood as suchness or the One Mind) is the basis of all phenomena, "the mind-ground."[35] Lacking self-nature, these phenomena are actually manifestations of that nature (which is none other than dharma-nature or suchness.)

The *Dasheng qixin lun* presents the One Mind as the ultimate source of reality. The One Mind has two modalities or aspects, which the text calls gateways, and these contain all dharmas, conditioned (existence that is subject to determination by the laws of cause and effect) and unconditioned. The gateway of the mind of suchness is the true mind—unchanging, eternal, and pure. Suchness (*zhenru* 真如; *tathātā*) is reality as it truly is, without any conceptual overlay. The gateway of the mind of arising and ceasing is cyclic existence (*saṃsāra*) in which the mind's propensity to awaken struggles against the mental and physical behaviors that arise from the mind's defilement by ignorance. Both the mind as suchness and the arising and ceasing mind are ultimately the One Mind but, because ignorance obscures the realization of the One Mind, deluded beings create false perceptions, and so become mired in suffering.

---

tradition within Mahāyāna Buddhism is associated with a cluster of texts, central to which is the *tathāgatagarbha* doctrine. For an overview of these texts, see for example, Michael Radich, "Tathāgatagarbha Sūtras" in *Brill's Encyclopedia of Buddhism*, Volume One: Literature and Languages, eds. Jonathan Silk, Oskar von Hinüber, and Vincent Eltschinger (Leiden: Brill, 2015), 261–273.

[33] Gregory, "The Vitality of Buddhism in the Sung," 6–7.

[34] On this connection, see also Gregory, *Tsung-mi and the Sinification of Buddhism* (Honolulu: University of Hawaii Press, 1991), 157–158; Imre Hamar, "The Manifestation of the Absolute in the Phenomenal World: Nature Origination in Huayan Exegesis," *Bulletin de l'École française d'Extrême-Orient* 94 (2007): 229.

[35] Zhiyan, *Dafangguang fo huayan jing souxuan fenqi tongzhi fanggui* 大方廣佛華嚴經搜玄分齊通智方軌 (The *Flower Garland Sutra*: A Categorization of Doctrine for the Enquiry into Its Mysteries and a Broad Avenue for the Access of Penetrating Insight into Its Meaning), T35.1732, 79b29-c30. Hamar, "The Manifestation of the Absolute in the Phenomenal World," 230, also proposes that the concept of *zhenxing yuanqi* 真性緣起 (dependent arising of the absolute nature), which occurs in Jingying Huiyuan's 淨影慧遠 (523–592) *Dasheng yi zhang* 大乘義章 (Essay

The *Dasheng qixin lun* succinctly addresses many of the doctrines of greatest importance to Buddhists in China between the fifth and seventh centuries in an attempt to reconcile seemingly contradictory ideas in Buddhist texts introduced from India.[36] The doctrine of the *tathāgatagarbha* is central here. In the *Dasheng qixin lun*, the *tathāgatagarbha* refers both to a latent buddhahood concealed by delusion, as well as to a more dynamic force that enables the mind of sentient beings to overcome darkness, ignorance, impurity, and karmic defilement. The doctrine of the *tathāgatagarbha* is also used to reveal the true meaning of suchness, or ultimate reality, as empty and free from delusion, yet also replete with perfect qualities.

The text's One Mind Two Gateways doctrine can be seen as an attempt to accommodate Yogācāra and Tathāgatagarbha teachings, in particular the concepts of *tathāgatagarbha* and *ālayavijñāna*. Traditional scholars also drew attention to what they distinguish as the Northern and Southern branches of the Dilun school, said to have been active in sixth century northern China. These commentators and doxographers identified the main difference between the two branches to have been whether defiled phenomena arise from suchness (Southern position) or from the *ālayavijñāna* (Northern position). If these accounts are taken as accurate, then the *Dasheng qixin lun* can be seen to be consistent with the Northern branch in presenting the *ālayavijñāna*—identified with the gateway of arising and ceasing—as the basis for defiled phenomena; and it is also consistent with the Southern branch in presenting suchness or *tathāgatagarbha*, which exists within the defiled *ālayavijñāna*, as the basis of everything, no matter defiled or undefiled.[37]

Coming into existence in the early seventh century, the Huayan school takes its name from its foundational scripture, the *Avataṃsaka-sūtra*

---

on the System of Mahāyāna), "strongly influenced" Huayan master Zhiyan's formulation of the concept of nature origination. Huiyuan is traditionally associated with the Dilun school.

[36] The authorship of the *Dasheng qixin lun* is attributed to the Indian poet Aśvaghoṣa (ca. 80–150 CE), and its Chinese translation is credited to the Indian monk Paramārtha (499–569). Although modern scholarship has shown that in language, style, vocabulary, and underlying models it has more in common with translators *other than* Aśvaghoṣa and Paramārtha, traditionally it was regarded as their text or, alternatively, as having been written by a member of Paramārtha's school.

[37] Zhanran, *Fahua xuan yi shi qian* 法華玄義釋籤 (Comments on the *Profound Meaning of the Lotus Sutra*), T33.1717, 792a11-15, T33.1717, 942c16-24. Keng Ching, "Yogācāra Buddhism Transmitted or Transformed? Paramārtha (499–569) and His Chinese Interpreters" (PhD diss., Harvard University, 2009), 344–345. See also Robert M. Gimello, "Chih-yen and the Foundations of Hua-yen Buddhism" (PhD diss., Columbia University, 1976), 146–147, 211, 294–297. The Tiantai master Zhiyi 智顗 (538–597) is recorded as attributing a similar distinction to the Dilun School and the Shelun School, respectively, with the former advocating that "dharma-nature" (*faxing* 法性; *dharmatā)—the functional equivalent of suchness—is the basis for all dharmas,

(*Huayan jing* 華嚴經; Flower Garland Sutra).[38] One of its key innovations was a reworking of the central Buddhist theory of dependent arising (*pratītya-samutpāda;* yuanqi 緣起)—everything arises from causes and conditions and has no inherent self-nature—into the doctrine of "the dependent arising of the dharma-realm" (*fajie yuanqi* 法界緣起), that is, the mutual inclusion of all aspects of reality: every single phenomenon contains and instantiates all phenomena, and is also contained in and instantiated by all phenomena. This doctrine, in turn, became the basis for the Huayan doctrine of the "unobstructed interpenetration of all phenomena" (*shi shi wu ai* 事事無礙).

Inspired by the *Dasheng qixin lun*'s teaching that the mind as suchness can merge with the arising and ceasing mind yet still retain its own identity, the Huayan master Dushun 杜順 (557–640) introduced the idea of the non-obstruction of Li and phenomena (*li shi wu ai* 理事無礙).[39] Huayan master Fazang 法藏 (643–712) subsequently identified this doctrine as the characteristic teaching of what he termed "the dependent arising out of the *tathāgatagarbha*" lineage tradition (*rulaizang yuanqi zong* 如來藏緣起宗), one of the four Buddhist lineage traditions (*zong* 宗) that he recognized.[40] The doctrine of the dependent arising out of the *tathāgatagarbha* effectively turned the theory of dependent arising (*pratītya-samutpāda*) into an ontology. The doctrine supports the idea that suchness (= *tathāgatagarbha*), an unconditioned dharma, is itself the

---

whereas the Shelun School maintains that everything arises from *ālayavijñāna*. See Zhiyi, *Mohe zhiguan* 摩訶止觀 (The Great Calming and Contemplation), T46.1911, 54a23-b8. A problem here is that Zhiyi's works were edited by his disciples, most importantly by Guanding 灌頂 (561–632). There is thus a question of how much of the information in Zhiyi's works reflects Zhiyi's views and how much was came from Guanding. As to whether the views attributed to Zhiyi in respect of the Shelun-Dilun distinction are historically accurate, this also remains unclear.

[38] Robert Gimello argues that Huayan was substantially the product of a reaction to the kind of Yogācāra represented by famous pilgrim and monk, Xuanzang 玄奘 (602–644), but it also drew variously on Madhyamaka and Tathāgatagarbha thought, in particular on texts such as the *Dasheng qixin lun*, and the Yogācāra associated with the Dilun school. See Robert Gimello, "Chih-yen and the Foundations of Hua-yen Buddhism," 441.

[39] In Sinitic Buddhist contexts, when contrasted with *shi* 事, Li 理 is synonymous with suchness (*tathatā*): reality as it truly is without any conceptual overlay. In order to distinguish this Buddhist usage I capitalize the term as Li in this Introduction and in my own chapter.

[40] In his system of doctrinal classification of Buddhist scriptures translated into Chinese, Fazang distinguished four lineage traditions: (1) attachment to dharmas through their characteristics (隨相法執宗), associated with Hīnayāna scripture; (2) real emptiness without characteristics (眞空無相宗), associated with Prajñā and Madhyamaka scriptures; (3) nothing but consciousness dharma characteristics (唯識法相宗) associated with Yogācāra scriptures; and (4) the dependent arising of the *tathāgatagarbha* associated with the *Dasheng qixin lun* and the *Ratnagotravibhāga* (*Bao xing lun* 寶性論; Treatise on the Jewel Nature) treatises and the *Laṅkāvatāra* (*Lengqie jing* 楞伽經; Sutra on [the Buddha's Entering the Country of] Lanka) and the *Ghana-vyūha* (*Dasheng miyan jing* 大乘密嚴經; Sutra of the Secret Adornment) sutras.

basis of conditioned and defiled phenomena. Fazang associated the concept of the "non-obstruction of Li and phenomena" (*li shi wu ai*) with this doctrine.

In doing so, however, he also subordinated it to the doctrine of the "unobstructed interpenetration of all phenomena" (*shi shi wu ai* 事事無礙), which he describes in terms of the harmonious identity of each determinate thing with all things and vice versa, in which not only does the whole determine the character of all of its parts but each part determines the character of the whole. Huayan theorists continued to debate the relative superiority of these two doctrines. Eventually, Zongmi (780–841) elevated the doctrine of the non-obstruction of Li and phenomena (*li shi wu ai*) to become the highest teaching of the Huayan school. Zongmi attached particular importance to the conditioned aspect of the One Mind, which, following Fazang and Fazang's teacher, Zhiyan, he referred to as nature origination (*xingqi* 性起).

It was in critical response to the Huayan doctrine of nature origination that Zhanran coined the term "nature inclusion" (*xingju* 性具).[41] Nature inclusion is the teaching that all dharmas, all things, including buddhahood, are present in each and every thing and that any dharma includes all other dharmas and is identical with all other dharmas. Everything has this nature of being present in and including every other thing.[42] Despite this attempt to distinguish Tiantai from Huayan, the Tiantai doctrine of nature inclusion (*xingju*) and the Huayan doctrine of "unobstructed interpenetration of all phenomena" (*shi shi wu ai* 事事無礙) are quite similar. As Brook A. Ziporyn notes in his chapter, both Huayan and Tiantai accept the claim that the buddha-nature is the absolute, the unconditioned, which therefore must be strictly omnipresent in all possible states. Crucially, however, "for Tiantai this all-inclusiveness means that buddha-nature must be non-external even to the delusions that seem to obstruct it. Hence Tiantai writers call this totality of unstained openness *and* delusion the buddha-nature, and say all determinations are 'inherently included' (*xingju* 性具) in this whole (indeterminacy plus delusion)."

By the early decades of the eleventh century, the question of the doctrinal superiority of non-obstruction of Li and phenomena (*li shi wu ai*) or nature origination (*xingqi*) vs. "unobstructed interpenetration of all phenomena" (*shi shi wu ai*) or what was then identified with the doctrine called "nature inclusion" (*xingju*), had moved beyond an internal Huayan

---

[41] Gregory, "Buddhism in the Sung," 7.
[42] Brook A. Ziporyn has coined the term omnipresent holism to refer to this idea.

debate to become a major focus of debate in renascent Tiantai Buddhism as well, as is evident in the so-called the Shanjia 山家/Shanwai 山外 (Home Mountain/Off Mountain) controversy in the Northern Song. The Home Mountain/Off Mountain controversy emerged as two groups sought to recover what they held to be the true teachings of Tiantai Buddhism after its decline during the Tang period.[43]

The core issue was whether Li should be ontologically privileged over things (*shi* 事), over dharmas, or whether there is a kind of ontological parity between, and indeed intersubsumption of, all dharmas, encapsulated in the idea that every dharma contained all other dharmas. As Brook A. Ziporyn relates in his chapter, Huayan posits an irreversible structural *dependence* priority of *shi* upon Li. Li is the root from which *shi* emerge, and *shi* "arise from" Li. In Tiantai, Li and *shi* are alternate one-sided interpretations of the same totality comprised of two opposites, the indeterminate (Li) and the determinate (*shi*).[44] Neither is more fundamental than the other, neither causes the other, and neither is the basis of the other unilaterally.

By the Northern Song (960–1127), Home Mountain leaders such as Zhili 知禮 (960–1028) were playing key roles in reviving or recreating the Tiantai tradition. And just as the proliferation of monasteries with public abbacies in the Northern Song had benefitted Chan, it also enabled Tiantai to develop an independent identity and an institutional base. Similarly, just as Chan clerics had forged close links with the educated elite, so too did Tiantai clerics. Consider the case of the leading Tiantai Off Mountain cleric, Zhiyuan 智圓 (976–1022). In the early years of the Northern Song, many senior Buddhist monks were instrumental in promoting a revival of Confucian social ideals and values. Together with "literatus monk" Zanning 贊寧 (919–1001) (also ordained in the Tiantai order), Albert Welter identifies Zhiyuan as a prominent member of what he refers to as "Confucian monks" (*ruseng* 儒僧). "These were monks who established strong reputations among secular literati for their literary abilities,

---

[43] Daniel B. Stevenson cautions that the Home Mountain and Off Mountain labels did not "actively enter the T'ien-t'ai lexicon until the thirteenth century" and that they "lend a misleading sense of partisanship and finality to a situation that was far less rigid than we might imagine.... It is better to think of the controversies of the early Sung not so much as full-fledged internecine rivalries as the explosion of diverse interpretive possibilities." Daniel B. Stevenson and Neal Donner, *The Great Calming and Contemplation: A Study and Annotated Translation of the First Chapter of Chih-i's Mo-ho chih-kuan* (Honolulu: University of Hawaii Press, 1993), 85, 86.

[44] As Ziporyn relates in his chapter: "The Buddhist indeterminate, however, is not a blank, which would still be determinate as something definite (i.e., pure white or black space that excludes all other colors), but rather is blank in the way that a mirror's brightness is blank, and hence neither inclusive of determinations nor exclusive of them."

including an acknowledged expertise over Confucian classics. The likes of Zanning and Zhiyuan openly accepted the Confucian premises of Chinese society, even going so far as to teach *guwen* principles to members of the Buddhist clergy."[45]

In an important study, Yu Yingshi 余英時 identifies Zhiyuan as the first figure in the Northern Song to promote *Zhongyong* 中庸 (Doctrine of the Mean),[46] and following an earlier proposal by Chen Yinke 陳寅恪 (1890–1969), Yu introduces some new evidence to strengthen the thesis that associates Zhiyuan with the origins of the Daoxue tradition of Neo-Confucianism.[47] Yu also speculates that the Daoxue interest in *Zhongyong* followed a path opened up by Buddhist clerics, in which certain Confucian texts became the focus of attention, and was accompanied by what he terms the "Confucianization" of Buddhism and the transformation of the clerisy under the influence of the social and cultural elite (*shidafu* 士大夫) during the early and middle periods of the Northern Song. Yu further argues that, in the early Northern Song period, the interpretative authority of *Zhongyong* was dominated by followers of Buddhism, with Hu Yuan 胡瑗 (993–1059) being the first Confucian of that period to write a book on *Zhongyong* that had any influence.[48]

Zhiyuan even styled himself as the Master of the *Mean* (Zhongyongzi 中庸子), and in his *Autobiography of Master of the* Mean (*Zhongyongzi zhuan* 中庸子傳), he promotes a kind of Buddho-Confucian ecumenicism: "Although the words of the Confucians and Buddhists differ, *li* (pattern) interconnects (夫儒釋者言異而理貫)"—this is because Buddhist and Confucian teachings both exhort people to advance towards

---

[45] Welter, *Yongming Yanshou's Conception of Chan in the* Zongjing Lu, 208. For Welter's related study on Zanning, see "Confucian Monks and Buddhist Junzi: Zanning's *Topical Compendium of the Buddhist Clergy* (*Da Song seng shi lüe* 大宋僧史略) and the Politics of Buddhist Accommodation at the Song Court," in *The Middle Kingdom and the Dharma Wheel: Aspects of the Relationship between the Buddhist Saṃgha and the State in Chinese History*, ed. Thomas Jülch (Brill, 2106). For more general studies of the engagement of Song literati with Buddhism, see Halperin, *Out of the Cloister*; Hong Shufen 洪淑芬, *Lun Ru-Fo jiaoshe yu Songdai Ruxue fuxing: yi Zhiyuan, Qisong, Zonggao wei li* 論儒佛交涉與宋代儒學復興— 以智圓、契嵩、宗杲為例 (Confucian-Buddhist Interactions and the Revival of Confucianism in the Song Dynasty: Zhiyuan, Qisong and Zonggao as Examples) (Taipei: Da'an chubanshe, 2008).
[46] On Qisong's "*Zhongyong* jie" 中庸解 (Interpretation of the *Mean*), see Douglas Skonicki, "A Buddhist Response to Ancient-style Learning," *T'oung Pao* 97, nos. 1-3 (2011): 21–24.
[47] Yu Yingshi's study focuses on both Zhiyuan and the Chan monk, Qisong 契嵩 (1007–1072): *Zhu Xi de lishi shijie: Songdai shidafu zhengzhi wenhua de yanjiu* 朱熹的歷史世界: 宋代士大夫政治文化的研究 (Zhu Xi's Historical World: Studies of Song Dynasty Elite Literati Political Culture), vol. 1 (Taipei: Yunchen, 2003), 115–126. On Qisong, see also Skonicki, "A Buddhist Response to Ancient-style Learning."
[48] Yu Yingshi, *Zhu Xi de lishi shijie*, vol. 1, 129–141; 145. See also Hong Shufen, *Lun Ru-Fo jiaoshe yu Songdai Ruxue fuxing*, 369–413.

goodness and keep far from badness.[49] His connections with senior officials at the court would, no doubt, have assisted in facilitating the dissemination of his ideas beyond the confines of his mountain hermitage.[50] Significantly, as the following selection of passages serves to illustrate, the Off Mountain privileging of the mind remained central to his thought, even as he pursued his ecumenical agenda:

> "The Mean" is what Nāgārjuna meant by "the middle path." [Someone] asked: "What does it mean?"
>
> [Master Zhongyong] replied: "Dharmas are transformations of the One Mind. The mind has no describable features so how could dharmas? [Try] to make [them] vanish and they will all the more readily be preserved—it is the nature [of the mind] inherently to include them. [Try] to preserve them and they will all the more readily vanish—their intrinsic reality does not exist. Neither vanished nor preserved—this highlights the meaning of the middle/mean. Even if they are [separately] dispatched, they cannot be separated. Even if mixed together, they cannot be made to be undifferentiated."
>
> 中庸者，龍樹所謂中道義也。曰：「其義何邪。」曰：「夫諸法云云，一心所變。心無狀也。法豈有哉。亡之彌存，性本具也。存之彌亡，體非有也。非亡非存。中義著也。此三者，派之而不可分，混之而不可同。」[51]

Dharmas are nothing other than expressions of the mind. Although devoid of their own intrinsic reality, the nature of mind is such that it inherently includes them. The "three" referred to here are "the middle" (*zhong* 中), "exist" (*cun* 存), and "vanish" (*wang* 亡). "Exist" and "vanish" are terms that have their *locus classicus* in Mencius's Ox Mountain fable (6A.8). Here they serve as the functional equivalents of two of Tiantai's Three Truths: the Provisionally Posited (*jia* 假), and Emptiness (*kong* 空). (The third of the Three Truths, Center [中], is represented by the middle [中].) The key point here is that all three—middle (= Center), existence (= Provisionally Posited), and vanished (= Emptiness)—apply equally and simultaneously to the mind. Zhiyuan has moved the focus from applying the Three Truths to dharmas generally, instead applying them to the mind.

---

[49] *Xianju bian* 閒居編 (Writings Compiled in Retirement), X56.949, 894a16-17.
[50] Yu Yingshi, *Zhu Xi de lishi shijie*, vol. 1, 145.
[51] *Xianju bian*, X56.949, 894b6-9.

Master Zhongyong then makes the relationship with the Three Truths even more explicit, invoking the terms emptiness, existence, and the middle:

> Some people are swayed by emptiness, whereas others are attached to existence.... [Someone] asked: "Which is better, to be swayed by emptiness or to be attached to existence?"
>
> [Master Zhongyong] replied: "Being swayed by emptiness is to go beyond it; being attached to existence is to fail to reach it."
>
> [The interlocuter asked]: "Then [it is better to be swayed by] emptiness?"
>
> [Master Zhongyong] replied: "'Going beyond it is no better than failing to reach it.' The middle path alone is best...." The middle path is the name given to the animation of the myriad dharmas and refers to the inherent nature [of the mind].[52] If one attains understanding of it, since there will be no attachment to emptiness and existence, is it likely that there will be attachment to the middle?

> 或蕩於空或膠於有。...曰:「蕩空,膠有孰良?」曰:「蕩空也過,膠有也不及。」[曰:]「然則空愈與」。曰:『過猶不及也。』唯中道為良。...中道也,妙萬法之名乎,稱本性之謂乎。苟達之矣,空有其無著,於中豈有著乎嗚呼?」[53]

This passage seems to be a prescription for avoiding the extremes of holding that there are ultimately existent things, things with intrinsic nature, and holding that ultimately nothing exists, that phenomena do not exist at all. The concluding sentence, however, further makes it clear that not even the middle/mean/Center should be reified. To reify is to exclude and to exclude is inconsistent with the doctrine of nature inclusion or inherent inclusion (*xingju*). To be attached to the middle/mean/Center would be to treat it either as determinate—"the Center" as distinct from "the non-Center"—which would render it merely provisionally posited; or to treat it as indeterminate—as standing beyond all determinations—which would render it as empty. Zhiyuan's apparently ecumenical agenda thus

---

[52] Cf. *miao wanwu* 妙萬物 "animating the myriad things," the *locus classicus* of which is "Shuo gua" 說掛 (Explaining the Hexagrams), *Zhou Yi* 周易 (Book of Change), *Shisan jing zhushu* 十三經注疏 (The Thirteen Classics with Annotations and Sub-commentaries), comp. Ruan Yuan 阮元 (1764–1849) (Taipei: Yiwen yinshuguan, 1985), 9.6a. Following the interpretation of Mou Zongsan 牟宗三, *Zhou Yi zhexue yanjiang lu* 周易哲學演講錄 (Lectures on the Philosophy of the *Zhou Book of Change*) (Taipei: Lianjing chuban shiye gongsi), 130. Here, that which animates the myriad dharmas is dependent arising.

[53] *Xianju bian*, X56.949, 894b13, 18–19, 23–25.

ultimately serves a distinctly Tiantai goal.⁵⁴ This is no mere intellectual one-upmanship—the stakes were real and tangible: to win over the hearts and minds of the educated elite.

I.2 Chapter Synopses

Between 1144 and 1152, Zhu had studied with Kaishan Daoqian 開善道謙 (d. ca. 1150), a leading disciple of Dahui Zonggao.⁵⁵ John Jorgensen sets the scene for his chapter, "The Radiant Mind: Zhu Xi and the Chan Doctrine of *Tathāgatagarbha*," by claiming that Zhu actually spent over a third of his life exposed to, and at times practicing, the Chan of Dahui Zonggao and his students, and only when he met Li Yanping 李延平 (1093–1163) in 1153 did he begin to have doubts about Buddhism and Chan, and only a decade after that did he begin to criticize Buddhism and vigorously repudiate Dahui's style of Chan. He argues that even though Zhu Xi vigorously rejected Dahui's Chan, he still retained or adapted certain key themes and motifs from Chan, which brought him closer to the positions of so-called Northern Chan masters Hongren 弘忍 (601–674) and his heir, Shenxiu 神秀 (d. 706), in particular to the idea of a radiant buddha-nature. Jorgensen prosecutes the strong case that Zhu Xi "ended up mirroring many of his opponents' doctrines as he responded to agendas already well established in Buddhist circles, central to which were interpretations of the *tathāgatagarbha* doctrine."

The focus of the chapter is Zhu Xi's choice of the term "lucid radiance" (*xuming* 虛明) to describe the nature of the mind.⁵⁶ Jorgensen maintains that Zhu was indebted to the term's use in seventh- and eighth-century Northern Chan⁵⁷ circles to describe the *tathāgatagarbha* (variously also

---

⁵⁴ In this connection, it is worth noting Skonicki's related observation that Chan monk Qisong's objective in positing a shared *dao* with the *dao* championed by Ancient-style learning partisans—the *dao* of the ancient sages—"was not to establish the foundations for a syncretic world view, but rather to demonstrate that the *dao* of the ancient sages was in fact the Buddhist *dao*." Moreover, this *dao* is the mind (which in turn is buddha-nature) and thus accessible to all. Skonicki, "A Buddhist Response to Ancient-style Learning," 13, 19–20.
⁵⁵ Shu Jingnan 束景南, *Zhu Xi nianpu changbian* 朱熹年譜長編 (Chronological Biography of Zhu Xi), 2 vols. (Shanghai: Huadong shifan daxue chuban she, 2001), vol. 1, 87, 103, 107, 116, 138, 151, 153.
⁵⁶ Recently, Douglas L. Berger, *Encounters of Mind: Luminosity and Personhood in Indian and Chinese Thought* (Albany: SUNY, 2015) has also drawn attention to the role of a pure, luminous mind (*prabhāsvara; ming* 明, *mingjing* 明淨, *qingjing* 清淨) that underlies the more common mind of sensations, emotions, and volitions, in the Chinese reception and development of Yogācāra thought. Surprisingly, the role of *tathāgatagarbha* receives little attention.
⁵⁷ Jorgensen emphasizes that this was the real Northern Chan of the seventh and eighth centuries rather than Shenhui's 神會 (684–758) polemical creation. The term "Northern Chan" was created

identified with "One Mind," suchness, buddha-nature or the nature of the mind). "Just as buddha-nature or *tathāgatagarbha* is not non-existent, so too Zhu conceives of the nature as filled with pattern. And just as pattern in the nature awaits to be discerned, so too the *tathāgatagarbha* has a *tathāgata*, a Thus Come One or buddha, waiting to be discovered. In both cases, that content—be it pattern, buddha or suchness—is to be preserved or protected. This is a major feature of Northern Chan practice as well as in Zhu's practice." Jorgensen also emphasises the similarities between Zhu Xi's appropriation of Mencius' "preserving the mind" (*cun xin* 存心) and Northern Chan's "maintaining the One Mind" (*shou yixin* 守一心), both of which are directed at stopping the mind losing its innate characteristic of pure radiance as it succumbs to the pursuit of things out of selfish desire.

He finds another connection between Zhu and Northern Chan is the shared notion that there is only one mind but it has two aspects. For Zhu these are the mind of the way (*daoxin* 道心) and the human mind (*renxin* 人心). For Northern Chan (following the *Dasheng qixin lun*), these are the mind as suchness and the arising and ceasing mind. Both agree that the latter aspect in each case—for Zhu, the human mind, for Northern Chan, the mind of arising and ceasing—obscures our perception of the "lucid radiance," which is mind of the way or the mind as suchness.

Jorgensen's principal thesis is that Zhu Xi's description of the nature in terms of a "lucid radiance" obscured by *qi* (vital stuff), actually drew on popular Northern Chan metaphors such as a pearl in muddy water or a mirror covered by dust, used to characterize the state of our inherent buddha-nature, which, by being gradually purified of misleading desires, could lead to sainthood or, in Zhu's case, to a state approximating sagehood. (In maintaining that not every person is able to become a sage, Zhu effectively rejected the *tathāgatagarbha* and Chan article of faith that all could become saints, or indeed, all will become buddhas.) He maintains that this Northern Chan view in turn drew on the Tathāgatagarbha tradition's motif of a "radiant" but obscured mind or *tathāgatagarbha* innate in all sentient beings. He also identifies Zhu's use of the image of a dust-covered mirror as evidencing that Zhu appropriated more from the *tathāgatagarbha* theory than just the concept of lucid radiance (*xuming*). For Jorgensen, the evidence suggests that Zhu Xi was "influenced, possibly indirectly or unconsciously, by this aspect of Northern Chan thought, probably as a result of criticizing the Chan of Mazu and Dahui that was important in Zhu Xi's

---

by Shenhui to refer to the teachings of Shenxiu, which he characterized as gradualist, contrasting it to the subitist teachings of "Southern Chan" associated with Huineng 會能 (trad. d. 713).

time," provocatively concluding that Zhu Xi formulated what was in effect a kind of Confucian "Northern Chan," as evidenced by the common belief in an empty, radiant mind, obscured by habituation and *qi,* which could be realized by gradual practice.

Although Zhu is well-known for his harsh criticisms of Buddhism,[58] in "Zhu Xi's Critique of Buddhism: Selfishness, Salvation, and Self-Cultivation," Justin Tiwald finds that "much of the contemporary scholarship on Zhu Xi's critique of Buddhism has called attention to various respects in which Zhu seems to misrepresent the explicit views of his Buddhist opponents, noting cases where Zhu's characterization seems to lack nuance, ignores exceptions, or mischaracterizes Buddhist doctrines in a rather flatfooted way." He finds that these attempts to reconstruct Zhu's critique have largely mischaracterized it by treating it as a critique of the Buddhists' explicit views. The success or failure of Zhu's critique is accordingly judged to depend in large part on simply whether he got the Buddhist views right—that is, whether he correctly describes them.

Tiwald instead develops a tightly knit set of arguments to show that Zhu tended to think that regardless of how subtle and defensible the Buddhists' explicit views may have been in principle, in practice these views amount to something very different. For example, in principle, Buddhists endorse an ethics of other-directed concern, and promote the cultivation of loving kindness and the "great compassion" of a bodhisattva. Zhu Xi, however, accused the Buddhists of being selfish—not because he believed that they actually endorsed selfishness or ethical egoism but because he believed that the Buddhists' own practices made it nearly impossible to cultivate genuine other-directed concern. For Buddhists, all routes to great compassion go through radical non-attachment, such that Buddhist monks have to jettison all special attachments even to their own families. In contrast, Confucian methods of moral cultivation build on the sort of other-directed concern that we learn in the family, which comes naturally and is more easily expanded to include others. The Confucian method is realistic, and through it other-directed care is realizable within the space of a single lifetime. The Buddhist methods are very unlikely to succeed, requiring heroic feats of self-transformation, and depending for their justification on highly speculative views about rebirth.

---

[58] Charles Fu notes: "Very few Neo-Confucian representatives in the Sung . . . , Yuan . . . , and Ming . . . dynasties had studied Buddhism as hard and seriously as Chu Hsi [Zhu Xi] did, nor had any of them attempted a genuine philosophical attack upon Buddhism as thoroughly and as devastatingly as he did." See his "Morality or Beyond: The Neo-Confucian Confrontation with Mahāyāna Buddhism," *Philosophy East and West* 23, no. 3 (1973): 377.

Tiwald approaches the question of Zhu Xi's relationship with Buddhism by examining three sets of criticisms Zhu developed in opposition to Buddhist views. He argues that the above sort of reframing of those criticisms makes them both more powerful and more faithful to Zhu's own understanding of them, as recorded in his letters, essays, and discussions with students. The first set of criticisms has to do with Buddhist soteriology, the fundamental priority of Buddhist salvation, which Zhu believed lent itself to egoism and perverted the more relationship-oriented nature of ethics itself. The second set of criticisms concerns Buddhist meditation, which in Zhu's view leaves Buddhists ill-equipped to take independent standards of right and wrong into account. Confucian "reverential attention" (*jing* 敬), he argued, is the better means by which to reshape one's intentions and emotions in light of objective standards. The final criticisms are of the Buddhist doctrine of emptiness. Here Zhu seems to be an uncharitable critic, suggesting that Buddhists treat all things as illusory and without any meaningful relationship to the larger world. Once again, however, Tiwald argues, a closer examination of the evidence shows that he was both aware of more defensible notions of Buddhist emptiness and, at the end of the day, unconvinced that Buddhist practices were conducive to realizing them.

Tiwald concludes that Zhu was not engaged merely with a fictional notion of Buddhism. Rather, the views and the arguments Zhu advanced in support of them were developed in direct response to Buddhist thought, revealing that Zhu participated in a genuine, shared dialogue with his Buddhist adversaries. And perhaps most importantly, "this dialogue took place at multiple levels, probing the connections between doctrines, presuppositions, and day-to-day practices in ways that stand apart from the more conceptual and scholastic disputes we associate with philosophy in medieval Europe and beyond."

In "Buddhism and Zhu Xi's Epistemology of Discernment," Stephen Angle focuses on the case of Zhu's theory of knowing to show how Zhu consciously repurposed Buddhist ideas to develop his own thought. Angle develops two parallel lines of argument. The first and more general argument is that despite Zhu's extended personal encounter with Buddhism, that is not the main reason key aspects of his thought resemble Buddhist ideas and modes of thought. Rather, the resemblance is due to the deep-rooted cultural embeddedness of Buddhist ideas and modes of thought. We are, however, exhorted to assess such resemblances, and indeed, influences, on a case-by-case basis, because they vary widely in nature and scope, and, crucially, in the means by which Zhu appropriated and repurposed them.

These more deep-rooted elements are associated with the first three of the four layers of Buddhist-Confucian interaction Angle identifies as having collectively shaped the ways in which Zhu was influenced by and reacted to Buddhism. The first layer consists of early developments within Sinitic Buddhism—such as the "buddha-nature" doctrine, a metaphysical "mind" (or heartmind), and the attention paid to holism and intersubjectivity, all of which became key conceptual resources in the process of cross-fertilization between Sinitic Buddhist and native Chinese traditions. The second layer is the gradual articulation of a shared Confucian-Buddhist-Daoist intellectual repertoire consisting of terms, phrases, and texts, which become common property of Tang-dynasty thinkers. The third layer consists of the varying attitudes towards and engagements with Buddhism on the part of first- and second-generation Daoxue figures. The fourth layer is Zhu Xi's own experience with Buddhism.

The second and more specific line of argument is despite the fact that Zhu's "epistemic theorizing is replete with terms and phrases that are strongly associated with, and in some cases originate from, Buddhist writing" and that "there are respects in which his theories appear to be structurally parallel with Buddhist theories," the similarities in terminology or structure actually mask deep differences. In order to understand how epistemic terms and categories that feature in earlier Buddhist sources eventually became important to Zhu Xi, Angle identifies three different attitudes to knowing presented in three influential Buddhist sources: a pragmatic approach (*Foxing lun* 佛性論 [Buddha-nature Treatise]), an approach emphasizing a deep and genuine knowing (Zongmi), and an approach that validates everyday perceptual experience (Mazu). While acknowledging that Zhu had studied a version of Mazu's approach (under Daoqian), and later had also developed a criticism of that approach consistent with Zongmi's critical views, Angle argues that such similarities mask important differences.

To that end, he sets out a schematic overview of Zhu's understanding of knowing, distinguishing three distinct types of knowing: (1) knowing a rule to which things should conform; (2) seeing an isolated instance of how things should be and being compelled to follow it; and (3) awakening to the underlying reason for why things are as they are. Against this background, he argues the case that Zhu repurposed the Buddhist term "*zhijue* 知覺" (perceptual awareness) to become a general term for the mind's (or heartmind's) various kinds of knowing activity, concluding that Zhu's epistemology was a conscious rejection of Dahui's radical Chan approach, and moreover was also responding to a discourse context, which, while deriving some of its underlying shape from the discourse shared with Zongmi, had quite distinct concerns and goals from those of Zongmi. In particular, the third type of knowing is characterized as being explicitly about seeing interconnections, about "unimpeded interconnecting" (*huoran guantong* 豁然貫通). "The key point about these holistic states of awakening and unimpeded interconnection, which distinguishes Zhu from Huayan and Chan descriptions of holistic states of enlightenment, is that for the Neo-Confucians, 'unimpeded interconnection' is still structured or centered in ways that we can at least partly articulate."

Finally, integrating the above two lines of argument, Angle concludes: "The ultimate picture will surely be one in which Zhu has strong, substantive connections to Buddhist teachings in some areas and not in others, all of this built on a foundation of deep, layered interactions over many centuries." As he cogently recommends, other chapters in this volume—as well as other scholarship on the Buddhist roots of Zhu Xi's thought—will, accordingly, need to be judged on a case-by-case basis.

In "The *Ti-Yong* 體用 Model and Its Discontents: Models of Ambiguous Priority in Chinese Buddhism and Zhu Xi's Neo-Confucianism," Brook A. Ziporyn continues to examine how Zhu repurposed Buddhist ideas to develop his own thought.

Ziporyn shows that although Tiantai, Huayan, and Zhu Xi all deploy the *ti-yong* model as a crucial component of their metaphysics, in certain key places they deploy it for different ends, "leading to subtle structural differences, which for them amounted to large philosophical consequences." To this end, he first develops a detailed comparison of these models in the Huayan and Tiantai schools, and then sets out to show how analogous structures to each of these are adapted to form parts of Zhu Xi's metaphysics.

Ziporyn distinguishes three different *ti-yong* models:

(1) The "classic *ti-yong* model" is associated in particular with early Chinese Buddhist sources and also non-Buddhist thinkers such as Wang Bi 王弼 (226–249). Like the root and branches of a tree, this model implies both strong contrast and strong continuity between *ti* and *yong*. Thus *ti* is one and unseen; *yong* is many and seen. *Ti* is prioritized over *yong*, *ti* is independent, and *yong* is always dependent on *ti* but not vice versa. *Ti* is the source or basis of *yong*. An important variation of this classic model is the "Huayan model," which Ziporyn characterizes as a radicalization of the classic *ti-yong* model and developed by representative figures such as

Dushun, Zhiyan, Fazang, Chengguan, and Zongmi. Strongly influenced by the *Dasheng qixin lun,* this model is often exemplified by the relation between the brightness of a mirror and the images appearing in the mirror, or between the wetness of water and the waves of the water. Here *ti* and the *yong* are coextensive—wherever there is *ti* there is *yong*. There is no *ti* outside *yong*, and no *yong* outside *ti*. They are, however, always distinct conceptually, and a one-way relation of dependence pertains to them: *yong* depends on *ti* but *ti* does not depend on *yong*. Crucially, however, the *ti* would not be apparent as *ti* if it were not functioning fully as the diverse *yong,* which are conceptually contrasted to it. This model applies both at the level of the mind or consciousness and its conceptual objects and at the metaphysical level, expressed in the relation between Li 理 and *shi* 事, between the sole ultimate reality and its multiple manifestations.

(2) The Tiantai model. Early Tiantai figures such as Zhiyi used the category of Center—a key category in the Tiantai doctrine of the Three Truths—rather than *ti-yong*, to describe the relation between Li and *shi*. As Ziporyn teases out in considerable detail, for Zhiyi, real particulars are assumed to be portions of the whole, their determinacy being nothing but a function of limitation and relationship to their opposites (i.e., a particular is determined relative to what it is not). The ground of reality is the Center, which is a part of *both* halves of any dyad—sameness and difference, ignorance and enlightenment, one and many, presence and absence, inside and outside, this and that, and so on—and yet also transcends both. Thus the Center is another term for the transcendent and yet also for the whole, the complete, the unbiased. This way of thinking allows Zhiyi to speak of the relation between Li and *shi* in terms of a relation between whole and part, center and periphery, biased and complete. In Zhanran, the *ti-yong* model derived from Huayan is adopted but modified to accord with the Center-periphery model of Zhiyi.

The Huayan view is that all *yong* are functions of, and coextensive with, the one same *ti*—all waves are coextensive with the same wetness—but where there is unity in the wetness there is multiplicity is the waves. In contrast, the Tiantai view of the relation between *ti* and *yong* is not that of one-many but of whole and part. Each part (*yong*) is also intersubsumptive with all other parts, and is thus itself inseparably the whole (*ti*). Moreover, gone is any sense of priority or one-way dependence. Thus each *yong* is a *ti*, and because *ti* and *yong* are coextensive, any particular *ti* is also the *yong* of any and all other *ti*. (Wetness is coextensive with wave but it is no less coextensive with color, happiness, third-world poverty, movement, space, Donald Trump, and so on.) *Ti* is both *ti* and *yong*, and *yong* is both *yong* and *ti*.

This ambiguity or bi-valence—being neither the same as nor different from—is a function of the Tiantai doctrine of Three Truths. Because *yong* (or *ti*) is both *ti* and *yong*, it is indeterminate: Viewed from one aspect it is *ti* and from the other it is *yong*; it is both and neither. To be indeterminate is to be empty, to lack a determinate identity; but to be empty is, in fact, to be determinate (i.e., "empty" as distinct from "non-empty"), and this determinacy is to be provisionally posited. Why is it merely provisional? It is provisional because the boundaries that demarcate it as distinct amount to an interface, and an interface is both and neither. An interface links two bounded things yet simultaneously separates them—to be provisional is to be both and to be neither. Yet precisely because it is both and neither it is also the Center. If viewed from the perspective of its being a whole that contains all opposed determinations, it is determinate (the whole as distinct from partial determinations), and to be determinate is to be provisionally posited. Conversely, if viewed from the aspect of its transcendence, its standing beyond all determinations, the Center is also emptiness, because to be indeterminate is to be empty.

(3) Zhu Xi's model. Drawing on this rich, if complex, theoretical background, Ziporyn proceeds to argue that around the age of forty Zhu Xi significantly changed his views about *li* and *qi*, no longer subscribing to a straightforward *ti-yong* relationship, instead seeming to mimic a move from the Huayan *ti-yong* model to the Tiantai *ti-yong* model. While retaining much of the still serviceable *ti-yong* language, Ziporyn finds that Zhu Xi specifically supplements the Huayan model with something structurally close to the Tiantai focus on Center-periphery relations and the relations between opposites. He argues that the mode of transcendence and pre-existence is also affected by this shift: Zhu Xi seems to want the kind of transcendence that pertains to the Center's transcendent-immanence with the peripheral opposites it unifies rather than the transcendent-immanence of wetness in waves or brightness in images. The second half of his chapter is an intricate and challenging argument to work out the philosophical and comparative significance of these points. In doing so, he presents us with an entirely new way to understand Zhu Xi's philosophical inventiveness and its profound correspondences with Buddhist thought.

Just as in Tiantai, where the Center as a whole is conceptually prior to and transcends its two parts (emptiness and the provisionally posited, indeterminate and determinate) yet is temporally simultaneous, so too for Zhu Xi, Taiji 太極 (Supreme Pivot) (=*li*) is the functional equivalent of the

Center—a union of opposites (*yin* and *yang*) that contains them but also transcends them. *Li* is conceptually prior to *qi*, yet also always coexistent with *qi*, immanent in *qi*.

At the same time, however, as with the relationship between Li and *shi* in Huayan, for Zhu Xi any particular configuration of *qi* depends on its *li* in a way that is not reversible. As expressed by Ziporyn, in Zhu Xi's case, "*any particular li is prior temporally to its manifestation as a particular configuration of qi.*" This is because any particular *li* is inherently present in the unity that is *li*, that is Taiji, and the entire *li* is fully present in each particular (*shi*). Where Zhu and Huayan radically part company is that in Huayan there is only one Li, and because it lacks any determinate nature it is equated with emptiness—a quality that enables it to interpenetrate with all phenomena.

For both Tiantai and Zhu Xi, the realm of Li/*li* is itself internally structured and articulated, while remaining unified and transcendental. Unlike the brightness of a mirror, it inherently possesses specific content. In the Tiantai case, the articulated differences, contrasts, and inter-nestings are referred to with the term "3000." In Zhu Xi's case, they are referred to as many individual principles/patterns of all things.

In the final chapter, "Monism and the Problem of the Ignorance and Badness in Chinese Buddhism and Zhu Xi's Neo-Confucianism," I also argue that key aspects of Zhu's metaphysics and philosophy of mind draw preponderantly on conceptual structures and problematics that evidence an unequivocal Buddhist pedigree, but which he adapted for his own philosophical ends. I advance two main theses, both of which link Zhu Xi to the *Dasheng qixin lun*. The first thesis again concerns the *ti-yong* polarity. The second and main thesis concerns the problem of the origin of ignorance. These theses are interwoven and developed concurrently.

Although the *ti-yong* polarity is generally still regarded as an endogenous Chinese philosophical construct, its philosophical development owes more to late Six Dynasties and Sui-Tang traditions of Sinitic Buddhist thought than to Wei-Jin Profound Learning (*xuanxue*).[59] The *Dasheng*

---

[59] Shimada Kenji 島田虔次, *Shushigaku to Yōmeigaku* 朱子学と陽明学 (Zhu Xi Learning and Yangming Learning) (Tokyo: Iwanami shoten, 1967), 4 even asserts that the systematic use of *ti* and *yong* as a dyad "can without the slightest exaggeration be said to be exclusive to Buddhist scriptures." For relevant studies, see also his "Taiyō no rekishi ni yosete" 体用の歴史に寄せて (On the History of *Ti-Yong*) in *Tsukamoto hakushi shōju kinen: Bukkyūshigaku ronshū* 塚本博士頌寿記念：仏教史学論集 (Collection of Essays on the History of Buddhism Presented to Dr. Tsukamoto in Commemoration of His Retirement), ed. Tsukamoto hakushi shōju kinenkai 塚本博士頌寿記念會 (Kyoto: 1961), 416–430, which provides a good overview of Six Dynasties sources. Funayama Toru 船山徹, "Taiyō shōkō" 體用小考 (On *Ti-Yong*), in *Rikuchō Zui Tō*

qixin lun presents the relationship between the two gateways as a *ti-yong* relationship, in which the unconditioned (suchness, *tathāgatabarbha*) pervades or is coextensive with the conditioned (*ālayavijñāna* or store consciousness, the locus of phenomenal experience). Moreover, suchness exists in the gateway of the mind of arising and ceasing (the adaption of *tathāgatagarbha* to phenomenal conditions, as *ālayavijñāna*) while *simultaneously extending beyond* the gateway of the mind of arising and ceasing (suchness *qua* the unconditioned), just as wetness exists in all waves but simultaneously extends beyond any particular wave.

What is distinctive about this particular conception of the *ti-yong* relationship is that it is used as a vehicle to convey the idea that the relationship between the unconditioned and the conditioned is one of immanent transcendence. Immanent transcendence is a realist metaphysical view (i.e., not a nominalism). It describes how, on the one hand, the referent wholly lies within the boundaries of a specifiable domain yet, on the other hand, it simultaneously extends beyond the boundaries of that domain.[60]

Just as Huayan master Fazang and various Northern Song Tiantai theorists describe the relationship between Li and phenomena (*shi*) also in terms of *ti-yong*, so too Zhu subsequently presented the relationship between Taiji/*li* and *qi* as a *ti-yong* relationship. More pertinently, his understanding of *ti-yong* is consistent with the model found in the *Dasheng qixin lun* and as described by various Huayan thinkers. According to this model, even though *ti* (the unconditioned) is coextensive with *yong* (the conditioned), *ti* remains unitary, and only *yong* are multiple. For Zhu Xi,

---

seishinshi no kenkyū 六朝隋唐精神史の研究 (Studies on the Psycho-Spiritual History in the Six Dynasties, Sui and Tang Periods), A Report of Grant-in-Aid for Scientific Research, ed. Usami Bunri 宇佐美文理 (Kyoto: Japan Society for the Promotion of Science, 2005), 125–135, provides an informative account of the earliest uses of *ti-yong* in Chinese Buddhist sources. I am grateful to Professor Funayama for generously providing a copy of this report.

[60] Elsewhere I have argued that that this particular conception of the *ti-yong* relationship can be traced to developments in Southern Chinese Buddhist circles during the latter half of the fifth century. (See my "Chinese Philosophy's Hybrid Identity," in *Why Traditional Chinese Philosophy Still Matters: The Relevance of Ancient Wisdom to the Global Age*, [ed.] Ming Dong Gu [London: Routledge, 2018].) It is a unique product of the fecund engagement of Buddhist constructs derived from both the Indian and Chinese traditions, or to use Chen-kuo Lin's felicitous phrase, "the result of a dialectical interplay between Sinification and Indianization." (Chen-kuo Lin, "Epistemology and Cultivation in Jingying Huiyuan's 'Essay on the Three Means of Valid Cognition,'" in [eds.] Chen-kuo Lin and Michael Radich, *A Distant Mirror: Articulating Indic Ideas in Sixth and Seventh Century Chinese Buddhism* [Hamburg: Hamburg University Press, 2014], 82). Its Sinified or Sinicized aspect is the *ti-yong* polarity; its Indianized aspect is the appropriation of the *ti-yong* polarity as a vehicle to express the idea of immanent transcendence, with specific reference to the unconditioned and the conditioned.

viewed from the perspective its transcendent aspect, Taiji is inherently imbued with the *li* of all phenomena, even before any particular phenomenon yet exists. Intrinsic reality does not exist without function—even if a particular function is yet to be activated—otherwise it would not be intrinsic reality. Conversely, any determinate phenomenon exists by virtue of being endowed with *li*. This is *li* or Taiji in its immanent aspect. The immanent and transcendent are aspects of a single whole that is Taiji. They refer to the two polar perspectives of that whole.

Zhu Xi did not stop there. His account of the mind of the way (*daoxin* 道心) and the human mind (*renxin* 人心); Taiji and *yin-yang*; and the "heaven-and-earth-bestowed nature" (*tiandi zhi xing* 天地之性) and the psychophysical nature (*qizhi zhi xing* 氣質之性) is, in each case, presented as a relationship of immanent transcendence of the *ti-yong* type. Each pair is used to affirm a consistent response to the following problem: "How can the unconditioned (the mind of the way, Taiji, the heaven-and-earth bestowed nature) be realized if our cognitive awareness is circumscribed by the conditioned nature of human existence?" Zhu's constant refrain, that the unconditioned is never apart from the conditioned yet its unconditioned nature is not in any way compromised by that relationship, bears a distinct family resemblance to a cognate formulation in the *Dasheng qixin lun*, where the ocean water is never separated from the wind, but whether the wind blows or not, the wet nature of the water remains unchanged. In both cases, the unconditioned (suchness, *tathāgatabarbha*, Taiji, *li*, the heaven-and-earth-bestowed nature, the mind of the way) is somehow able to be coextensive with the conditioned (the *ālayavijñāna*, *qi*, the psychophysical nature [*qizhi zhi xing*], the mind of humans) yet simultaneously also extend beyond the conditioned; and the relation between the unconditioned and the conditioned is expressed in terms of the *ti-yong* polarity.

Whether Zhu's understanding of "pattern" and "*qi*" and the *Dasheng qixin lun*'s account of "the gateway of the mind as suchness" and "the gateway of the mind as arising and ceasing" are merely isomorphic or whether this correspondence can also be linked to more specific agencies of influence and appropriation, is a question that lies beyond the scope of my chapter.[61] Of greater significance to our understanding of Zhu Xi's thought is that the research introduced in that chapter—as in other chapters in this volume—reveals the vital role that Buddhist resources

---

[61] My own view is that they are homologues: The similarity of their shared structures is due to their being modified descendants of a common ancestor.

played in Zhu Xi's philosophical repertoire, and in doing so, opens up new ways of understanding what Zhu Xi was trying to achieve as a philosopher.

The second and main thesis of my chapter concerns the problem of the origin of ignorance. Robert Gimello maintains that the problem of the origin of ignorance was an issue that Mādhyamika, Yogācāra, and Tathāgatagarbha thinkers all failed to resolve, be it in India or in China. The Mādhyamika's apophatic focus on emptiness effectively dismisses the functional role that conventional reality can play in identifying those agencies that perpetuate ignorance. The Yogācāras make ignorance seem a natural state of the mind but have difficulty in showing how that state of mind can lead to the generation of enlightenment through the external agency of "permeation by hearing" (*śruta-vāsanā*; residual impression left by listening [to the correct exposition of the truth]). The Tathāgatagarbha tradition was confronted with the problem of how to reconcile the doctrine of the mind's inherent state of enlightenment with the doctrine that ignorance is present since beginningless time.[62] Given the fundamental role that ignorance plays in the second of the Four Noble Truths and as the first link in the Twelve Links of Conditioned Origination, the import of this issue was not trifling.

The *Dasheng qixin lun* is significant for its discussion of why it is so difficult to attain buddhahood and why so few are aware of their inherent buddha-nature. Specifically, it explores why most beings are enmeshed in delusion, given that the mind is inherently awoken (*benjue* 本覺). The text provides a concise restatement of the complexities of the ten-stage path of bodhisattva (enlightened being) practice in Mahāyāna Buddhism, which enables deluded beings to free themselves from their false perceptions and suffering. The title, *Giving Rise to Faith in the Great Vehicle*, refers to the arousing of an aspiration to enter that path. The text attempts to guide the novice towards its soteriological goal by means of a number of strategies. One key strategy is via a monism, which is deployed to show the pernicious effects of, but also the illusory nature of, ignorance. By drawing on analogies that present ignorance as external to suchness, however, the text leaves itself vulnerable to the charge that it introduces a dualist analogy into a monistic ontology.

As introduced in the first part of my chapter, in failing to provide a consistent account of the origin of ignorance, the *Dasheng qixin lun* was

---

[62] Gimello, "Chih-yen and the Foundations of Hua-yen Buddhism," 222–274 passim.

construed as also failing to provide a satisfactory account of how badness, evil and suffering arise, thus undermining its own soteriological goal. Beginning with early commentators such as the Huayan master Fazang in the early Tang and continuing through to Tiantai masters of the Northern Song, a rich diversity of arguments was developed to preserve a monistic ontology yet also account for the origin of ignorance. Many such accounts were framed in terms of the relationship between Li 理 and phenomena (*shi* 事), with Li representing suchness, and phenomena representing dharmas.

The second part analyzes attempts by two groups of Tiantai thinkers—the Home Mountain and Off Mountain masters—to reconcile the origin of badness with a monistic ontology. As with Huayan theorists, their arguments were framed in terms of the relationship between Li and *shi*. One of the main philosophical issues separating the Home Mountain and Off Mountain masters concerned this relationship. The Home Mountain masters deconstruct the problem of ontological dualism and the attendant issue of the origin of ignorance by arguing that ignorance is not an external condition, separate from intrinsic reality. Li is phenomena and phenomena (including ignorance) are Li. The Off Mountain masters also deconstruct the problem, but do so by denying that ignorance (qua phenomena) has a self-nature. Only Li has self-nature, not phenomena.

The third part argues that Zhu Xi was able to reconcile the origin of badness with a monistic ontology in such a way that it provided a more compelling case for affirming the phenomenal world, the life-world, as the ground for ethical practice. I endeavor to show that Zhu Xi's understanding of the *li-qi* relationship, posited as one of immanent transcendence, is a further development of the rich and complex body of Buddhist discourse that arose in the Tang and Northern Song about Li 理 and *shi* 事, which had attempted to reconcile the origin of ignorance and badness with a monistic ontology. Zhu's solution was to develop a monistic ontology in which the conditions that make badness possible are not associated with pattern (*li* 理) but rather are associated with *qi*, but with the crucial stipulation that there can be no pattern without *qi*. In doing so, I maintain, he also provided a new solution to the problem of badness—one that avoided the radical proposals entailed in Buddhist attempts to deal with the issue for over half a millennium. This example underscores why an understanding of the Buddhist models Zhu had at his disposal can yield new insights into how he constructed and defended the monistic ontology that is the centerpiece of his metaphysics, ethics, and philosophy of mind.

I.3 Concluding Remarks

On the question of Neo-Confucianism's philosophical borrowings from Buddhism, Peter Bol maintains that these borrowings "were more accidental than purposeful. Ideas about all things sharing the same principle and, above all, the importance given to the 'mind' in moral cultivation were in origin Buddhist but by Song times had become current in literati society." He further relates that even though certain ideas were Buddhist in origin they had become shared assumptions by the Song era.[63] The evidence garnered in this volume suggests, rather, it is only by analyzing precisely how key concepts such as *li* and *qi*, mind and the nature, *ti* and *yong* and so forth were understood and used by individual thinkers such as Zhu Xi that their significance as components of a specific body of philosophical thought can be determined. In turn, that determination can be achieved only by understanding the Buddhist contributions to the development of these and related concepts and to the theoretical debates that informed that development over the course of centuries.

This volume presents a range of "case studies" to show just how Zhu Xi both engaged with and also drew upon a diverse repertoire of Buddhist ideas and conceptual structures, repurposing them for his philosophical project. Stephen Angle maintains that the main reason key aspects of Zhu Xi's thought resemble Buddhist ideas and modes of thought is due to their deep-rooted cultural embeddedness. Despite these resemblances, he argues that the theoretical differences between Zhu's epistemology and various Buddhist positions "are real, deep, and were well understood by Zhu himself." As with Justin Tiwald, he finds that Zhu's concerns were primarily motived by principled, philosophical reasons for insisting that key aspects of Buddhist teachings are wrong and pernicious. At the same time, however, Angle's focus on Zhu's theory of knowing also highlights how Zhu consciously repurposed the Buddhist term "*zhijue* 知覺" (perceptual awareness) to develop his epistemology. Such repurposing attests to sustained, focused, and conscious engagement rather than accidental borrowing.

John Jorgensen similarly sets out a rich body of evidence to show that it was in reaction to doctrines associated with the Mazu-Linji-Dahui lineage of Chan that the mature Zhu actually embraced key aspects of Tathāgatagarbha thought as the theoretical underpinning of his philosophy

---

[63] Bol, *Neo-Confucianism in History*, 104, 164.

of mind and the nature, albeit now repurposed for Zhu's own Confucian project.

The *ti-yong* polarity—which by Song times certainly had already become a shared conceptual resource—provides another prominent example of philosophical repurposing. Brook A. Ziporyn advances a detailed series of arguments to show that Zhu Xi made the *ti-yong* model a crucial component of his metaphysics by modifying it to align with the Tiantai doctrine of the Three Truths. In doing so, he presents an entirely new interpretation of Zhu Xi's philosophical appropriation of Zhou Dunyi's Taiji Diagram and its essay, and key concepts such as Taiji, *li*, and *yin-yang*.

My chapter shows that Zhu's conception of immanent transcendence is based on a series of theoretical refinements and elaborations of the *ti-yong* polarity made by Buddhist theorists, but appropriated by Zhu for his own philosophical ends. I argue that this Buddhist theoretical background is essential to understanding why Zhu framed the relationship between *li* and *qi* within a monism, which in turn underpins his philosophy of mind and moral philosophy.

CHAPTER 1 | **The Radiant Mind**

Zhu Xi and the Chan Doctrine of Tathāgatagarbha

JOHN JORGENSEN

FOR MUCH OF his life, Zhu Xi 朱熹 (1130–1200) held that Buddhism was the most dangerous rival teaching to Confucianism. It was worse than the teachings of Yang Zhu, Mozi, and Daoism. "The Buddhists are people who have the most refined and subtle doctrines that affect people, and in this dynasty many of the most excellent people have fallen for it" (佛氏最有精微動得人處，本朝許多極好人無不陷焉。). Zhu proceeds to claim that the Buddhists are those "who most delude people. When you first see that their theories are reasonable, then the more you follow their theories, the more you harm people" (只為釋氏最能惑人。初見他說出來自有道理，從他說愈深，愈是害人。).[1] In fact, this critical attitude was actually a major reversal in Zhu Xi's thought, and his rejection of Chan, and Buddhism more generally, was a gradual process.

Zhu Xi's predecessors in Daoxue[2] had studied Buddhism, especially Chan Buddhism, and referred to Chan teachings and texts, and associated with Chan monks.[3] Zhu Xi himself referred to many Chan masters

---

[1] Li Jingde 黎靖德, comp. *Zhuzi yulei* 朱子語類 (Topically Arranged Conversations of Master Zhu) 8 vols. (Beijing: Zhonghua shuju, 1986; hereafter *Zhuzi yulei*), *juan* 24, 587.

[2] The Learning of the [Confucian] Way. In a narrow sense, this term was applied to those Northern Song (960–1126) thinkers who studied the teachings of a lineage of thinkers from Confucius to Mencius and who attempted to resurrect those teachings by giving them a new interpretation. The chief re-interpreters or self-proclaimed heirs to this lineage of the Way (*daotong* 道統) were Zhu Xi and Cheng Yi 程頤 (Yichuan 伊川; 1033–1107). See Peter K. Bol, *"This Culture of Ours": Intellectual Transitions in T'ang and Sung China* (Stanford, CA: Stanford University Press, 1992), 28. See also John Makeham's Introduction to this volume.

[3] Zhang Zai, *Zhang Zai ji* 張載集 (Collected Writings of Zhang Zai) (Beijing: Zhonghua shuju, 1978), 381; Shao Yong, *Shao Yong ji* 邵雍集 (Collected Writings of Shao Yong)

and texts, most often to Dahui Zonggao 大慧宗杲 (1089–1163), the most influential Chan master of the day.⁴ Zhu had also exchanged letters with Kaishan Daoqian 開善道謙 (d.u.), a disciple of Dahui Zonggao, and he had studied Buddhism, and Daoism to a lesser extent, for around two decades. He is even said to have become "enlightened" at the age of fifteen or sixteen when Daoqian confronted Zhu with the "point of the story" (*huatou* 話頭) in Zhaozhou's 趙州 (778–897) celebrated riddle, "Does a dog have buddha-nature?"⁵ This involvement with Chan is not surprising, as Chan in the early Northern Song had imperial support, with the *Jingde chuandeng lu* having imperial imprimatur and the prime text of Linji Chan, the *Tiansheng guangdeng lu* 天聖廣燈錄 (Supplementary Lamp Record Published in the Tiansheng Era) having a preface penned by Emperor Renzong (r. 1022–1063).⁶

Zhu Xi had become concerned that earlier and contemporary contributors to Daoxue were influenced by Chan.⁷ This anxiety of influence was due to the fact that Chan was very close doctrinally to some of the ideas Zhu and his comrades were promoting; and that Dahui was undermining support

---

(Beijing: Zhonghua shuju, 2010), 300, 582; for the Cheng brothers, Song Siyŏl 宋時烈, comp., *Chŏngsŏ bullyu* 程書分類 (The Cheng Brothers's Writings Topically Arranged), 2 vols. (Shanghai: Shanghai cishu chubanshe, 2006), 460, 537 (a Chan *gong'an*), 668 (citation of *Jingde chuandeng lu* 景德傳燈錄 [Record of the Transmission of the Lamplight Compiled during the Jingde Era]); A. C. Graham, *Two Chinese Philosophers: Ch'êng Ming-tao and Ch'êng Yi-ch'uan* (London: Lund Humphries, 1958), xxi.

⁴ For example, on Dahui Zonggao, *Zhuzi yulei*, *juan* 4, 80; on Caodong, *juan* 6, 120; a mention of *Chanyuan qinggui* 禪苑清規 (Rules of Purity in the Chan Monastery), *juan*7, 126; a metaphor from Chan *kanhua* 看話 practice, *juan* 8, 132; quotation of Dahui, *juan* 8, 137 and *juan* 41, 1057; on Yanshou 延壽 (904–975), Chan and Tiantai, *juan* 8, 14; quotation of Zhaozhou, *juan*10, 1731. See also Galen Sargent, "Tchou Hi contre le bouddhisme," *Mélanges publiés l'Institut des Hautes Études Chinoises* 1 (1957), 4. Zonggao is referred to by name in no less than thirteen paragraphs in *juan* 126 of the *Zhuzi yulei*.

⁵ Fukushima Shun'ō 福嶋俊翁, "Chūgoku ni okeru Zen bunka" 中国に於ける禅文化 (Chan Culture in China) in *Fukushima Shun'ō chosakushū* 福嶋俊翁著作集 (Collected Writings of Fukushima Shun'ō) (Tokyo: Mokujisha, 1938, reprint 1974), vol. 3, 161–162. Zhaozhou Congshen 趙州從諗 was a Chan master in a lineage from Mazu Daoyi 馬祖道一 (706–788). Zhaozhou was famed for his sharp tongue and wit, so his Chan gained the name "eloquent Chan," and many of his verbal responses were made into *gong'an* 公案 or Chan cases. The "point of the story," sometimes translated as "critical phrase," is the *huatou*, a reduction of the *gong'an* to a single word or phrase, a technique invented by Dahui Zonggao. The crucial element in the practice of *huatou* is doubt, not the words. The most famous *huatou* was Zhaozhou's response to the question, "Does a dog have buddha-nature?" which was *wu* 無 ("It does not"). See Ibuki Atsushi 伊吹敦, *Zen no rekishi* 禅の歴史 (History of Chan/Zen) (Kyoto: Hōzōkan, 2001), 67, 121.

⁶ Albert Welter, *Monks, Rulers, and Literati: The Political Ascendancy of Chan Buddhism* (New York: Oxford University Press, 2006), 186–187.

⁷ On Wang Tianshun 王天順 and Lu Jiuyuan 陸九淵 (1139–1193), see *Zhuzi yulei*, *juan* 17, 379–380; on Li Ao's 李翱 (772–841) theory of eliminating emotion, see *juan* 59, 1381; on Zhang Wugou 張無垢, see *juan* 126, 3037.

among the educated gentry for Daoxue or more broadly for Confucianism. Zhu, however, thought that Buddhism was misguided philosophically, and that these errors led to morally problematic consequences.[8] In particular, even the Buddhist bodhisattva vow to postpone one's own liberation until all sentient beings were liberated was labeled insincere or selfish by Daoxue leaders.[9] Zhu's prime concern was not personal salvation but the moral robustness of society and the state, especially when the Southern Song state in which Zhu lived was threatened from within by inappropriate distribution of power, including what he thought were excessive resources dedicated to Buddhism, and from without by the state of Jin. Zhu tried to remedy the situation through education in "funadamentalist" Confucian values.[10]

It seems that the main element held in common by Chan and Confucianism was the idea of a common human nature that is basically good, and which provides for people to become a saint or sage. It was this similarity in a core doctrine that probably motivated Zhu Xi to devote so much energy to differentiating his teachings from those of Chan.

Dahui Zonggao (Miaoxi 妙喜) was the greatest Chan rival for Zhu Xi. Dahui's teachings had great appeal among the scholar-gentry, in part because Dahui directed some of his teachings specifically to the gentry (he wrote at least sixty-two letters to forty gentry).[11] Another reason was because Dahui borrowed ideas about doubt from the Daoxue pioneer Zhang Zai 張載 (1020–1077),[12] and the technique of focusing on a single word,[13] which he adapted from the poetics of Huang Tingjian 黃庭堅 (1045–1105), a disciple of the Daoxue school of Fan Zhen 范鎮 (1007–1088) and Lü Gongzhu 呂公著 (1018–1089), which derived from Zhou Dunyi 周敦頤 (1017–1073).[14] He applied this practice of focusing on one or two words as a simplification of the practice of *gong'an* 公案 (Japanese *kōan*). That is, Dahui had made his Chan more like practices found in Daoxue

---

[8] See the chapters by Stephen Angle and Justin Tiwald in this volume.
[9] See Justin Tiwald's chapter.
[10] Brian McKnight, "Chu Hsi and His World," in *Chu Hsi and Neo-Confucianism*, ed. Wing-tsit Chan (Honolulu: University of Hawaii Press, 1986), 419, 421.
[11] Araki Kengo 荒木見悟, *Daie sho: Zen no goroku 17* 大慧書、禅の語録 17 (Dahui's Letters, Chan Recorded Sayings 17) (Tokyo: Chikuma shobō, 1969), 252.
[12] Zhang Zai, *Zhang Zai ji*, 268, 275, 286 ("To learn you must have doubt").
[13] Such as in the famous *huatou* of *wu* 無 referred to above: Zhaozhou asked, "Does a dog have buddha-nature?" "No (*wu*)."
[14] John Jorgensen, *A Handbook of Korean Zen Practice: A Mirror on the Sŏn School of Buddhism* (*Sŏn'gakwigam*) (Honolulu: University of Hawaii Press, 2015), 27–28. For Huang Tingjian's Daoxue lineage, see Huang Zongxi 黃宗羲 (1610–1695), *Song Yuan xue'an* 宋元學案 (Song and Yuan [Confucian] Case Studies), 2 vols. (n.p., Zhongguo shudian, 1990), chap. 19, 1, 4.

Neo-Confucianism. Moreover, Dahui was a great patriot, lending him gravity among the serious scholar gentry.[15] Zhu Xi was very familiar with Dahui's teachings and in his youth, he practiced Dahui's Chan, a likely stimulant to the development of Zhu's own ideas.[16]

I contend that Zhu gradually shifted away from Dahui Zonggao's practice and its theoretical bases that he had subscribed to from his teens to early twenties as he developed a new formulation of Confucianism that he thought would be more socially responsible and politically useful. For Zhu, this meant moving away from practice that was primarily directed at personal salvation or that amounted to being all words but no action.[17] And yet even as Zhu rejected the radical elements of Dahui's Chan, under the influence of Li Yanping 李延平 (Tong 侗;1093–1163), in his own readings of the Confucian classics, questions from students and so on, he retained or adapted certain key themes and motifs from Chan, which brought him closer to the positions of so-called Northern Chan, in particular to the idea of a radiant buddha-nature.[18] This buddha-nature or *tathāgatagarbha* is innate in all human beings and according to the charges laid against "Northern Chan" by its rivals, can be perceived only by the gradual, not sudden, removal of contaminants or selfish desires through a practice that is like removing the dust covering an inherently bright mirror.[19] The comparison I wish to develop in this essay is between the radiant buddha-nature of the *tathāgatagarbha* tradition of Buddhism popular in Chan

---

[15] For more on the relation of Zhu Xi and Dahui, see Yanagida Seizan 柳田聖山, "Bukkyō to Shushi no shūhen" 仏教と朱子の周辺 (On Buddhism and Zhu Xi), *Zen bunka kenkyū kiyō* 8 (1976): 1–30.
[16] Araki, *Daie sho*, 2.
[17] For the claim Buddhism is concerned merely with personal salvation, see *Zhuzi yulei, juan* 95, 2443, and also Justin Tiwald's chapter in this volume. This is despite the prevalence of the bodhisattva vow not to enter nirvana until all sentient beings are saved.
[18] The term "Northern Chan" was created by Shenhui 神會 (684–758) in the 720s to denigrate his rivals. Shenhui claimed to be the heir of the teachings of Huineng 慧能 (trad. d. 713), the leader of "Southern Chan." The features of "Southern Chan" were sudden enlightenment and a lineage that purported to extend from Huineng right back to the Buddha. On the other hand, "Northern Chan" was alleged to teach gradual enlightenment, to practice freezing the mind in trance, and to belong to a divergent lineage. Atsushi, *Zen no rekishi*, 40–44; John Jorgensen, *Inventing Hui-neng the Sixth Patriarch: Hagiography and Biography in Early Ch'an* (Leiden: Brill, 2005), 62–68 for the life of Shenhui. Shenhui's charges were incorrect and polemical. Shenxiu 神秀 (d. 706), the alleged leader of Northern Chan, taught sudden enlightenment, as did other "Northern Chan" masters. See the *Wu fangbian* 五方便 (The Five Expedient Means) translated in John McRae, *The Northern School and the Formation of Early Ch'an Buddhism* (Honolulu: University of Hawaii Press, 1986), 172, 209, 292n153A. Shenhui probably took the idea of "sudden enlightenment" from some of Shenxiu's pupils. See Jorgensen, *Inventing Hui-neng*, 52, 61, 481.
[19] For the difficulty of separating so-called Northern Chan—a term imposed by others—from the earlier Chan of the Dongshan Famen 東山法門, see John McRae, *The Northern School and the Formation of Early Ch'an Buddhism*, 8–10.

and the radiance of the human nature posited by Zhu Xi. To describe the buddha-nature, the Northern Chanists employed the metaphor of a pure, radiant mind (pearl or mirror) covered by something (muddy water or dust) that has to be discovered by gradual practice and preserved. As root metaphors for the human condition, this provided a foundation stone for Zhu's teachings, and thus my comparison of the structures of the mind and human nature deals with similarities that are more than superficial, even though Northern Chan and Zhu had different goals.[20]

1.1 The Chan of Zhu Xi's Youth

Zhu Xi was exposed to Chan from his earliest years. A curious child, at the age of five or six (*sui*) he allegedly asked, "What is the intrinsic reality of heaven? What is external to (beyond) it?"[21] Zhu Xi's father had connections with Buddhists and Daoists,[22] and it is possible that Zhu Xi was instructed in elementary Confucian teachings around the age of five by the Chan monk Yuanwu Keqin 圓悟克勤 (1063–1135), author of the famous *Biyan lu* 碧巖錄 (Blue Cliff Record), a classic collection of Chan *gong'an* and responses to them.[23] Keqin had been born into a Confucian household and was later also the teacher of Dahui Zonggao. In a letter to Li Yanping, who was later to be his Confucian teacher, Zhu Xi states that

---

[20] For root metaphors, see Earl R. MacCormac, *Metaphor and Myth in Science and Religion* (Durham, NC: Duke University Press, 1976), xiii, 93 ("A root-metaphor is the most basic assumption about the nature of the world or experience that we make when we try to give a description of it"), and 141 ("we believe that such an assumption . . . will yield fruitful explanations"). Comparing Zongmi and Zhu Xi, Stephen Angle (note 5 of his chapter in this volume) cites Jeffrey Lyle Broughton, *Zongmi on Chan* (New York: Columbia University Press, 2009), 20, in support of his claim that the metaphor and the structures based on it may differ in content according to context. In fact, the differences in content between Northern Chan and Zhu were not so great, for both talked of mind and nature, and Zhu's compassion for others, feeling shame, and discussions of ritual are similar to Northern Chan talk of compassion, repentance or contrition, and precepts, even if the talk of meditation and wisdom may have been different. Different contexts for a metaphor do not necessarily negate influence, for metaphors can be bridges between new and old theories. See MacCormac, *Metaphor and Myth*, 36.

[21] *Zhuzi yulei, juan* 45, 1156.

[22] Yun Yŏnghae 윤영해, *Chuja ŭi SŏnPulgyo pipan yŏn'gu* 주자의선불교비판연구 (Study of Zhu Xi's criticism of Chan Buddhism) (Seoul: Minjoksa, 2000), 68, citing *Zhu Xi ji* 朱熹集 (Collected Works of Zhu Xi), eds. Guo Qi 郭齊 and Yin Bo 尹波 (Chengdu: Sichuan jiaoyu chubanshe, 1996), *juan* 84, 4344.

[23] Yun, *Chuja*, 70, citing the *Kuya manlu* 枯崖漫錄 (Desultory Records of Master Kuya) *juan* 2, 16. The *Kuya manlu*, compiled in 1263 by a member of Zonggao's lineage, states: "While [Yuanwu] was at Damu Chan cloister, he taught Confucian studies to Hui'an Zhu Wengong." This would have to have been when Zhu Xi was five years old or younger.

he had studied Chan in his youth.[24] Before Zhu's father died when Zhu Xi was fourteen, he had entrusted his son's education to his friends Hu Xian 胡憲 (Jixi 籍溪; 1082–1162) and Liu Zihui 劉子翬 (Pingshan 屏山; 1101–1147) who, while formally Confucians, were much interested in Buddhism and Daoism.[25] Zhu Xi often stayed with Liu Zihui, who loved Buddhism, as Zhu himself recorded.[26] Through the social circles of Liu Zihui, Zhu may have personally came into contact with Dahui Zonggao, possibly when Zhu was just a boy of five to seven years (*sui*) of age. Zhu studied Chan with Kaishan Daoqian, a disciple of Zonggao. Zhu's later teacher, Li Yanping, wrote: "At first Yuanhui (Zhu Xi) practiced at [Dao]qian's place in Kaishan [Monastery]. Therefore it was entirely an internal experience" (元晦初從謙開善處下工夫來。故皆就裏面體認。).[27] In his collection of Chan stories compiled circa 1183, Zhu Xi's contemporary Xiaoying Zhongwen 曉瑩仲溫 (b. 1116) wrote that when Daoqian was in Jianyang he received the devotion (*gui* 歸) of Liu Baoxue 劉寶學, Pingshan's elder brother, and Zhu Yuanhui 朱元晦 (Zhu Xi).[28]

It is evident that Zhu Xi had studied the Chan largely as taught by Zonggao and that Zhu was probably influenced in this by his father's friend, Liu Pingshan, who may even have been related to Daoqian, Zonggao's disciple.[29]

It was only due to discussions with Li Yanping, whom Zhu first met when he was twenty-four or later, that Zhu began to have his doubts about Chan and Buddhism in general.[30] He may have been prompted by misgivings about his own "enlightenment" as well as that claimed by some monks.[31] Perhaps, as a junior bureaucrat, the assistant magistrate of

---

[24] "When young I studied Chan." Cited by Yun, *Chuja*, 72, from *Li Yanping ji* 李延平集 (Li Yanping's Collected Writings), *juan* 3. See also *Zhuzi yulei*, *juan* 104, 2620 ("'When you, master, wrote the *Account of Conduct of Yanping*, you said, 'He [Yanping] sat in silence and cleansed his mind, and he examined the four beginnings before they were manifested as images in *qi* [or were manifested in one's temperament].' What about these words?' [Zhu said], 'My master himself said that this was a defect. . . . When I was young I still did not have knowledge and I also studied Chan. It was only Master Li who strenuously said [Chan] is wrong"; cited in Yun, *Chuja*, 107).
[25] Yun, *Chuja*, 69.
[26] *Song Yuan xue'an*, 43.1a, 659a; and 43.6a, 661: "Zhu Xi laughed and said, 'Pingshan only wanted to talk of the Buddhists and Daoists and he received their transmissions'."
[27] *Li Yanping ji*, *juan* 1, 5, cited by Yun, *Chuja*, 88.
[28] Cited in Yun, *Chuja*, 93.
[29] See Yun, *Chuja*, 90.
[30] For the date of the first meeting, see Chen Lai 陳來, *Zhuzi zhexue yanjiu* 朱子哲學研究 (Research into Zhu Xi's Philosophy) (Shanghai: Huadong Shifan Daxue chubanshe, 2000), 35–43, who concludes the influence on Zhu began in 1158 when Zhu was twenty-eight.
[31] *Zhuzi yulei*, *juan* 104, 2630.

Tongan, Zhu found Buddhist teachings of little relevance to governance and social disputes. He wrote that even after the death of Liu Pingshan in 1147 and up until his meeting with Li Yanping in 1153, he got nothing from Confucianism.[32]

Zhu, did not, however experience a sudden conversion to Confucianism. As he later recalled, at first he thought Li did not understand Chan:

> Later I went to take up a post at Tongan. I first met Master Li when I was twenty-four or twenty-five and I spoke with him. Master Li only said [Chan] is incorrect. I rather suspected that Master Li did not understand this [Chan] and questioned him two or three times. . . . I subsequently put Chan aside temporarily. My intent was to be neutral, but my Chan [practice] was still present of itself (*zizai*).[33] I read the books of the sage [Confucius] thoroughly day after day. I became aware that the words of the sages and wise men gradually had a taste [made sense]. Then I turned back to look at the theories of the Buddhists and gradually [I saw] the flaws [in Buddhism] and many defects emerged.
>
> 後赴同安任。時年二十四五矣，始見李先生，與他說。李先生只說不是。某却倒疑李先生理會此未得，體三質問。...某遂將那禪來權易閣起。意中道，禪亦自在，且將聖人書來讀。讀來讀去，一日復一日，覺得聖賢言語漸漸有味。却回頭看釋氏之說，漸漸破綻，罅漏百出。[34]

His subsequent rejection of Chan and Buddhism was a gradual process that took years.[35] As Zhu said on another occasion:

> It was only Master Li who strenuously said that [Chan] is wrong. As I later thought it through, it was on this side [Confucianism] in which the taste grew. As soon as this side could grow a little, that side [Chan] shrunk a little. By now [Chan] has melted away with nothing left.
>
> 只李先生極言其不是。後來考究，却是這邊味長。才這邊長得一寸，那邊便縮了一寸，到今銷鑠無餘矣。[36]

---

[32] *Zhuzi yulei*, juan 104, 2619.
[33] This may refer to the idea in Zonggao's *huatou* practice that once one has practiced it intensively for a considerable time, the *huatou* topic automatically presents itself.
[34] *Zhuzi yulei*, juan 104, 2620.
[35] *Zhuzi yulei*, juan 126, 3040.
[36] *Zhuzi yulei*, juan 104, 2620.

This was not a sudden conversion from Chan to Confucianism, but a slow, possibly grudging, change of mind, in which traces of Chan influence possibly remained. Yun Yŏnghae thinks this process of conversion took ten years and that Zhu fully realized the differences between Confucianism and Buddhism, as well as Daoism, only by the age of thirty-three, after which Zhu had the confidence to start actively criticizing Buddhism.[37]

The main reasons for Zhu's shift from Chan to the sort of Confucianism advocated by Li are not spelled out in detail, but some of the issues were doctrinal. According to the epilogue to a record of Yanping's dialogues, *Yanping wenda lu* 延平問答錄:

> When Wengong (Zhu) was the assistant magistrate of Tongan, he went back and forward over Yanping's words. If he got something from them he would completely discard what he had learned and treat [Yanping] as his teacher. . . . Master Wengong told me [Zhao Shixia], "When I first studied, I still regarded unclear and broad-ranging words as essential. I loved the identical and disliked the different. I delighted in the great and despised the minor. I thought, 'How can there be so many things if all the patterns under heaven are meant to be but one?' I had my doubts about this and did not agree. When I was an official at Tongan, in my spare time I went over and over Yanping's words and I thought about them. It was only then I realized that he was not deceiving me. Yanping said, 'Where Confucianism differs from the heresy [Buddhism] lies in [their respective accounts of] pattern is one yet is differentiated in particulars. [Although both] have no concerns about pattern being one, [where the Buddhists] are open to criticism is on the issue of the differentiation of particulars. This is the crux of the matter.'"
>
> 文公領簿同安，反復延平之言。若有所得者，於是盡棄所學而師事焉。. . . 文公先生嘗師夏：「余之始學亦務為用侗之言、好同而惡異、喜大而恥於小。於延平之言則以為何為多事，若是天下之理一而已。心疑而不服。同安官餘，以延平之言反覆思之，始知其不我欺矣。蓋延平之言曰：『吾儒之學所以異於異端者、理一分殊也。理不患其不一、所難者分殊耳。此其要也。』」[38]

---

[37] Yun, *Chuja*, 97.
[38] *Yanping wenda lu*, epilogue by Zhao Shixia 趙師夏, in Zhu Xi, *Zhuzi yishu* 朱子遺書 (Posthumous Writings of Master Zhu) (Kyoto: Chūbun shuppansha, 1975; reproduction of a Lü shi Baogao tang 呂氏寶誥堂 woodblock print of the Kangxi era), 84 (in consecutive pagination of the modern volume), "Yanping wenda houlu," 9a-b (in internal pagination of the woodblock text).

Li Yanping taught a method for the realization of the singular pattern or coherence inherent in all divergent particulars, thus underscoring the value and worth of phenomenal reality. The implication is that the Buddhists rejected the phenomenal world in the singular pursuit of abstractions. Li insisted, "Study only in the context of daily functions or in reference to phenomena. [By doing so] surely one can gradually unite oneself and things. If you do not do so then it is only talk" (唯於日用處便下工夫，或就事上便下工夫。庶幾漸可合為己物。不然只是說也。).[39] In other words, Li advocated that students could gradually come to empathize with other things (and perceive coherence thereby) in the daily functions of life via quiet sitting and cleansing the mind. Zhu said that Li "sat in silence, cleansed his mind, and investigated the four beginnings before they emerged as images of *qi* (temperament)" (默坐澄心，觀四者未發已前氣象。).[40] This was important because "before these (four beginnings) have emerged all the patterns are complete in me" (未發之前，萬理備具。).[41]

Although Zhu described Li's practice as defective, it has some intriguing similarities with aspects of Chan, such as "the everyday mind is the Way" of Mazu Daoyi[42] and some Northern Chan ideas such as "cleansing the mind" by silent sitting. For example, Northern Chan master Jingjue 淨覺 (683–ca. 750) characterizes the Chan meditation method as found in the *Laṅkāvatāra-sūtra* (The Sutra on the Buddha's Entering the Country of Lanka) as follows: "One should just silence the mind and one will know by oneself. Nurture the spirit with no-mind, calm the body with no thoughts, rest in peace and sit in purity, protect/maintain the innate and return to the true" (只可默心自知、無心養神、無念安身、閑居淨坐、守本歸真。).[43] Jingjue also cited Huike 慧可 (487–593), the purported second patriarch of Chan: "If erroneous thoughts do not arise, quietly sit in purity, and the sun of great nirvana will naturally be radiant and pure" (若妄念不生、默然淨坐、大涅槃日、自然明淨。).[44] Perhaps Yanping's words reminded Zhu of forms of Chan decried by Zonggao as "silent illumination Chan": "At present mistaken teachers often take silent illumination

---

[39] "Yanping dawen" 延平答文 (Yanping's letters of reply), 199, cited Yun, *Chuja*, 105.
[40] *Zhuzi yulei, juan* 104, 2620.
[41] *Zhuzi yulei, juan* 62, 1509; see also 1496 for everyday life.
[42] Jinhua Jia, *The Hongzhou School of Chan Buddhism in Eighth- through Tenth-Century China* (Albany: State University of New York Press, 2006), "ordinary mind is the Way," 68–71.
[43] In his *Lengqie shizi ji* 楞伽師資記 (Record of the Masters of the *Laṅkāvatāra-sūtra*), translated in Yanagida Seizan 柳田聖山, *Shoki no Zenshi: Zen no goroku 2* 初期の禅史：禅の語錄2 (Early Chan History: Chan Recorded Sayings 2) (Tokyo: Chikuma shobō, 1971), 93.
[44] Yanagida, *Zen no goroku 2*, 146.

and quiet sitting to be the ultimate method" (今時邪師輩、多以默照静坐、為究竟法。).⁴⁵

Zhu's rejection of Chan and Buddhism was a gradual process. His early training was the Chan of Zonggao, in particular the practice of *huatou*. Zhu's early mentors, especially Liu Pingshan, were knowledgeable of Chan and had exchanges with Zonggao. After Pingshan's death, Zhu began to entertain doubts, especially after he took up an administrative post in Tongan. There he debated with Li Yanping, who taught the Confucianism of Cheng Mingdao 程明道 (1032), Cheng Yichuan, and Yang Shi 楊時 (1053–1135). It took some years for Zhu gradually to be won over to this new version of Confucianism. Although the stages in the process are unclear, Zhu gradually rejected elements of Chan, probably the more radical forms such as those of Mazu's Hongzhou Chan 洪州禪 and the *huatou* Chan of Zonggao, who claimed a lineage back to Mazu via the iconoclastic master Linji Yixuan 臨濟義玄 (d. 866). It is possible that the writings of Guifeng Zongmi 圭峰宗密 (780–840), who advanced some criticisms of Hongzhou Chan, especially of the idea that "functions are the [buddha]-nature"⁴⁶ and that "the everyday mind is the Way," prompted Zhu to agree with Li Yanping that this teaching was wrong, if not dangerous to the social order.⁴⁷ Zhu definitely read some of Zongmi's works, but it is not clear when he did so.

This gradual rejection of elements of Chan teaching resulted in Zhu's advocating certain doctrines that resemble what by Song times had come to be denigrated as "Northern Chan," the negative view of which was largely created through early versions of the *Platform Sutra* and the characterizations made by Zongmi. In the 720s, Shenhui (684–758) attacked the group connected with Shenxiu (d. 706) for teaching gradual enlightenment, freezing the mind in trance, and of not belonging to a lineage that allegedly stretched back in a succession of patriarchs, one per generation, to the Buddha.⁴⁸ Shenxiu, his teacher Hongren 弘忍 (601–674), and their students called themselves Dongshan Famen 東山法門, and never used the term "Northern Chan" to refer to themselves. Rather,

---

⁴⁵ Araki, *Daiesho*, 71.
⁴⁶ Jia, *Hongzhou*, 76–79, on "buddha-nature manifests in function" and Zongmi's criticism. See also *Zhuzi yulei*, juan 62, 1497; juan 57, 1348; and juan 126, 3029 for "manifestations are the function."
⁴⁷ See *Zhuzi yulei*, juan 68, 1685.
⁴⁸ Atsushi, *Zen no rekishi*, 40–44; John Jorgensen, *Inventing Hui-neng the Sixth Patriarch: Hagiography and Biography in Early Ch'an* (Leiden: Brill, 2005), 62–68 for the life of Shenhui.

Dongshan Famen was pluralistic in its teachings, allowing for various practices including mindfulness of the Buddha (*nianfo* 念佛), which could range from chanting the name of the Buddha to contemplation of the Buddha. Dongshan Famen taught that *shouyi* 守一 or "protecting the one" had two levels of meaning: a form of concentration on a single line (*yi* or one) like a line on the horizon, and maintaining the One Mind, the mind in its pure state as described in the *Dasheng qixin lun* 大乘起信論 (*Treatise on Giving Rise to Faith in the Great Vehicle*).[49]

Importantly, it allowed for gradual and sudden enlightenment.[50] Students with different obstructions to enlightenment were taught practices suitable to their condition, but these practices often went under the same name. This ambiguity was really a subtle interpenetration of elementary and advanced practices.[51] Zongmi, who claimed to be in a lineage from Shenhui, somewhat misleadingly used the metaphor of a bright jewel covered by blackness to characterize this Northern Chan of Shenxiu and others as gradualist. The Northern Chanists allegedly tried to wipe away the black color and only when this gradual practice was finished did they claim to see the bright jewel.[52]

Although it is possible that Zhu Xi partially derived his understanding of Northern Chan teachings from Zongmi, Zhu's own ideas are in many ways closer to the teachings of Shenxiu's group— to the real "Northern Chan"—rather than the misrepresentation referred to as "Northern Chan" by Shenhui, Zongmi, and Song dynasty Chan writers. Given that Zhu had practiced sudden enlightenment Chan for around the first two decades of his life, and given his initial resistance to Yanping's theories because of their resemblance to the rival Caodong school's 曹洞宗 "silent illumination" (*mozhao* 默照) Chan[53] and possibly doctrines such as gradual enlightenment, it is not unreasonable to suggest that Zhu remained influenced by the structures of Chan thought, its practices, metaphors, and language as

---

[49] John Jorgensen, "Two Themes in Korean Buddhist Thought", *Han'guk Pulgyohak* 7 (1982): 208–213.
[50] McRae, *Northern Ch'an*, 140–144, especially 143–144 on gradual improvement in brightness.
[51] Jorgensen, "Two Themes in Korean Buddhist Thought," 210.
[52] Broughton, *Zongmi on Chan*, 14. See notes 18 and 19 above, and comments by John McRae, *The Northern School and the Formation of Early Ch'an Buddhism*, 5–6. Some Northern Chan teachers taught sudden enlightenment, so Zongmi's comments reveal that he accepted the anti-Northern Chan (Shenhui's coinage) propaganda of Shenhui and therefore need to be challenged.
[53] See Atsushi, *Zen no rekishi*, 122 for silent illumination Chan. Zonggao, who claimed to be a member of the Linji lineage of Chan, alleged that members of the rival Caodong lineage of Chan did not aim to achieve enlightenment but instead simply sat meditating in silence while waiting for enlightenment to arise of its own accord. In contrast, Zonggao advocated a life-and-death struggle to obtain enlightenment, often using violent imagery.

he formulated his own version of Confucianism. He consciously rejected certain Chan ideas, such as sudden enlightenment, but he is likely to have retained some elements of Chan even when they were couched in Confucian terms. As he repudiated radical Chan ideas such as sudden enlightenment and the view that human beings are in a sense already enlightened and require neither sustained practice nor moral discipline to realize this, what remained influential on his thinking were Northern Chan motifs of a "lucid radiant" mind or *tathāgatagarbha*, which, by being gradually purified of misleading desires, could lead to sainthood or a state approximating sainthood. Both Zhu and (the real) Northern Chanists compared this radiant mind or nature to a mirror. In the metaphor, this mirror was covered by adventitious dust that had to be gradually brushed away for that radiance to be seen. On the other hand, the pure, radiant mind had to be preserved or protected.

1.2 Human Nature and the Buddha-Nature or *Tathāgatagarbha*

The belief that all people possess a human nature that is good and which provides a potential for sagehood was fundamental to Zhu Xi's ideas about human nature and the way, possibly, to become a sage. Whereas ordinary people are not sages because that nature is obscured by turbid *qi* or selfish desire, sages have pure *qi* and no selfish desires. For example, after referring to several passages in *Lunyu, Zhongyong*, and *Daxue*, some referring to human nature or mind, Zhu said:

> The many words and sayings of the sages and worthies only teach people to be enlightened (*ming*) to the heavenly pattern and to extinguish human desire. The heavenly pattern is bright (*ming*). . . . Human nature is originally bright (*ming*), like a pearl submerged in filthy water such that its radiance (*ming*) cannot be seen. If you remove the filthy water the pearl is of itself bright (*ming*), just as it has always been. If you can understand that it is concealed by human desires then that is enlightenment (*ming*).
>
> 聖賢千言萬語，只是教人明天理，滅人欲。天理明。...人性本明，如寶珠沉溷水中，明不可見；去了溷水，則寶珠依舊自明。自家若得知是人欲蔽了，便是明處。⁵⁴

---

⁵⁴ *Zhuzi yulei, juan* 20, 207.

The main Buddhist doctrine that came to dominate Sinitic Buddhist thought was *tathāgatagarbha* 如來藏 or buddha-nature 佛性: the innate capacity to be buddha (enlightened) that the practitioner of Buddhism needed to discover, or the innate capacity that had to be developed via prolonged practice.[55] The buddha-nature according to Chan and most Chinese Buddhists had to be discovered. The *tathāgatagarbha* or buddha-nature is usually described as light/enlightenment covered by adventitious contaminants (literally "guest dusts"; 客塵) that have to be removed for it to be discovered. The image used by Zhu Xi above is clearly derived from the *tathāgatagarbha* element within Chan thought. For example, in writing about the fourth patriarch of Chan, Daoxin 道信 (580–651), the Northern Chan master Jingjue, said, "The mind then can be bright (*ming*) and clear like a bright (*ming*) mirror" (心即得明淨心如明鏡), citing the *Mahāparinirvāṇa-sūtra* (Nirvana Sutra) as proof text.

> "The nature of the mind of sentient beings is for example like a pearl sunk in water. When the water is muddy the pearl is hidden, when the water is clear the pearl is revealed." . . . As it is defiled by greed, anger and perverted views, [these frustrations/*kleśa* mean] that sentient beings do not awaken to [the fact] that the nature of the mind is originally and constantly pure. Therefore students differ in their awakening and have such differentiations. In brief, this comes from differences in natural capacity and conditions.
>
> 衆生心性譬如宝珠没水。水濁珠隱；水清珠顯。. . . 貪、瞋、顛倒所染，衆生不悟心性本來常清淨。故為学者取悟不同，有如此差別。今略出根緣不同。[56]

Although Jingjue's *Lengqie shizi ji* was probably lost by Zhu Xi's time, sutras and treatises using these metaphors were available. Other Chan texts, such as Dahui's *yulu*, used similar metaphors.[57]

---

[55] Douglas L. Berger, *Encounters of Mind: Luminosity and Personhood in Indian and Chinese Thought* (Albany: State University of New York Press, 2015), 6, 107, 111–112, and 199 emphasizes the role of Vijñānavāda, especially the works of Paramārtha (499–569) in the development of ideas of a "luminous mind." Contrary to this claim, I maintain it was the idea of the buddha-nature or *tathāgatagarbha* that dominated Chinese Buddhism. Even the interpretation of the "luminous consciousness" or *amalavijñāna* of Paramārtha was later made in terms of *tathāgatagarbha*. See Michael Radich, "The Doctrine of *Amalavijñāna* in Paramārtha (499–569) and Later Authors to Approximately 800 CE," *Zinbun* 41 (2008): 138, 151, 154, 156, and 162.
[56] Yanagida Seizan, *Zen no goroku 2*, 205 for text, 211 notes, which indicate that the same metaphor is found in the *Ratnagotra-vibhāga* (*Baoxinglun* 寳性論; Treatise on the Jewel Nature), one of the fundamental treatises on *tathāgatagarbha*.
[57] See *Dahui yulu* 大慧語錄 (Record of Dahui), T47.1998A, 912c9-11, Yanshou 延壽 (904–975), *Zongjing lu* 宗鏡錄 (Records of the Source-Mirror), T48.2016, 517c05-14, 518b13ff, 626b5-7.

Zhu adopted the word *ming*, brightness or radiance, due to the salience he gave to the phrase *zai ming ming de* 在明明德 (resides in illuminating/being enlightened to the bright/radiant virtue) of the *Daxue*. First, Zhu thought "bright virtue" is something inherent in the mind as it is endowed by heaven.[58] This "bright virtue" is the nature of humaneness, rightness, ritual propriety, and wisdom.[59] It is entirely marvelous. The sages teach

---

The metaphors of the mirror or still water for the mind can be found in pre-Buddhist Chinese texts, but with the exception of one metaphor used in the *Huainanzi* 淮南子 of the second century CE, none of these metaphors mention the mind-mirror being covered over by something. See Burton Watson, *The Complete Works of Chuang Tzu* (New York: Columbia University Press, 1968), 69 ("Men do not mirror themselves in running water"); 97 ("Be empty, that is all. The Perfect Man uses his mind like a mirror"); 142 ("Water that is still gives back a clear image. . . . The sage's mind in stillness is the mirror of Heaven and Earth"); 372 ("His movement is like that of water, his stillness like that of a mirror."). Again, the closest metaphor in *Zhuangzi* is that of water mixed with something, not covering it. Watson, *Chuang Tzu*, 169 ("It is of the nature of water that if it is not mixed with other things, it will be clear."). In all of these metaphors, there is nothing to be discovered, like the pearl, in the water, whether clear or turbid, or a bright mirror beneath the dust. There is also no mention of anything like dust being removed. Xunzi (third century BCE) used another metaphor, that of a pan of water, which, if kept level and is not shaken, will act like a mirror. (For a translation of this passage, see section 1.5.1 of this chapter). In this case, however, the mind or pan of water contains the mud. When the pan is held level and unshaken by the superior man, the mud settles to the bottom. This accords with Xunzi's theory that human nature is evil (the mud) and that only by moral training (that is, holding the pan of water level and undisturbed) can humans be made good or that water be made to be still and reflective. This stillness and clarity is not a goal in itself; it is a preparation for proper learning. Erin M. Cline, "Mirrors, Minds, and Metaphors," *Philosophy East and West* 58, no. 3 (2008): 341–343. The mud is not covering over something intrinsically bright like a pearl. The closest metaphor is that found in the second chapter of the *Huainanzi*, which seems to be developing a metaphor found in *Zhuangzi*, which says, "But I've heard that if the mirror is bright, no dust settles on it. . . . When you live around worthy men a long time, you'll be free of faults." Watson, *Chuang Tzu*, 70. Here the context refers to the company one keeps. In other words, an enlightened person will not have evil people in his or her company. The *Huainanzi* passage reads, "A clear mirror cannot be soiled/buried by dust; a pure spirit cannot be troubled by desires. . . . When the external [world] and the inner [mind/spirit] are not connected and one desires [the mind] to be in contact with [external] things one conceals the primal light [of the spirit]" (夫鑒明者，塵垢弗能薶；神清者，嗜欲弗能亂。...外內無符而欲與物接，弊其元光。). *Huainanzi, Sibu congkan* edition, 2.10b; my translation; passage cited in Paul Demiéville, "Le miroir spirituel," in *Choix d'Études Bouddhiques* [Leiden: Brill, 1973], 140. Although this resembles the metaphor used by Jingjue and Zhu Xi, for *Huainanzi* the clear mirror can never have dust land on it and hence is always clear (see also Berger, *Encounters of Mind*, 52 ["able to preserve his luminosity undiminished"]); for Jingjue and Zhu Xi the innately clear mirror has dust on it already, which obscures it. The pearl or mirror must be discovered or the dust removed. As Demiéville wrote (141–142), the notions of humans recovering a pure spirituality or an absolute interior within themselves via cleansing were absent in Chinese antiquity. Thus the structures, intentions, and even the language of the metaphors used by Zhu Xi and Jingjue were similar, but despite superficial resemblances, were very different from the pre-Buddhist Chinese metaphors of the mirror and the mind.

[58] "What Heaven provides to humans and things is called the mandate/decree; what humans and things receive is called the nature, and that which is lord over the body is called the mind. That which is obtained from Heaven and which is a brilliant radiance, which is correct and great, is called bright virtue." *Zhuzi yulei, juan* 14, 260.

[59] *Zhuzi yulei, juan* 14, 260.

that one should "illuminate this bright virtue." Moreover, it is "the study of oneself" because "the brightness exists in humans and is not something invited in from outside." Therefore,

> The line "resides in illuminating the bright virtue" of the *Daxue* should always be taken up as a topic of investigation (*changchang tisi* 常常提撕). If people can do so they will advance. This is because their source can be discovered from this. People have only one mind as their basis and if one preserves this mind one will know that there is a thread running through things.
>
> 大學「在明明德」一句，當常常提撕。能如此，便有進步處。蓋其原自此發見。人只一心為本。存得此心，於事物方知有脈絡貫通處。[60]

The word *tisi* in this context suggests a likely origin in the *huatou* practice of Zonggao.[61] The term is found in a letter from Zonggao to Liu Pingshan,[62] telling him to always investigate this topic 時時提撕 (*shishi tisi*).[63] Zhu thus seems to be using *ming ming de* as a Confucian *huatou*.

Zhu glossed *ming ming de* as follows: "People all have this radiance; it is simply covered over by physical desires. By scraping this [covering] away, only then will the radiance gradually become clear (人皆有個明處，但為物欲所蔽，剔撥去了。只就明處漸明將去。)."[64] Zhu also stated that this bright virtue is obscured by external things,[65] a characteristic that recalls the *tathāgatagarbha* as described by Jingjue. Even more pertinently, as we shall see, when someone compared *ming ming de* to polishing a mirror, Zhu commented: "A mirror will be bright (*ming*) after it is polished, which is like a person's bright virtue (*ming de*). It has always been bright. Even though the obscuration is extreme, the emergence of the good beginnings can never be interrupted" (鏡猶磨而後明。若人之

---

[60] *Zhuzi yulei, juan* 14, 261.
[61] *Tisi* has a number of meanings such as "to grasp" as in grabbing hold of an ear; to instruct or educate; or to urge or stir up. Dictionaries of Chan give various meanings, including "investigation," all citing Dahui. *Chanzong dacidian* 禪宗大辭典 (Large Dictionary of Chan), compiled by Yuan Bin 袁賓 and Kang Jian 康健 (Wuhan: Chongwen shuju, 2010), 406a: (1) to indicate, show/present, and (2) investigate, search (探究); *Zengaku daijiten* 879d: (1) teacher directs the students, to entice and lead, and (2) study and investigate (工夫參究); Iriya and Koga, *Zengo jiten*, 320a: "the instruction of the practitioner by the master."
[62] Araki, *Daiesho*, 95.
[63] See Araki, *Daiesho*, 51, 200, 208, 226, 229, with reference to always "investigating" (*tisi*) used in relation to the Zhaozhou *huatou*, and 230 for its being used in conjunction with "preserving the mind" (*cunxin* 存心).
[64] *Zhuzi yulei, juan* 14, 262.
[65] *Zhuzi yulei, juan* 14, 262.

明德，則未嘗不明。雖其昏蔽之極，而其善端之發，終不可絕。).⁶⁶ Thus the "bright virtue" seems to be equated with the four beginnings. Zhu even compared *ming de* to a bright pearl "that is always shining bright but at times requires rubbing. If it is covered over by physical desires, then this pearl will be muddied, but the nature of the shining light is self-so (*zizai*), just as it has always been" (明德如明珠，常自光明，但要時加拂拭耳。若為物欲所蔽，即是珠為泥涴，然光明之性依舊自在。).⁶⁷

It is important to note the similarity in the structure between Zhu Xi's idea of the human nature's being fundamentally bright or luminous but concealed by human desires and Northern Chan master Jingjue's idea that the innately pure mind or nature of the mind is covered by greed, anger, and so on. The metaphor used by both men is almost identical. Moreover, the word *ming* 明, with many meanings, such as bright, light, radiance, luminosity, and to clarify or enlighten, is in both cases related to the mind's nature. Although there are references to *ming* in the sense of "enlightenment" or "numinous" in relation to the (human) nature in the Confucian tradition,⁶⁸ there does not appear to be much weight given to it, at least until Zhu focussed on it. In contrast, *ming* is of central importance in Buddhism, as it means "enlightened" in contrast to *wuming* 無明 (Sanskrit *avidyā*) or "ignorance." It also means "to know," "to clarify" (from Sanskrit verb root *vid*), and "bright" or "numinous" (Sanskrit *prabhā*).⁶⁹

Moreover, the doctrine that "consciousness is intrinsically pure but defiled by adventitious contaminants" can be traced to early Buddhist groups such as the Mahāsāṅghika,⁷⁰ and the idea that the mind is light

---

⁶⁶ *Zhuzi yulei*, juan 14, 261.
⁶⁷ *Zhuzi yulei*, juan 15, 308.
⁶⁸ See *Zhongyong* 21, "The enlightenment (*ming*) that comes from sincerity is called the nature; the sincerity that comes from enlightenment is called the teaching" (自誠明、謂之性。自明誠、謂之教。). Zhu Xi's gloss on this sentence is unfortunately not very enlightening. See *Zhuzi yulei*, juan 62, 1495.
⁶⁹ A frequent description of *tathāgatagarbha* in Sanskrit is *prabhāsvara* (明淨), for which see Takasaki Jikidō 高崎直道, *Nyoraizō shisō no keisei: Indo Daijō Bukkyō shisō kenkyū* 如来蔵思想の形成：インド大乗仏教思想研究 (The Formation of Tathāgatagarbha Thought: Studies in Indian Mahāyāna Buddhist Thought) (Tokyo: Shunjūsha, 1974), 434, 704, and 754. Here it means "clear" (see Monier-Williams, *A Sanskrit-English Dictionary* [London: Oxford University Press, 1899], 684), from the root *pra√bhās* and not *pra√bhā*, although these have almost identical meanings. *Prabhāsvara* is usually translated into Chinese as 清淨 or "pure/pristine" when it is an adjective for *tathāgathagarbha* or mind. Berger, *Encounters of Mind*, 92, 110–111 translates *prabhāsvara* and *qingjing* 清淨 as "luminous," but I have maintained a distinction between "purity" and "luminosity" or rather "radiance."
⁷⁰ Alex and Hideko Wayman, *The Lion's Roar of Queen Śrīmālā* (New York: Columbia University Press, 1974), 42.

or radiant goes back even further.[71] This light is covered over, with such analogies as grain being covered by a husk or a buried treasure,[72] or "gold covered by pebbles and sand" in the *Ratnagotra-vibhāga* or a lantern in a flask.[73]

This structure of a bright or radiant mind covered over by contaminants also appears in the writings of some of Zhu Xi's Daoxue predecessors such as the Cheng brothers. This aspect of Zhu Xi's position seems to be a development of ideas advanced by Cheng Mingdao, who wrote, "All human minds have knowledge; it is just that being concealed by human desire they lose the virtue [or 'pattern' in one version] of heaven" (人心莫不有知惟蔽於人欲則亡天德也。). This theme was further developed by Mingdao's brother, Cheng Yichuan, who criticized the claim that "the inborn is what is meant by the nature" (生之謂性)—attributed to Mencius's sparring partner, Gaozi 告子 (fl. fourth century BC)—on the grounds that "the nature is *qi*" (性即氣), where "nature" means something natural, like the way water always flows downwards, and as it flows it inevitably becomes muddied, but "the purity of the water means the nature is good" (水之清則性善之謂也). This, in turn, prompted the question of why the pure water or human nature is muddied or concealed:

[Someone] asked: "If human nature is basically bright (*ming*), why is it concealed?"

[Yichuan] replied, "This demands understanding. Mencius says that human nature is good, but Xunzi and Yang Zhu did not know about the nature. For that reason, Mencius alone stood out among Confucians. This was because he could clarify (*ming*) the nature. The nature is entirely good; and what is not good is the material capability.[74] The nature is pattern. As for

---

[71] Peter N. Gregory, *Tsung-mi and the Sinification of Buddhism* (Honolulu: University of Hawaii Press, 2002), 181n27; Robert M. Gimello, "Bodhi," in *Encyclopedia of Buddhism*, 2 vols., ed. Robert E. Buswell, Jr. (New York: Macmillan Reference, 2004), 52 on "natural purity of mind" (*cittaprakṛtiviśuddhi*) or "underlying radiance of mind" (*prabhāsvaratvaṃcittasya*). Note, here I prefer "underlying purity of mind" as a translation of the latter. For detailed discussion of this in relation to various attempts to explain Bodhidharma's *biguan* 壁觀 (wall meditation) and to its background, see John Jorgensen, "The Earliest Text of Ch'an Buddhism," (MA diss., Australian National University, 1979), 196–198, including discussion of the Tibetan translation of part of this text, the *bKa-thang sde-lnga*, which glosses *biguan* as *lham-me*, "clarity" or "light." Conze traced the idea that "thought in its substance is luminous through and through and through, but has become defiled by adventitious taints," back to the *Aṅguttara Nikāya*, 1.8-10. Edward Conze, *The Large Sutra on Perfect Wisdom* (London: Luzac and Co., 1961), 9.

[72] Sallie B. King, *Buddha Nature* (Albany: SUNY Press, 1991), 12.

[73] Wayman, *Lion's Roar*, 47.

[74] See James Legge, *The Chinese Classics*, 5 vols., 2nd ed., rev. (Taipei: Wenshizhe chubanshe, 1972 reprint; hereafter Legge), vol. 2, 402 on *cai* 才 meaning *cai* 材.

pattern, from Yao and Shun [mythical sage emperors] to the person in the street, it is one. The material capability is endowed by *qi*, and *qi* is pure and turbid/muddied. Those endowed with pure *qi* are the worthies, and those endowed with the turbid *qi* are the benighted."

問：「人性本明，因何有蔽？」曰：「此須索理會也。孟子言人性善是也。雖荀、楊亦不知性。孟子所以獨出諸儒者，以能明性也。性無不善，而有不善者才也。性即是理，理則自堯、舜至于塗人，一也。才稟於氣，氣有清濁。稟其清者為賢，稟其濁者為愚。」⁷⁵

It is evident from the passages and references cited above about the concealing of the radiant mind that Zhu Xi adopted elements of Buddhism, and some of the theories of his Daoxue predecessors that seem to have been influenced by Buddhism, in order to build his own system of thought. Part of his motivation was to refute Buddhism, Chan in particular, and part was to strengthen his system of thought. Zhu developed his thought over time, responding to questions from students and to contradictions that became evident when the ideas of his predecessors, passages from the Confucian Classics, and his earlier thought were compared and put to the test.[76] Given that the Buddhist theories about *tathāgatagarbha* and the buddha-nature also developed over time, with many disputes, discerning the interaction between Zhu Xi's thought and Buddhism is not an easy task, and this is probably why little attention has been paid to it in modern times.[77] This present chapter is no more than a preliminary study.

---

[75] *Er Cheng ji* 二程集 (Collected Works of the Two Chengs), 2 vols. (Beijing: Zhonghua shuju, 1981 (Rpt. 2004), vol. 1, 204.
[76] Yun, *Chuja*, 98–103 posits four stages in Zhu's career.
[77] One of the earliest scholars to notice this connection, although largely via the (pseudo) *Shoulengyan jing* 首楞嚴經 (*Śūraṃgama-sūtra*), which maintains a very distinctive position, was Lin Ketang 林科棠, *Song Ru yu Fojiao* 宋儒與佛教 (Song Confucians and Buddhism) (Shanghai: Shangwu yinshuguan, 1928; reprint Taipei: Taiwan shangwu yinshuguan, 1966), esp. 16, 29. This was followed by Tsuchida Tomoaki, "Mind and Reality: A Study of the 'Shoulengyanjing'" (unpublished PhD diss., Harvard 1986), who analyses Zhu Xi's reactions to the *Shoulengyan jing*. Another analysis is provided in Lin Zhenguo 林鎮國, "Zhenli yu yishi— cong foxing lunzhengdao Zhu-Lu yitongde erzhong zhexue luixing" 真理與意識：從佛性論爭到朱陸異同的二種哲學類型 (Truth and Consciousness: From Debates about Buddha-nature to Differences and Similarities between the Philosophical Models of Zhu Xi and Lu Xiangshan), *Guoli Zhengzhi Daxue xuebao* 28 (2012): 1–46. P. J. Ivanhoe, *Confucian Moral Self Cultivation* (Indianapolis: Hackett, 2001), 45–46, writing about the mirror used as a metaphor for the mind, states "this view of human nature deeply influenced the notion of Buddha-nature which developed among Chinese Buddhists and then, in turn, had a profound influence on the Neo-Confucian conceptions of human nature." He claims that such hybrid notions led Zhu to transform Mencius' account of human nature into a recovery model, not a development model. Ivanhoe identifies *li* and *xin* (heartmind) as having undergone similar processes of hybridization. This may be true for *li* and *xin*, and the mirror as a metaphor for the mind probably did influence the Chinese Buddhist

1.3 Definitions of the Nature

Zhu Xi accused the Buddhists—particularly Chan Buddhists, whom he singled out for attention by referring to their famous slogan of "directly point at the human mind, see the nature [of the mind] and become buddha"[78]—of confusing the mind with the nature. When discussing whether or not dead wood has a nature, Zhu said to his interlocutor:

> Where you are mistaken is in taking the mind to be the nature, exactly like the Buddhists. It is just that the Buddhists polish that mind to the finest degree. Like with a lump of something, after they peel away a layer, they then peel away another layer until reaching the end where one cannot peel off any more. It is by this means that they polish to obtain the refined light of that mind, which they then regard as constituting the nature. They really do not know that this is precisely what the sages call the mind. Therefore [Xie] Shangcai [1050–1103] said, "What the Buddhists call the nature is precisely what the sages call the mind. What the Buddhists call the mind is precisely what the sages call intention." The mind should simply obtain this pattern. The Buddhists never perceived this pattern, so they took sensation and movement to be the nature. With seeing, hearing, speaking, and appearance, the sages saw there is a pattern in seeing, a pattern in hearing. . . . The Buddhists only take that capacity to see, capacity to hear . . . as the nature, and no matter whether the sight or hearing is clear or unclear . . . they take this to be the nature.
>
> 子融錯處是認心為性，正與佛氏相似。只是佛氏磨擦得這心極精細，如一塊物事，剝了一重皮，又剝一重皮，至剝到極盡無可剝處，所以磨弄得這心精光，它便認做性，殊不知此正聖人之所謂心。故上蔡云：「佛氏所謂性，正聖人所謂心；佛氏所謂心，正聖人所謂意。」心只是該得這理。佛氏元不曾識得這理一節，便認知覺運動做性。如視聽言貌，聖人則視有視之理，聽有聽之理，言有言之理。... 佛氏則只認那能視、能聽 ... 便是性。視明也得，不明也得；聽聰也得，不聰也得 ... 它都認做性。[79]

---

debates, but as already noted, the *Zhuangzi* metaphor cited makes no reference to the mirror being covered or polished; the perfect person merely reflects or responds. There is no reference to how this is achieved, and so this is more like the position of "Huineng" and not like Northern Chan or Zhu, where the obscuring dust needs to be removed before this spontaneous response can occur. In this *Zhuangzi* passage there is no hint of "recovery" or "discovery."

[78] See for example, *Zhuzi yulei, juan* 97, 2500 in the context of a discussion of Chan and the nature.
[79] *Zhuzi yulei, juan* 126, 3019–3020.

Zhu equated this Chan Buddhist viewpoint with the ideas of Gaozi, an opponent of Mencius, and he accused them of regarding the functions of the body and the mind as being the nature.[80] He also claimed that the nature according to the Confucians was real (實); that is, it contained the patterns of the Way, such as humaneness and rightness, but that the nature of the Buddhists was empty (空).[81] Given these accusations concerning the understanding of mind and the nature (the mind, the nature of the mind, human nature, buddha-nature), we need to examine the definitions of these terms by the Buddhists and the Confucians as represented by Zhu Xi.

Nature or *xing* 性 has been defined in many ways. In Chinese Buddhism, the word *xing* 性 was used to translate a number of Indic words or affixes, including *dhātu* (also rendered as *jie* 界), glossed sometimes as buddha-nature or *tathāgatagarbha*;[82] *svabhāva* or that which is so of itself (*zixing* 自性, *zi you xing* 自有性); *prakṛti* or an essence, something that cannot be changed by external influences; and *gotra* or seed and lineage (*xing* 姓). It was also used to represent the affixes *tva* or *tā* (-ness).[83] For Chinese Buddhists, there is a buddha-nature (*foxing* 佛性) and a dharma-nature (*faxing* 法性), but because buddha-nature is revealed through understanding that both dharmas and human beings are empty of anything substantial,[84] therefore the buddha-nature can be the same as the dharma-nature.[85] The dharma-nature is equated with

---

[80] *Zhuzi yulei*, juan 126, 3020–3022.
[81] *Zhuzi yulei*, juan 4, 64.
[82] Hirakawa Akira 平川彰, "Nyoraizō to wa nanika" 如来蔵とは何か (What is *rulaizang*?) in *Nyoraizō to Daijō kishin ron* 如来蔵と大乗起信論 (*Tathāgatagarbha* and *Dasheng qixin lun*), ed. Hirakawa Akira (Tokyo: Shunjusha, 1990), 67, on the identity of buddha-nature and *tathāgatagarbha*. See also Sallie B. King, *Buddha Nature* (Albany: SUNY Press, 1991), 3–4, 14. This remains a core topic of the so-called Critical Buddhism debate, proponents of which allege that most of Chinese Buddhism, but especially Chan, constituted a "*dhātuvāda*" (doctrine about true reality) that posited a *dhātu* (locus) or essential existent behind everything, and so was not Buddhist. This debate had actually begun in Republican China. For references to these early debates on *tathāgatagarbha*, see *Transforming Consciousness: Yogācāra Thought in Modern China*, ed. John Makeham (Oxford and New York: Oxford University Press, 2014), "Introduction," 6, and on the Critical Buddhism debate, 34–35. See also Jamie Hubbard and Paul L. Swanson, eds., *Pruning the Bodhi Tree: The Storm over Critical Buddhism* (Honolulu: University of Hawaii Press, 1997). For the complexity of the term *dhātu*, see Gregory, *Tsung-mi*, 8–9.
[83] See entries on *shō* and *busshō* in Nakamura Hajime 中村元, ed., *Bukkyōgo daijiten* 仏教語大辞典 (Large Dictionary of Buddhist Terms), 3 vols. (Tokyo: Tōkyō shoseki, 1975).
[84] See *Foxing lun* 佛性論 (The Buddha-nature Treatise): "The buddha-nature reveals suchness through the emptiness of humans and dharmas" (佛性者即是人法二空所顯眞如。). T31.1610, 787b4-5.
[85] See Zhiyi 智顗 (538–597), *Weimo jing lüeshu* 維摩經略疏 (Brief Commentary on the *Vimalakīrti-nirdeśa-sūtra*)："Causal conditions are the buddha-nature and the buddha-nature is the dharma-nature" (因緣即是佛性，佛性即是法性。). T38.1778, 681a26.

dharmatā, dharmasvabhāva, and even *dharmadhātu*, which can mean the constituents of reality (including the mind) in themselves, their essence, or their cause.[86]

As Zhu's prime target of criticism with respect to the nature was Chan, the definitions of the nature by Chan Buddhists are crucial for understanding Zhu's criticism. The buddha-nature in Chan is an innate potential that the practitioner needs to discover rather than an innate potential that had to be developed via prolonged practice. The most influential theorist of Chan, Zongmi 宗密 (780–841), discussed the "nature" of buddha-nature. Distinguishing two kinds of Chan, the "School of Emptiness" (*kongzong* 空宗) and the "School of the Nature" (*xingzong* 性宗), he identified the latter with the "School of the Tathāgatagarbha" or the "School of the Buddha-nature" and the former approximately with the school of *prajñāpāramitā* (perfection of wisdom) and Madhyamaka.[87] He described the way in which these two schools differed in their account of the "nature" and the "nature of the mind" as follows:

> The School of Emptiness has always regarded the fundamental source of all dharmas as being the nature; the School of the Nature mostly regards the source of the dharmas as being the mind. . . . Those who view it to be the mind [use] the *Śrīmālā[-sūtra]*, which says, "The self-nature is the pristine mind," and the *Dasheng qixin lun*, which says, "All dharmas from the very beginning . . . are nothing but this One Mind." . . . Precisely because the intrinsic nature that is spoken of by this school is not merely empty and quiescent, but rather, of itself, is constant awareness, it should be viewed as the mind.
>
> 空宗一向目諸法本源爲性；性宗多目諸法本源爲心。 . . . 目爲心者，《勝鬘》云：「自性清淨心」。《起信》云：「一切法從本已來。. . . 唯是一心」。. . . 良由此宗所説本性不但空寂，而乃自然常知，故應目爲心也。[88]

---

[86] See *busshō* in Nakamura, *Daijiten*, and Gregory, *Tsung-mi and the Sinification of Buddhism*, 8–9.
[87] Zongmi does not explicitly identify the "School of Emptiness" with any particular school of Buddhism, but the identification made here is on the basis of texts he refers to. See Gregory, *Tsung-mi and the Sinification of Buddhism*, 211–212; Broughton, *Zongmi on Chan*, 30, 32. Kamata Shigeo 鎌田茂雄, *Chanyuan zhuquan ji duxu* 禪源諸詮集都序 (Preface to the Collected Writings on the Chan Source), in *Zen no goroku* 禅の語録 9 (Chan Recorded Sayings, 9) (Tokyo: Chikuma shobō, 1971), 178 notes that there are elements in Zongmi's description of the "School of Emptiness" that are not Madhyamaka (Sanlun).
[88] *Chanyuan zhuquan ji duxu*, T48.2015, 406a26-b3.

In other words, according to the School of the Nature (or *tathāgatagarbha*) the word "nature" also implies "mind." Another difference over the nature is described as follows:

> The reason that the intrinsic reality of the "nature" in each case is different [even though the word "nature" is the same] is as follows. The School of Emptiness takes [the fact that] dharmas have no nature [or are of the nature of nothingness] to be the nature; the School of the Nature takes the intrinsic reality of the numinous light (*ming*) that is always present and not empty to be the nature.
>
> 「性」字二體異者：空宗以諸法無性爲性；性宗以靈明常住不空之體爲性。[89]

Zongmi identified with the School of Nature, and this "school" generally dominated Chan from the late Tang period onwards.

There is a further use of "nature" in the *Shoulengyan jing*, an apocryphal sutra composed in China before 730 in which Chan was implicated.[90] The earliest references to this text were made by Chan masters, but by the eleventh and twelfth centuries it had become very popular beyond Chan, with commentaries written on it by members of the Tiantai, Huayan, and Chan schools, as well as by the leading statesmen and scholars Wang Anshi 王安石 (1021–1086) and Zhang Shangying 張商英 (1043–1121).[91] Zhu was familiar with the *Shoulengyan jing*, for he mentions it a number of times with regard to change over time[92] and with regard to Mazu's identification of the nature with function.[93] Zhu was particularly critical of the *Shoulengyan jing*'s doctrine of the mind and the nature.[94]

The use of the term *jianxing* 見性 in the *Shoulengyan jing* is not the usual sense of *jianxing* found in Chan, where it is used to mean to "see the [buddha]-nature," as is described in the *Xuemo lun* 血脈論 (Treatise on the Blood Line), a scripture falsely attributed to Bodhidharma: "If you wish to see the Buddha be sure to see the nature. The nature is the Buddha" (若欲

---

[89] T48.2015, 406b3-5. Both passages are quoted in Yanshou, *Zongjinglu*, a work that Zhu Xi had probably read.
[90] Jorgensen, *Inventing Hui-neng*, 510–515.
[91] Tsuchida, "Shoulengyan jing," 2–3, 5–8.
[92] *Zhuzi yulei*, juan 72, 1788 ("As the first paragraph of fascicle two of the *Lengyan jing* writes . . . ").
[93] *Zhuzi yulei*, juan 126, 3022, commenting on a quotation from *Dahui yulu*, T47.1998A, 829c24-27.
[94] Tsuchida, "Shoulengyan jing," 183, 188.

覓，須是見性；性即是佛。).⁹⁵ This can be understood to mean seeing, or realizing the potential to become a buddha, in which emptiness is posited as a potential.

In contrast, the *Shoulengyan jing* posits a "nature" that perceives and could be identified as a ground or what the Japanese Critical Buddhists of the twentieth century would call a "topos" or *dhātu*. Thus the *Shoulengyan jing* writes of a "seeing essence-nature."⁹⁶ This could be taken as being an ontological essence, which would be contrary to the Buddhist doctrines of emptiness and conditional origination. The Tang Chan master, Nanyang Huizhong 南陽慧忠 (d. 774), was particularly critical of this view and accused certain "southerners" of altering a "platform sutra" and of maintaining the heretical doctrine of the eternal soul. According to Huizhong, these "southerners" maintained:

> In this body I have a soul-nature. The nature knows pain and itching. When the body is destroyed, the soul departs. It is like a householder leaving his blazing house. The house is not eternal but the householder is.
>
> 我此身中有一神性。此性能知痛癢。身壞之時神則出去。如舍被燒舍主出去：舍即無常，舍主常矣。⁹⁷

There are two contenders for the object of this accusation of heresy: the Chan lineage of Daoyi and the *Shoulengyan jing*. Zongmi thus characterized Mazu's Chan as follows:

> Giving rise to the mind and stirring up thoughts, snapping fingers and moving the eyes . . . are all the functions of the entire intrinsic reality of buddha-nature, beyond which there is no separate function. The entire intrinsic reality craves, hates, and is stupid. . . . All of this is buddha-nature.
>
> 起心動念、彈指動目 . . . 皆是佛性全體之用；更無別用。全體貪嗔癡。. . . 此皆是佛性。⁹⁸

---

⁹⁵ *Xuemo lun*, T48.2009, 373c08.
⁹⁶ "The Buddha said to the great king, 'Although your face is wrinkled, this seeing/perceiving essence-nature has never been wrinkled" (佛言大王，汝面雖皺而此見精性未曾皺。), T19.945, 110b29-c1; see also *Zongjing lu*, T48.2016, 673a17-18.
⁹⁷ *Jingde chuandeng lu*, T51.2076, 437c26-29.
⁹⁸ *Zhonghua chuanxindi Chanmen shizi chengxi tu* 中華傳心地禪門師資承襲圖 (Chart of the Master-Disciple Succession of the Chan Gate that Transmits the Mind-Ground in China) in Kamata Shigeo 鎌田茂雄, *Chan yuan zhuquanji duxu* 禪源諸詮集都序 (Preface to the Collected Writings on the Chan Source), in *Zen no goroku* 禅の語録 9 (Chan Recorded Sayings, 9) (Tokyo: Chikuma shobō, 1971), 307. Only Kamata's edition contains this exact paragraph.

The following comments are attributed to Mazu:

> [See] that the nature of numinous awareness really lacks rising and ceasing. . . . The present seeing, hearing, perceiving, and knowing has always been your intrinsic nature. It is also called intrinsic mind. There are no buddhas apart from this. The mind inherently exists; it is not constructed by provisional positing.
>
> 而靈覺之性實無生滅 。... 今見、聞、覺、知元是汝本性，亦名本心。更不離此心別有佛。此心本有，今有不假造作。[99]

There were thus schisms in Chan over how to deal with the "nature," be it buddha-nature or the nature of the mind.[100] These schisms correspond to the divisions between the "weak" *tathāgatagarbha* thesis and the "strong" *tathāgatagarbha* thesis proposed by the contemporary scholar Ching Keng. The weak thesis refers to the idea that all sentient beings share the *tathāgatagarbha* because they are pervaded by suchness, for which we may read also "emptiness." On the other hand, the strong thesis asserts that the pure *tathāgatagarbha* is the basis of the impure storehouse consciousness or *ālayavijñāna*, as an "ontological basis of all conditioned dharmas," a thesis that had a Chinese origin.[101]

The question of the status and role of *xing* in Zhu Xi's thought is likewise complex and contested.[102] For Zhu Xi, the nature is necessarily a conjoining of *li* and *qi*, but the quality of *qi* is crucial:[103]

> Humans and things are born together in heaven and earth, innately sharing one pattern but differ through their endowment of *qi*. That which is endowed with clear and pure *qi* are humans; that which is endowed with turbid and impure *qi* are things.
>
> 人物并生于天地之間，本同一理，而稟氣有異焉。稟其清明純粹則為人；稟其昏濁偏駁則為物。[104]

---

[99] *Zongjing lu*, T48.2016, 492a19-24. This text also appears in the *Mazu yulu*.
[100] For more discussion of this, see Jorgensen, *Inventing Hui-neng*, 517, 624–627.
[101] Ching Keng, "Yogâcāra Buddhism Transmitted or Transformed? Paramârtha (499–569) and His Chinese Interpreters" (PhD diss., Harvard University, 2009), 40, 422–424. Note Ching Keng maintains that the *Laṅkāvatāra-sūtra*, a core text for Chan, may have advocated the strong thesis, although he has his reservations. I contend that Chan mostly evidences the weak thesis.
[102] Chen Lai, *Zhuzi*, 194.
[103] For a more detailed account, see John Makeham's chapter in this volume.
[104] From *Mengzi huowen, juan* 1.6a, 289c, in *Zhuzi yishu*.

Furthermore, the endowment of *qi* in humans has the potential to obscure the purity of the nature, which is *li*:

> The nature is like sunlight. What humans and things receive of it are not the same, just as the light received through an aperture [literally a crack] has [differences] in amount [according to the size of the aperture]. . . .
>
> Somebody said, "The nature of humans and things is the same."
>
> Zhu said, "The nature of humans and things is inherently the same, it is just that their endowment of *qi* is different. It is like water—there is nowhere it is not clear. When poured into a white bowl it is of the same color and when put in a black bowl it also is of the same color [as the bowl]. . . ."
>
> He also said, "It is very difficult to speak of the "nature." One may say that it is the same, and one may say it is different. It is like the sun [shining through] a crack; the length and size of the cracks themselves are not the same but there is only this [one] sun."
>
> 性如日光，人物所受之不同，如隙竅之受光有大小也。... 或說：「人物性同。」曰：「人物性本同，只氣禀異。如水無有不清，朱放白椀中是一般色，及放黑椀中又是一般色，放青椀中又是一般色。」... 又曰：「性最難說，要說同亦得，要說異亦得。如隙中之日，隙之長短大小自是不同，然却只是此日。」¹⁰⁵

This same idea is expressed in the following metaphor, when illustrating the thesis that complete sincerity is totally visible, but is obscured by formed *qi*, which differs according to its level of turbidity:

> He pointed to a lantern in front of him, saying, "It is like this lamp—its inherent nature has never not been brightness. The psychophysical [nature] is not the same. This is like when thick paste-paper is used as the lamp shade, and so the lamp is not very bright (*ming*), and when thin paste-paper is used then the lamp is brighter than the lamp covered with thick paste-paper. . . . If you remove the lamp-shade then the lamp[light] is completely visible. The pattern of this [sincerity being completely visible] is exactly like this."
>
> 因指面前燈籠曰：「且如此燈，乃本性也，未有不光明者。氣質不同，便如燈籠用厚紙糊，燈便不甚明；用薄紙糊，燈便明似紙厚者。... 撤去籠，則燈之全體著見，其理正如此也。」¹⁰⁶

---

¹⁰⁵ *Zhuzi yulei*, juan 4, 58.
¹⁰⁶ *Zhuzi yulei*, juan 64, 1572.

The image of the lamplight being covered or blocked replicates a metaphor used for the *tathāgatagarbha* in the *Aṅgulimālīya-sūtra* (*Yangjuemoluo jing* 央掘魔羅經; Aṅgulimāla Sutra):[107]

> This buddha-nature resides within afflictions like a lamp inside a pitcher. When the pitcher is broken then it can appear. The pitcher refers to the afflictions and the lamp refers to the *tathāgatagarbha*.
>
> 是佛性煩惱中住。如瓶中燈。瓶破則現。「瓶」者謂煩惱,「燈」者謂如來藏。[108]

In Buddhism, it is mental afflictions that conceal the buddha-nature, whereas with Zhu Xi it is turbid *qi* that obscures the *li* inherent in human nature. Before the nature is constituted in humans, it is pure *li*.

Although Zhu describes how this aspect of the nature, the "inherently-so nature," "changes" or "transforms" into the psychophysical nature,[109] he denied that there are two different natures, the psychophysical nature and the inherent nature:

> Human nature is inherently good, but as soon as it falls into the psychophysical it is polluted and can be bad. Even though it is polluted and can be bad, still the inherent nature is present herein, just as it has always been.
>
> 人性本善而已,才墮入氣質中,便薰染得不好了。雖薰染得不好,然本性却依舊在此。[110]

There is only one nature, which is inherently good but which can also take on a polluted modality by virtue of its *qi*-constitution in humans:

> The proper nature is like water, and the nature of psychophysical *qi* is like scattering in some soy and salt, so that it takes on the same taste [as the soy or the salt].
>
> 好底性如水,氣質之性如殺些醬與鹽,便是一般滋味。[111]

---

[107] This sutra was translated by Guṇabhadra (394–468), who was feted by Chan for his translation of the *Laṅkāvatāra-sūtra*.
[108] T02.0120, 526b24-25.
[109] Chen Lai, *Zhuzi*, 205.
[110] *Zhuzi yulei*, juan 95, 2432
[111] *Zhuzi yulei*, juan 4, 68. The character *sha* 殺 is incorrect. It should be *za* 雜.

This comment was directed both at Cheng Yichuan and the Buddhists:

> If it were not for the psychophysical then the heavenly ordained nature would have no place to lodge. With respect to people's endowment of *qi*, however, there are differences of purity and degree. Hence, with respect to the impartiality of what heaven ordains[112] there are also differences of grade and quality. Crucially, however, [both] must be deemed to be the nature. [On one occasion] when I had I met with Bingweng (Pingshan) he said, "What [Cheng] Yichuan said about the psychophysical nature is just like what the Buddhist books mean by 'The saltiness in [sea]water and the glue in paint.' "

> 天命之性，非氣質則無所寓。然人之氣禀有清濁偏正之殊，故天命之正，亦有淺深厚薄之異，要亦不可不謂之性。舊見病翁云：「伊川言氣質之性，正猶佛書所謂『水中鹽味，色裏膠清。』」[113]

Although the wording here best fits with the *Fu dashi xinwang ming* 傅大士心王銘 (Mahāsattva Fu's Mind-king Inscription) attributed to Fu Xi 傅翕 (497–569) in the *Jingde chuandeng lu*,[114] the idea is also similar to that mentioned by Yanshou 延壽 (904–975) in his *Zongjing lu*[115] when he was discussing the Janus-faced characteristics of the seventh *vijñāna* (consciousness), the *manas*:

> ... which likewise does not commit the error of holding that there are two natures common to the self. It is like a salty taste in water. Hold onto the water alone; do not hold onto the salt. [It is just that] the water and the salt originally are not intermixed.

> 亦不犯所執我中通二性過。如水中鹽味。但執是水不執於鹽。水與鹽元不相離。[116]

---

[112] That which heaven ordains is the nature.
[113] *Zhuzi yulei*, juan 4, 67.
[114] T51.2076, 456b26. This work, in fact, shows traces of Mazu Chan and thus cannot date from before the ninth century or have been written by Fu Dashi. See also the discussion of this passage in John Makeham's chapter in this volume.
[115] Yongming Yanshou was a scholarly Chan master who wrote the massive *Zongjing lu* (Records of the Source-Mirror) in one hundred fascicles to demonstrate that Chan and Buddhist doctrines are "two aspects of a single unity," a unity that is provided by the mind. Albert Welter, *Yongming Yanshou's Conception of Chan* (Oxford: Oxford University Press, 2011), 5. Zhu Xi was definitely aware of Yanshou's ideas. See note 4 of this chapter.
[116] T48.2016, 723c12-14.

Human nature is nothing other than this inherent nature in a human body, a particular form of pattern. Commenting on Cheng Yichuan's ideas, Zhu wrote:

> Before people or things are born, we can speak only of pattern and not of the nature. This is what he meant by "in heaven it is called 'what is ordained.'" "As soon as it called the 'nature' then it is already not the nature." "As soon as it is called the 'nature'" refers to when humans are born then this pattern has already fallen into the formed *qi*, and it is no longer completely the intrinsic reality of the nature. Therefore he said, "Then it is already not the nature." This is what he means by "In humans it is called the nature." In general humans have this formed *qi*, so when this pattern is first present in the formed *qi* that is called the "nature." As soon as we call it the "nature," then it is already involved with being born and being together with the psychophysical, which cannot be regarded as the intrinsic reality of the nature.
>
> 人物未生時，只可謂之理，說性未得，此所謂「在天曰命」也。「纔說性時，便已不是性」者，言纔謂之性，便是人生以後，此理已墮在形氣之中，不全是性之本體矣，故曰「便已不是性也」，此所謂「在人曰性」也。大抵人有此形氣，則是此理始具於形氣之中，而謂之性。纔是說性，便已涉乎有生而兼乎氣質，不得為性之本體也。[117]

For Zhu Xi, the "nature" is endowed with qualities such as humaneness, rightness and so on, but he characterized the Buddhists as entertaining the misconception that the nature is empty and devoid of content:

> Within the nature there are only the patterns of humaneness, rightness, ritual propriety, and wisdom—these are real patterns. We Confucians take the nature to be real; the Buddhists take pattern to be empty (*xu*). As for their doctrine that refers to nature as the mind, it is unacceptable. People nowadays often take the mind to speak of the nature, but first we must recognize [what the mind is] before we can speak [of the nature]. Bida recorded that, "If you refer to that which has knowing and awareness as being the nature, [in fact] you are only talking about the word 'mind'." If there is the nature ordained by heaven then there will be the psychophysical. If you take the nature that is ordained by heaven to be based in the mind, then where will the psychophysical nature be placed? It can be said to be like "The human

---

[117] *Zhuzi yulei, juan* 95, 2430.

mind is precarious, the mind of the Way is subtle." Both are mind—it is not the case that only the mind of the Way is the mind and the human mind is not the mind.

蓋性中所有道理，只是仁義禮智，便是實理。吾儒以性為實，釋氏以性為空。若是指性來做心說，則不可。今人往往以心來說性，須是先識得，方可說。必大錄云：「若指有知覺者為性，只是說得『心』字。」如有天命之性，便有氣質。若以天命之性為根於心，則氣質之性又安頓在何處！謂如「人心惟危，道心惟微」，都是心，不成只道心是心，人心不是心！118

As this passage possibly contains an allusion to Zongmi's ideas about the mind, it behooves us to follow Zhu's advice to first examine what is meant by the mind.

1.4 Definitions of the Mind and Its Relation to the Nature

This section will examine the relationship of the mind to the nature, especially as discussed by Zongmi, which contained criticisms of Mazu's Chan. Zhu shared Zongmi's criticisms but seems to have applied them indiscriminately to all branches of Chan.

Zongmi based much of his theory about the mind on the doctrines found in the *Dasheng qixin lun*, which divides the mind into two modalities or "gateways," the mind as suchness and the mind as rising and ceasing:

> The unchanging is the nature, and the according with conditions is the characteristic. You should know that the nature and the characteristics are both references to the One Mind. Now, the reason the schools of the nature (*tathāgatagarbha*) and of the characteristics (Faxiang/Yogācāra) criticize each other is precisely for not recognizing the true mind. Every time they hear mention of the word "mind" they say it refers only to the eight consciousnesses, not knowing that the eight consciousnesses are references to the true mind's according with conditions. Therefore bodhisattva Aśvaghoṣa [in the *Dasheng qixin lun*] took the One Mind to be Dharma, and took the two gateways of suchness and rising-and-cessation to be its meanings.

---

[118] *Zhuzi yulei, juan* 4, 64.

不變是性；隨緣是相。當知性相皆是一心上義。今性相二宗互相非者，良由不識眞心。每聞心字將謂只是八識，不知八識但是眞心上隨緣之義。故馬鳴菩薩以一心爲法，以眞如生滅二門爲義。[119]

Zongmi then elucidated the different meanings given by the two schools to the word "mind," and analyzed the four different types of mind found in Buddhism.[120] Among these he found some contradictions:

> [Some sutras] vilify the mind as a thief that should be controlled and eliminated, and others praise the mind as being the Buddha and encourage us to practice. . . . Some say that the mind is produced by dependence on cognitive objects while others say that the mind produces the cognitive objects. Some say that quiescence is the mind while others say that mental concern [that is, the mental appropriation of cognitive objects] is the mind.
>
> 或毀心是賊，制令斷除；或讚心是佛，仙令修習。. . .[121] 或云託境心生；或云心生於境。或云寂滅爲心；或云緣慮爲心。[122]

Zongmi proceeds to discuss the One Mind as it features in the Laṅkāvatāra-sūtra:

> "The quiescent [nirvana] is called the One Mind. The One Mind is the tathāgatagarbha." The tathāgatagarbha is also the Dharma-body that is wrapped up, as the Śrīmālā-sūtra preaches.[123] Therefore know that these four kinds of mind are of a single intrinsic reality. Thus the Miyan jing (Ghanavyūha-sūtra; Sutra of Secret Adornment) says, "The Buddha preached that the tathāgatagarbha (the name of the Dharma-body when wrapped-up [in afflictions]) is the ālaya [store consciousness]." Those of bad insight cannot know that the garbha [store] is the ālayavijñāna. (Those who maintain that the intrinsic reality of suchness and the ālaya are different are [those of] bad insight.) The pristine store of the tathāgata and the ālaya of the conventional world are like gold and a ring, which turn into each other, and yet have no differentiation. (The ring etc. are metaphors for the ālaya, the gold a metaphor for suchness, and both are called the tathāgatagarbha.)

---

[119] Chanyuan zhuquanji duxu, T48.2015, 401b27-c3.
[120] Hṛdaya, the physical heart; object-perceiving mind or eight consciousnesses; citta, the collecting mind, the eighth consciousness or ālayavijñāna; and the real mind or hṛdaya that is the tathāgatagarbha.
[121] T48.2015, 401c11-12
[122] T48.2015, 401c13-14.
[123] T12.353, 221c.

Even though they are of the same intrinsic reality, the characteristics of true and false are distinct, and basic and derivative are also differentiated. The first three [types of mind] are characteritics; the last one is the nature. There is a reason characteristics arise on the basis of the nature, just as there is a reason for bringing the characteristics together and subsuming them to the nature. [The reason is that] the nature and characteristics are unimpeded; both are One Mind.

「寂滅者名為一心。一心者即如來藏。」如來藏亦是在纏法身，如《勝鬘經》說。故知四種心本同一體。故《密嚴經》云：「佛說如來藏 (法身在纏之名) 以為阿賴耶 (藏識)。」惡慧不能知藏即賴耶識 (有執真如與賴耶體別者是惡慧。) 如來清淨藏，世間阿賴耶，如金與指鐶展轉無差別。(指鐶等喻賴耶，金喻真如；都名如來藏。) 然雖同體，真妄義別本末亦殊。前三是相，後一是性。依性起相蓋有因由；會相歸性非無所以。性相無礙，都是一心。[124]

In other words, all is the mind, the One Mind, or *tathāgatagarbha*, which like gold can be in the state of true suchness, gold as it is, but can also unfold into different forms (characteristics or images) like the golden ring or *ālayavijñāna*. This description resembles Zhang Zai's theory about an omnipresent *qi* that evolves into various forms or condensations (*qizhi* 氣質).

The comparison of One Mind and *qi* is further complicated by the fact that Chan was split between two positions on the nature of the mind; that of the Mazu branch and that of the Heze (Shenhui) branch. Zongmi claimed allegiance to the latter:

> The School of Directly Revealing the Nature of the Mind says that all dharmas, whether existent or empty, are all nothing but the true nature. The true nature is without characteristics and is unconditioned. Its intrinsic reality is not anything, meaning it is not ordinary person or saint, not cause or result, not good or bad and so on. However, the functioning of this intrinsic reality can create all kinds [of dharmas, things], meaning it can be an ordinary person or be a saint, and can manifest form and manifest characteristics.
>
> In referring to the nature of the mind there are, furthermore, two kinds. One, [Mazu Chan,] says that that which at present can speak and act, crave, be angry, be kind, and be patient, creates good and evil and experiences

---

[124] Kamata, *Zengen shosenshū tojo*, 70; T48.2015, 401c29-402a8.

suffering and bliss and so on, is precisely your buddha-nature, and it is precisely this that has always been the Buddha. . . . The Way is precisely this mind and one cannot take the mind to turn around and cultivate the mind. Evil is also this mind, so one cannot take the mind to turn around and eliminate it from the mind. Only when one does not eliminate and does not cultivate, leaving it up to the free action [of the mind], is it called release. The nature is like empty space, it neither increases nor decreases, so what use is there in [trying to] augment it? Simply accord with the time and the place, and halt the work [of karma] and nourish the spirit, and the holy foetus will grow and emerge, a natural divine marvel. . . .

The second, [Heze Chan,] says that the dharmas are like a dream, which is what the saints all say. Therefore the erroneous thought-moments are fundamentally quiescent, and the sense-realms [contaminating cognitive objects] are intrinsically empty. The mind of quiescence and emptiness is an unobscured numinous knowing. It is precisely this quiescent and empty knowing that is your true nature, which allows for delusion and allows for enlightenment. The mind intrinsically knows by itself, and does not depend on conditions to be produced and does not arise due to cognitive objects. The single word "knowing" is the gate of the many marvels. Because of beginning-less delusion, one erroneously grasps the body and the mind to be the self, and gives rise to thoughts of craving and anger et cetera. . . . The mind itself has no thoughts, so when thoughts arise be aware [of this process], and if you are aware of them, they will become non-existent. The marvellous gate of cultivation depends on this alone.

直顯心性宗者說一切諸法，若有、若空，皆唯眞性。眞性無相無爲。體非一切，謂非凡、非聖、非因、非果、非善、非惡等。然即體之用而能造作種種，謂能凡、能聖、現色、現相等。於中指示心性復有二類。一云：即今能語言、動作、貪、嗔、慈、忍、造善惡、受苦樂等，即汝佛性，即此本來是佛。. . . 道即是心，不可將心還修於心。惡亦是心，不可將心還斷於心。不斷、不修任運自在，方名解脫。性如虛空，不增、不減，何假添補？但隨時、隨處，息業、養神，聖胎增長，顯發自然神妙。. . . 二云：諸法如夢，諸聖同說。故妄念本寂，塵境本空。空寂之心靈知不昧。即此空寂之知是汝眞性，任迷、任悟。心本自知，不藉緣生不因境起。「知」之一字衆妙之門。由無始迷之故，妄執身心爲我，起貪、嗔等念。. . . 心自無念，念起即覺，覺之即無。修行妙門唯在此也。[125]

---

[125] T48.2015, 402c15-403a6.

Both of these Chan schools hold that the nature of the mind is undifferentiated and identical to all dharmas, but its functions lead to differentiations. The Mazu Chan position seems similar to the strong *tathāgatagarbha* of the *Shoulengyan jing* in that buddha-nature, which is the mind, creates or underlies all perceptions and actions. This implies that one does not intentionally practice to remove evil, or use the mind to see the mind. On the other hand, the Heze position seems closer to the weak *tathāgatagarbha* theory in that it emphasizes emptiness of the nature and of all dharmas (of which mind is one). Although this emptiness presents a potential for both delusion and enlightenment, in its unconditioned state it is a numinous knowing. It is this numinous knowing that underlies all that is perceived. As Zongmi writes:

> Directly indicate that the numinous knowing is exactly this nature of the mind, and everything else is vain and erroneous. Therefore it is said, "It is neither what is cognized by consciousness nor is it the mind's cognitive objects and so on."

直指靈知即是心性。餘皆虛妄。故云：「非識所識，非心境等」。[126]

> Since it is this mind that manifests and gives rise to dharmas, each and every dharma is this true mind. It is like the events appearing in a person's dream—every event is entirely the person; or like the metal used to make implements—every implement is the metal; or like the reflections appearing in a mirror—every reflection is the mirror. Therefore the *Huayan* [*jing*] says, "Know that all dharmas are the mind itself [or self-nature of the mind] . . . " [and] the *Dasheng qixin lun* says, "The three worlds are empty constructs that are created by nothing but mind. Apart from the mind, there are no six sensory fields. . . . All dharmas are produced from the mind's giving rise to deluded thoughts. All discriminations are precisely the mind's discriminating itself. The mind, however, does not see the mind for there are no characteristics to be apprehended. For this reason, all dharmas are like images in a mirror." The *Laṅkāvatāra-sūtra* says, "Quiescent cessation is called the One Mind, and the One Mind is called the *tathāgatagarbha*, which permeates and gives rise to the creation of all destinations of [re]birth, creating good and evil."

既是此心現起諸法，諸法全即眞心。如人夢所現事，事事皆人；如金作器，器器皆金；如鏡現影，影影皆鏡。... 故《華嚴》云：「知一

---

[126] T48.2015, 405c7-8.

切法即心自性。...」《起信論》云：「三界虛漢唯心所作，離心則無六塵境界。...一切分別即分別自心。心不見心，無相可得。故一切法如鏡中相。」《楞伽》云：「寂滅者名爲一心。一心者名如來藏。能遍興造一切趣生。造善造惡。」[127]

The mind perceives when it relates to objects, with each of the consciousnesses taking specific sense-data as its object. This is the mind that arises and ceases. The mind, however, also creates its objects, in the sense that the raw sense data is processed, coordinated, and categorized via language, memory, and discrimination. On the other hand, the nature of the mind is a numinous knowing, which is enlightenment, and corresponds to suchness. Yet all is One Mind.

Zhu also asserts that there is only one mind, which is differentiated according to what it perceives. Zhu further distinguished mind before it emerges or is manifested and after it emerges. According to the modern scholar, Chen Lai, Zhu Xi appropriated the Buddhist differentiation of the agent (*neng* 能) and object (*suo* 所), the perceiver and the perceived, quoting Zhu as follows:

> Humans have only one mind, yet that which perceives pattern is the mind of the Way, and that which perceives sound, color, smell, and taste is the human mind.... The mind of the Way and the human mind are intrinsically just a single thing. It is just that what they perceive is not the same.
>
> 人只有一箇心，但知覺得道理底是道心，知覺得聲色臭味底是人心。...道心、人心，本只是一箇物事，但所知覺不同。[128]

The human mind can exist only in formed *qi*, and the mind of the Way is therefore also within formed *qi*. They are not differentiated ontologically but rather by the human mind's propensity to succumb to selfish desire:

> To eat when hungry and drink when thirsty is the human mind. [Consideration of] which circumstances in which to eat and drink or not to eat and drink is the mind of the Way. To be called human is to have a body of *qi*, and so the human mind is comparatively close to other humans [as bodies]. Although the mind of the Way has been previously attained, yet it is blocked by a layer of the human mind. Therefore it is difficult to see. The mind of the Way is

---

[127] T48.2015, 405c13-21.
[128] *Zhuzi yulei, juan* 78, 2010. Chen Lai, *Zhuzi*, 213–214.

like clean water in muddied water, which is seen only to be muddy and not seen to be clean. Therefore it is subtle and hard to see.

饑食渴飲，人心也；如是而飲食，如是而不飲食，道心也。喚做人，便有形氣，人心較切近於人。道心雖先得之，然被人心隔了一重，故難見。道心如清水之在濁水，惟見其濁，不見其清，故微而難見。[129]

This account of the mind of the Way resembles the *tathāgatagarbha* or One Mind of the *Dasheng qixin lun* and other Buddhist texts.[130] These texts claim that the One Mind has two aspects: the mind of desires that interacts with the impermanent objects of perception and the mind of suchness that sees these objects for what they are, impermanent and empty of essence or substance.

In early Chan, the suchness aspect of the One Mind was to be protected or maintained, as was taught by the fifth patriarch, Hongren (601–674), whom Yanshou quoted as follows:

> To simply protect/maintain the One Mind is the aspect of the mind as suchness. [In that state] no dharmas or actions emerge from one's own mind. It is the mind alone that knows that the mind has no shape or materiality. The patriarchs use [this] mind to transmit the mind.
>
> 但守一心即心眞如門。一切法行不出自心。唯心自知心無形色。諸祖只是以心傳心。[131]

Zhu Xi at times uses similar language about preserving the mind of the Way, echoing this Northern Chan language. In commenting on a line from the *Shangshu*, Zhu said:

> The human mind is really precarious; the mind of the Way is really subtle. What criteria are there for saying that the mind of the Way is subtle and marvelous? One really needs to select the refined [mind] and really needs to be focused in protecting/maintaining it.
>
> 人心直是危，道心直是微。且說道心微妙，有甚準則？直是要擇之精。直是要守之一。[132]

---

[129] *Zhuzi yulei, juan* 78, 2011.
[130] For further discussion of Zhu's thought and its connection with the *Dasheng qixin lun* see John Makeham's chapter in this volume.
[131] *Zongjinglu*, T48.2016, 940a16-18.
[132] *Zhuzi yulei, juan* 78, 2014.

At other times Zhu approaches the "nothing-but mind" aspect of *tathāgatagarbha* thought when he commented on the same line from the *Shangshu*, saying that this line refers to both the mind and to things:

> If there is this mind then there is this thing, for it is due to this thing that later this mind is born.¹³³ How can there be a thing that is not created from out of this mind? It is like the mouth speaking—which is because the mind wants to speak.
>
> 有這箇心，便有這箇事；因有這箇事後，方生這箇心。那有一事不是心裏做出來底？如口說話，便是心裏要說.¹³⁴

As described by Yanshou, the human mind flows on without interruption:

> It is like ordinary people each separately giving rise to the mind/thoughts, they being already arisen, currently arising, and rising in the future, without limit and without interruption or end. This mind flows on continually without cessation.
>
> 譬如凡夫各別生心：已生、現生及以當生、無有邊際、無斷、無盡；其心流轉相續不絕。¹³⁵

Zhu Xi's similar description of the mind as flowing without interruption¹³⁶ provides some insight into his understanding of the relationship between the mind and the nature:

> However, in the body of humans, the functioning of perception is controlled by none other than the mind. . . . However, as soon as it is calmed and things do not come to it, and thoughts have yet to sprout, then the one nature will be entirely plain, and the meaning of the Way will be completely present, which is the so-called equilibrium. This then is why the mind is taken to be the intrinsic reality, and yet is quiescent and unmoving. When it moves [it is because] things come into intercourse with

---

¹³³ This suggests that a thing, or an action, is created by the mind, but also that the mind arises because of a thing. The context is about selecting the mind of the Way and focusing only on it.
¹³⁴ *Zhuzi yulei*, juan 78, 2017.
¹³⁵ T48.2016, 650b14-16.
¹³⁶ *Zhuzi yulei*, juan 63, 1538.

it, and thoughts sprout in it. . . . However, the calmness of the nature must be active.

然人之一身，知覺運用莫非心之所為。...然方其靜也，事物未至，思慮未萌，而一性渾然，道義全具，其所謂中，是乃心之所以為體而寂然不動者也。及其動也，事物交至，思慮萌焉。...然性之靜也而不能不動。[137]

As with the position of many Buddhists, Zhu is saying that the mind only becomes evident as thoughts or emotions once it engages with things. If the mind can be disengaged and calmed, then the nature of the mind can become clear, which is the mind of the Way.

The empty mind is similar to the pleroma—something empty that is filled. As Zhu wrote:

The nature is like the field of the mind. It fills in the emptiness in [the mind], and is nothing other than pattern. The mind is the home of the divine/spirit light (*shenming*) and is the controller of the body, and so the nature is the many patterns, which are obtained from heaven and are present in the mind.

性如心之田地，充此中虛，莫非是理而已。心是神明之舍，為一身之主宰。性便是許多道理，得之於天而具於心者。[138]

Although Zhu Xi's interpretation of the mind and the nature differs from that found in the Mazu school of Chan Buddhism, as represented by Zongmi, it nevertheless shares a number of similarities with the Northern Chan understanding of the *tathāgatagarbha*, which is based on the *Dasheng qixin lun*. Both agree that there is one mind that has two aspects, the human mind or the mind of rising and cessation, and the mind of the Way or the mind of suchness. The human mind flows continuously as it interacts with its environment and the other aspect of mind becomes evident when this flow is calmed. Both agree that the human mind obscures our perception of the mind of the Way or suchness. Moreover, their respective descriptions of the mind of the Way and the mind as suchness are similar. Both Northern Chan and Zhu Xi also state that the one mind, at least in its pure aspect, must be protected.

---

[137] *Zhu Xi ji, juan* 32, 1403–1404.
[138] *Zhuzi yulei, juan* 98, 2514.

1.5 Descriptions of the Fundamental Mind as Radiant

Zhu Xi and Northern Chan also share two related descriptions of the pure mind (the mind of the Way and the mind of suchness, respectively). One relates to a lucid radiance[139] or light and the other to a bright mirror.

1.5.1 Lucid Radiance

In Chinese Buddhist literature, as distinct from that translated into Chinese, the term "lucid radiance" is often used to describe the buddha-nature or the *tathāgatagarbha*. An example from Chan literature occurs in the legendary encounter between fourteenth patriarch of Chan, Nāgārjuna (second to third century) and his disciple Kāṇadeva, the fifteenth patriarch. Kāṇadeva said, "The *samādhi* (contemplative concentration) that lacks characteristics is shaped like the full moon; the meaning of buddha-nature is vast lucid radiance" (無相三昧形如滿月。佛性之義廓然虛明。).[140] The term *xuming* also occurs in the *Shoulengyan jing*: "Grasp the mind as lucid radiance, as purely being wisdom. The nature of insight is bright and round/perfect" (執心虛明純是智慧。慧性明圓。).[141] Zongmi relates this description to the *tathāgatagarbha* and to the theories of the *Dasheng qixin lun* in a commentary on the *Yuanjue jing* 圓覺經 (Sutra of Perfect Awareness/Enlightenment), a Chinese apocryphon closely related to Chan:

> Awareness is lucid radiance that illuminates numinously, without any discriminatory thoughts and ideas. Therefore the *Treatise* [*Dasheng qixin lun*] says, "'Awakening' means that the intrinsic reality of the mind is

---

[139] *Xuming* 虛明. The word *xu* has many meanings, such as "empty" or "false," and is often glossed as *kong* 空. Zhu sometimes uses *xu* in the sense of empty as can be seen where he says the Buddhist *li* is empty but the Confucian *li* is real. However, it can also be read as "in vain," or "without desire," or to "be without thought." As *Zhuangzi* states, "Emptiness is the fasting of the mind" 虛者心齋 (Watson, *Chuang Tzu*, 58). In Chinese poetry and non-philosophical literature the compound *xuming* was thought to mean mind in some cases (see Morohashi Tetsuji 諸橋轍次, ed., *Dai KanWa jiten* 大漢和辭典 (Large Chinese-Japanese Dictionary), (Tokyo: Daishūkan, reduced reprint 1966), no. 32709.329, citing Li Shan's 李善 (d. 689) commentary to Ren Fang's 任昉 (460–508) "Wang Wenxian jixu" 王文憲集序 (Preface to Wang Wenxian's Collected Writings) in Xiao Tong 蕭統 (501–531), *Wenxuan* 文選 (Literary Selections). In poetry it is a description of a scene as "clear and bright," and resembles words such as *xuying* 虛映 (Morohashi no. 32709.10; clear water in which everything is clearly reflected) and *xuying* 虛瑩 (Morohashi no. 15; shiny, like pure jade). Therefore I have translated it as "lucid radiance," although some ambiguity remains, and it can also mean "empty and radiant" in some contexts.
[140] *Jingde chuandeng lu*, T51.2076, 210b11-12.
[141] T19.945, 142a5-6.

free from conceiving. Being free from the characteristics of conceiving is identical to the realm of space: it is all-pervasive. The unitary characteristic of the dharma-realm is precisely the uniform dharma-body of the Tathāgata." . . . The explanatory commentary says, "This is a passage explaining the intrinsic awareness in the aspect of arising and cessation of the *tathāgatagarbha*."

覺者。虛明靈照無諸分別念想。故《論》云：「所言『覺』義者謂心體離念。離念相者等虛空界，即是如來平等法身」。. . . 釋曰：「此是釋如來藏心生滅門中本覺之文也。」[142]

"Lucid radiance" is thus a description of awareness of or enlightenment to the pure aspect of the *tathāgatagarbha*. Yanshou also quotes texts that associate lucid radiance with intrinsic awareness and non-conceptual insight,[143] and links the term with the School of the Nature (or *tathāgatagarbha*) identified by Zongmi: "The School of the Nature takes the intrinsic reality that is the ever-present lucid radiance that is not empty to be the nature" (性宗以虛明常住不空之體爲性。).[144] Dahui Zonggao, the master of Zhu Xi's former teacher (Kaishan Daoqian) and later arch-rival, also cited these words, saying, "Just as when water is clear and unmoving then this lucid radiance is self-illuminating" (如水之湛然不動，則虛明自照。).[145] This harks back to the description of buddha-nature or mind as "bright" and the characterization of both mind and dharmas as empty (of self-nature) or *śūnya* (*kong* 空) but still real.[146]

Zhu Xi frequently used the same descriptors of *xuming* to characterize the mind. Thus he describes the mind as "bright" and "empty," which enables it to be filled with pattern. Rather like Dahui, Zhu declared,

---

[142] *Dafangguang yuanjue xiuduoluo liaoyi jing lüe shuzhu* 大方廣圓覺修多羅了義經略疏註 (Short Commentary on the *Sutra on the Perfect Enlightenment*), T39.1795, 527a19-21. All translations from the *Dasheng qixin lun* in this chapter are drawn from the pre-copyedited manuscript of the forthcoming annotated translation by John Jorgensen, Dan Lusthaus, John Makeham, and Mark Strange, *Treatise on Giving Rise to Faith in the Great Vehicle* (New York: Oxford University Press).

[143] *Zongjing lu*, T48.2016, 605b15-16.

[144] *Zongjing lu*, T48.2016, 616a27-28.

[145] *Dahui yulu*, T47.1998A, 924c2-3.

[146] For Zongmi, the School of Emptiness takes all dharmas to be empty, whereas the School of Nature takes the radiant mind to be not empty, a higher level of understanding that incorporates the understanding maintained by the School of Emptiness. According to Kamata Shigeo, *Zengen shosenshū tojo: Zen no goroku 9*, 162, this pairing of empty and not empty is derived from the *Śrīmālā-devī siṁhanāda-sūtra*'s idea of the empty *tathāgatagarbha* and the non-empty *tathāgatagarbha*. In the first case, one tries to be free from all afflictions or frustrations, but in the second one does not try to be free from them, but rather positively affirms them. Kamata thinks that Zongmi's idea of "non-emptiness" is more strongly based on the *Dasheng qixin lun*.

"Because the one mind of humans is clear, lucid and radiant, like the emptiness of a mirror or the balance of a set of scales, serving as the lord of the entire person, it is certainly the intrinsic suchness of true reality" (人之一心湛然虛明如鑑之空、如衡之平，以為一身之主者，固其真體之本然。).[147] The explanation for this is that the mind must be bright like a mirror to reflect things, and empty so that it can be a potential and so filled. If it is already filled with something, it can no longer reflect something else:

> The human mind is like a mirror. If previously it does not have a reflected image then when things come it will reflect and show that thing's beauty or ugliness. If there is already a reflected image in it, how can it reflect [this newly arrived thing]? The human mind is inherently clear, lucid and radiant, so when things come to it, it is influenced by them and responds, and naturally one can see their height and weight, and when the phenomena have passed, then as before, it must be empty/lucid.
>
> 人心如一箇鏡，先未有一箇影象，有事物來，方始照見妍醜。若先有一箇影象在裏，如何照得！人心本是湛然虛明，事物之來，隨感而應，自然見得高下輕重。事過便當依前恁地虛，方得。[148]

According to Chen Lai, this description of the mind is derived from Xunzi's chapter *Jiebi* 解蔽 (Dispelling Ignorance) because Zhu Xi uses several images in these descriptions such as *shenming* 神明, empty, and still.[149] Xunzi also wrote that people can understand the Way:

> because it is empty, unified, and still. The mind is constantly storing up things, and yet it is said to be empty (*xu*).... Man is born with an intellect, and where there is intellect there is memory. Memory is what is stored up in the mind. Yet the mind is said to be empty because what has already been stored up in it does not hinder the reception of new impressions. Therefore it is said to be empty.... Emptiness, unity, and stillness—these are the qualities of great and pure enlightenment.... The mind is the ruler of the body and the master of its god-like intelligence.
>
> 虛壹而靜。心未嘗不臧也，然而有所謂虛。．．．人生而有知，知而有志；志也者，臧也；然而有所謂虛；不以所已臧害所將受謂之

---

[147] *Zhu Xi ji*, juan 51, 2512.
[148] *Zhuzi yulei*, juan 16, 347.
[149] Chen Lai, *Zhuzi*, 218.

虛。. . .虛壹而靜，謂之大清明。. . . 心者，形之君也，而神明之主也。[150]

A metaphor used by Xunzi also has some resemblance to Zhu's ideas about the obscuring of the mind of the Way:

> The mind may be compared to a pan of water. If you place the pan on a level and do not move it, then the heavy sediment will settle to the bottom and the clear water will collect on top, so that you can see your beard and eyebrows in it and examine the lines of your face. But if a faint wind passes over the top of the water, the heavy sediment will be stirred up from the bottom and the clear water will become mingled with it, so that you can no longer get a clear reflection of even a large object. The mind is the same way.
>
> 故人心譬如槃水，正錯而勿動，則湛濁在下，而清明在上，則足以見鬚眉而察理矣。微風過之，湛濁動乎下，清明亂於上，則不可以得大形之正也。心亦如是矣。[151]

For Zhu Xi, however, the mind is embedded in formed *qi*, which obscures or covers the brightness of the mind, depending on the muddiness or clarity of the *qi*. It is not that the muddiness or sediment is stirred up; the *qi* covers or obscures as soon as it takes form. Rather than from Xunzi, the descriptor *xuming* for the mind is more likely to have been derived from the characteristics of the *tathāgatagarbha* as championed by Northern Chan in the seventh and eighth centuries.

Part of Zhu's inspiration probably also came from Zhang Zai's comment on the opening passage of *Mencius* 7A. Zhang said: "The combination of emptiness (*xu*) with *qi* has the name 'nature'." Zhu commented: "The word 'emptiness/lucidity' (*xu*) refers to pattern. When pattern and *qi* combine, this is the reason there are people. . . . Lucid radiance (*xuming*) is not dulled. This [non-obscuration] is [due to] pattern's being fully present within [the nature] without the slightest diminution" (「虛」字便說理，理與氣合，所以有人。. . . 虛明不昧，此理具乎其中，無少虧欠。).[152] When asked, "Why does the combination of emptiness and *qi* have a nature?" Zhu responded: "One should say, 'Emptiness is

---

[150] Burton Watson, trans., *Hsün Tzu: Basic Writings* (New York and London: Columbia University Press, 1963), 127–129.
[151] Watson, *Hsün Tzu*, 131.
[152] *Zhuzi yulei, juan* 60, 1431.

the nature; *qi* is the person.' As the empty/lucid radiance (*xuming*) of *qi* lodges in them, therefore 'the combination of emptiness and *qi* has the name nature'" (問:「合虛與氣何以有性?」曰:「.... 當言『虛即是性,氣即是人』。以氣之虛明寓於中,故『合虛與氣有性之名』。」).[153]

Thus "emptiness" is the nature, is pattern, which resembles the "emptiness" (*kong*) of buddha-nature. *Xu*, as with the Buddhists, here cannot mean 'nothing' or the absence of anything. Rather, it means something like "without shape or form," but not "lacking content." Just as pattern does not have a presence without *qi* in Zhu's philosophy, so too the *Dasheng qixin lun* states it is erroneous to think that "empty space (*xukong*) is the nature of a Thus Come One (buddha)" (即謂虛空是如來性).[154] In other words, the buddha-nature is not non-existent. Just as buddha-nature or *tathāgatagarbha* is not non-existent, so too Zhu conceives of the nature as filled with pattern. And just as pattern in the nature awaits to be discerned, so too the *tathāgatagarbha* has a *tathāgata*, a Thus Come One or buddha waiting to be discovered. In both cases, that content—be it pattern, buddha or suchness—is to be preserved or protected. This is a major feature of Northern Chan practice as well as in Zhu's practice. As the *Dasheng qixin lun* says, "Therefore, the [One] Mind is complete and is called the the Dharma-body or the store of the Thus Come One" (是故滿足名爲法身如來之藏。).[155]

Contrary to Zhu's assertion that the Buddhists take the nature to be empty (*kong*),[156] the buddha-nature does have content or characteristics. As described in the *Poxiang lun* 破相論 (Treatise on the Refutation of Characteristics) (also known as the *Guanxin lun* 觀心論 [Treatise on Observing the Mind]) attributed to Shenxiu 神秀 (d. 706), the famous Northern Chan master, quoting the *Shidi jing* 十地經 (*Daśabhūmika-sūtra* [The Ten Stages Sutra]): "The adamantine buddha-nature is radiant like the orb of the sun" (十地經云。眾生身中有金剛佛性。猶如日輪體明。).[157] It is also "awareness" (*juexing* 覺性),[158] an "awareness that is the root of all merits" (一切功德因覺爲根).[159] Hongren, the fifth Chan patriarch, quoted

---

[153] *Zhuzi yulei*, juan 60, 1432.
[154] T32.1666, 580a2.
[155] T32.1666, 579b7-8.
[156] See passage cited at the end of Section 1.3. See also Stephen Angle's discussion in his chapter in this volume.
[157] T48.2009, 367a7-8.
[158] T48.2009, 367a11.
[159] T48.2009, 367a15.

the same line from the *Shidi jing* to demonstrate that the [buddha]-nature is "pure."[160] Zhu Xi's assertion was wrong, so if he was not misrepresenting his rivals, perhaps what he meant was that "reality" is something rather more specific such as concrete practices rather than general qualities.

It is clear that Zhu Xi and the Buddhists, in particular the Chan Buddhists, shared the use of the term *xuming* (lucid radiance). The Buddhists used it to describe the *tathāgatagrabha*, buddha-nature, or awareness, which were also said to be empty (*kong*). Zhu used *xuming* as a characterization of the mind, but *xu*, at least when standing alone, could also mean empty. The implication is that the mind is empty or lucid so that it can be filled with pattern just as a mirror is empty or lucid so that it can reflect images. The Buddhists likewise claimed that "emptiness" (*kong*) of the buddha-nature or *tathāgatagarbha* does not mean empty of content, as it is suchness or awareness. Given that Zhu seems to have obtained the use of *xuming* in a philosophical or religious sense from the Buddhists, his assertion that the nature of the Buddhists is empty of content is best regarded as a distortion for rhetorical purposes.

1.5.2 The Brightness of the Mind and the Metaphor of the Mirror

Zhu also used the image of a mirror being covered by dust, suggesting that he took more from the *tathāgatagarbha* theory than just *xuming*. As we have seen above, Zhu Xi's comparison of the mind or human nature with a pearl in filthy water was almost identical to the metaphor used by the Northern Chan master Jingjue, who, as we have noted, compared the purity of the mind to a mirror. In discussing a line from the *Lunyu* on Yan Yuan's 顏淵 being humane for three months,[161] Zhu Xi said:

> Humaneness and the mind are intrinsically one thing. When they are separated by selfish desires, then the mind is contrary to humaneness, and they become two things. If selfish desires do not exist, then the mind and humaneness are not contrary to each other and they form one thing. The mind is like a mirror, humaneness is like the brightness (*ming*) of the mirror. The mirror has always been bright, but as soon as it is concealed by dust and dirt it is no longer bright. If the dirt and dust are entirely removed, then the mirror is bright.

---

[160] T48.2011, 377a24-26.
[161] *Lunyu*, VI.5, Legge, vol. 1, 186.

曰：「仁與心本是一物。被私欲一隔，心便違仁去，却為二物。若私欲既無，則心與仁便不相違，合成一物。心猶鏡，仁猶鏡之明。鏡本來明，被塵垢一蔽，遂不明。若塵垢一去，則鏡明矣。」¹⁶²

Zhu's knowledge of this metaphor probably came from Chan texts. Even one of the earliest Chan works, the *Zuishangsheng lun* 最上乘論 (Treatise on the Highest Vehicle) or *Xiuxin yaolun* 修心論 (修心要論) (Treatise on Cultivating the Mind) attributed to Hongren, states:

> I have personally realized that the buddha-nature of sentient beings is always already pure, but is like a clouded-over sun, so I just clearly protect that inherently true mind. When the clouds of erroneous thoughts have ended, the sun of insight appears. Why does one further need knowledge acquired through learning to discern all the meanings and patterns of the suffering of birth and death and the matters of the three times? It is like polishing a mirror so that the dust is removed and the brightness appears of itself.
>
> 我既體知衆生佛性本來清淨如雲底日，但了然守本眞心。妄念雲盡，慧日即現。何須更多學，知見所生死苦一切義理及三世之事？譬如磨鏡塵盡，明自然現。¹⁶³

This text and its metaphors represent the Northern Chan position, a supposed gradualism. It is unclear whether Zhu Xi had access to this particular text, for it has been found only at Dunhuang and in a 1570 print made in Korea,¹⁶⁴ but there is a long paraphrase in Yanshou's *Zongjing lu*, suggesting that the *Xiuxin yaolun* was still in circulation as late as the early Song.¹⁶⁵

The metaphor of the mirror, however, most famously appears in the *Platform Sutra*'s depiction of the fictional verse contest between Shenxiu, the purported leader of Northern Chan, and Huineng, the founder of Southern Chan. Again, although it is uncertain as to whether Zhu Xi actually read a version of the *Platform Sutra*,¹⁶⁶ he definitely knew about

---

¹⁶² *Zhuzi yulei*, juan 31, 781.
¹⁶³ T48.2011, 378a2-6.
¹⁶⁴ T48.2011, 379b15.
¹⁶⁵ McRae, *Northern School*, 316n67; T48.2016, 462a.
¹⁶⁶ Zhu lived before the standard editions were finalized, and he would not have had access to the Dunhuang version. He possibly had access to other now-lost versions.

Huineng,[167] and he read the *Jingde chuandeng lu*[168] in which the verse exchange is described. Shenxiu's verse is as follows:

> The body is the bodhi tree,
> The mind is like a bright mirror.[169]
> At all times diligently wipe it clean
> So that no dust remains.
>
> 身是菩提樹，心如明鏡臺。時時篇拂拭，莫遣有塵埃。[170]

Huineng replied later with his own verse:

> Bodhi is intrinsically not a tree,
> The mind-mirror likewise not a mirror.
> From the beginning there is not a single thing,
> So why is it necessary to wipe away the dust?
>
> 菩提本非樹，心鏡亦非臺。本來無一物，何假拂塵埃？[171]

Zongmi, in his *Zhonghua chuanxindi Chanmen shizi chengxi duxu*, introduced the "Northern Chan" position as follows:

> Sentient beings have an aware nature, just as a mirror has a bright (*ming*) nature, but frustrations cover it and it is not seen, just as a mirror is darkened by dust. If you follow the verbal teaching of the master, you [should] eliminate erroneous thoughts and when the thoughts have ended the nature of the mind will be awakened and all will be known. It is like polishing away the dark dust; when the dust is eliminated the intrinsic reality of the mirror will be bright and clear and it will reflect everything.
>
> 北宗意者。眾生本有覺性。如鏡有明性。煩惱覆之不見。如鏡有塵闇。若依師言教。息滅妄念。念盡則心性覺悟。無所不知。如磨拂昏塵。塵盡則鏡體明淨無所不照。[172]

---

[167] Mentioned *Zhuzi yulei, juan* 126, 3040.
[168] Mentioned *Zhuzi yulei, juan* 138, 3286.
[169] This line is usually translated, "The mind is like a bright-mirror stand," which makes no sense. Paul Demiéville, "Le miroir spirituel," in *Choix d'Études Bouddhiques* (Leiden: Brill, 1973), 121n1, claims that *tai* 臺 is used as a counter word for mirrors (particule spécificative des miroirs).
[170] T51.2076, 222c21-22.
[171] T51.2076, 223a6-7.
[172] X63.1225, 333a13-16.

After quoting Shenxiu's verse, Zongmi evaluated it as follows:

> This simply is an image of the conditioned arising[173] of defilements and purity, and is the gate [method of teaching/entry] of opposing the flow [of *saṃsāra*] and rejecting habituation. [It evinces] a non-awareness that erroneous thoughts are intrinsically empty and that the nature of the mind is intrinsically pure. As the enlightenment is as yet incomplete, how can the practice [now] be declared true?
>
> 評曰：此但是染淨緣起之相，反流背習之門，而不覺妄念本空，心性本淨。悟既未徹，修豈稱真？[174]

I think Zhu Xi rejected Zongmi's evaluation, for Zhu asserted the need to clear the dust away gradually, as we find in his comments on the words *ming ming de* 明明德 (to illuminate bright virtue) of the *Daxue*.[175]

> One inherently has this bright virtue. . . . One inherently has his good knowing, good capability, it is just that it is concealed by selfish desires and for that reason is dull and not bright. The words "illuminating the bright virtue" seek out the means by which one illuminates it. It is like a mirror. Intrinsically it is a bright thing, and it is due to its being clouded over by dust that it therefore cannot reflect [images], so it is necessary to polish away the dust and dirt, and only after that is the mirror bright again.
>
> 謂本有此明德也。. . . 其良知、良能，本自有之，只為私欲所蔽，故暗而不明。所謂「明明德」者，求所以明之也。譬如鏡焉：本是箇明底物，緣為塵昏，故不能照；須是磨去塵垢，然後鏡復明也。[176]

Whereas for Zhu Xi enlightenment is gradual, Zongmi advocated sudden enlightenment followed by gradual cultivation or refinement. Zhu is thus closer to the Northern Chan of Hongren or to his heir, Shenxiu, who famously was accused of teaching gradual enlightenment.

---

[173] *Pratitya-samutpāda*, also translated "conditioned origination" or "co-dependent origination."
[174] Kamata, *Zengen shosenshū tojo: Zen no goroku 9*, 298; X63.1225, 33a19-20.
[175] These words are at the beginning of the text; see Legge, vol. 1, 356.
[176] *Zhuzi yulei*, juan 14, 267.

1.6 What Covers or Obscures the Radiance?

Using the metaphor of the mirror for the mind, Zhu Xi said that it was covered by dust:

> What thing is the so-called Way? The mind is just like a mirror. If it is simply without an obscuration by dust pollutants then its intrinsic reality will be bright (*ming*) of itself, and when things come it will be able to reflect [them]. Now, if you wish to recognize this mind yourself, this would be like using the mirror to reflect itself and thereby see the mirror. Since this is illogical then this is not different from using the one mind to also recognize the same mind.[177]
>
> 所謂道者又何物耶？心猶鏡也。但無塵垢之蔽，則本體自明物來能照。今欲自識此心，是猶欲以鏡自照而見夫鏡也。既無此理，則非別以一心又識一心。

Zhu here raises two issues: the mirror's being obscured and using one's own mind to recognize one's own mind. The first issue can be related to *tathāgatagarbha* doctrine because the Buddhist texts that write about the *tathāgatagarbha* state that the contaminants or "dusts" that obscure it are "adventitious" (*ke* 客; *āgantuka*), a "stranger" or "guest" that lodges for a limited time. The *Vimalakīrti-nirdeśa-sūtra* (*Weimojie jing* 維摩詰經), a popular sutra known to Zhu Xi[178] and to the Cheng brothers,[179] states: "bodhisattvas cut out adventitious contaminants and frustrations." In his commentary on this sutra, Sengzhao, also known to Zhu Xi,[180] wrote: "When the mind encounters external conditions/objects, as frustrations arise without reason, they are called adventitious contaminants/sense-data" (心遇外緣煩惱橫起故名客塵。).[181] These adventitious contaminants that obscure the pure mind function just like the "dust pollutants" (塵垢) that Zhu says obscure the mirror or the pure mind.

The earliest Chan text, the *Erru sixing lun* 二入四行論 (Treatise on the Two Entrances and Four Practices), found also in the *Jingde chuandeng*

---

[177] *Zhu Xi ji, juan* 49, 2369.
[178] *Zhuzi yulei, juan* 126, 3013, 3028.
[179] *Chŏngsŏ bullyu*, 679.
[180] *Zhuzi yulei, juan* 126, 3025; *juan* 122, 2953; *juan* 130, 3115.
[181] Sengzhao, *Zhu Weimojiejing* 注維摩詰經 (Notes on *Vimalakīrti-nirdeśa-sūtra*), T38.1775, 378b6-10, cited in Yanagida Seizan 柳田聖山, *Daruma no goroku: Zen no goroku 1* 達摩の語錄：禅の語錄 1 (Recorded Sayings of Bodhidharma: Chan Recorded Sayings 1) (Tokyo: Chikuma shobō, 1969), 39.

lu of 1004, illustrates this obscuration of the *tathāgatagarbha* when describing the entry (into enlightenment) via principle/theory (理入) as opposed to entry via practice:

> Deeply believe that living beings, ordinary and saint, share one true nature and it is only because it is covered by adventitious contaminants and deluded conceptualizations that it is unable to be revealed. . . . This then is in profound agreement with principle. [When] there is no discrimination, one is quiescent and without [intentional] activity. This is called entry via principle.
>
> 深信含生同一眞性。但爲客塵妄想所覆不能顯了。. . . 此即與理冥符。無有分別。寂然無爲。名之理入。[182]

This is basic *tathāgatagarbha* doctrine, and so Zhu Xi's description of selfish desires as being like a "guest" or "adventitious"[183] is a clear echo of this doctrine, a doctrine first clearly promoted in the *Śrīmālādevī-siṁhanāda-sūtra* (*Shengman shizihou yisheng dafangbian fangguang jing* 勝鬘師子吼一乘大方便方廣經 [The Sutra of Queen Śrīmālā of the Lion's Roar]): "The *tathāgatagarbha* that is the pristine self-nature is defiled by adventitious afflictions and by severe afflictions" (此性清淨。如來藏而客塵煩惱、上煩惱所染。).[184] The afflictions (*kleśa*; *fannao* 煩惱)—defilements that frustrate progress towards enlightenment—overlap with desire, especially craving, and emotions such as anger.[185]

It is clear that Zhu was drawing on Buddhist sources for the linkage between selfish desires and their guest-like externality and temporary nature, for he makes a reference to a famous metaphor that is found in the *Lotus Sutra*:

> It is simply because [the thoughts of the person used in this example] mostly resided externally that this person is said to be a guest. If one is reverential then one can always reside in the house, and not needing to go outside for a long time one is likely to be the host. Once one is the host then from then on

---

[182] *Jingde chuandeng lu*, T51.2076, 458b22-26.
[183] *Zhuzi yulei*, juan 31, 786: "Since humaneness is the subject [lord of the house] of the words 'For three months [Yan Hui's mind] was not contrary [to humaneness],' humaneness is the host (lord of the house), and selfish desires are the guest" (蓋「三月不違」底是仁爲主，私欲爲客。). This is a comment on *Lunyu* 6.5.
[184] T12.353, 222b23-24, cited in Hirakawa, "Nyoraizō to wa nanika," 39; the Sanskrit is *āgantuka-kleśa* as attested by the *Laṅkāvatāra-sūtra*.
[185] King, *Buddha Nature*, 2.

one leaves rarely. The analogy of the prodigal son [carrying] a jewel [hidden in his clothes] in the Buddhist sutras is also appropriate [to this situation].

只是以其多在外，故謂之客。敬則常在屋中住得，不要出外，久之亦是主人。既是主人，自是出去時少也。佛經中貧子寶珠之喻亦當。[186]

Furthermore, Zhu linked the mind as pure mirror and selfish desires as being like the dust that covers the mirror when he commented on Yan Hui's not acting contrary to humaneness for three months.[187]

Zhu Xi also related this idea of afflictions to his personal experience, confessing that the frustrations he had suffered led him to existential questions: "When I was five or six years old my mind was frustrated/vexed (煩惱) [by the questions]: What is the intrinsic reality of heaven? What is that external thing?" (某五六歲時，心便煩惱箇天體是如何？外面是何物？).[188] Zhu did not use the term "adventitious dust" in his philosophy, but he was aware of it because in a poem "On the morning my long-lived mother was born" (Shou mu sheng zhao 壽母生朝) he wrote:

The immortal in the past lived in the room of Zilin.
One morning he fluttered down to the outer bounds of space.
He had long been enlightened [to the fact] that the guest dusts have no self-nature.

全人昔住紫琳房。一旦翩然下太荒。久悟客塵無自性。[189]

Zhu thus adopted the Buddhist idea of contaminants, metaphorically described as dusts, covering the radiant mind, but he differed from the Buddhists on the source of that contamination. Whereas the Buddhists claimed that the dust on the mirror-mind were the afflictions, which are mental states or a malfunctioning of the mind—in other words, they are produced by beings themselves but appear to be adventitious—Zhu asserted that formed *qi*, which has a physical nuance (but a consequence of which may be selfish desires), was the covering and was definitely due to something external:

[Yuan] Yafu said, "[Human] nature is like the sun and moon; the muddying of it by *qi* is like clouds and fog." The master agreed. . . . [Zhu Xi said]: "The

---

[186] *Zhuzi yulei*, juan 31, 786. The *Lotus Sutra* reference is for example to T9.262, 29b2-9.
[187] *Zhuzi yulei*, juan 31, 781. Translated on page 78 of this chapter.
[188] Fukushima, "Chūgoku," 161. *Zhuzi yulei*, juan 45, 1156.
[189] *Zhu Xi ji*, juan 2, 107.

nature is the source of all things, but the endowment of *qi* is pure or turbid, and so there is the difference between the sage and the benighted."

亞夫曰：「性如日月，氣濁者如雲霧。」先生以為然。...「性者萬物之原，而氣稟則有清濁，是以有聖愚之異。」[190]

For the Buddhists, the adventitious dusts or afflictions are due to karma: to one's deeds and intentions of the past, including past lives. This is mental, but the idea of shared karma (*gongye* 共業) implies that the "physical" environment in which one is reborn is also due to karma. In contrast, Zhu Xi held that *qi* came from heaven. In other words, it was a given. It is clear that Zhu Xi could not accept the Buddhist theory of karma because otherwise, given his adoption of the Buddhist idea of a radiant mind being covered by contaminants, the theoretical underpinnings of his teachings would be difficult to differentiate from those of Chan Buddhism. Therefore, instead he used the idea of *qi* that had already been used in Confucian thought to explain why there are differences between people. In a long discussion of *qi*, emotions, and the nature, Zhu said that the (human) nature and *qi* have to be discussed together. Asked, "Does *qi* come from heaven?" he said:

"The nature and *qi* both come from heaven. The nature is only pattern; as for *qi*, it already pertains to shape and image. The goodness of the nature is certainly what people share in common; *qi* is what has the inequalities." Accordingly [Zhu] pointed to the air [heavenly *qi*, sky] and said, "If the sky is clear and expansive, that is excellent *qi*. . . . When it is clouded over and dark, that is bad *qi*." . . . He also said, "Poverty and wealth, nobility and meanness, the long life or short life of people are all unequal due to their being mixed up with *qi*, yet no-one pays any attention. There are those whose *qi* is clear and thin, and those whose *qi* is turbid and thick."

「性與氣皆出於天。性只是理，氣則已屬於形象。性之善，固人所同，氣便有不齊處。」因指天氣而言：「如天氣晴明舒豁，便是好底氣。...到陰沉黯淡時，便是不好底氣。...又曰：「人之貧富貴賤壽夭不齊處，都是被氣滾亂了，都沒理會。有清而薄者，有濁而厚者。」[191]

There are comparable passages in the *Lengqie shizi ji* 楞伽師子記 (Records of Teachers and Disciples of the *Laṅkāvatāra*[*-sūtra* School]) by

---

[190] *Zhuzi yulei*, juan 4, 76.
[191] *Zhuzi yulei*, juan 59, 1387.

Northern Chan master Jingjue. Writing of Huike, the so-called second patriarch of Chan, Jingjue quoted the *Shidi jing* on the adamantine buddha-nature: "It is only covered and blocked by the thick clouds of the five *skandha*s so that sentient beings cannot see it."[192] The *skandha*s are the psychosomatic aggregates that constitute a person. They can be compared to the *qi* in Zhu's system that constitutes humans and all things, but they are due to karma. Jingjue also quoted Daoxin, the fourth Chan patriarch as saying the following about practice:

> If one attains the abiding mind and has no further concerns with objects; is calm in concentration according to one's endowment; and also attains cessation of the afflictions according to one's endowment, one will therefore not create new [karma]. That is called release.
>
> 若得住心、更無緣慮、随分寂定、亦得随分息諸煩惱畢、故不造新、名為解脱。[193]

These passages show that in both Zhu's system of thought and the *tathāgatagarbha* doctrine the radiance is covered over by varying levels of obstruction. They also raise the problem of endowments (*fen* 分) and whether people can do anything about them, which in turn is related to the question of how the mind can enlighten itself when it is covered over by elements, mental or material, that prevent it from perceiving its intrinsic radiance.

1.7 Endowments

Zhang Zai, one of the Daoxue founders, introduced the old idea of "endowments" into the discussion of *qi* and the differences in ability to see the radiant mind: "The admirable or bad quality of a person's *qi*, and the patterns of being noble and base, long-lived or short-lived, are all due to the fixed endowment one receives" (人之氣質美惡與貴賤、夭壽之理，皆是所受定分。).[194] This endowment is related to a person's *ming* 命 or fate. "And so, to realize the mandate fully one is able to protect only what is endowed by heaven. The inherent

---

[192] Yanagida, *Zen no goroku 2*, 146.
[193] Yanagida, *Zen no goroku 2*, 249.
[194] *Zhang Zai ji*, 266; Ira Kasoff, *The Thought of Chang Tsai (1020–1077)* (Cambridge, UK: Cambridge University Press, 1984), 73.

endowment, however, cannot be added to" (然至於命者止能摛全天之所稟賦，本分者且不可以有加也。)[195] This endowment is determined naturally, is "mandated by heaven," and seems akin to the karma of the Buddhists.

We find such ideas in both Confucian and Buddhist history.[196] Some Buddhists maintained that there are two fundamental categories of beings: those who can become Buddha and those who cannot. The latter are called *icchantika*, and supposedly lack buddha-nature. The issue of whether all humans possess buddha-nature divided opinions in China. Many of the southern Chinese aristocracy or gentry (including monks) of the Northern and Southern Dynasties period believed that only the high-born possessed buddha-nature, and the others, the *icchantika*, lacked it. Common people were thus considered ineligible for buddhahood, just as the possibility of sagehood was denied to the masses in contemporary interpretations of Confucianism.[197]

On the basis of the concept of *śūnyatā* and passages such as that in the *Śrīmālādevī-sūtra*, "To know the *tathāgatagarbha* is to know *śūnyatā*,"[198] Daosheng 道生 (ca. 360–434) and others asserted that all sentient beings have the buddha-nature. Despite this becoming the popular view in China, in the early seventh century, Xuanzang introduced the theory that there were five types of nature or *gotra* (*xing* 姓), including the *icchantika*. This idea was firmly rejected by other Buddhist groups.

On the other hand, Confucians also asserted that there were grades of human nature based on the type of *qi* that people were endowed with. This was discussed in detail by Huang Kan 皇侃 (488–545), a leading Confucian thinker:

> Human nature is what people are endowed with when they are born. Habits are the matters a person regularly performs in accordance with the

---

[195] *Zhang Zai ji*, 234.

[196] See for example, Li Shen 李申, *Rujiao baoying lun* 儒教報應論 (Confucian Theories of Retribution/Recompense), (Beijing: Guojia tushuguan chubanshe, 2009), for a collection of pre-Buddhist materials that show "Confucians" believed in "retribution."

[197] Walter Liebenthal, "The World Conception of Chu Tao-sheng," *Monumenta Nipponica* 12 (1956): 92–93; Tōdō Kyōshun 藤堂恭俊, in Tōdō Kyōshun and Shioiri Ryōdō 塩入良道, *Ajia Bukkyōshi: Chūgoku hen I: Han minzoku no Bukkyō: Bukkyō denrai kara Zui-Tō made* アジア仏教史　中国編I 漢民族の仏教 (The History of Asian Buddhism: China, Volume 1, Buddhism of the Han People) (Tokyo: Kōsei shuppansha, 1975), 171–172 stresses the difficulties that Daosheng 道生 (ca. 360–434) faced in having his doctrine of the buddha-nature of all sentient beings accepted due to the contemporary strict status distinctions between commoner and aristocrat. For the inability to learn to become a sage, see later section.

[198] Wayman, *Lion's Roar*, 99; Takasaki Jikidō, *A Study on the Ratnagotravibhāga (Uttaratantra): Being a Treatise on the Tathāgatagarbha Theory of Mahāyāna Buddhism* (Rome: Istituto Italiano per il Medio ed Estremo Oriente, 1966), 37.

inclinations he develops after he is born. All people are born with the *qi* given by heaven and earth. Although there are, in addition, differences in the purity of *qi*, everyone is endowed with *qi*.[199]

This idea of differences in endowments of *qi* was probably based on the theories of Wang Chong 王充 (27–ca. 100). Huang argued that there are three grades of human nature, the differences being due to the clear and turbid qualities of *qi*. Two grades, those of the saint and the benighted person, cannot be changed, the endowment being fixed at birth. Huang calls these grades *fen* 分. These views remained current in the Tang dynasty and the three grades ranging from pure *qi* to turbid *qi* can be found in Kong Yingda's 孔穎達 (574–648) *Liji zhengyi* 禮記正義 (Correct Interpretation of the Book of Rites) and in the writings of Han Yu.[200]

The term *benfen* 本分 (inherent endowment), used by Zhang Zai and by Zhu Xi,[201] was also adopted by Dahui Zonggao.[202] The earliest occurrences known of *benfen* are probably those in the *Xunzi*, where the term is used to mean something like "the thing itself," as in, "to see the clue/beginning [such as the four beginnings of Mencius] is not as good as seeing the main portion (*benfen*)."[203] It is, however, the idea of *fen* as allotment or endowment that appears in the commentary on the *Zhuangzi* by Guo Xiang 郭象 (d. 312) and Xiang Xiu 向秀 (ca. 221–ca. 300) that was crucial. There it means "inborn 'share' of capacities . . . inclinations." The commentary states, "Each has inherent allotment (*benfen*) obtained as inherent nature; nobody can escape from it, and nobody can add to it."[204]

The term *benfen* first appears in Chan literature in the *Zutang ji* 祖堂集 (Hall of Patriarchs Collection) of 952 in an entry on Lingyan Huizong 靈巖慧宗:

A monk asked, "What is my own innate endowment?" The master said, "What are you doing throwing away the true gold and picking up the rubble?"

僧問、如何是學人自己本分事。師云、拋却真金拾得瓦礫。[205]

---

[199] John Makeham, *Transmitters and Creators: Chinese Commentators and Commentaries on the Analects* (Cambridge, MA: Harvard University Asia Center, 2003), 99.
[200] Makeham, *Transmitters*, 99, 102, 109, 115, 166.
[201] *Zhang Zai ji*, 234; *Zhuzi yulei, juan* 6, 101; *juan* 13, 243; *juan* 22, 520.
[202] Araki, *Daiesho*, 13, 236, 239–240, 222.
[203] *Xunzi*, "Feixiang 非相" (Contra Physiognamy) chapter, *juan* 3, 7a, *Sibu beiyao* edition.
[204] Erik Zürcher, *The Buddhist Conquest of China* (Leiden: Brill, 1959), 90–93, mod.
[205] Sun Changwu 孫昌武, Kinugawa Kenji 衣川賢次, and Nishiguchi Yoshio 西口芳男, eds., *Zutang ji*, 2 vols. (Beijing: Zhonghua shuju, 2007), 448.

Later, Yuanwu Keqin wrote to Dahui sometime after 1125 asserting that all the actions of Mazu and Huangbo in their enlightenment process and teaching "were based on their innate endowment."[206] For Chan, *benfen* meant a mental capacity, the nature of the mind, which is a potential.[207]

Zhu Xi was certainly cognizant of the Chan use of *benfen*, for when he was commenting on the passage in *Mengzi* 6B.10, "Zhongni (Confucius) did not do extraordinary things," Zhu noted, "This says that the sage [Confucius] did not do an iota more than his *benfen*, like a person who deserves eight blows of the staff and received only eight blows" (「四尼不為已甚」，言聖人所為，本分之外不加毫末。如人合喫八棒，只打八棒。).[208]

Whether *qi* is allotted by heaven (nature) or by karma that has no beginning, the idea of an allotment or endowment (*fen*) that differs from individual to individual, and extends through all sentient existence, had implications for an individual's capacity to become enlightened or to "see the nature," be it the good human nature of Mencius or the buddha-nature of Chan.

1.8 Who Can See the Radiance? Can All People Become Sages?

Both *tathāgatagarbha* writings and Zhu Xi claim that the primal radiance of the mind is obscured or hidden by adventitious contaminants or by turbid *qi*, the endowment or allotment of which varies from individual to individual. Only the sages have entirely pure *qi*. Only the buddhas in nirvana have exhausted all karma. As such, do all people

---

[206] Araki, "Kaisetsu," in *Daiesho*, 246.
[207] The authority on Chan/Zen terminology, Mujaku Dōchū 無著道忠 (1653–1744), glosses one of Dahui's uses of *benfen* as follows: "The adept of the original endowment is your own mind and nature, which is your original endowment." *Daei Fugaku Zenji shokōroju* 大慧普覚禪師書栲栳珠 (Pearls in the Basket of Chan Master Dahui Pujue's Letters) facsimile of manuscript (Kyoto: Zenbunka kenkyūsho, 1977), 505b. Mujaku also glossed it as "original capacity" or "original capacity applicable to yourself" (本来當己之分量 . . . 定分) in his *Kattō gosen* 葛藤語箋 (Notes on Chan Terminology) (Komazawa University, Zenshū jiten hensansho, 1959), 78a-79a.
[208] *Zhuzi yulei, juan* 57, 1339. The reference to eight blows was very popular in Chan, often short for "eight blows the equal of thirteen." See Komazawa Daigaku Zengaku Daijiten hensansho 駒沢大学禅学大辞典編纂所, comp., *Zengaku daijiten* 禅学大辞典 (Large Dictionary of Zen), 3 vols. (Tokyo: Daishūkan shoten, 1977), 1024b. This was also a term from the theater, meaning the eight blows were delivered so hard that they were the equivalent of thirteen. Eight blows was the lightest punishment by caning.

have the capacity to remove or to see through these contaminants, or is it rather a matter of how much the contamination varies that determines whether people can see through the contamination regardless of their innate capacities?[209]

Proponents of the *tathāgatagarbha* or buddha-nature theory had long asserted that all sentient beings have buddha-nature and so can discern their buddha-nature or become a buddha. This in turn was related to the bodhisattva vow in Mahāyāna Buddhism, which promised the bodhisattva would not enter nirvana until all beings are liberated. This Buddhist idea of a universal potential for sainthood, buddha-nature, was initiated in China by Zhu Daosheng 竺道生 (ca. 360–434). Daosheng said that after a process of gradual practice, likened to chopping down a tree, anybody who did so could be suddenly enlightened (all at once), just as the tree is cut through with the last strike. Daosheng's views were publicized by the noted poet Xie Lingyun 謝靈運 (385–433) in his "Bianzong lun" 辯宗論 (Distinguishing between Confucian and Buddhist Teachings) of 422, a text that influenced Chan, especially the notion of a universal buddha-nature and the association of subitism with the south.[210]

Tang Yongtong, the first modern scholar to deal with the topic of whether sagehood could be learned, quoted Cheng Yichuan to the effect that all people could learn to be a sage, but Tang argued that in the pre-Qin period "Confucians" maintained that all people could become a sage, a Yao, or a Shun, but not by learning. In other words, in the pre-Qin period, a sage is born (and anyone could be so born), not made. Sagehood is innate, not acquired.[211] This view was countered during the Han dynasty in texts

---

[209] See Makeham's related discussion in Chapter 5 of this volume, where he discusses whether Zhu Xi maintained that a person's *qi* constitution determines "limits on the mind's cognitive, affective, and volitional awareness and hence its capacity to exercise appropriate control over its moral decision-making."

[210] The idea that it was Daosheng and Xie who provided the idea for Daoxue of the possibility of anybody becoming a sage was first raised by Tang Yongtong 湯用彤 in his essay, "Xie Lingyun 'Bianzong lun' shu hou" 謝靈運辨宗論書後 (Postscript to Xie Lingyun's Distinguishing between Confucian and Buddhist Teachings) reproduced in his *Wei Jin xuanxue lungao* 魏晋玄學論稿 (Essays on Wei-Jin Dark Learning) (Shanghai: Shanghai guji chubanshe, 2001), with an introduction by the compilers. For the influence on Chan, see Jorgensen, *Hui-neng*, 457, 471.

[211] Donald J. Munro, *The Concept of Man in Early China* (Stanford, CA: Stanford University Press, 1969), 2, 14, states that there is a natural equality among humans in that all have an "evaluating mind" or a "biological equality," and the sages Yao and Shun "were just the same as other men" and that any person could achieve that status by diligence. The passage cited from *Mencius*, 4B.32, however, does not mention diligence or learning. Rather, Mencius says that "things which are the same in kind are like (*si* 似) one another.... The sage and we are the same in kind." In contrast, Xunzi does say that a person can become a Yao or a Shun (13). On the other hand, Confucius said, "The sage and the man of *jen*; how dare I rank myself with them?" Munro

such as *Lunheng* 論衡 (Discourses Weighed in the Balance) and *Hanshu* 漢書 (History of the Former Han Dynasty). The Daoist text *Baopuzi* 抱朴子 (The Master Who Embraces Simplicity) added the theory that an immortal is endowed with a different kind of *qi* (禀異氣).²¹² According to the authors of the introduction to Tang's work, by the post-Han period, even Wang Bi 王弼 (226–249) stated, "that which makes a sage superior to other people is his numinous perspicacity (or divine light/enlightenment [神明])," which suggests that one could not learn to be a sage but that learning was still valued. The compilers of Tang's volume also note that Huang Kan stated that one could get close to being a sage by learning, but could not bridge the last gap, probably because of the endowment of *qi*. Indeed, Huang was indebted to Wang Bi for some of his ideas. Huang Kan also seems to have believed that Confucius did not learn because he was "innately endowed with knowledge," and that therefore it was impossible for others to learn to be a sage.²¹³

Tang argues that before Huang Kan lived, Daosheng had proposed that all sentient beings could become a buddha or sage. Xie Lingyun even notes that the Confucians of his day maintained that even Yan Yuan was unable to become a sage.²¹⁴ Based on Daosheng's theory, Xie insisted that buddhahood can be attained but not learned. Daosheng, however, stipulated that gradual practice and guidance were necessary before one was capable of sudden enlightenment.²¹⁵ Whatever the case, for Tang Yongtong, Daosheng's

---

comments here that there was some confusion between the "ideal man" and the "actual man" (72) and concludes that "For the Confucians, the sage-king was a lofty ideal, whose status was rarely reached" (115). Generally then, Confucius and Mencius say that humans are of the same kind or category, and can become similar to the sage by emulation or education, but are not able to become sages. Even Confucius was not a sage by his own admission. Xunzi, however, did allow that people could become sages by effort. I consider this insufficient to dismiss Tang's general thesis.

²¹² Tang, "Xie Lingyun," 103–104.

²¹³ Makeham, *Transmitters*, 110, 112, 116–117, 119, 123.

²¹⁴ Tang, "Xie Lingyun," 104–105; *Bianzong lun*, in *Guang hongming ji* 廣弘明集 (Expanded Collection of Writings Illuminating and Propagating Buddhism), T52.2103, 225a1, 226a24-25; Makeham, *Transmitters*, 153.

²¹⁵ "Introduction," 34–36. The passage is T52.2103, 225a3-6, Makeham, *Transmitters*, 153; Jorgensen, *Hui-neng*, 471: "'Silent illumination is subtle and marvellous, not permitting gradations. [Because] the accumulation of learning is limitless, why should it not end of itself?' Now I would reject the gradual enlightenment of the Buddhists and adopt [their proposition] that one can reach [sainthood] and I would reject the [thesis] of the Confucians that [sagehood] is just out of reach and adopt [their proposition] of the Immediate Attainment" (寂鑒微妙不容階級。積學無限何爲自絕。今去釋氏之漸悟而取其能至。去孔氏之殆庶而取其一極。). As indicated by my quotation marks, I think that the attempt to merge the two theories was made by Xie, not by Daosheng, who still maintained a gradual build-up by practice until a sudden breakthrough, as in the analogy of cutting down a tree. Daosheng's own writings confirm that gradual cultivation is required before sudden enlightenment is possible. See Chen Peiran 陳沛然, *Zhu Daosheng* 竺道生 (Taipei: Dongdatushu gongsi, 2011), 146. See also Jorgensen, "The Earliest Text of Ch'an

intervention brought a radical change in the conception of the sage, something that provided a basis for Cheng Yichuan's claim that one could learn to be a sage, despite the blockage of *qi*.[216] Significantly, there is evidence that Daosheng also took up the issue of *qi* and buddha-nature. Asked by an opponent, Faxian 法顯 (c. 337–ca. 422), "Is [it the case] that with the exception of the *icchantika*, all [beings] have buddha-nature?" Daosheng replied:

> All [sentient beings] who are endowed with the two modes of *qi* [*yin* and *yang*] are themselves the proper cause for attaining nirvana, whereas undergoing rebirth in the three realms is a result only of delusion. The *icchantika* is in the category of beings with life, so how could they alone be without buddha-nature? This [idea about the *icchantika* being without buddha-nature] is due to this sutra's [the *Nirvana Sutra*] being incompletely translated.
>
> 稟氣二儀者皆是涅槃正因，三界受生蓋惟惑果。闡提是含生之類，何得獨無佛性？蓋此經度未盡耳。[217]

In other words, all sentient beings, including *iccantika*, are innately endowed with buddha-nature. In Daosheng's time, one finds mention of the endowment of *qi* in a number of texts written by Chinese Buddhists,[218] but the link Daosheng establishes between a person's *qi* endowment and a universal potential to become a saint seems to have had the greatest subsequent influence.[219]

After Daosheng made the above statement, he claimed he was vindicated by a new translation of the *Nirvana Sutra*, one which explicitly stated that all beings without exception have buddha-nature, the potential to become a buddha. Later, some of the Daoxue followers adopted the possibility that

---

Buddhism" (MA diss., Australian National University, 1979), 47–62, especially 53–54 on the metaphor of chopping wood.

[216] Tang, "Xie Lingyun," 104.

[217] Ensō 圓宗 (d. 865), *Ichijō busshō enichi shō* 一乘佛性慧日抄 (Abstract of the Sun of Insight of the Buddha-nature of the One Vehicle), T70.2297, 173c10-13, quoting the *Mingseng zhuan* 名僧傳 (Biographies of Famous Monks) completed by Baochang 寶唱 (fl. 502) in 519. (For Baochang's text, see Zürcher, *Buddhist Conquest*, 10). Also see Chinkai 珍海 (d. 1152), *Sanron genshō mongi yō* 三論玄疏文義要 (Essentials of the Meanings of the Profound Commentaries of the Three Treatises [by Jizang])), T70.2299, 290c25-28.

[218] Notably in the *Hongming ji* 弘明集 (Collection of Writings Illuminating and Propagating Buddhism) and later in some works by Zongmi, who appears to have been influenced by them. Requires further investigation.

[219] For example, see Zongmi's *Yuanren lun* 原人論 (Inquiry into the Origin of Humanity) as cited by Berger, *Encounters of Mind*, 134.

all people could become a sage, but most, following Huang Kan, who was influenced by the *Bianzong lun*, did not accept this universal potential for sainthood.[220] Daosheng's influence on Chan was profound, for his ideas appear in the earliest text of Chan Buddhism,[221] and although later Chan thinkers like Zongmi reversed Daosheng's order of gradual practice and sudden enlightenment, Daosheng's influence continued. Therefore, Tang Yongtong's argument that Daosheng contributed to Daoxue has some validity, but it must be borne in mind that leading Daoxue figures such as Zhu Xi were ambivalent about the possibility that sagehood was achievable by all, maintaining that it was possible for Yan Yuan to become a sage, but because he remained hindered by the desire to become a sage he needed to stop making an effort.[222] This lack of desire at the end of strenuous practice resembles the practice of *huatou* by Dahui, which condemned anticipation:

> By putting in place before you the mind that seeks for enlightenment, you are doing no more than creating an obstacle for yourself. Try this method of practice [referring to *huatou*], and as time goes by you will naturally fumble about [respond freely]. If you desire to use the mind to anticipate enlightenment . . . then you will be unable to gain enlightenment from this moment until Maitreya is incarnated [in the inconceivably distant future].
>
> 以求悟證之心在前頓放，自作障難，非干別事。公試如此做工夫，日久月深自然築著磕著。若欲將心待悟將心待休歇 . . . 到彌熊下生，亦不能得悟。[223]

In contrast, if the endowment of *qi* is determined by heaven—and in several places Zhu suggests that Confucius was born a sage[224]—that would be a fatal flaw in any moral teaching that held out hope for becoming a sage or saint. Moreover, it seems it may also have been impossible to recognize a sage:

> [Someone asked:] "Zheng Xuan's 鄭玄 [127–200] commentary on the *Analects* states: 'Only a sage can know a sage.' Is it probable that the

---

[220] Jorgensen, *Hui-neng*, 470; Makeham, *Transmitters*, 150–151.
[221] Jorgensen, "The Earliest Text of Ch'an Buddhism," 59–61.
[222] Makeham, *Transmitters*, 248.
[223] Araki, *Daiesho*, 15; T47.1998A, 917c8-11.
[224] "Someone asked, 'Confucius could speak about the rituals of the Xia and the Yin and yet he had no evidence of that, for at that time the documents were insufficient/lacking. So where did Confucius get this knowledge?' [Zhu Xi] said, 'The sage himself was born with the knowledge and intelligence; there was nothing he could not comprehend'" (或問：「孔子能言夏殷之禮而無其證。是時文獻不足，孔子何從知得？」曰：「聖人自是生知聰明，無所不通。」), *Zhuzi yulei*, juan 25, 614.

first 'sage' here is the person and the second 'sage' is only the Way of the sage?"

Zhu Xi replied, "It is indeed the person. Only after there is the person can the Way of ultimate sincerity begin to be manifest."

鄭氏注云：「『唯聖人乃能知聖人。』恐上面聖人是人，下面聖人只是聖人之道耳。」曰：「亦是人也。惟有其人，而後至誠之道乃始實見耳。」²²⁵

Elsewhere, in commenting on the lines in *Analects* " . . . I learn from below and reach what is above. The only one who understands me is perhaps heaven" (下學而上達，知我者其天乎。),²²⁶ Zhu said:

"I learn from below and reach what is above" means to penetrate thoroughly the affairs and principles of heaven and humans so that not the slightest gap remains. What the sage [Confucius] means by "reach what is above" is simply that everything is suddenly here and that he does not need first to learn from below and only then to turn around to reach what is above. The sage is heaven, and [ordinary] people are unable to be like heaven. Heaven alone is without the many defects and failings of people and so it alone is able to know him [Confucius]. Heaven does not truly have a knowledge that knows. However, so long as the sage has this pattern, then heaven also has this pattern. Hence, what is marvellous about the sage is that he alone is in accord with it [heaven]. The Buddhists also say, "Only a buddha can know a buddha." This is precisely what is meant.

「下學上達」，是天人事理，洞然透徹，無一毫之間隔。聖人所謂上達，只是一舉便都在此，非待下學後旋上達也。聖人便是天，人則不能如天。惟天無人許多病敗，故獨能知之。天非真有知識能知，但聖人有此理，天亦有此理，故其妙處獨與之契合。釋氏亦云：「惟佛與佛，乃能知之。」正此意也。²²⁷

In the end, Zhu Xi followed Huang Kan in denying the possibility that every person is able to become a sage.²²⁸ In this respect Zhu effectively rejected the *tathāgatagarbha* and Chan article of faith that all could

---

²²⁵ *Zhuzi yulei*, juan 32, 1597.
²²⁶ *Analects*, 14.35.
²²⁷ *Zhuzi yulei*, juan 34, 889, translation tentative. The Buddhist text quoted is the *Lotus Sutra*, T9.262, 5c10-11.
²²⁸ Makeham, *Transmitters*, 250.

become saints, or indeed, all will become buddhas. As Zongmi said of the One Vehicle teachings,[229] "All sentient beings have buddha-nature, and all that has mind will certainly become a buddha" (一切眾生皆有佛性。凡是有心定當作佛。).[230]

In contrast, Zhu Xi insisted said that animals (a subset of sentient beings) could not realize the Way or become sages. According to Zhu, animals were allotted only a portion of the principles of morality, whereas humans were granted these principles in full. When asked, "If the nature of dogs and oxen is not the same as the nature of humans, how can the world have multiple natures?" Zhu Xi replied, "Humans have filial piety, brotherliness, loyalty, and trust, and do not dogs and oxen also serve their parents and serve their masters with loyalty?" (問:「犬牛之性與人之性不同，天下如何解有許多性？」曰:「人則有孝悌忠信，犬牛還能事親孝、事君忠也無？」).[231] Elsewhere he similarly maintained:

> It is crucial that we discriminate difference within sameness and sameness within difference. At their beginning, how have their [natures] ever been different? As soon as their [natures] fall into the [realm of] *qi*, only the crude aspects are the same. Humans and animals both eat when hungry and drink when thirsty, pursue benefit and avoid harm. If you do not recognize this principle, you are the same as them. . . . "The common people throw this difference away, the gentleman preserves it,"[232] so you must preserve this state of difference and only then can you be distinguished from animals. You cannot say that creeping and crawling things with intelligence/life all have buddha-nature, for then you will be the same as them [animals].
>
> 須是去分別得他同中有異，異中有同，始得。其初那理未嘗不同。才落到氣上，便只是那粗處相同。如飢食渴飲，趨利避害，人能之，禽獸亦能之。若不識箇義理，便與他一般也。...「庶民去之，君子存之」，須是存得這異處，方能自別於禽獸。不可道蠢動含靈皆有佛性，與自家都一般。[233]

---

[229] The "One Vehicle" is an idea derived from the *Lotus Sutra*, according to which there is only one true vehicle to carry sentient beings to nirvana. This one vehicle contains all the other vehicles the Buddha taught as expedients adapted to the various capacities for understanding of students. See Gregory, *Tsung-mi*, 102.
[230] Kamata, *Zengen shosenshū tojo*, 201; T48.2015, 408c21.
[231] *Zhuzi yulei, juan* 59, 1377.
[232] Mencius 4B.19: "That whereby people differ from animals is slight. The common people throw this difference away while the gentleman preserves it."
[233] *Zhuzi yulei, juan* 59, 1389.

For Zhu Xi, the Buddhist notion of buddha-nature is akin to the nature spoken of by Gaozi in the *Mencius*. The difference between humans and animals is really due to the differences in *qi*, which determines how much is revealed of the moral principles they are all endowed with. Mencius, he said, unlike Gaozi and the Buddhists, was not speaking about the differences between animals and humans in terms of the *qi* they were endowed with, but about their moral natures, nature as principle:

> "When asked, 'It is like with ants who have rulers and subjects . . . is this not also principle?' Zhu said, 'They have [that is, reveal] only a little of it, unlike humans who can possess [reveal] it entirely.'"
>
> 或問：「如螻蟻之有君臣 . . . 此亦是理。」曰：「他只有這些子，不似人具得全。」[234]
>
> As with the submissiveness of oxen . . . and the righteousness of ants, even though this is the nature of the five [moral] constants, they only receive a little of them, unlike humans who receive them in their entirety.[235]
>
> 如牛之性順 . . . 螻蟻之義，即五常之性。但只稟得來少，不似人稟得來全耳。

Zhu elaborated on these topics of preserving that which is innately endowed and the difference between humans and animals in order to criticize Buddhism:

> Such categories as hunger for food and thirst for drink are both the same for animals. The Buddhists say, "Function is the nature." When asked, "What is function?" the Buddhists say, "In the eye it is called seeing, in the ear it is called hearing . . . in the feet it is running around; it is present throughout all the myriads of realms and it is included in a speck of dust." This is saying they are the same as with animals. What differentiates humans from animals is that "Between father and child there is affection between ruler and subject there is righteousness . . . between old and young there is sequence, and between friends there is trust." The Buddhists have never been able to preserve [this difference].
>
> 饑食渴飲之類，皆其與禽獸同者也。釋氏云：「作用是性。」或問：「如何是作用？」云：「在眼曰見，在耳曰聞 . . . 在足運奔，徧現俱

---

[234] *Zhuzi yulei, juan* 59, 1377. I am grateful to an anonymous reviewer for the Press for correcting my earlier reading of this passage.

[235] *Zhuzi yulei, juan* 62, 1490.

該沙界，收攝在一微塵。」此是說其與禽獸同者耳。人之異於禽獸，是「父子有親，君臣有義...長幼有序，朋友有信」。釋氏元不曾存得。[236]

Despite this, Zhu had to allow that principle or the Way was present in everyday activity because *Zhongyong* 1 states: "One cannot depart from the Way even for an instant" (道不可須臾離), which Zhu glossed as follows:

> *Zhongyong* is talking about principles that are combined in daily functions and normal activity. For example, "To be a lord consists only of being humane, to be a subject consists only in being respectful, to be a son consists only in being filial."... The Buddhists do not understand the Way of normal activity, wanting only to emptily maintain that one thing, which they call the Way, yet of course is not the same [as the Way] of the *Zhongyong*.
>
> 《中庸》所言是日用常行合做底道理，如「為人君止於仁，為人臣止於敬，為人子止，為人子止於孝」。... 蓋釋氏不理會常行之道，只要空守著這一箇物事，便喚做道，與中庸自不同。[237]

The target of Zhu Xi's criticisms was Mazu Chan, for he refers to a famous verse by one of Mazu Daoyi's pupils, Layman Pang:

> If you say that eating, drinking, working, and breathing are the Way, that cannot be accepted, as it would have the same fault as Layman Pang's hymn, "Divine powers and marvelous functions [lie in] carting water and toting firewood."... The Buddhist words "Functions are the nature" are like this. Paying no heed to right and wrong, the only thing they maintain is that [wearing] clothes, eating, working, breathing, seeing and hearing are the Way. Claiming that my ability to speak and to act... is divine power and marvelous function is to pay no heed to principle. Within all of this Confucians must investigate principle—that alone is the Way. A Chan elder said, "There is a true man of no rank in this lump of red meat...." He merely acknowledges this, toying with it.
>
> 若便謂食飲作息者是道，則不可，與龐居士「神通妙用，運水搬柴」之頌一般，亦是此病。... 佛家所謂「作用是性」，便是如此。他都不理會是和非，只認得那衣食作息，視聽舉履，便是道。說我這箇

---

[236] *Zhuzi yulei*, juan 57, 1348; see similar passage in *Zhuzi yulei*, juan 59, 1376, which specifically refers to Chan and *Mencius*.
[237] *Zhuzi yulei*, juan 62, 1496.

會說話底,會作用底 . . . 便是神通妙用,更不問道理如何。儒家則須是就這上尋討箇道理方是道。禪老云「赤肉團上,有一無位真人。」 . . . 云云。他便是只認得這箇,把來作弄。[238]

Zhu is accusing the Chan Buddhists of not understanding that the Way consists of investigating principle, and is not to be found merely in actions or functions. The Chan elder here is the famous Linji Yixuan (d. 866), who by Zhu Xi's time had been deemed to be the source of the dominant form of Chan, and who was recognized to be in the Mazu lineage. In some respects, Zhu's attack on Mazu Chan was echoing the criticisms made by Zongmi of Mazu (Hongzhou) Chan:

> The idea of Hongzhou is that giving rise to mind [thoughts], snapping fingers and moving eyeballs, what is done and what is acted on, is in its entirety the function of the buddha-nature, and there is no other function. The entirety of craving, anger, and stupidity, of doing good and doing evil, experiencing pleasure and experiencing pain, these are all buddha-nature, just as flour makes all kinds of food, each [item of food] is flour. The intent is to investigate this body [made up] of the four elements, of bone and flesh, throat, tongue, molars and teeth, of eyes and ears and hands and feet [to show that] they are entirely unable on their own to speak, see, hear, move and act. If in a moment life ends, before the body has deteriorated in the slightest, the mouth cannot speak and the eyes cannot see, the ears cannot hear, the feet cannot walk. . . . Therefore we know that the capacity to speak, move and act must be [due to] buddha-nature. If we break down each of the four elements, bones and on flesh down, then none of them can crave, be angry, or frustrated. Therefore we know that craving, anger, and frustrations are all buddha-nature. The intrinsic reality of buddha-nature is not all the differentiated types, and yet it is creator of all differentiated types. That its reality is not various types means that this buddha-nature is neither saint nor commoner, neither cause nor effect, neither good nor evil. . . . "[Buddha-nature] is creator of the various types" means that because this nature is the function of intrinsic reality, it can be commoner and can be a saint, . . . it can be good and can be evil . . . it can be a buddha and it can be a sentient being, and it can crave and be angry and so on. If this reality-nature is covered over then ultimately it cannot be seen and cannot be verified, just as the eye by itself cannot see the eye and so on. If we refer to its responsive

---

[238] *Zhuzi yulei,* juan 62, 1497.

function, then raising up, moving and operating are all this [buddha-nature] and there is no other dharma that can verify what is to be verified. This idea is based on the *Laṅkāvatāra-sūtra*, which says: "The *tathāgatagarbha* is the cause of the good and not good, and can universally give rise to and create all the destinations of rebirth, experience pleasure and pain, that accompany the causes." Again, in the "Buddha Discourses on the Mind" [chapter] the sutra says, "There are Buddha worlds where raising eyebrows and moving eyeballs, smiling . . . are all matters pertaining to the Buddha." Once one is enlightened to and understands this principle, all is naturally true and self-so. Therefore, what is cultivated in practice should in principle conform to this, and so one does not give rise to the mind [thought] of eliminating evil, does not give rise to the mind of cultivating the Way, for the Way is the mind, and one cannot use the mind to cultivate the mind. Evil is also the mind, so one cannot use the mind to eliminate the mind. . . . There is no dharma to be embraced, no buddha to be made. It is just like empty space that neither expands nor contracts. What need is there to augment it?

洪州意者，起心動念、彈指動目、所作所為，皆是佛性全體之用，更無別用。全體貪、嗔、癡、造善、造惡、受樂、受苦：此皆是佛性，如麵作種種飲食，一一皆麵。意以推求此身四大、骨、肉、喉、舌、牙、齒、眼、耳、手、足，並不能自語言、見、聞、動作。如一念命終，全身都未變壞，即便口不能語、眼不能見、耳不能聞、腳不能行 . . . 故知能言語動作者必是佛性。且四大、骨、肉，一一細推，都不解貪、嗔、煩惱。故知貪、嗔、煩惱並是佛性。佛性體非一切差引種種，而能造作一切差別種種。體非種種者，謂此佛性非聖、非凡、非因、非果、非善、非惡 。. . .「能作種種者」謂此性即體之用，故能凡、能聖、能因 . . . 能善、能惡 。. . . 能佛、能眾生，乃至能貪、嗔等。若覷其體性則畢竟不可見不可證，如眼不自見眼等。若就其應用，即舉、動、運、為，一切皆是，更無別法而為能證所證。彼意准《楞伽經》云：「如來藏是善不善因，能遍興造一切趣生，受苦、樂與因俱。」又〈佛語心〉經云：「或有佛刹揚眉、動睛、笑 . . . 等皆是佛事。」既悟解之理，一切天真自然。故所修行理宜順此，而乃不起心斷惡，亦不起心修道。道即是心，不可將心還修於心；惡亦是心，不可將心還斷於心 。. . . 無法可拘，無佛可作，猶如虛空不增不減，何假添補？[239]

The first thing that both Zongmi and Zhu Xi found objectionable was the antinomian implications of the claim that practice, especially moral practice,

---

[239] Kamata, *Zengen shosenshū tojo*, 307–308; X63.1225, 33a22-333b30.

was not required.²⁴⁰ For Zhu in particular this doctrine was completely antithetical to his stress on the principles that had to be sought and preserved so that humans did not descend to the level of animals. For Zhu, only humans could become sages (but only by birth), but for Chan Buddhists, who believed in rebirth, all beings, including animals, could eventually become a buddha or a saint. Northern Chan Buddhists, unlike Mazu Chan, stressed the observance of the precepts (moral rules) and the *pāramitā*s as a means of cleansing the mind.²⁴¹ Because Zhu rejected the potentially antinomian views of Mazu or his heirs and instead valued moral cultivation, once again Zhu is closer to Northern Chan than to Mazu and Zonggao or even Zongmi.

1.9 What Sees the Radiance? Is It the Radiant Mind Seeing the Radiance or Is It the Mind Seeing the Nature That Is Radiant?

The *Laṅkāvatāra-sūtra* that Zongmi cited in the above passage to represent the position of Mazu Chan contains a discussion of nothing-but mind and its relation with objects. Guṇabhadra (394–468) translates it in verse:

> If there is no cognitive object there will be no mind,
> So how can there be nothing-but consciousness/cognition?
> By taking it that there are supports for cognitive objects,
> The mind of sentient beings can occur.
> Without a cause the mind will not be produced,
> So how can there be nothing-but consciousness?
> Suchness and nothing-but consciousness
> Are what act in ordinary beings and the saints.
> . . .
> Due to the grasper and the grasped
> The mind can arise.
> The mundane mind is like this,
> Therefore it is not nothing-but mind.
> The body with the support of the earth reflects an image,
> Just as a dream is produced from the mind.
> Although the mind is made of two parts,
> The mind does not have two characteristics/forms.

---

²⁴⁰ Gregory, *Tsung-mi*, 246–251.
²⁴¹ Shenxiu, *Poxiang lun* 破相論 (Treatise on the Refutation of Characteristics), T48.209, 357c1-358a8. This text was traditionally attributed to Bodhidharma, but it is almost identical with Shenxiu's *Guanxin lun*.

Just as the knife does not harm itself,
Or the finger does not touch itself,
The mind does not see itself.
This matter is also like this.
Where there is no reflected image,
There is no rising based on something else.

無境則無心　云何成唯識
以有所緣境　衆生心得起
無因心不生　云何成惟識
眞如及惟識　是衆聖所行

. . .

由能取所取而心得生起
世間心如是　故非是唯心
身資土影像　如夢從心生
心雖成二分　而心無二相
如刀不自割　如指不自觸
而心不自見　其事亦如是
無有影像處　則無依他起[242]

If there is only mind and no external objects, if all is the *tathāgatagarbha* or radiance, how can the mind see itself? There would be no point in practice. If there are coverings obscuring the empty, radiant mind or nature of the mind, then how can the mind see itself?

The motifs of the mind seeing the mind or the sword cutting itself go back to a conflict in India between the Mādhyamikas and Yogācāras. "The Vijñānavādin [Yogācāra] especially compared the self-luminous *citta* [mind] to a lamp which shines in darkness, an idea attacked by Mādhyamikas."[243] Śāntideva (fl. eighth c.), for example, argues: "As the blade of the sword does not cut itself, neither does the mind know itself. If it is thought that the self is like a lamp that illuminates, that lamp cannot be illuminated, since it is not covered by darkness."[244]

The Mādhyamikas, however, had to concede that consciousness or cognition required objects, for "As it is said that a child is born out of the father and mother relationship, so also does consciousness arise from the bond between the eye and material."[245]

---

[242] T16.670, 634b3-14.
[243] Marion L. Matics, *Entering the Path of Enlightenment: Śāntideva's* Bodhicaryāvatāra (London: George Allen & Unwin, 1970), 116.
[244] Matics, *Entering the Path of Enlightenment*, 213. Śāntideva, of course, was not the initiator of this idea, but rather was drawing upon it.
[245] See Inada, *Nāgārjuna*, 53.

The *Laṅkāvatāra-sūtra* took up this challenge, saying, "The mind is apprehended by one's own mind. There is no dharma that arises without a cause, the mind and dharmas in themselves are pristine" (心取於自心，無法無因生，心法體清淨。).[246] There are conditions or objects, which are not separate from the mind, and these are also empty. As the sutra states in the preceding lines:

> If [dharmas] rise only in the mind,
> This would be like being on a wall in empty space.
> Why would they not arise?
> If you have the slightest contemplation of their characteristics,
> Then mind will arise from objects/conditions.
> [But] if they rise from causes and conditions,
> One cannot say nothing-but mind.[247]
>
> 若但心中生　　如虛空壁中
> 何故而不生　　若有少相觀
> 心則從緣生　　若從因緣生
> 不得言惟心

This topic is often referred to in Chan sources and so it is unsurprising that Yanshou took it up, saying that "the mind cannot see the mind because there are no characteristics/forms (相) to be obtained, which clarifies the meaning that dharmas have no existence." He then quoted the *Laṅkāvatāra-sūtra* and commented as follows:

> It is like being in a dream. Because the things perceived [seem] really to exist then there are the two aspects/characteristics of the seer and the seen. What is [perceived] in a dream, however, [does not exist] and these two dharmas [of seer and seen] really do not exist. The three realms and all minds are like this dream. Apart from the mind there is nothing that can be discriminated. Therefore it is said that all discrimination is discrimination of your own mind, and that in reference to your own mind you cannot see it of itself. It is like the knife and finger and so on. Therefore it is said that mind does not see mind, since there is nothing else to be seen, and also one cannot see oneself. Because the seen does not exist the seer is not established. The two aspects of subject and object cannot be obtained.

---

[246] Bodhiruci's (d. ca. 535) translation, T16.671, 567c10-11.
[247] T16.671, 567c7-9.

Therefore there are no forms [or aspects of mind] obtainable. Also, because the One Mind moves in accordance with ignorance (*wuming*) to create the five kinds of consciousness, it is said that the three realms are nothing-but the functioning of the mind.

若如夢中：所見諸事是實有者，即有能見、所見二相。而其夢中實無二法。三界諸心皆如此夢。離心之外無可分別。故言一切分別即分別自心，而就自心不能自見，如刀指等。故言心不見心，既無他可見，亦不能自見。所見無故，能見不成。能、所二相皆無所得，故言無相可得。又一心隨無明動作五種識故，説三界唯心轉也。[248]

In discussing this topic, Yanshou also refers to Mazu Chan. This increases the likelihood that Zhu Xi was aware of this topic and found it useful for the prosecution of his own agenda. Yanshou wrote:

When ignorance comes to a permanent end then it reverts to the source that is the One Mind. Nothing else arises or moves. Therefore it is said that one can see the nature of the mind and that the mind is always present. There being nothing to improve on is called ultimate awareness. Before one has arrived at the source of the mind dream, thoughts are not yet exhausted. Wishing to extinguish their movement to gaze at that other shore [nirvana], one will now already see the nature of the mind and the characteristics of the dream will all end. Perceive that your own mind is intrinsically without any operation. Now that ignorance is calmed and halted then there will always of itself be One Mind. This is done by realizing that the Buddha-stage has no thought-moments. This is initiating the cause and verifying the result. Great master Mazu said, "If you wish to recognize the mind, it is only the present words that are your mind. We call this mind 'Buddha.' It is also [called] the real characteristic Dharma-body Buddha, and is called the Way. It is like a mani-pearl that accords with the color [it encounters]. When it touches green then it is green, when it touches yellow then it is yellow. In reality it is not any color, just as a finger does not touch itself, or like a knife does not cut itself, or a mirror does not reflect itself. Each of the states of the seen [aspect] that accord with objects can be given this name. . . . Because sentient beings do not recognize their own mind, deluded emotions erroneously give rise to various karma and receive the recompense. . . .

---

[248] *Zongjing lu*, T48.2016, 823a16-27.

The present seeing, hearing, and perceiving have always been your inherent nature, and is also called the inherent mind. There is no other Buddha apart from the mind. This mind has always existed and its existence now does not rely on its having been created. It was originally pure and is now pure. It does not need to be wiped clean. Its own nature is nirvana.... It is your nature of the mind that inherently of itself is the Buddha.... Baozhi ... said, 'Great wisdom is not different from stupidity. What use is there in searching for the precious gem outside of it? There is a bright pearl of itself inside the body.'"

無明永盡歸一心原；更無起動。故言得見心性，心即常住。更無所進名究竟覺。未至心原，夢念未盡。欲滅此動望到彼岸，而今既見心性，夢相都盡。覺知自心本無流轉。今無明靜息，常自一心；是以證知佛地無念。此是舉因而證果也。馬祖大師云：「汝若欲識心，秖今語言即是汝心。喚此心作佛。亦是實相法身佛。亦名爲道。... 如隨色摩尼珠；觸青即青，觸黃即黃。體非一切色：如指不自觸，如刀不自割，如鏡不自照。隨緣所見之處各得其名。... 爲眾生不識自心，迷情妄起諸業受報。... 今見、聞、覺、知元是汝本性，亦名本心。更不離此心別有佛。此心本有，今有不假造作。本淨今淨。不待瑩拭。自性涅槃。自性清淨。... 是汝心性本自是佛。... 志公 ... 云：『大智不異於愚。何用外求珍寶？身震自有明珠。』」。[249]

In other words, in Mazu's formulation of the *tathāgatagarbha* the purity or radiance is always present and does not require any intentional searching for it to be seen. It is simply left to shine. Like a mirror, it cannot reflect itself, and once one has given up on trying to find it and lets go of all of one's discriminatory tendencies, the inner light will be revealed by itself. For Mazu, the activities or functions themselves when performed naturally are the nature. It is not about finding principles; it is about performing them. The Hongzhou school with which Mazu is affiliated saw the actions of searching and investigating to be intentional and thus misleading.

Zhu agreed that the mind cannot see itself ("Since this is illogical, this is not different from using one mind to recognize the same mind"),[250] but he did not agree that there is nothing but the mind, instead maintaining that the mind can see itself via other things. He also distinguished the mind from the nature, but said they are difficult to differentiate:

---

[249] *Zongjing lu*, T48.2016, 492a5-18, 492a23-29.
[250] *Zhu Xi ji, juan* 49, 2369.

[Someone] asked: "Since the nature is real, if we speak of it in terms of stimulus and response and emptiness and radiance (*xuming*) then [will not] the mind have many meanings?"

[Zhu Xi] replied: "If you say that these two things [mind and nature] are one, then whichever one you arrive at, originally they cannot be separated, and also of themselves are hard to distinguish. If you discard the mind then there is nothing through which to see the nature, and if you discard the nature there will also be nothing through which to see the mind.... Humaneness, righteousness, propriety, and wisdom are the nature."

曰：「性却實。以感應虛明言之，則心之意亦多。」曰：「此兩箇說著一箇，則一箇隨到，元不可相離，亦自難與分別。捨心則無以見性，捨性又無以見心。...仁義禮智是性。」[251]

Zhu Xi also criticized the "seeing the nature" of Chan:

> The Buddhists say that all principles are entirely emptiness; we Confucians say that all the principles are all real. As a consequence of this single divergence there are the differences of impartial and selfish, and righteousness and profit. Now the students of Buddhism say "Recognize the mind and see the Buddha." They do not know what mind they [are to] recognize, and what nature [they are to see].

佛說萬理俱空，吾儒說萬理俱實。從此一差，方有公私、義利之不同。今學佛者云「識心見性」，不知是識何心，是見何性。[252]

Zhu definitely knew the Chan sources, for he cited a dialogue between an Indian king and a youthful Bodhidharma on the question of seeing the buddha-nature, found in the *Jingde chuandeng lu*. This was connected with Zhu's concerns over Mazu's teaching that the nature is a function of the mind, such as in the following passage:

> The Buddhists solely take functions to be the nature. For example, a certain king asked a certain venerable monk, "What is the Buddha?" "Seeing the nature is the Buddha." "What is the nature?" "Function is the nature." "What is function?" End quote. The Chan school also has a *gāthā* that says, "In the future, when the venerable answered the king/ Why didn't the king ask the venerable,/ 'When it is not yet functioning, where is the nature?'"

---

[251] *Zhuzi yulei*, juan 5, 88.
[252] *Zhuzi yulei*, juan 17, 380.

釋氏專以作用爲性。如某國王問某尊者曰：「如何是佛？」曰：「見性爲佛。」曰：「如何是性？」曰：「作用爲性？」曰：「如何是作用？」曰云云。禪家又有書者云：「當來尊者答國王時，國王何不問尊者云：『未作用時，性在甚處？』」[253]

This exchange is summarized from the hagiography of Bodhidharma in the *Jingde chuandeng lu*,[254] the hagiography being a reflection of the Hongzhou Chan of Mazu.

Zhu also maintained that things are real and so we can examine the mind via things. When someone asked him about the Buddhist theory of examining the mind, he replied:

> The mind is that whereby a person controls the body. It is one and not two, it is the lord, not the guest; it commands things and is not commanded by things. Therefore if you use the mind to examine things then you will apprehend the principle of things. Now, if there is something by means of which one looks back on the mind, then outside of this mind there is another mind, and it can control this mind. If so, then what [the Buddhists] call the mind, is it one or two? Is it the lord/host or is it the guest? Does it command things or is it commanded by things?

> 夫心者，人之所以主乎身者也，一而不二者也，爲主而不爲客者也，命物而不命於物者也。故以心觀物，則物之理得；今復有物以反觀乎心，則是此心之外復有一心，而能管乎此心也。然則所謂心者，爲一耶，爲二耶？爲主耶？爲客耶？爲命物者耶, 爲命於物者耶？[255]

In other words, Zhu accused the Chan Buddhists of maintaining that there are actually two minds, not simply One Mind. He apparently did not accept Mazu's assertion that the nature is seen or manifested (*jian* 見) in the functioning of the inherent nature, which is the inherently radiant mind. Rather, Zhu probably thought that one aspect of one mind is seen by another aspect of that mind because one (type of) mind cannot see the same (type of) mind. He may have read Shenxiu's statement that the realization of *guanxin* is the realization that "seeing that one's own mind gives rise to functions that are differentiated into two types . . . the pure mind . . . and the polluted mind" (了見自心起用有二種差別。. . . 一

---

[253] *Zhuzi yulei*, juan 126, 3021.
[254] T51.218b10-13.
[255] *Zhu Xi ji*, juan 67, 3540.

者淨心、二者染心。).²⁵⁶ These are compared to the pure sun hidden by obscuring clouds or a lamp inside a jar.²⁵⁷

Zhu may have understood the relations of the two types of mind, which he called in his Confucian system the "mind of the Way" and the "human mind," drawing on the *Dasheng qixin lun*'s two aspects of the One Mind: the mind of suchness and the mind of rising and ceasing.²⁵⁸

Zhu may also have been drawing on the Yogācāra (Faxiang) idea of a seeing part (*jianfen* 見分) and a seen part (*xiangfen* 相分) in the mind. In two poems, Zhu wrote:

> The supreme principle has no words, eliminating shallow and deep,
> The numerous dust motes in every world do not encroach on the other.
> If you say that the transmission beyond the teachings is true,
> Then that is Gautama [Buddha] having two minds.²⁵⁹

至理無言絕淺深，塵塵刹刹不相廆。如云教外傳真的，却是瞿曇有兩心。

> It is unlikely that Gautama [really] has two minds,
> So do not take this idea and annoy the Confucian scholars.
> If you wish to know the joys to be found in the distress of living in a mean narrow lane,²⁶⁰
> Simply investigate why Confucius thrice broke the bindings of the *Book of Change*.

未必瞿曇有兩心，莫將此意攪儒林。欲知陋巷憂時樂，只向韋編絕處尋。²⁶¹

Zhu's reference to a true transmission beyond the doctrinal teachings is to the Chan idea of "transmitting mind to mind" (以心傳心) and "a separate transmission beyond the [doctrinal] teachings"(教外別傳). He is claiming that the Buddhists are confused about the mind and seeing the nature of the

---

²⁵⁶ *Poxiang lun*, T48.209, 366c29-367a2.
²⁵⁷ *Poxiang lun*, T48.209, 367a8-9.
²⁵⁸ McRae, *The Northern School and the Formation of Early Ch'an Buddhism*, 223 ("the most fundamental assumptions of the *Awakening of Faith* are identical to those of Northern Ch'an doctrine").
²⁵⁹ The words "transmission beyond the teachings" reflect the Chan motto of "a special/separate transmission beyond the teachings" which was a "transmission from mind to mind." Zhu appears to be saying that the Buddha had two minds, one that orally taught Buddhism in general, and another that transmitted Chan by a mental transmission.
²⁶⁰ Allusion to *Analects* 6.9.
²⁶¹ Both poems are from *Zhu Xi ji, juan* 6, 273.

mind. He is claiming that the Buddhists entertain both a reflexive examination of the mind and an examination of the mind by contemplating external things, which he asserts means the Buddhists are positing the existence of two minds. For Zhu there is only one mind.

Zhu largely concurred with Chan followers who said the mind cannot see itself. If the radiant mind is covered by contaminants such as turbid *qi* or habituation (*xiqi*) due to selfish desires, how can the obstructed mind see itself? Zhu maintained that one can see the principles inherent in human nature within phenomena and actions (functions) such as the rescue of a child about to fall into a well by the spontaneous reaction of a bystander. Mazu's Chan asserted that the radiant mind should just be allowed to shine forth by having no intention and because phenomena lack reality and so functions are in themselves the nature of the mind. The *Laṅkāvatārasūtra*, Yanshou, and possibly early Chan maintained that the mind does not see the mind because the mind has no characteristics to be seen. The earliest Chan text, the [*Damo*] *sixing lun* 達摩四行論 (The Four Practices of Bodhidharma) states, "the buddha-mind cannot be known by having a mind" (佛心不可以有心知)[262] in the sense that "having a mind" is intentional and hence deluded. Accordingly, both early Chan and Zhu Xi saw it as problematic to attempt to use the deluded mind or the human mind (*renxin* 人心) to see the buddha-mind or mind of the Way (*daoxin* 道心).

1.10 What Influences a Person's Inability to See the Radiance?

Zhu Xi and Chan Buddhists agreed that something prevented people from seeing the inherent radiance of their mind or nature of the mind. Chan stated that all people could see it. Zhu said that one could only be born a sage, i.e., that one could never perfectly purify one's *qi*. However, even if a person cannot become a sage because of the fixed endowments of turbid and pure *qi*, Zhu allows that one can become close to being a sage. There is a key passage in *Lunyu* 17.2, "[Humans] are close in their nature; they grow distant through habit/practice" (性相近也，習相遠也。). Citing this passage, Zhu wrote:

---

[262] *Sŏnmun chwaryo* 禪門撮要 (*Sŏn* Essentials), in *Zengaku sōsho* 2 禪學叢書之二 (Zen Studues 2), comp. Yanagida Seizan 柳田聖山 (Kyoto: Chūbun shuppansha, 1974), 22 (woodblock, 18b). I have followed this text rather than the one used in Yanagida Seizan, *Daruma no goroku: Zen no goroku*, 162, which lacks the second *xin* 心, which parallelism suggests should be there.

The nature is pattern. The pattern that should be conformed to is that there is nothing that is not good. Therefore, in speaking of the nature, Mencius was referring to the inherent nature. Because it is necessary for it to depend on something to be established, the psychophysical endowment [i.e., *qi*] that is received cannot be without differences in degree and density. Confucius said, "By nature [people] are close." His reference to the nature also referred to the psychophysical nature.

性即理也。當然之理，無有不善者。故孟子之言性，指性之本而言。然必有所依而立，故氣質之禀不能無淺深厚薄之別。孔子曰：「性相近也」，兼氣質而言。[263]

The source of moral goodness in people is their "inherent" or "heaven-and-earth-bestowed nature" (天地之性), something that all people share in common. When this nature takes on its psychophysical constitution, however, this innate goodness needs to be recovered/uncovered. Until it is recovered, people are close to one another merely by virtue of the fact that they are all endowed with different constitutions of *qi*, which, to varying degrees, obscures realization of that which is innate.

"Habit" in this *Analects* passage resembles the Buddhist idea of *xiqi* 習氣 (*vāsanā*) sometimes translated literally as "habit-energy," which is an "impression, the result of past deeds and experience on the personality" or "habits" or "propensity."[264] *Xiqi* is closely related to the frustrations (*fannao* 煩惱; *kleśa*), in particular the "three poisons" of craving, anger, and stupidity. Even after these frustrations have been eliminated, impressions or influences remain and can still prevent enlightenment. Xuanzang's disciple Kuiji 窺基 (632–682) glossed *xiqi* as follows: "*Xiqi* is the presently operating *qifen* 氣分 that is constituted through habituation, and so is called *xiqi*" (言習氣者是現氣分熏習所成，故名習氣。).[265] The word *qifen* here has the sense of "endowment" or "allotment" of *qi*.

The combination of the frustrations and *xiqi* can be found in many Buddhist texts, such as the *Mahāprajñāpāramitā-sūtra* (*Da bore boluomiduo jing* 大般若波羅蜜多經; Large Perfection of Wisdom Sutra): "If a bodhisattva, a great being, desires to uproot all frustrations and *xiqi*, he should learn . . ." (若菩薩摩訶薩。欲拔一切煩惱習氣。應學 . . .).[266] Another

---

[263] *Zhuzi yulei*, juan 4, 67–68.
[264] Franklin Edgerton, *Buddhist Hybrid Sanskrit Grammar and Dictionary, Volume II: Dictionary* (New Haven: Yale University Press, 1953), 478b.
[265] *Cheng weishi lun shuji* 成唯識論述記 (Notes on Demonstration of Nothing-but Consciousness), T43.1830, 298c9-10.
[266] Translated by Xuanzang, T5.220, 12c4.

example is in the *Fangguang da zhuangyan jing* 方廣大莊嚴經, a translation of the famous *Lalitavistara* made in 683 by Divākara. Writing about becoming a bodhisattva, it says:

> He, able to cut off the dirt and impurities,
> And cravings, anger, stupidity, the *xiqi*,
> His body will shine on worlds in all directions,
> Outshining all the radiant bodies.
>
> 能斷諸垢濁，貪瞋癡習氣，身照十方剎，暎蔽眾光明。[267]

In a later example, after discussing and citing passages about the clear mirror in which, like the body of the Buddha, all images are displayed to all the worlds of sentient beings, Yanshou states:

> It is simply covered by frustrations and *xiqi* and [yet] there is no [Buddha] body that is not manifest. It is like a bright lamp in a jar, the light of which is not extinguished. This is called the *tathāgatagarbha*.
>
> 但為煩惱習氣所覆，無體不現。如瓶內淨，燈光不滅；名如來藏。[268]

There are hundreds of such examples, and they can be found in the *Huayan* (*Avataṁsaka*) and *Laṅkāvatāra* sutras, and in the *Zongjing lu* and the works of Zongmi, works known to the Zhi Xi and other Daoxue figures. The frustrations and *xiqi* referred to in these explanations of the *tathāgatagarbha* and the buddha-nature doctrines operate just like the *qi* or *qizhi* that covers human nature, as described by Zhu Xi and other Daoxue thinkers. Thus Yanshou even states that *xiqi* and "frustrations have [differences in] density, and *xiqi* have [differences in] degree" (煩惱有厚薄。習氣有淺深。),[269] just as Zhu Xi was later to describe *qi* as having differences in purity.

1.11 Preserving or Protecting the Radiant Nature or Mind by Practice

If it is claimed that the mind or the nature, whether buddha-mind or buddha-nature, mind of the Way or human nature, is essentially radiant

---

[267] T3.187, 588b1-2.
[268] *Zongjing lu*, T48.2016, 473b10-11.
[269] T48.2016, 633b4-5.

and pristine, then it follows not only that one should try to discover it and reveal it by eliminating the obscuring factors, but also that one maintain, protect, and preserve it. Both Zhu Xi and Northern Chan advocated practicing these methods.

Zhu adopted a theme from *Mencius* about the preservation of the mind (*cunxin* 存心), which he applied to the maintaining or keeping of the moral principles in the "empty and radiant" (*xuming*) human nature. Similarly, the Northern Chan masters, especially Hongren, spoke of "maintaining" or "protecting the One Mind" (*shou yixin* 守一心) as a key practice. In order to tease out the broader significance of this, let's first look at related issues in *Mencius*, beginning with the opening passage to *Mencius* 7A:

> Those who exhaust [fully understand] their mind (*jin qi xin*) know their nature. If one knows one's nature one will know heaven. Preserving one's mind and nurturing one's nature is the means by which to serve Heaven.
>
> 盡其心者，知其性也。知其性，則知天矣。存其心，養其性， 所以事天也。

There is considerable variation in how this passage, especially *jin qi xin*, has been understood.[270] Zhu introduces the idea of the "empty radiance" into his interpretation. When asked, "If the mind is limitless, how can you talk of exhausting the mind?" Zhu replied:

> There is nothing that is not controlled by the intrinsic reality of the mind, and its functions operate everywhere. Now if one fully traces principle and comprehensively interconnects it such that one can know everything, one will definitely fully comprehend its intrinsic reality that controls everything and its functions that operate everywhere. It is for this reason that when peacefully settled in a quiet place, the empty radiance (*xuming*) [of the mind] clearly penetrates and there is not a hair's breadth of doubt. With that [empty radiance] preserved in one's breast [mind], then when phenomena arrive and things come, even if it were all the things in the world or something one had never encountered with one's senses before, there will be nothing that is not clearly distinguished and easily solved. This is

---

[270] For example, compare D. C. Lau, *Mencius*, 182, "For a man to give full realization to his heart" and W.A.C.H. Dobson, *Mencius* (Toronto: University of Toronto Press, 1963), 143, "the man who has stretched his mind to the full," and Legge, *Chinese Classics*, vol. 2, 448, "exhausted all his mental constitution." For Zhu's selection of earlier Daoxue thinkers' comments on this passage, see his *Mengzi jingyi* 孟子精義 (Essential Meanings of *Mencius*) in *Zhuzi yishu*, 752–753.

what is meant by comprehending fully the mind. As for mind, it certainly has no limit.

或問：「心無量者也，此其言盡心何也？」曰：「心之體無所不統，而其用無所不周者。今窮理而貫通以至於可以無所不知，則固盡其無所不統之體無所不周之用矣。是以平居靜處虛明洞達，固無毫髮疑慮。存於胸中，至於事至物來則雖舉天下之物，或素所未嘗接於耳目思慮之間者，亦無不判然迎a而解。此其所以為盡心，而所謂心者，固未嘗有限量也。」[271]

For Zhu, *jinxin* is to comprehend the mind fully by tracing principle/pattern in all that it encounters, when in an appropriate state of meditative composure. The empty radiance of the mind that derives from quiet sitting thus becomes like the bright, clear mirror that reflects all that appears before it. In addition, it permits a judgment of those phenomena.

Zhu distinguished *jinxin* (comprehending the mind fully) and *cunxin* (preserving the mind), the latter being a more preliminary practice or a precondition for *jinxin*:

Jinxin and *cunxin* are not the same. *Cunxin* is a matter of holding on to and preserving or letting go and vanishing.[272] This is what students first devote their efforts to. *Jinxin* means to fathom principle/pattern to its utmost, comprehensively interconnecting on a vast scale. What is called knowing the nature is the matter of thoroughly fathoming principle.

蓋盡心與存心不同。存心即操存求放之事。是學者初用力處。盡心則窮理之至，廓然貫通之謂。所謂知性即窮理之事也。[273]

The mind encompasses all principles and all principles are present in the one mind (*yixin*). If one cannot preserve the mind then one cannot fathom principles fully and if one cannot fathom principles fully then one cannot comprehend the mind fully (*jinxin*).

心仲萬理，萬理具於一心。不能存得心，不能窮得理；不能窮得理，不能盡得心。[274]

---

[271] *Mengzi huowen* 孟子或問 (Questions and answers on *Mencius*) in *Zhuzi yishu*, 13.1a, 322.
[272] Allusion to *Mencius* 6A.8: "Confucius said, 'Hold onto it and you will preserve it; let it go and it will vanish. Its comings and goings have no set time and no one knows whither it goes.' Was it not the mind that he was referring to?" 孔子曰：「操則存，舍則亡；出入無時，莫知其鄉。」惟心之謂與！
[273] *Zhu Xi ji*, juan 61, 3162.
[274] *Zhuzi yulei*, juan 9, 155.

Zhu was greatly concerned to distinguish Confucian practice from Buddhist practice, and *jinxin* was one way he tried to do so:

> [Someone] asked: "In comprehending the mind fully and in knowing the nature, is it the sage alone who does not need to have recourse to preserving [the mind] and nurturing [the nature]?[275] The Buddha never needed to have recourse to preserving [the mind] or nurturing [the nature]. How could he possibly aspire to be a sage?"
>
> [Zhu Xi] replied: "to comprehend the mind fully, to know the nature, to preserve the mind, and to nurture the nature are our Confucian [practices]. They resemble Buddhist [practices] but they are not the same. It is simply that the reasoning they employ in preserving, nurturing, knowing, and comprehending fully is, in all cases, wrong. With our Confucian "comprehending the mind fully" it is simply that in comprehending fully the mind of the ruler and minister, father and son and so on we see that there is a principle. What the Buddhists call comprehending the mind fully and knowing the nature revert entirely to emptiness. What they preserve and nurture is [in fact] closing one's eyes—they pay not the slightest heed to the way of principle."
>
> 問：「盡心、知性，不假存、養，其惟聖人乎！佛本不假於存、養，豈竊希聖人之事乎？」曰：「盡、知、存、養，吾儒、釋氏相似而不同。只是他所存、所養、所知、所盡處，道理皆不是。如吾儒盡心，只是盡君臣父子等心，便見有是理。性即是理也。如釋氏所謂『盡心、知性』，皆歸於空虛。其所存、養，却是閉眉合眼，全不理會道理。」[276]

For Zhu, comprehending the mind fully enables one to discern the principles inherent in human nature. By "mind," Zhu Xi means the "mind of the Way," not the "human mind." For Zhu, the Buddhists saw only the human mind and not the mind of the Way.

In turn, reverential attention (*jing* 敬) is the key to preserving the mind:

> If one takes reverential attention to be the ruler, then internally and externally one is solemn and while neither forgetting [the mind] nor actively assisting it, the mind preserves itself. If one does not know to take reverential attention to be the ruler and one wants to preserve the mind, then this

---
[275] Allusion to *Mencius* 7A.1.
[276] *Zhuzi yulei, juan* 60, 1432.

would be tantamount to taking one mind to grasp another mind. . . . The difference between Confucianism and Buddhism hinges on nothing more than this distinction. If it were said, "One always sees this mind shining brilliantly,"[277] then that would be to have two rulers [as the Buddhists do]. Is the light the true mind or the seer the true mind?

以敬爲主，則震外肅然，不忘不助，而心自存，不知以敬爲主，而欲存心，則不要將一箇心把捉一箇心。. . . 儒釋之異，亦只於此便分了。如云「常見此心光爍爍地」，便是有兩箇主宰了。不知光者是真心乎？見者是真心乎？[278]

Reverential attention is the key to preserving the mind of the Way, but this preservation must be natural, not something intended. Zhu elaborated on this concept in his essay on the Buddhist investigation of the mind (*guanxin* 觀心), a key term in Northern Chan practice:[279]

> The precariousness of the human mind is the sprout of human desires; the subtlety of the mind of the Way is the depths of heavenly principle. [Yet] the mind is one. It is merely a difference of name [related to being] correct or incorrect....It is not that the Way is one mind and the human mind is one mind, and still one more mind to meticulously focus on them. Here what is meant by holding on to and preserving is not this [mind] holding on to that [mind] and preserving it. . . . It is not inertly and resolutely sitting in order to maintain its brilliant but non-functioning awareness that is called holding onto and preserving. As for what is called "fully comprehending the mind" (*jinxin*), that is investigating things (*gewu*), fathoming principle, and comprehensively interconnecting on a vast scale, such that one has the means to exhaust fully the principles inherent in the mind. As for what is called "preserving the mind," that is being reverentially attentive so as to straighten the internal [i.e., the mind] and being righteous so as correct the external [i.e., the body]. . . . By preserving the mind one is able to nurture the nature and serve heaven. This is because one personally experiences it [the mind] and does not lose it, such that one has the wherewithal to accord with principle just the way it is. How can this be

---

[277] The last part of this sentence, "shining brilliantly," can be found in *Jingde chuandeng lu*, T51.2076, 466c20-21, with reference to the buddha-nature.
[278] *Zhu Xi ji, juan* 31, 1325.
[279] Shenxiu, for example, wrote a *Guanxin lun*, in which *guanxin* "was the very crux of the Buddhist religion." See McRae, *Northern School*, 199.

using the mind to understand the mind fully or using the mind to preserve the mind, as if there were two things that propped one another up and could not be without each other?

> 夫謂人心之危者，人欲之萌也；道心之微者，天理之奧也。心則一也，以正不正而異其名耳....非以道爲一心，人爲一心，而又有一心以精一之也。夫謂操而存者，非以彼操此而存之也....非塊然薈坐以守其烱然不用之知覺而謂之操存也。若盡心云者，則格物窮理廓然貫通而有以極夫心之所具之理也；存心云者，則敬以直震、義以方外....存心而可以養性事天，以其體之不失而有以順夫理之自然也。是豈以心盡心，以心存心，如兩物之相持而不相舍哉。²⁸⁰

Several reasons may be proffered for Zhu's concern with *cunxin* in particular. First, Mencius states that the practice of *cunxin* is what differentiates the *junzi* or superior person from ordinary people. This he does by practicing humaneness and propriety or rites.²⁸¹ The gloss in the Tang dynasty commentary says *cun* means *zai* 在, or to be present in, meaning that the content of the mind is humaneness and propriety.²⁸²

Cunxin is also a common term in Buddhist texts, where it has a range of meanings from "keeping in mind" or "mindfulness" to "preserving the mind." Moreover, it resembles the Northern Chan practice of "protecting/maintaining the mind" (*shouxin*). For example, Yanshou quoted an advanced method of Northern Chan, which is clearly derived from the *Dasheng qixin lun*: "Protect the One Mind alone, which is the gateway of the mind of suchness" (但守一心即心真如門。).²⁸³ Jingjue wrote of one of the Northern Chan teachings: "Maintain the One and do not shift, movement and calm are always present, which enables students to see buddha-nature clearly and soon enter into the gate of *dhyāna* (contemplative trance)" (守一不移。動靜常住、能令学者明見佛性、早入定門。).²⁸⁴ Hongren used the metaphor of the radiant sun that is covered over by clouds to describe the innate purity of the mind's being obscured by defilement.²⁸⁵ In other words, he used the metaphors associated with the radiant mind that we find in *tathāgatagarbha*-based texts. And because the innate purity of the mind is obscured he proposed that one should "maintain

---

²⁸⁰ "Guanxin shuo," *Zhu Xi ji, juan* 67, 3541.
²⁸¹ *Mencius* 4B.28.
²⁸² *Shisan jing zhushu*, 2730c.
²⁸³ *Zongjing lu* 97, T48.2016, 940a16-17.
²⁸⁴ *Lengqie shizi ji* in Yanagida, *Zen no goroku* 2, 225.
²⁸⁵ T48.2011, 377a.

the innate true mind so that erroneous thoughts do not arise" (守本眞心 妄念不生。).²⁸⁶ This is the fundamental teaching of Hongren's text, the essential practice. When asked, "How does one know that maintaining the true mind is the basis of nirvana?" he replied:

> Nirvana in reality is calm cessation, unconditioned and restful bliss. Since my mind is already the true mind, erroneous conceptions are eliminated. Because erroneous conceptions are eliminated, [the mind] includes correct thoughts. Because correct thoughts are present, calm illuminating wisdom arises. Because calm illuminating wisdom arises one completely discerns the dharma-nature. And because one completely discerns the dharma-nature one attains nirvana. Therefore know that maintaining the innate true mind is the basis of nirvana.
>
> 問曰：何知守本眞心是涅槃之根本？答曰：涅槃者體是寂滅、無爲、安樂。我心既是眞心妄想斷。妄想斷故則具正念。正念具故寂照智生。寂照智生故窮達法性。窮達法性故則得涅槃。故知守本眞心是涅槃之根本。²⁸⁷

This pristine mind can be realized in two ways: by "maintaining the true mind" and by removing the dust:

> Since I know through personal realization that the buddha-nature of sentient beings is inherently pure like the sun that is covered by clouds, I just clearly maintain (*shou*) the intrinsically true mind. When the erroneous thought-clouds are eliminated (*jin*) the sun will appear. What need is there of much further study? . . . It is for example like polishing a mirror and when the dust is completely removed the radiance naturally appears.
>
> 我既體知衆生佛性本來清淨如雲底日，但了然守本眞心。妄念雲盡慧日即現。何須更多學？...譬如磨鏡塵盡明自然現。²⁸⁸

Similarly, Daoxin, the fourth Chan patriarch, used *shou [yi]xin* as both an elementary and advanced practice, both as visualizing technique and as a practice to "protect/maintain the inherently true mind."²⁸⁹ The practice

---

²⁸⁶ T48.2011, 377c3.
²⁸⁷ T48.2011, 377c14-18.
²⁸⁸ T48.2011, 378a2-6. For an account of *shouxin* and its origins, see McRae, *Northern School*, 136–144.
²⁸⁹ It also meant controlling one's breathing. *Lengqie shizi ji*, in Yanagida, *Zen no goroku 2*, 241, and Hongren, T48.2011, 378a.

of "protecting the mind" was common to both beginning and advanced students, although it had different meanings.[290]

Zhu Xi's "preserving the mind" and Northern Chan's "maintaining the mind" are very similar. Both aim to stop the mind from losing its innate characteristic of pure radiance due to pursuing things out of selfish desire. This outflow from the mind has to be halted, and so it is guarded or preserved, which in turn aids in the realization of that purity. Moreover, both Zhu and Northern Chan teachers are said to have advocated a gradual practice or cultivation. This similarity may be pure coincidence, but may well be indebted to the similar structure of the *tathāgatagarbha* theory of pure radiance that Northern Chan had as a core doctrine and Zhu Xi's theory of a nature that was empty radiance and possessed the principles of the Way, something I contend was inspired in part by *tathāgatagarbha* theory. Both demanded preservation or maintaining.

1.12 Conclusion

In this chapter I have examined the structural similarities of the thought related to the human condition as expressed in root metaphors used by Northern Chan Buddhism and by Zhu Xi. The core theme is the radiance of the mind or human nature that is covered by obscuring contaminants. This is expressed through metaphors that came from *tathāgatagarbha* doctrine and were used especially by Northern Chan; namely, that of a bright pearl covered by muddy water or a bright mirror covered by dust. These metaphors had many implications for ideas about the mind, human nature or buddha-nature, and practice and related developments can be detected in Northern Chan and in the thought of Zhu Xi. The evidence suggests that Zhu Xi was influenced, possibly indirectly or unconsciously, by this aspect of Northern Chan thought, probably as a result of criticizing the Chan of Mazu and Dahui that was important in Zhu Xi's time.

Zhu spent over a third of his life exposed to, and at times practicing, the Chan of Dahui and his students. He only gradually rejected Dahui's Chan and Buddhism in general, reaching conclusions that have structural similarities with Northern Chan thought. Zhu and Northern Chan stressed the radiance of the pure mind, whether it was called the nature of the

---

[290] John Jorgensen, "Two Themes in Korean Buddhist Thought," *Han'guk Pulgyohak* 7 (1982): 211–212.

mind or buddha-nature or mind of the Way. There were, however, multiple definitions of the "nature" in the key concepts of human nature, buddha-nature and nature of the mind, as well as differing definitions of mind. In Chan teachings, which varied considerably, there were two definitions of the nature of the mind, and based on one of these, Zhu accused Buddhists of confusing the mind with the nature. He also asserted that the "nature" of the Buddhists was empty of moral content.

Furthermore, Buddhists had differing definitions of the mind. Many Chan Buddhists, especially Northern Chan Buddhists, equated the "One Mind" with the *tathāgatagarbha*. Based on the *Dasheng qixin lun*, this One Mind was said to have two modalities, suchness and rising-and-ceasing. Zhu also spoke of "one mind" that has two aspects, the mind of the Way and the human mind. In both Northern Chan and Zhu's thought, these are differentiated by desire or attachment, and this desire leads to the mind's flowing on as it interacts with the environment. The pure or radiant aspect becomes evident only when the flow is stopped.

The pure aspect of the mind or its nature is described by Chan and Zhu as "lucid radiance" (*xuming*). Both used the bright mirror as a metaphor for this pure aspect, a metaphor I contend was derived from *tathāgathagarbha* texts. Northern Chan and Zhu claimed that the removal of dust on the mirror is a gradual process, unlike Dahui who maintained that the removal is sudden. The dust that covers the mirror is described as adventitious. For Zhu, the covering is called *qi*, which has a physical component, whereas for *tathāgatagarbha* advocates the coverings are mental afflictions, although some spoke of the coverings as *skandha*s that likewise have a physical component.

Zhu maintains that the differences in the covering are due to different "endowments" (*fen*), which in turn are mandated by the natural order (heaven). The Buddhists spoke of "inherent endowment" (*benfen*), more applicable to a being's capacity, and the result of karma from innumerable past lives. Zhang Zai, Dahui Zonggao, and Zhu Xi all spoke of *benfen*. If beings differ in the depth of the obscuring contaminants or inherited capacities, the question that follows is: "Can all beings become sages or saints?" Zhu and some other Confucians insisted that only sages are born with pure *qi*, which does not obscure the innate radiance. In other words, sagehood cannot be acquired. In contrast, *tathāgatagarbha* believers, especially Chan Buddhists, asserted that all beings can become saints/buddhas.

These assumptions in turn prompted the question of how the radiant mind/nature can be seen if the radiance is obscured, given that there is only one mind. Mazu claimed that the mind—which is identical to buddha-nature—can itself be seen in everyday functions; it performs and is manifested, rather than discovered. The implication is that there is no point in practicing to find that radiance. For the moralist Zhu Xi, this was anathema. Like Northern Chan, Zhu asserted that moral practice was necessary. Despite agreeing with some Northern Chan monks who said that the mind cannot see itself, just as the eye cannot (directly) see itself, Zhu accused Chan Buddhists of teaching a doctrine of two minds, not one mind.

Furthermore, according to Zhu. what stopped people from seeing the radiance is *xi* (habit), and according to Chan Buddhists, among others, it is *xiqi* (habit-energy/force). Northern Chan and Zhu also spoke of protecting or preserving the radiant mind or nature. This was often described as a preliminary practice, as a way to stop losing the radiance.

The metaphor of radiance covered by obscuring contaminants had doctrinal implications for Northern Chan and for Zhu Xi. Both tried to describe what the radiance and the contaminants are. Both outlined how it was possible to remove the covering and the practices that enabled one to do so. Although some elements contributing to the structure of the extended metaphor may be traced to early interactions between Buddhism and Confucianism, for example to Daosheng in the first half of the fifth century, it was Zhu Xi in the twelfth century who orchestrated the implications of the metaphor in detail.[291] His thought has structures and language shared with Northern Chan because he adopted the same root metaphors as Northern Chan, even though the wine in the old bottles may have been new.

In addition to the above theme, Zhu addressed many other aspects of Chan, including whether the nature extended into the insentient or the inert, and the role of emotion and selfish desires in practice. Zhu Xi also advocated gradual practice, rather like Northern Chan and the *Dasheng qixin lun*.

It appears that much of the structure of the philosophical system built by Zhu Xi and his Daoxue predecessors was deeply informed by *tathāgatagarbha* thought, especially as developed or implemented by Northern Chan. It was not just the structure—even Zhu's vocabulary choices are replete with Chan and general Buddhist terms, such as the six sense-faculties and conditions. He even employs terms like "mind-ground" (*xindi* 心地) when describing the mind as inherently bright or

---

[291] While I acknowledge the long history of Confucian and Buddhist interaction as mentioned by Stephen Angle in his chapter of this volume, I am not so certain that Zhu's "own experiences [with Buddhism] play a minor role" (page 164 note 29).

radiant (*xindi ben zi guangming* 心地本自光明),²⁹² which is essentially a description of the *tathāgatagarbha*. (Zongmi had already used "mind-ground" as a synonym for buddha-nature.²⁹³) There are not just similarities in structure and vocabulary between Chan *tathāgatagarbha* thought and the sort of Confucian philosophy developed by Zhu Xi. There are also identifiable pathways through which Zhu Xi learned this Buddhist doctrine and vocabulary, for Zhu had clearly read Zongmi's writings and was well-versed in the teachings of Dahui Zonggao.

It is Zhu's notion of the mind's radiance being covered by a polluting or turbid *qi* that evidences the greatest debt to *tathāgatagarbha* thought as expressed by various branches of Chan. There were, however, different views on *tathāgatagarbha* or buddha-nature among the branches of Chan, some more radical than others. The radical position that sought to identify the *tathāgatagarbha* with the functions of everyday life (and thus removing the need to practice) contrasts with the positions held by such figures as Zongmi and the Northern Chan proponents of the *Dasheng qixin lun*, who did not identify function with the *tathāgatagarbha* and who advocated practice, including moral practice. Zhu tended towards this latter position.

Despite his deep indebtedness to Chan *tathāgatagarbha* thought, Zhu attacked Chan, especially Hongzhou Chan of Mazu, because he regarded its rejection of the need to practice to be antinomian and thus the greatest enemy of the Confucian project. He probably regarded Hongzhou Chan as the source of Dahui's Chan, his rival for the hearts and minds of the scholar-gentry. We know, for example, that Dahui quoted Mazu as well as the *Jingde chuandeng lu* dialogue between the youthful Bodhidharma and the Indian king about buddha-nature being function.²⁹⁴ We also know that Zhu also quoted this passage and attacked its ideas,²⁹⁵ indicating his concerns over the allure of this doctrine.

Zhuzi yulei arguably evidences more Chan *tathāgatagarbha* influence than Zhu's other works and those of the earlier major Daoxue thinkers²⁹⁶ because the struggle with Dahui's Chan had become more intense than the rivalry that had existed between Chan and the earlier Daoxue thinkers, and also because *Zhuzi yulei* records Zhu's attempts to counter the influence

---

²⁹² *Zhuzi yulei*, juan 12, 209.
²⁹³ Kamata, *Zengen shosenshū tojo*, 13 and notes 15–16. The word "mind-ground" appears in many Chan texts.
²⁹⁴ *Dahui yulu*, T47.1998A, 829c.
²⁹⁵ *Zhuzi yulei*, juan 126, 3021.
²⁹⁶ Here I am not including the lesser-known works by Yang Shi and others.

of Chan he perceived in the ideas of his own students and interlocutors.[297] What is revealed through this collection and other Daoxue collections is the growing influence of Chan, the main propagator of *tathāgatagarbha* thought. Without this *tathāgatagarbha* framework, with its many implications, Daoxue would lack much of its core structure, even vocabulary, and perhaps its raison d'être. In the end, Daoxue, especially that of Zhu Xi, formulated a kind of Confucian "Northern Chan" because it claimed there was an empty, radiant mind obscured by habituation and *qi*, which could be realized by gradual practice—all doctrines of the Northern Chan of the early Tang period. While Zhu would have strenuously denied this contention, he was also interacting with people such as Liu Pingshan and Zhang Jiucheng who were openly attempting to reconcile Buddhism and Confucianism or create a new synthesis. Zhu was trying to do the opposite, but like many who attempt to oppose something strenuously, he ended up mirroring many of his opponents' doctrines as he responded to agendas already well-established in Buddhist circles, central to which were interpretations of the *tathāgatagarbha* doctrine.

---

[297] A work of the *yulu* genre, itself originally a Chan product, *Zhuzi yulei* was not such a systematic text. It collects Zhu's sayings and comments, which were compiled years after his death, not necessarily in chronological order. Deng Aimin 鄧艾民, "Preface," *Zhuzi yulei, juan* 1, 8. See Yanagida Seizan 柳田聖山, "Goroku no rekishi" 語錄の歷史 (The History of Recorded Sayings), *Tōhō gakuhō* 57 (1985): 211–663, esp. 230–253; Judith Berling, "Bringing the Buddha Down to Earth: Notes on the Emergence of the *Yü-lu* as a Buddhist Genre," *History of Religions* 27 (1987): 56–88.

CHAPTER 2 | Zhu Xi's Critique of Buddhism
Selfishness, Salvation, and Self-Cultivation

JUSTIN TIWALD

NO WELL-ROUNDED STUDY of the Buddhist influences on Zhu Xi 朱熹 (1130–1200) would be complete without an examination of his disagreements with the Buddhists. If we take Zhu's remarks at face value, a great deal of his work was animated by his desire to rid China of the (mostly baleful) influence of Buddhism, and Zhu often clarified his own views by juxtaposing them with Buddhist alternatives. There are different ways to go about reconstructing Zhu's objections to Buddhism. The most prevalent has been what we might call the method of comparing explicit doctrines, in which one looks at Zhu's characterization of specific Buddhist views, checks to see whether they are faithful to Buddhist writings and teachings, and, where his characterizations are accurate, proceeds to weigh his arguments against them. But this method has not yielded a great deal of insight. Much of the contemporary scholarship on Zhu Xi's critique of Buddhism has called attention to various respects in which Zhu seems to misrepresent the explicit views of his Buddhist opponents, noting cases where Zhu's characterization seems to lack nuance, ignores exceptions, or mischaracterizes Buddhist doctrines in a rather flatfooted way.[1]

---

[1] The most important contemporary work on Zhu's criticisms of Buddhism include Cai Zhenfeng 蔡振豐, "Zhuzi dui Fojiao de lijie ji qi xianzhi" 朱子對佛教的理解及其限制 (Zhu Xi's Understanding of Buddhism and Its Limits) in *Dongya Zhuzixue de quanshi yu fazhan* 東亞朱子學的詮釋與發展 (Interpretations and Development of Zhu Xi Learning in East Asia), ed. Cai Zhenfeng 蔡振豐 (Taipei: Taiwan daxue chuban zhongxin, 2009), 177–213; Charles Wei-hsun Fu, "Morality or Beyond: The Neo-Confucian Confrontation With Mahāyāna Buddhism," *Philosophy East & West* 23.3 (1973): 375–396; Charles Wei-hsun Fu, "Chu Hsi on Buddhism" in *Chu Hsi and Neo-Confucianism*, ed. Wing-tsit Chan (Honolulu: University of Hawaii Press, 1986), 377–407; and Galen E. Sargent, *Tchou Hi contre Le Bouddhisme* (Paris: Impremerie Nationale, 1955).

In this chapter, I hope to show that the method of comparing explicit doctrines, taken on its own, largely misses the point of Zhu's critique. He neither believed nor intended for most of his major criticisms to represent Buddhist doctrine accurately. Zhu was more interested in the views that Buddhist theories and practices presupposed than the positions that they explicitly endorsed, and more interested in the shape that Buddhist doctrines took when put to the test by practitioners. Here the debate is joined in two somewhat different areas of inquiry.

The first has to do with the implicit presuppositions of certain Buddhist practices. For example, while some Buddhists may say that they take the heartmind (*xin* 心) to be one thing rather than two, they might nevertheless endorse meditative practices that presuppose two different heartminds: an (active) heartmind that observes and a (passive) heartmind that is observed.[2] And while some Buddhists might pay lip-service to the notion that there are objective grounds by which to distinguish right from wrong, they might nevertheless exclusively recommend methods of insight—such as meditation or pure introspection—that make it difficult to acquaint oneself with those objective grounds.[3]

The second area has to do with the real-world consequences of Buddhist doctrines and practices, such as the actual psychological effects of meditation, or the state of mind formed by years of striving for non-attachment and freedom from suffering. One of Zhu's ways of describing Buddhism's failures, adopted from Cheng Hao 程顥 (1032–1085), is to say that Buddhists arrive at abstract understandings of the fundamental nature and purpose of things without taking into account ordinary human experience, which he characterized as "penetrating to what's above" without "learning what's below."[4] Historically, these were the areas of inquiry that both Zhu and the Buddhists thinkers cared about most, and they are the ones I propose to address here.

---

[2] As Zhu proposes in "Guanxin shuo" 觀心說 (Explanation of Observing the Heartmind). See *Zhu Xi ji* 朱熹集 (Collected Works of Zhu Xi), eds. Guo Qi 郭齊 and Yin Bo 尹波 (Chengdu: Sichuan jiaoyu chubanshe, 1996), *juan* 67, 3540–3542.

[3] See Section 2.3, below.

[4] *Zhuzi yulei* 朱子語類 (Topically Arranged Conversations of Master Zhu) (Beijing: Zhonghua shuju, 1986), *juan* 44, 1140. "Learning what's below" (*xiaxue* 下學) and "penetrating to what's above" (*shangda* 上達) are references to *Analects* 14.35. Zhu takes this characterization of the disconnect in Buddhist inquiry from Cheng Hao. See Cheng Hao 程顥 and Cheng Yi 程頤, *Henan Chengshi yishu* 河南程氏遺書 (Surviving Works of the Chengs of Henan), *juan* 13, no. 7 (hereafter *Yishu*, 13.7), in *Er Cheng ji* 二程集 (Collected Works of the Two Chengs) (Beijing: Zhonghua shuju, 1981), 139.

In this chapter I attempt to fill out this crucial dimension of Zhu's response to the Buddhists by examining some of his major lines of argument against the Buddhists. As we will see, Zhu takes many of his cues from Cheng Hao and Cheng Yi 程頤 (1033–1107), but also sees himself as improving in various ways on their criticisms. For this reason I will also spend some time explicating the pre-existing criticisms of Buddhism that he treated as starting points for his own. I begin, in Section 2.1, with a brief summary of Zhu's personal experiences with Buddhism and a short description of the main Buddhist views as Zhu understood them. In the subsequent sections I will look at Zhu's criticisms of Buddhist soteriology, meditation, and metaphysics. As I hope to illustrate, in each of these areas Zhu shows some sensitivity to the differences between the explicit doctrines and the implicit theoretical and practical commitments of Buddhism, and his critique of Buddhism is much stronger for it.

2.1 Buddhism from a Song Confucian's Point of View

Zhu Xi's acquaintance with Buddhism was based both on direct experience with Chan Buddhist teachers and some familiarity with Buddhist scriptures and philosophical discourses. He began to study Buddhism in earnest at the age of fifteen or sixteen, and he developed a fascination with Buddhist thought and meditative practices, which lasted until the age of thirty when doubts about Buddhism and the urgings of his father led him to undertake formal study with the Neo-Confucian master Li Tong 李侗 (1093–1163), thereby joining a lineage that descended from (and aligned itself with) the Cheng brothers.[5] He met or exchanged letters with some prominent monks in his time, including a disciple of the influential Chan monk Dahui Zonggao 大慧宗杲 (1089–1163), of whom he was largely critical, as well as an unspecified monk whom Zhu Xi credits backhandedly for providing him with the high-flown ideas that he used to pass the civil service exam, and possibly Dahui himself.[6] Zhu also read a great number of Buddhist works, both scriptures and secondary philosophical and religious works by later Buddhists.

Chan was both the most prevalent form of Buddhism in his day, and also the form with which he had the most experience. But he intended many

---

[5] Fu, "Chu Hsi on Buddhism," 377–379.
[6] Wing-tsit Chan, *Chu Hsi: New Studies* (Honolulu: University of Hawaii Press, 1989), 509–520; *Zhuzi yulei, juan* 106, 2620. For a close study of some of the ideas and terminology that Zhu shares with Dahui, see John Jorgensen's contribution to this volume.

of his criticisms for Buddhism more broadly. Zhu recognized that there were major differences between Buddhist source texts and the thinkers and practitioners with which they were associated, and he paid particular attention to the differences between the Buddhism that originated in barbarian lands and Sinitic Buddhism, the latter of which he took to have been substantially altered and reconceived in Daoist terms.[7] For the most part, when Zhu criticized the Buddhists of his day he had Chan Buddhists in mind, but in his criticisms of Buddhist texts and historical figures he tended to find shortcomings that he believed to apply to the broader sweep of Buddhism, sometimes to the Buddhism of a particular period or origin (barbarian, Sinitic) and sometimes to the core doctrines and practices of the entire tradition.

In *Zhuzi yulei* Zhu shares his views about several Buddhist sutras and takes many of them to be authentic expressions of Buddhist wisdom, although he contends that significant portions were fabricated by Chinese authors, repackaging Daoist ideas and adding Chinese rhyme schemes.[8] He also read some secondary works of Buddhism, including at minimum the *Zhao lun* 肇論 (Treatises of Sengzhao), the *Dahui yulu* 大慧語錄 (Recorded Sayings of Dahui), and works of Guifeng Zongmi 圭峰宗密 (780–841).[9] In his review of the evidence that Zhu was familiar with Buddhist texts, Wing-tsit Chan concludes that Zhu's understanding of the Buddhist works, while often wrong, was nevertheless informed by much more extensive reading than that of his prominent Confucian contemporaries.[10]

Buddhism as Zhu understands it could be distinguished from other fundamental teachings in several ways. We might distinguish it by its central *views* or beliefs (like the doctrine of emptiness), by specific *practices* it recommends (like meditation), or by the *behaviors* and ways of life it encourages in its most devoted followers (like observing dietary restrictions or monasticism). Zhu Xi sees Buddhism as problematic in all three

---

[7] Cai, *Zhuzi dui Fojiao de lijie ji qi xianzhi*, 183–188.
[8] *Zhuzi yulei*, juan 126, 3025.
[9] *Zhuzi yulei*, juan 68, 1685; *juan* 126, 3009, 3028, 3029. Sengzhao 僧肇 (378–413) was the leading figure in the *Sanlun* 三論 ("Three-Treatise") school of Buddhism, a Sinitic adaptation of the Mādhyamika Buddhism of Nāgārjuna in India (ca. 150–ca. 250). Zongmi was a prominent monk with affinities to both Huayan 華嚴 and Chan Buddhism, although he was a critic of the most radical antinomian sects of Chan thought. See Ming-wood Liu, *Madhyamaka Thought in China*, Sinica Leidensia, vol. 10 (Leiden: E. J. Brill, 1994) and Peter N. Gregory, *Tsung-Mi and the Sinification of Buddhism* (Honolulu: University of Hawaii Press, 2002).
[10] Including Lu Xiangshan 陸象山 (1139–1193) and Chen Liang 陳亮 (1143–1194). See Chan, *Chu Hsi*, 525.

respects, but sometimes he points to a deeper and more pervasive distinguishing characteristic: *ultimate aspirations or goals*. One of Buddhism's defining features is its commitment to personal salvation, conceived as nirvana, the extinguishment of suffering. Most Chinese Buddhists (like most self-avowed Mahāyāna Buddhists) see this as a secondary aim, subordinate to the greater goal of achieving enlightenment. But their interest in salvation nevertheless strikes many of Zhu's Confucian predecessors and contemporaries as selfish or self-centered (*si* 私), and incompatible with the sort of love and other-directed care necessary for a good and virtuous life.[11] Furthermore, Zhu himself objects not only to the Buddhist preoccupation with personal salvation, but also to the background conception of moral goodness that it presupposes. On the Buddhist view, we suffer in large part because we are deeply attached to life generativity and various goods most closely associated with it, including growth and procreation. It is our attachment to life that keeps us forever stuck in a cycle of birth and death (Sk. *saṃsāra*), escape from which is the point of achieving nirvana. For Zhu and his Neo-Confucian predecessors, by contrast, the very point is to participate in a process of what they describe as "ceaseless life production," or "ceaseless life generativity," the most crucial elements of which are self-preservation, growth, and procreation.[12] Having certain sorts of attachments—expressed in the form of love and other virtuous feelings—is a necessary condition for participation in this process. Without having a strong emotional investment in (that is, attachment to) this process, Zhu fears, Buddhists could not participate in the most important and ethically valuable activities and relationships. As we will see, Zhu thinks that because Buddhists seek a good that transcends or stands outside of ceaseless life production and repudiate attachments to life production itself, there was a very real sense in which Buddhists cannot have an ethics or morality at all.[13]

Zhu and his Northern Song predecessors also develop several arguments against specific Buddhist doctrines. One of these is the Buddhist doctrine of rebirth. The other is the Buddhist doctrine of emptiness, perhaps the most challenging of Buddhist philosophical views. In a nutshell, the Buddhist doctrine of emptiness holds that all things are illusory in the

---

[11] *Zhuzi yulei, juan* 126, 3032.
[12] "Ceaseless life production/generativity" (*shengsheng bu xi* 生生不息) is a paraphrase of a remark that appears in "Great Appendix" to the *Zhou Yi* 周易 (Book of Change), *Shisan jing zhushu* 十三經注疏 (The Thirteen Classics with annotations and sub-commentaries), comp. Ruan Yuan 阮元 (1764–1849) (Taipei: Yiwen yinshuguan, 1985), 7.13b.
[13] *Zhuzi yulei, juan* 126, 3012.

following sense: They lack their own independent identity and existence. Things like wealth, health, vision would not have the particular essential or defining features that they appear to have, without other things to confer that identity on them (or more precisely, with which they mutually confer identities). In the language of Buddhist semantics and metaphysics, all things are "empty" of "self-nature." This is, however, the most general description of the doctrine of emptiness. Specific ways of conceptualizing and explaining it varied from one Buddhist school or thinker to the next. Some Buddhists maintain that what appears to be the self-nature of things is conferred upon them by our minds or conscious activity, others say that the putative self-nature of things is (mutually) conferred by their relation to other things and to the entire system (the universe) to which they belong, as a rafter gets identity in part by the function it plays in making a house.[14]

Among Buddhist *practices*, perhaps most disconcerting for Zhu is the attempt to achieve enlightenment through meditation and the expectation that full devotees (Buddhist monks and nuns) remove themselves from family life and relationships.[15] By the time of the Cheng brothers, the sort of meditation that most interested Neo-Confucians was "quiet-sitting" (*jingzuo* 靜坐). For Zhu's purposes two features of this practice stand out: First, he sees this form of meditation as a passive mode, the sort of thing that one does when unengaged and not interacting with the world. Second, Zhu largely thinks that meditation should be directed inward. The object of one's concentration, he maintains, is supposed to be one's own heartmind. In point of fact, not all Buddhist thinkers see meditation as passive, nor as exclusively inward, and Zhu concedes as much.[16] But Zhu appears to take such cases to be either peripheral to or out of step with the

---

[14] The former is a rough characterization of what is usually translated as the "Yogācāra" or "Nothing but Consciousness" school of Buddhism, in China most famously associated with Xuanzang 玄奘 (602–664). The latter describes the view of the "Huayan" school, whose best known philosophical spokesperson is Fazang 法藏 (643–712).

[15] This criticism pre-dates the rise of Song dynasty Neo-Confucianism by many centuries and was forcefully advanced by the Tang dynasty Confucian philosopher Han Yu 韓愈 (768–824). See Han Yu's "Yuan dao" 原道 (On the Way) in *Changli xiansheng ji* 昌黎先生集 (Han Yu's Collected Writings), *Sibu beiyao* 四部備要 (The Essential Collection of the Four Divisions) (Shanghai: Zhonghua shuju, 1927–1936), 11.1a–11.5a, translated by Philip J. Ivanhoe in *On Ethics and History: Essays and Letters of Zhang Xuecheng* (Stanford, CA: Stanford University Press, 2009), 133–137.

[16] Philip B. Yampolsky, *The Platform Sutra of the Sixth Patriarch: The Text of the Tun-Huang Manuscript With Translation, Introduction, and Notes* (New York: Columbia University Press, 1967), 117, 136–137; *Zhuzi yulei, juan* 30, 772.

actual practices of ordinary Buddhists in his era, or thinks that more active forms of meditation are unworkable for most practicing Buddhists.

2.2 Objections to the Goal of Buddhist Salvation

The most important elements of Buddhist soteriology concern the state of salvation itself, the means to that state, and finally the background theory of value or purpose that makes salvation worth aspiring to. On most Buddhist views, salvation is above all the elimination of human sorrow and misery, and the process by which it is achieved is more akin to attacking the underlying psychological sources or roots of those sorrows and miseries, rather than the sorrows and miseries themselves. There are different ways of characterizing these underlying sources. One of the best-known formulations states that the cause of suffering is "craving" or "desire" (yu 欲). Others stress that desire itself comes from a sense of attachment to things—sometimes to material goods or reputation, sometimes to relationships, and even to the very reality of permanent things and phenomena, most especially the reality of the self, or at least the self as we normally understand it. Eliminating such attachments is supposed to help us in ways that are both obvious and subtle. Most obviously, if we are no longer attached to things like fine clothing, long life or a good reputation, we will have less anxiety about gaining or losing such things, and this in turn will make us less attached to many other things that we want because they are means to fine clothing, long life or a good reputation, such as money. More subtly, our attachment to the goods we encounter over the course of our lives in this world is responsible for the fact that we continue to be reborn in this world. It is because we are attached to things of this world that we are stuck in the cycle of life and death.

2.2.1 First Critique of Buddhist Soteriology: Selfishness

For Zhu, this general soteriological vision has dangerous implications. A cluster of them falls under the general observation that if personal freedom from the suffering of life really is the ultimate purpose of Buddhist practice, then Buddhists are essentially engaged in a selfish or self-centered enterprise. In making these charges, a term he frequently uses to describe Buddhist practitioners is *si* 私, variously translated as "selfish," "self-centered," "self-interested," and "private." Generally speaking, there are three ways of understanding this charge. The first is that Buddhists are selfish in the sense that they devote their lives to obtaining something personally beneficial—escape from *their own* suffering—and, perhaps even worse, that they are driven by a strong interest in their own welfare (that is, they are selfish not just in behavior but also in motivation).[17] A second and subtler argument is that they simply fail to take the interests of others into full consideration, so that they neglect the welfare of others no matter how much or little their personal goals may be directed toward their own interests. Unlike the first form of selfishness, this one is more negative: It's about what Buddhists *do not* do (they do not take an interest in others) rather than what they *do* (seek their own good or benefit). The third form of selfishness lies not in behavior or motivation, but in how Buddhist practitioners *conceive* of themselves: what picture, vision or self-understanding they adopt when considering themselves and their interests. Strictly speaking, Zhu Xi thinks, humane or benevolent people should see themselves as a complete, life-generating system, forming "one body with heaven, earth and the myriad things." Even if they recognize themselves as numerically distinct from one another, they nevertheless understand themselves as belonging to a larger whole, much as different parts of the body belong to the whole body. Zhu shares this idea with the Cheng brothers and takes it to be a core element of the Confucian vision.[18]

The charge that Buddhists are selfish is something of a commonplace in Neo-Confucian texts, but one of the most adamant proponents of this view is Cheng Yi. Cheng explains that the Buddhist aspiration to leave the cycle of life and death is born of fear, so that their motive for adhering to Buddhism is their desire to escape personal hardship:

> Buddhism simply seeks to frighten people with its teachings about life and death. It is odd that in the course of the past two thousand years no one has realized this, which only goes to show how successfully it has frightened people. The sages and worthies [of the Confucian tradition] regarded life and death as a matter of one's lot; they saw nothing to fear about them and so did not discuss life and death. Buddhists are afraid of life and death and so all they can do is talk about them incessantly. The most common sorts of people fear many things and are easily motivated by self-interest. As for Chan Buddhists, although they say they are not like this, in its essence, their

---

[17] *Zhuzi yulei*, juan 126, 3032.
[18] Cheng and Cheng, *Yishu* 2A.17, in *Er Cheng ji*, 15; Zhu Xi "Ren shuo" 仁說 (Treatise on Humaneness), *Zhu Xi ji*, juan 67, 3542–3544.

teaching comes down to the same idea: in everything they desire personal benefit.

佛學只是以生死恐動人。可怪二千年來，無一人覺此，是被他恐動也。聖賢以生死為本分事，無可懼，故不論死生。佛之學為怕死生，故只管說不休。下俗之人固多懼，易以利動。至如禪學者，雖自曰異此，然要之只是此箇意見，皆利心也。[19]

Here Cheng Yi maintains that the chief motivating factor in Buddhism is its promise of salvation, which is freedom from the suffering inherent in the cycle of life and death. Buddhism, he suggests, plays on ordinary people's pre-existing fears of this state, and despite their protests to the contrary they never really overcome these fears. Cheng also adds the interesting claim that the Confucian tradition does not just ignore such fears or draw on other, overriding drives; it ultimately neutralizes them, alluding to the widespread Neo-Confucian view that Confucian sages are able to put their own lives into perspective, seeing that there are much greater values at stake in human existence.

We might think Cheng Yi is simply making the point that Buddhists play on people's fears in order to win their devotion to Buddhist practices and institutions. But later in the same discussion, Cheng makes it clear that he is not just talking about devotion; he is also talking about belief or faith (*xin* 信): Those who study closely the Buddhist teachings about life and death, he says, "believe these teachings out of a desire for personal benefit."[20] This has still more disturbing implications by the lights of most Neo-Confucian philosophers, for it suggests not just that they are selfishly motivated but also that their belief is insincere, thereby lacking in that crucial element—sincerity or integrity (*cheng* 誠)—that makes true virtue possible.[21]

For as long as this criticism has been made, sympathetic readers of Buddhism have observed that it seems deeply unfair to the prominent role of ethical precepts and compassion in the course of Buddhist spiritual development. It is true that many Buddhists think the final destination or goal is personal liberation from suffering, but en route to that goal they

---

[19] *Yishu* 1.10, in *Er Cheng ji*, 3; translation modified from Justin Tiwald and Bryan W. Van Norden, *Readings in Later Chinese Philosophy: Han Dynasty to the 20th Century* (Cambridge: Hackett, 2014), 158 (hereafter *Readings*).
[20] *Yishu* 1.3, in *Er Cheng ji*, 3; translation modified from Tiwald and Van Norden, *Readings*, 158.
[21] Fuji Michiaki 藤井倫明, *Zhuzi sixiang jiegou tansuo* 朱熹思想結構探索 (Investigations into the Structure of Zhu Xi's Thought) (Taipei: Taida chuban zhongxin, 2011), 9–34.

are required to take on a way of life in which selfish motives have no role at all. This is nowhere more evident than in the figure of the bodhisattva, a kind of enlightened being who is close enough to nirvana that he or she could leave the cycle of life and death behind, but chooses instead to work for the salvation of all other beings. In the Mahāyāna tradition of Buddhism that dominated China, Buddhists should eventually take what they called a "bodhisattva vow," promising to refrain from leaving the world until all other beings have achieved enlightenment. Bodhisattvas are marked out by what Buddhists call "great compassion," an attitude of genuine care and concern for all things, powerful enough to lead them unflinchingly to acts of great self-sacrifice in their service to others. To be sure, laypeople are first inspired to take up the Buddhist life because they want to be free from personal suffering—Buddhists admit this much. But clearly, that original motive is supposed to fall away in the course of one's development, and it hardly seems fair to charge truly compassionate and generous Buddhists with selfishness just because they had self-interested reasons at the outset.[22]

This is an important line of defense against the charge of selfishness, but it is not the end of the matter. While it is true that Neo-Confucian critics sometimes ignore the prominent place of bodhisattvahood in Buddhist thought and practice, most are, of course, well aware of the objection, and one can find them grappling with it in their letters and treatises, sometimes in response to indignant defenders of Buddhism who find the selfishness criticism unfair.[23] Here I will take some time to identify and make sense of these parts of the works of Cheng Yi and Zhu Xi. This will give us a chance to consider further the nature of selfishness, the theory of value presupposed by a familiar Buddhist account of salvation and enlightenment, and a surprising array of important philosophical differences between Buddhism and Confucianism as Zhu construes them. In what follows, it will be useful to have a quick and easy way of referring to the

---

[22] And we could add here that the Confucians are really no better: The Confucian founders themselves routinely attempted to sell others on the advantages of the Confucian Way by appealing to the fact that those with it would be more effective at governing, would have more influence, and would be more likely than not to fulfill their most important goals and interests. See for example, *Mengzi* 1A:1 and 1A:7.

[23] For example, see the "Yu Wang Shunbo" 與王順伯 (Letter to Wang Shunbo) by Zhu's contemporary Lu Xiangshan 陸象山 (1139–1193), in *Lu Jiuyuan ji* 陸九淵集 (Collected Works of Lu Jiuyuan) (Beijing: Zhonghua shuju, 1980), *juan* 2, 16–21, in Philip J. Ivanhoe, trans., *Readings from the Lu-Wang School of Neo-Confucianism* (Cambridge, MA: Hackett Publishing, 2009), 51–55.

general line of defense just described, so let us call it the Objection from Bodhisattva Ethics.

To start we can consider three arguments that come most readily to Neo-Confucians like Cheng Yi and Zhu Xi. The first is that the selfishness charge is essentially an empirical one, about what drives Buddhists *in fact* and not about what drives them in principle or forms the ideological basis of their doctrines and practices. Cheng Yi is careful to note that he has in mind what Chan Buddhists really worry about, not what they say they worry about, and he is also concerned with the more public rhetoric that disseminators of Buddhism use to attract ordinary people to Buddhism. But it is difficult to say how much purchase this sort of argument should have. Most Buddhist practitioners fall short of the ideal, just as assuredly as most career-minded Confucians, and both Buddhists and Confucians admit as much.

A second available response is to say that while Buddhists may see bodhisattvahood as a necessary step to Buddhist enlightenment, and admittedly a very long (even infinitely long) one, they nevertheless see personal enlightenment as playing an important justificatory role. The great compassion of the bodhisattva is justified insofar as it is a means to personal enlightenment or a constituent of personal enlightenment, or so it seems. This is not unlike the familiar claim that Christian altruism is warranted in part because the Christian God commands it rather than justified on its own merits. In effect, it suggests that even if an adherent is *in fact* driven by altruistic motives, it is still the case that she *would* have adopted different motives altogether, had it been necessary for soteriological purposes, and there is an unsettling sort of selfishness in this justificatory scheme. This indeed is how I read one line of argument by Lu Xiangshan 陸象山 (1139–1193), one of Zhu's regular interlocutors.[24] To my knowledge neither Cheng Yi nor Zhu Xi make such a claim, but the fact that it is articulated by Lu suggests it may have been one of the kinds or senses of Buddhist selfishness that Zhu had in mind.

Although Zhu does not face the Objection from Bodhisattva Ethics squarely, his passing remarks on Buddhist compassion and the bodhisattva's psychology indicates that he was aware of the issue, and there are the makings of a response in them. One argument would appeal to the second notion of selfishness mentioned at the beginning of this subsection, the notion that defines selfishness not by what it has (selfish motives) but

---

[24] "Yu Wang Shunbo," in *Lu Jiuyuan ji*, 17.

rather by what it lacks (concern for others). Zhu claims that the mark of a budding bodhisattva is the ability to maintain self-control, and that, at least on some Buddhist accounts, one can achieve this control only by overcoming even the most natural and deep-seated affections for family. Zhu describes someone whose parents are murdered but remains unfazed, with no perturbation of the heartmind and no longing for the dead. Certain Buddhists, he says, characterize this as an important step on the path toward bodhisattvahood, the stage at which one "first commits the heartmind to becoming a bodhisattva" (初發心菩薩).[25] This represents a kind *reductio ad absurdum* for Buddhist non-attachment.

A Buddhist interlocutor would be quick to point out that while a bodhisattva (or proto-bodhisattva) may remain unperturbed by the death of a parent, he or she would nevertheless have care or concern of another kind, better characterized as compassion or kindness. The *Yulei* indicates that Zhu Xi had considered views about this line of thinking as well. In two revealing exchanges Zhu explains that Buddhist compassion, while a form of care or concern, is nevertheless a peculiar kind, far removed from the kind that arises naturally from intimacy and family bonds. To clarify, he deploys the technical distinction between "conditioned compassion" (*you yuan ci* 有緣慈) and "unconditioned compassion" (*wu yuan ci* 無緣慈). The former is the sort of compassion that is contingent on one's relationship to someone or something (e.g., being related as a child, sibling, friend, or member of the same species), while the latter is a kind of compassion that one has for all things, regardless of one's relationship to them.[26]

I will supply these passages in full in the next section. For now it should be enough to note that care of the unconditioned kind must have a very different psychological basis, putting it at much greater distance from the natural psychological constitution of most people. By contrast, Confucian humaneness is nearer at hand, for it builds on natural attachments and other-directed concern for family members, whereas Buddhists want to sever those attachments and construct altruism in an entirely different way. Earlier I suggested that it might be unfair of the Confucians to separate non-ideal Buddhist practitioners from non-ideal Confucian practitioners—surely ordinary members of both traditions fall beneath the high bar of altruism expected of them. But now we see why it might be mistaken to paint both the ordinary, flawed Confucian and the ordinary, flawed Buddhist

---

[25] *Zhuzi yulei*, juan 126, 3019.
[26] *Zhuzi yulei*, juan 126, 3031.

with the same brush. Whereas Confucians may fall short of their ideal form of altruism, at the very least their other-directed concern is more readily accessible through the love and compassion that they naturally feel for their near and dear, something that they can grasp and build on right from the start. Discernable progress is evident in most decent Confucians within the space of a single lifetime. For Zhu, this too is a major advantage of Confucianism over Buddhism: It can justify its aims without appealing to speculative theories about future lives, because its methods can bear fruit in this life.

2.2.2 Second Critique of Buddhist Soteriology: Foundations of Ethics

A more contested issue in all of this concerns Buddhist stances toward life production (*sheng sheng*). As we have seen, Zhu takes Buddhists to repudiate attachments to life and its related goods (growth and procreation), and aim ultimately for a state without life or death, production or destruction.[27] But insofar as Buddhists aim to achieve a state that neither produces nor extinguishes life, Zhu thinks they presuppose a system of values that is fundamentally at odds with moral virtue, for morality and the virtues are at bottom concerned with promoting life, not with one's own liberation from life and death. There is a sense, in other words, in which any norm grounded in personal transcendence of life is not a *moral* or *ethical* norm at all, but something else—a soteriological norm, perhaps. Or so it seems on a close reading of Zhu's remarks about Buddhist prescriptions and the very nature of ethics and goodness, remarks I will piece together here.

Let us start with a charitable reconstruction of a Buddhist view on life production. It would be unfair to say that Buddhists think life production and its associated goods (growth, development, intergenerational continuity) have no value at all. The better way to put the Buddhist view is to say that life production, however valuable, is not the sort of thing that devoted Buddhists should become attached to. A Buddhist can treat something as valuable and worth promoting without being attached to it.[28] Furthermore, the value of life production diminishes for those who are nearest to enlightenment, so that it is something worth promoting for people at certain stages of spiritual development but not worth promoting for others. Huiyuan's 慧遠 (334–416) "Shamen bu jing wangzhe lun" 沙門不敬王者論

---

[27] *Zhuzi yulei*, juan 126, 3012.
[28] My thanks to Brook A. Ziporyn for pointing out the significance of this distinction in Buddhism.

(On Why Buddhist Monks Do Not Honor the King) provides an illuminating Buddhist account of these distinctions.[29] Huiyuan structures his argument around the presupposition that a Buddhist's attitudes toward life production will depend on the particular kind of practitioner he or she is. Most will be lay Buddhists, that is, Buddhists who stay in the home and family, where they cannot help but participate in family life and become emotionally invested in the nurturing and reproductive activities around which it is organized: "Complying with the transformations of the temporal world becomes the common practice and they do not strip away what comes naturally to them" (順為通而不革其自然也).[30] But the attitude of monastic Buddhists is different:

> Those who have left the family are guests beyond the temporal world. In their outward behavior they are cut off from external things. Their doctrine leads them to understand that the reason they are burdened by suffering is because they have a body, and that they can put an end to their suffering by not preserving the body. They understand that life production (*sheng sheng*) depends on being subject to the transformations of the temporal world, and by refraining from following the transformations they seek out the great ancestral source of the world (*zong* 宗). Because seeking out the great ancestral source does not depend on following the transformations of the temporal world, they do not value the resources required for participation in the cyclical changes. Because putting an end to their suffering does not depend on preserving the body, they do not value the benefits of life.
>
> 出家則是方外之賓。跡絕於物。其為教也。達患累緣於有身。不存身以息患。知生生由於稟化。不順化以求宗。求宗不由於順化。則不重運通之資。息患不由於存身。則不貴厚生之益。[31]

Whether a Buddhist is attached to and values life production thus depends in part on whether he or she is a lay or monastic Buddhist. Lay Buddhists maintain some attachments to life and thus regard it as having some value or benefit to themselves. This passage might be taken to suggest that the

---

[29] For a complete but somewhat dated translation see Leon Hurvitz, "'Render Unto Caesar' in Early Chinese Buddhism," in *Liebenthal Festschrift*, ed. Kshitis Roy (Santiniketan: Visvabharati, 1957), 80–114. I will be quoting the selected translation in Tiwald and Van Norden, *Readings*, 75–80.

[30] Tiwald and Van Norden, *Readings*, 76. For the original passage, see "Shamen bu jing wangzhe lun," T52.2102, 30a22-23.

[31] Tiwald and Van Norden, *Readings*, 76–77, slightly modified, my brackets. "Shamen bu jing wangzhe lun," T52.2102, 30b06-10.

opposite is true for monastic Buddhists: They should neither be attached to life nor value it. Huiyuan's view, however, is more nuanced. To be sure, monastic Buddhists do aim to free themselves of attachments to their own life, and they also regard it as having little intrinsic value for themselves, but Huiyuan is careful to say that Buddhist monks, while not themselves beneficiaries of the contributions that their parents and rulers make to their own life, nevertheless share the goals of a benevolent son or ruler, wanting the people in their care to flourish by participating properly in processes of life production:

> Although they do not occupy the positions of kings or nobles they are truly in harmony with the ultimate [standards of] august rulership, giving life to the people through non-interference and leniency. Therefore, within the family they deviate from [the normal tendency to] attach great importance to natural relationships, but do this without violating their filial responsibilities. Outside the family they refrain from honoring their lord, but do this without losing their reverence for him. Seeing it this way, one will understand that when someone transcends the transformations of the temporal world in order to seek out the great ancestral source of the world, then the *li* 理 [that moves him] is profound and his righteous conduct is sincere.
>
> 雖不處王侯之位。亦已協契皇極。在宥生民矣。是故內乖天屬之重。而不違其孝。外闕奉主之恭。而不失其敬。從此而觀。故知超化表以尋宗則理深而義篤。[32]

So the monastic Buddhist does regard life production and growth as having intrinsic value after all, albeit in a circumscribed way, limited to those who do not have the ready option of overcoming their attachments to life.

When Zhu Xi criticizes the Buddhists for putting the path to salvation before ethics, he does not take them to task for denying the value of life production, but rather for their insistence that people ultimately shed their *attachments* to life production. I find two major arguments along these lines. The first is to suggest that Buddhists' fascination with their religious goals introduces a new notion of moral goodness (*shan* 善) that is at odds with most sensible and conventional understandings of it. Normally, he suggests, people understand moral goodness as consisting in helping others and participating in ethical relationships with others. But Buddhism introduces a new set of moral norms that are not properly linked to either of

---

[32] Tiwald and Van Norden, *Readings*, 78. *Shamen bu jing wangzhe lun*, T52.2102, 30b17-20.

these things. In one exchange, a student asks Zhu about an old adage: "Get rid of the Buddhist shrines, then all of the world will know how to turn to goodness" (除卻浮屠祠廟，天下便知向善). Zhu takes this to be a reference to the practice of venerating the Buddha and other Buddhist figures, one of the chief purposes for visiting temples:

> From the time that Buddhism entered China, this term "good" has fallen into error. People now regard revering the Buddha as a form of goodness. If one repairs a bridge or builds a road this benefits people. If one takes maintaining a Buddhist diet and establishing a temple to be forms of goodness, wherein does that goodness lie? The meaning of the expression "get rid of the Buddhist shrines, then all of the world will know how to turn to goodness" is that once the people of the world are not drowning in that [erroneous understanding of goodness] they will naturally have filial piety for their parents and respect for their elders, acting as good people. Now *this* is goodness.
>
> 自浮屠氏入中國，善之名便錯了。渠把奉佛為善。如修橋道造路，猶有益於人。以齋僧立寺為善，善安在？所謂除浮屠祠廟便向善者，天下之人既不溺於彼，自然孝父母，悌長上，做一好人，便是善。[33]

A second set of arguments for some sort of attachment to life production has to do with the crucial part such attachments play in human relationships. Here I find two general claims in Zhu. The first is that without some attachment to life and life-producing processes, people would not be able to develop the natural sense of gratitude on which virtues are based. The second is that a special interest in the life and growth of others is the very material of human relationships, so that if one does not have someone whose life they value more than others, then in a sense she does not have relationships at all. I turn to these arguments next.

Many of the chief virtues we associate with loyalty and devotion to superiors tend to rely on gratitude for their development. Consider the foundational virtue of filial piety. Ideally, filial piety is not just a matter of serving one's parents; it is a matter of serving them happily, willingly, and without reluctance or regret. Serving them faithfully but grudgingly may be difficult, but at least it is something we can force ourselves to do. By contrast, we cannot make ourselves happy about serving our parents through sheer force of will. In order to reach the state where filial behavior

---

[33] *Zhuzi yulei*, juan 126, 3033 (emphasis added).

comes effortlessly or naturally (as is necessary for filial piety as a full or complete virtue), we need a more whole-hearted and authentic expression of filial devotion. And to cultivate that, many (or most) of us rely on the feeling of gratitude that arises from awareness of the goods we have been given by our parents. This includes gratitude for such things as food and clothing lovingly rendered. On a widely shared Confucian view, moreover, it should include gratitude for our very bodies and lives, which we would not have were it not for our parents.[34] As we saw above, Huiyuan suggests that monastic Buddhists do not feel any particular gratitude for being given the opportunity to live and grow by their parents, nor, in the case of the ruler, for protecting and providing for them. Zhu finds this view to be pervasive among Buddhists, saying that "they regard the body the parents gave them by birth as a temporary abode, as though they can just freely pick a new home to move into after the old home has collapsed" (而以父母所生之身為寄寓。譬以舊屋破倒，即自挑入新屋), which interferes with the natural operations of *tianli* 天理 (heavenly pattern) that manifest in proper human relationships.[35]

Probably Zhu's most fundamental objection to the intrusion of Buddhist soteriological principles into ethics concerns the role of relationships. As we saw earlier, Zhu found it odd to think that venerating Buddhist figures could qualify as an act of goodness (*shan*) whereas acts such as respecting one's elders and repairing bridges are subordinate. A more conspicuous objection in Zhu's works is that Buddhists abandon ethics outright because they abandon relationships outright. Human relationships (*renlun* 人倫), and performing one's role-specific responsibilities well, are the very stuff of ethics (*lunli* 倫理) as understood by Zhu and his contemporaries. Zhu argues that by encouraging people to shed their attachments to specific other people and to replace these partial forms of care with the universal and impartial compassion of the bodhisattva, Buddhists essentially promote the eradication of human relationships. If one does not have a strong, emotional investment in certain people, and care about their interests more than the interests of strangers or, for that matter, members of other species, then for all intents and purposes one does not have relationships at all, and

---

[34] "Our bodies, hair, and skin are received from our parents and we dare not damage or injure them. This is the beginning of filial piety." See *Xiaojing* 孝經 (Classic of Filial Piety), *Shisan jing zhu shu* edition, *juan* 1, 3a.

[35] *Zhuzi yulei*, *juan* 126, 3013. For more on the role that gratitude plays in cultivating filial piety, see Philip J. Ivanhoe, "Filial Piety as a Virtue," in *Working Virtue: Virtue Ethics and Contemporary Moral Problems*, eds. Rebecca Walker and Philip J. Ivanhoe (Oxford: Oxford University Press, 2007), 297–312.

thus no ethics (*lunli*) to speak of. Here Zhu's criticisms of the Buddhists echo Mencius' memorable claim that Mohists, by virtue of practicing impartial care (*jian'ai* 兼愛), are for all intents and purposes "without fathers."[36] Zhu makes this point by building on the Buddhist distinction between "conditioned" and "unconditioned" compassion:

> The Chan school takes the mutual care between fathers, sons, older and younger brothers to be "conditioned compassion." But if one regards oneself as being different in kind from, say, tigers and wolves, and yet one's care reaches out to them such that one will, for example, use one's own body to feed a tiger, this is "unconditioned compassion," which they take to be true compassion.
>
> 禪家以父子兄弟相親愛處為有緣之慈。如虎狼與我非類，我卻有愛及他，如以身飼虎。便是無緣之慈，以此為真慈。[37]

On Zhu's understanding, what distinguishes conditioned compassion is that it is subject to one's existing circumstances and relations, contingent on standing in a certain relationship to the one for whom one feels compassion (e.g., as a parent, sibling, or friend) and thus discriminates between those objects and other potential and worthy objects of care. Unconditioned compassion is not contingent on having a certain relationship to the other, and is thus undiscriminating. He makes these connections in the following set of remarks:

> [A student asked about the proposal that Buddhist compassion is a form of care that lacks distinctions of degree between family and others.] The teacher responded: "The Buddhists speak of 'unconditioned compassion.' I remember a place in which [a Buddhist author] describes 'the great compassion that originates from the nature, which is unconditioned.'[38] This is because what the Buddhists call compassion arises in the absence of any conditions, and simply is care directed at all things. As for the case of caring for one's parents, they rashly take that to be subject to conditions. And so they abandon their parents and fail to nurture them but if they encounter a starving tiger they will sacrifice their bodies in order to feed it. How could this possibly be morally correct?"

---

[36] *Mencius* 3B9.
[37] *Zhuzi yulei*, juan 126, 3031.
[38] This is a reference to the doctrine of nature origination—that is, the view that our true nature, as true suchness (*zhenru* 真如), is the basis of all things, which is itself uncaused or unconditioned.

先生曰：「釋氏說『無緣慈』。記得甚處說：『融性起無緣之大慈。』蓋佛氏之所謂慈，並無緣由，只是無所不愛。若如愛親之愛，渠便以為有緣；故父母棄而不養，而遇虎之飢餓，則捨身以食之，此何義理耶？」[39]

Zhu is too quick to take at face value the claim that practitioners of unconditioned (and thus non-discriminating) care should feed themselves to starving animals. Many Buddhist recommendations are intended as therapy rather than as action-guiding prescriptions, meant not to specify a rule of behavior but rather to shock our moral sensibilities and thereby pave the way for radical shifts in thought. And even when they are meant to be action-guiding prescriptions, they are often highly particularistic, meant for people of a certain stage in their spiritual development and in certain extraordinary circumstances, not just any practicing Buddhist. In these respects Zhu misrepresents the Buddhists.

But Zhu's underlying worries about Buddhist compassion present a more formidable challenge. Whether or not Buddhists see personal salvation as valuable in its own right, they still treat salvation as a regulative ideal, setting forth a course of personal development in which special relationships recede and a more general kind of care—care without distinctions—becomes the dominant ethical feeling. Even if this sort of compassion is admirable, it is open to the Confucian to say that Buddhists are trading in their ethics for their soteriological principles, for there is little room for ethics in a social landscape without relationships, and relationships require care with distinctions.

All of this appears to suggest that for Zhu, Buddhists who put their soteriology before their "ethics" do not *have* an ethics in the proper sense. The terms *shan* (goodness) and *lunli* (proper human relations) are misapplied. I take this to be the *reductio ad absurdum* that Zhu is offering as a response to Buddhists taken on their own terms. As mentioned at the outset of this chapter, however, Zhu is less interested in Buddhist doctrines as such and more interested in what becomes of them in the hands of Buddhist practitioners, given the tendencies of human nature and other facts on the ground. At this level, Zhu's criticism is quite different. Ordinary practitioners, he thinks, do not lack an ethics in the proper sense, because there are powerful drives in our nature that make it difficult to overcome

---

[39] *Zhuzi yulei, juan* 126, 3031–3032. I thank Philip J. Ivanhoe, John Jorgensen, and John Makeham for their helpful clarifications of conditioned and unconditioned compassion in the Buddhist tradition.

attachments to others and withdraw from human relationships entirely. The upshot for most Buddhist monastics is something of a false consciousness. Monks take themselves to have eliminated human relationships but what we see instead, he suggests, are ersatz families formed in the context of the monastic community, with relationships between monks that closely approximate those between parent and child or older and younger siblings:

> Even though Buddhists and Daoists extinguish human relationships they cannot escape them. They may lack father-son relationships but they pay obeisance to their teachers, who accordingly regard their disciples as sons. The older apprentices become the "elder brothers" and the younger ones become the "younger brothers." This is just to defend a false version [of human relationships] while the [Confucian] sages and worthies preserve the authentic one.
>
> 如佛老雖是滅人倫，然自是逃不得。如無父子，卻拜其師，以其弟子為子；長者為師兄，少者為師弟。但是只護得箇假底，聖賢便是存得箇真底。[40]

Here again, Zhu implies that a major advantage of Confucian, family-based approaches to ethics is that they can be made consistent with the deep-seated dispositions embedded in human nature, such that one can adopt the Confucian way of life in a wholehearted or sincere (*cheng*) way, without internal conflict or cognitive dissonance. Buddhists, by contrast, demand impossibly heroic feats of self-transformation, which puts sincerity out of reach.[41] On Zhu's view, sincerity is impossible for Buddhists because the inclination to form close relationships is an ineradicable part of our nature. Even if we think it can be eradicated, however, it is fair to say that such an achievement would be exceedingly rare, and, I worry, probably not worth the toll that it would take on the human psyche.

2.3 Objections to Buddhist Practices: Mental Discipline

As I use the term here, "mental discipline" refers to a variety of techniques and habits that help to sustain certain (usually rarified) states of mind, such as peace of mind, open-mindedness, selflessness, or vigilance. Among the mental disciplines that most occupied the Buddhists and Zhu Xi, two of the

---

[40] *Zhuzi yulei, juan* 126, 3014
[41] *Zhuzi yulei, juan* 126, 3016.

most prominent were meditation and self-monitoring for selfish biases and motives. The second was of much interest to Buddhists and Neo-Confucian thinkers alike, but it stands out as a locus of much debate and theorizing in Neo-Confucian discourse. Many Neo-Confucian philosophers, including Zhu, were deeply convinced that selfish motives and biases were pervasive, deeply rooted and remarkably difficult to detect. Moreover, because these motives and biases are the biggest obstacle to good on-the-ground moral decision-making, eradicating them is one of the greatest tasks for people who aspire to be good. One might say that getting this mental discipline right was as important to the reflective twelfth- or thirteenth-century Chinese thinker as was having the right understanding of humankind's relationship to God for their Western contemporaries. Their views on the topic in question weighed heavily in their peers' overall assessment of their thought and work.

The chief form of mental discipline taught by Buddhists is meditation. And the form of meditation of the greatest interest to Zhu Xi was what he usually called "quiet sitting" (*jingzuo* 靜坐), used to describe an array of practices which, done rightly, were supposed to bring about a state of quietude or tranquility. To be sure, Buddhists advocated many different kinds of meditation, some of them more active and contemplative.[42] But it was quiet sitting that most interested him, as he saw it as a relatively promising technique for achieving mental stability and self-control, and it was the technique adopted by other influential Confucians of his day, including both his own teacher Li Tong as well as Zhang Jiucheng 張九成 (1092–1159), one of his bitterest of rivals.[43]

The most succinct way of putting Zhu's critique of Buddhist meditation was to say that while it provided a kind of tranquility, that tranquility was incomplete without some further source of mental self-mastery accessed through "reverential attention" or *jing* 敬, a term also translated as "inner mental attentiveness," "seriousness," or, more simply, "reverence." Generally speaking, Zhu tended to highlight two respects in which mere meditative tranquility was incomplete. First, so long as it remains

---

[42] The major dispute among Buddhists of the Song dynasty was between advocates of "Silent Illumination Chan," a kind of quiet sitting meditation, and "Gong'an Introspection Chan," which aimed to provide enlightenment through contemplation of Buddhist koāns. See Morten Schlütter, "Silent Illumination, Kung-an Introspection, and the Competition for Lay Patronage in Sung Dynasty Ch'an," in *Buddhism in the Sung*, eds. Peter N. Gregory and Daniel A. Getz Jr. (Honolulu: University of Hawaii Press, 1999), 109–147.

[43] On Li, see John Jorgensen's chapter; on Zhang, see Ari Borrell, "*Ko-wu* or *Kung-an*? Practice, Realization, and Teaching in the Thought of Chang Chiu-ch'eng," in Gregory and Getz, *Buddhism in the Sung*, 62–108.

relatively passive, meditation at best prepares us only to maintain our mental discipline. Zhu, however, was also concerned with the moral side of personal cultivation and insight, which requires active participation.[44] People thus need some ability to keep the heartmind under control even when engaged in emotion-eliciting affairs like trading in the marketplace, household management, politics, and any variety of other activities that are prone to disturb our peace of mind and precipitate loss of control.[45] Zhu explains at length:

> Someone asked about the Buddhist practice of entering into meditative stability and the Daoist practice of counting breaths. Master Zhu said: "They can be flawless in their dealings with external matters only so long as they maintain tranquility [i.e., and not in periods of activity]. Mencius also emphasized [the practice of] preserving the *qi* of nighttime, but [unlike the Buddhists and Daoists] he also thought we have to pay attention to 'what we do during the daylight hours'."[46]
>
> Someone responded: "Why don't we Confucians imitate their practices [of meditation]?"
>
> Master Zhu answered: "As soon as they open their eyes they fall back on their old ways and lose it, and they just to hold on to [their old ways] with a firmer grip. This isn't as good as our Confucian way of refusing to look, hear, speak or move when it's not ritually appropriate,[47] while being vigilant and fearful about [the intentions in ourselves that] we do not see or hear. 'Straighten the inner life by means of reverential attention; square the outer life by means of righteousness.'[48] All that comes to them externally they obstruct completely."
>
> Someone said: "The Buddhists are concerned only with making efforts to 'not see and not hear,' without any of that [Confucian] effort to [avoid seeing and hearing what] isn't ritually appropriate."
>
> Master Zhu responded: "That is correct."
>
> Accordingly, Cai Yuanding [(1135–1198), one of Zhu's students] said: "There are things in the world that people must do. If, like the

---

[44] *Zhuzi yulei, juan* 126, 3018.
[45] Charles Wei-hsun Fu, "Chu Hsi on Buddhism," 393–394; *Zhuzi yulei, juan* 126, 3019. Zhu Xi also turned this line of criticism on the founding figure Zhou Dunyi 周敦頤 (1017–1073), who appeared to think that tranquility provided the self-mastery necessary for virtuous behavior. See *Zhuzi yulei, juan* 94, 2371.
[46] *Mencius* 6A8.
[47] *Analects* 12.1.
[48] *Zhou yi*, 1.26b, *Shisan jing zhushu*.

Buddhists, they concerned themselves only with achieving the stability of sitting meditation, what would they do? The sun and moon must move [across the sky], and heaven and earth must proceed [along their paths]."

Master Zhu responded: "[The Buddhists] neither move nor proceed, so they are certainly incorrect. Those in our generation [of Confucians] do move and proceed, it's just that their activities are erroneous in certain respects. For example, take the wild pleasure and anger of the present day—how can these not be in error? [The Buddhists] go too far while people of the present day do not go far enough."

問釋氏入定，道家數息。曰：「他只要靜，則應接事物不差。 孟子便也要存夜氣，然而須是理會『旦晝之所為』。」曰：「吾儒何不傚他恁地？」曰：「他開眼便依舊失了，只是硬把捉；不如吾儒非禮勿視聽言動，戒慎恐懼乎不睹不聞，『敬以直內，義以方外』，都一切就外面攔截。」曰：「釋氏只是『勿視、勿聽』，無那『非禮』工夫。」曰：「然。」季通因曰：「世上事便要人做，只管似它坐定做甚?日月便要行，天地便要運。」曰：「他不行不運，固不是。吾輩是在這裏行，是在這裏運，只是運行又有差處。如今胡喜胡怒，豈不是差！他是過之，今人又不及。」⁴⁹

A second point of Zhu's is that meditation-induced tranquility has no necessary connection to the larger world. The goal of meditation is to quiet the heartmind, not necessarily to make one more responsive to the interests of others, nor to the demands of a larger-scale social or biological order. Zhu allows that meditation helps the practitioner to rein in unruly emotions and desires, but without some more outward-looking orientation that meditatively achieved mastery of the emotions will be for naught, wasted on arbitrary ends, or made to serve more deeply entrenched subjective inclinations. To put the point in terms more recognizable to Zhu's contemporaries, the "human way" (*rendao* 人道) is ultimately rooted in the "way of heaven" (*tiandao* 天道), so we need some source of self-control that is accountable to the latter.⁵⁰ This would be a source that closely tracks the larger good of harmonious life generation, and Zhu found reverential attention well-suited for that role. In providing attention, it allows us to focus on the issue at hand without the noise of other worries, wants and needs; in providing reverence, it

---

⁴⁹ *Zhuzi yulei, juan* 126, 3019.
⁵⁰ Araki Kengo 荒木見悟, *Fojiao yu Rujiao* 佛教與儒教 (Buddhism and Confucianism), trans., Liao Zhaoheng 廖肇亨 (Taipei: Lianjing chubanshe, 2008), 335.

harnesses the unique motivational power of awe and appreciation of the grandeur of things far greater than ourselves.[51]

One might turn the tables and suggest that while Zhu recommends practicing reverential attention in active states, he does so at the expense of meditative tranquility. We live in both active and passive states and both require some sort of self-mastery (for a variety of reasons having to do with peace of mind, rest or relief from turmoil, and self-understanding, among other things). So a more self-effacing Buddhist might concede that his or her methods of mental discipline excel at tending to the passive parts of life at the expense of the active parts, but add that the situation is the reverse for Zhu.[52]

Some things said by other Neo-Confucian philosophers might be taken to suggest that the practice of reverential attention is meant for the active side of human life alone.[53] But Zhu Xi characterizes reverential attention as something that runs through both passive and active states. When rightly done, he thinks, reverential attention will be at work even in a state of meditative tranquility. Zhu draws a helpful analogy between the kind of self-control required for the heartmind with the kind of self-control required for the eye: The same power to direct the eye is present whether open or shut. His argument for this is partly experiential: He believes that his own more successful experiments with quiet sitting were driven in some way or another by reverential attention.[54] But just as importantly, Zhu maintains that mental discipline should not just govern the mind *in* active and passive mental states; it should govern the shift *between* active and passive mental states: Some periods and circumstances are better suited for quiet sitting than others, and sometimes we need to get up and attend to business or hit the books instead.[55] Expanding on his analogy, we might say that the very

---

[51] Stephen C. Angle, *Sagehood: The Contemporary Significance of Neo-Confucian Philosophy* (New York: Oxford University Press, 2009), 155. As Angle shows, the Neo-Confucian thinkers see attention as an important component of many of the feelings, attitudes, and forms of mental discipline that their methods of cultivation are meant to encourage, not limited to *jing* (*Sagehood*, 150–156).

[52] The Cheng brothers and Zhu Xi actually endorsed the view that Buddhists in general excel at achieving tranquility through quiet sitting. This might be the one concession that Zhu most consistently makes to Buddhist practices. See Cai, *Zhuzi dui Fojiao de lijie ji qi xianzhi*, 196–197.

[53] Wang Yangming 王陽明, *Chuan xi lu* 傳習錄 (A Record of Practicing What Has Been Transmitted), in *Chuan xi lu zhushu* 傳習錄注疏 (An Extended Commentary on *A Record of Practicing What Has Been Transmitted*), ed. Deng Aimin 鄧艾民 (Jilong: Fayan chubanshe, 2000), §117.

[54] *Zhuzi yulei, juan* 12, 214.

[55] "As the heartmind is master of the self in activity or tranquility, in speech or silence, so too the gentleman practices reverential attention in activity or tranquility, in speech or silence" (蓋心主乎一身，而無動靜語默之間，是以君子之於敬，亦無動靜語默而不用其力焉。), *Zhu Xi ji, juan*

same source of control that directs the eye when open or closed should direct the opening and closing of the eyelids as well.⁵⁶

These worries about Buddhist forms of mental discipline are of a piece with a more general worry about the search for some source of ethical direction. This is because, as Zhu saw it, the proper way to acquire ethical direction is by finding it in our nature. Certain inclinations that come naturally to us are motivated by an inherent love of life (*sheng*) and sense of continuity with others. The meaner parts of our psychology (especially self-centered desires) are so good at hiding themselves from us, and so tenacious, that the only realistic way of overcoming them is by drawing and building on these pre-existing inclinations to care about life and the larger whole. Given all of this, it was absolutely essential that whatever forms of mental discipline we learn, they help us tap into those parts of our nature, and Zhu saw Buddhist practices as working against these natural tendencies. At best, Zhu argued, Buddhist practices help the contingent ("human") heartmind to win control over itself, but the real goal should be to make our (good) nature win control over the contingent heartmind, for the former has a built-in moral directedness that the latter does not.

To be sure, many Buddhists also took themselves to be seeking for a source of built-in directedness, which they found in their own preferred conception of our nature, "buddha-nature." But for the most part, Confucian philosophers in the Cheng-Zhu line believed that the actual techniques that the Buddhists taught were capable of controlling only the heartmind's subjective tendencies in service of other subjective tendencies, not in service of a nature truly predisposed to care about life and continuity. This criticism was put most concisely in a saying popularized by Zhu Xi: "What the Buddhists call the nature is what the [Confucian] sages call the heartmind."⁵⁷ Zhu explains what he means by this in a memorable lesson to his students:

> The Buddhists are cognizant only of that which can see hear, speak, think, and move, and consider that to be the nature. But they accept seeing whether it is clear or unclear, they accept hearing whether it is keen or not, they

---

32, 1419, translation modified from Julia Ching, "Chu Hsi on Personal Cultivation," in *Chu Hsi and Neo-Confucianism*, ed. Wing-tsit Chan (Honolulu: University of Hawaii Press), 283.

⁵⁶ *Zhuzi yulei, juan* 96, 2469.

⁵⁷ The complete expression is "what the Buddhists call the nature is precisely what the sages call the heartmind, and what the Buddhists calls the heartmind is precisely what the sages call intentions" (佛氏所謂性，正聖人所謂心；佛氏所謂心，正聖人所謂意。), a criticism that Zhu credited to Xie Liangzuo 謝良佐 (1050–1103). See *Zhuzi yulei, juan* 126, 3019–3020.

accept speech whether it does or does not accord, and they accept thoughts whether they are percipient or not. Either way it is of no concern to them. They regard them as the nature no matter which direction they go.

佛氏則只認那能視、能聽、能言、能思、能動底，便是性。視明也得，不明也得；聽聰也得，不聰也得；言從也得，不從也得；思睿也得，不睿也得，它都不管，橫來豎來，它都認做性。[58]

The debate with the Buddhists about mental discipline is thus joined at two levels: The first concerns the general or theoretical description of the sort of thing that Buddhists and Zhu Xi understand themselves to be doing, and the second concerns what the Buddhists' and what Zhu's practices are doing in fact. Chinese philosophers of the Northern and Southern Song were keenly aware of the fact that theories about one's moral practices may not accurately describe how the practices work, and to this extent their debates about mental discipline moved fluidly between both the theoretical and practical levels, making for a vast body of discourse that appeals deeply to those of us who are both philosophically inclined and interested in genuine self-improvement. This is but a small slice of that much larger discourse.

2.4 Objections to Buddhist Doctrine: Emptiness

Much of Buddhist enlightenment consists in coming to grips with the doctrine that all things of the phenomenal world (or, on some versions, all things simpliciter) are empty. What this means depends a great deal on the particular school of Buddhism that advocates it, but for the sake of better understanding Zhu Xi's objections, we can make some rough generalizations that should help shed light on his criticisms. When a Buddhist claims that something is empty, he or she likely means that it has no nature or essence of its own. Pick a certain property or feature of a phenomenon that seems to be an important part of its very nature, as many people think "consciousness" is a crucial property for mind or "going from one place to another" is an essential feature of movement. Buddhists agree that in some profound sense, it is a fundamental error to describe that feature (or cluster of features) as being in the phenomenon

---

[58] *Zhuzi yulei*, juan 126, 3019–3020. This general line of criticism mirrors one that the prominent Buddhist philosopher Zongmi made of other Buddhists. For a reconstruction of these parallels between Zongmi's and Zhu Xi's criticisms see Peter N. Gregory, *Tsung-Mi and the Sinification of Buddhism*, 295–311.

itself. They might say that the feature is just a projection of our own minds (as the Yogācāra Buddhists do). They might say that there is no particular reason to regard one feature as essential or necessary for its existence, that the selection is arbitrary and dependent on conventions (as Madhyamika Buddhists do). Or they might invoke the peculiarly Buddhist notion that the phenomenon cannot contain a self-nature insofar as the existence of those natural qualities depends on other things and can change over time (as most Chinese Buddhists do). Finally, a Buddhist might not invoke arguments at all, but simply insist that the phenomenon's lack of nature or essence is just how it appears if correctly perceived, which is possible only after a great deal of training. Just as a person who is blind from birth can neither see nor conceive of colors, those who have not cultivated Buddhist insight cannot see the emptiness of things firsthand and cannot fully grasp or conceive of it either.

There are many criticisms of Buddhist emptiness in the extant works of Zhu Xi and those Confucian philosophers he most admired, although some (as we shall see) are more pragmatic than philosophical. Let us begin with a brief overview of the philosophical ones. Like most Neo-Confucians, Zhu thinks that for every manifest phenomenon (*yong* 用, also translated as "function") there must be an intrinsic reality (*ti* 體) for without the intrinsic reality there would be no way to explain certain regularities we find in the ongoing changes of things (as the seasons change but exhibit regularities in their changes), nor would we be able to explain how it is that some phenomena go right or wrong. These regularities or underlying structures are the *li* 理 (patterns, principles) that play a systematic role in explaining or accounting for things. Furthermore, Zhu prides himself on having a more sophisticated conception of the underlying *li*, neatly captured in the catchphrase "*li* is one yet is differentiated in particulars" (*li yi fen shu* 理一分殊).[59] On this view, we should not expect that the underlying *li* (pattern) of all things should be directly evident from the

---

[59] Many Neo-Confucians thought the "differentiated in particulars" half of the famous phrase served as a concise and deep explanation of the differences between themselves and the Buddhists. The Buddhists, they said, accepted that *li* is one, but they could not appreciate that it manifested itself in many different ways, in part because they denied the ultimate existence of *qi*. This influential take on Buddhism apparently came from Li Tong 李侗, the transformational teacher of the young Zhu Xi; see William Theodore de Bary, *Learning for Oneself: Essays on the Individual in Neo-Confucian Thought* (New York: Columbia University Press, 1991), 81–82. The Neo-Confucians also thought the Buddhists' inability to accept *qi* (and *qi*-based things like the bodily self) left them without any real specifics with which to build an intelligible, ethically engaging worldview, forcing them to fall back on abstract doctrine and mystery. This too is another facet of their criticism that Buddhists ignore the many ways in which *li* can be allotted. See Fu, "Chu Hsi on Buddhism," 377–380, and Luo Qinshun 羅欽順, *Kun zhi ji* 困知記 (Knowledge Painfully

phenomena of the world. The particular nature and purpose of a thing is determined in part by *qi* 氣, which sets its own rules for (and limitations on) the operation of things, much as a complete picture of the *li* requires that we not reject or ignore the bodily self (*shen* 身).[60] This adds another layer of experience and explanation before we can identify the ultimate reality of things.

On Zhu's own understanding, the major metaphysical dispute between Buddhists and Confucians like himself is that for the Buddhists, *li* is vacuous or empty (*xu* 虛 or *kong* 空) while for the Confucians it has substance and content (*shi* 實). What it means to say that *li* is empty is somewhat unclear, because, as we will see, Zhu takes this to be a description of the de facto philosophical stance that Buddhists adopt, not their professed views on the matter. At the very least it suggests that there are no structures or values in the phenomenal world, the world of everyday experience. Whatever structures or values we think we find in the world are illusory. For Zhu, however, *li* does have content, and that content is life production (*sheng sheng*). When we fully grasp the intrinsic reality underlying the change of seasons, human relationships, even the decay of organic life, what we find is that all things belong to a larger, interlocking whole in which life promotes life.[61]

One way of capturing all of the aforementioned criticisms of Buddhist metaphysics is to say that the Buddhists simply did not try hard enough to find the sources of order and value underlying things. From Zhu's point of view, the Buddhists look at an ever-changing world and assume it has no underlying system or structure, when keener insight reveals that there are regularities in the midst of the changes, and these regularities presuppose some sort of constant, underlying regulative apparatus at work, keeping the changes in steady rotation like a fixed and stable pivot maintains the steady rotation of a wheel. This criticism is certainly uncharitable to Buddhists and Buddhist metaphysics, but it underscores the importance (for thinkers like Zhu) of finding some sort of constant underlying the fluctuations of the world. Constants are necessary both to show that things are ultimately real and that there are stable, reliable standards to which they should be held.[62] One of the Cheng brothers highlights this point.

Acquired) (Beijing: Zhonghua shuju, 1990), II.59. See John Jorgensen's chapter in this volume on resonances between Zhu Xi's and Buddhist interpretations of the one-many relationship.

[60] Araki, *Fojiao yu Rujiao*, chap. 3, sections 3–4.

[61] For an extended discussion of the "substance" or "content" of *li* see Stephen C. Angle and Justin Tiwald, *Neo-Confucianism: A Philosophical Introduction* (Cambridge, UK: Polity, 2017), chap. 2.

[62] As Zhang Zai puts the point, "intrinsic reality" refers to "that which is never absent" in the midst of the processes of the life, growth and death of things. See *Zhengmeng he jiao ji shi*

Students of Chan say: "The life of plants, trees, birds and beasts is all illusion." I say: "You consider it illusory because they grow in the spring and summer and then decay when autumn and winter come, and you similarly conclude that human life is also an illusion. Why not give this answer: things are born and die, are completed and decay, there is this *li* naturally; how can they be considered illusory?"

學禪者曰：「草木鳥獸之生，亦皆是幻。」曰：「子以為生息於春夏，及至秋冬便卻變壞，便以為幻，故亦以人生為幻，何不付與他。物生死成壞，自有此理，何者為幻？」[63]

Occasionally Zhu Xi is more charitable. In two lessons recorded in the *Yulei*, Zhu seems to concede that he and likeminded Confucians have largely focused their metaphysical critique on a superficial conception of emptiness, and that there is a more promising Buddhist conception that they largely overlook. The superficial one, he suggests, implies that empty things are literally nonexistent and contain nothing (*wu wu* 無物), which he takes to be the basic sense of what Buddhists call "mysterious emptiness" (*xuan kong* 玄空) and "stubborn emptiness" (*wan kong* 頑空, also "biased emptiness"). Zhu is less forthcoming about the deeper conception, which he calls "true emptiness" (*zhen kong* 真空) but—quite shockingly—he acknowledges that the ethical implications of this deeper conception are not unlike the ethical implications of Zhu's own metaphysics of *li*:

> [Buddhists] speak of "mysterious emptiness" and also speak of "true emptiness." Mysterious emptiness is just a kind of emptiness in which there is nothing at all. But in the case of true emptiness things do exist, making it roughly equivalent to what we Confucians speak of. But they don't at all concern themselves with heaven, earth, and the four directions, only with understanding a single heartmind [rather than the larger world].

說「玄空」，又說「真空」。玄空便是空無物，真空卻是有物，與吾儒說略同。但是它都不管天地四方，只是理會一箇心。[64]

正蒙合校集釋 (上) (Collation and Variorum of *Rectifying Ignorance*), ed. Lin Yuechang 林樂昌 (Beijing: Zhonghua shuju, 2012), *juan* 21, 303.

[63] *Yishu*, 1.10, in *Er Cheng ji*, 4; translation slightly modified from Graham, *Two Chinese Philosophers*, 89.

[64] *Zhuzi yulei, juan* 126, 3013.

Here Zhu seems to imply that Buddhist emptiness could ground a meaningful ethics after all, but suggests somewhat mysteriously that the more robust notion of emptiness does Buddhists little good without showing greater interest in the world outside of themselves. In a second passage Zhu shows even less patience with the finer points of Buddhist emptiness:

> There's also the theory of what's called "stubborn emptiness" and "true emptiness." What's stubbornly empty is like dead ashes and dried up wood. In true emptiness one is able to take in all of existence and respond appropriately to change. But this too is only emptiness. There is no need to study it thoroughly at present. As Cheng Yi said, "One needs only to judge [a Buddhist doctrine] on the basis of its practical manifestations [ji 跡, lit. 'footprints']."
>
> 又有所謂「頑空」、「真空」之說。頑空者如死灰槁木，真空則能攝眾有而應變，然亦只是空耳。今不消窮究他，伊川所謂「只消就跡上斷便了。」[65]

In this latter set of remarks, Zhu declines to examine the finer points of Buddhist metaphysics because he thinks it unnecessary. All one needs to do is to look at the implications of the metaphysics for human behavior, and that is enough to show that the Buddhists must have gotten something fundamentally wrong (surely no metaphysics that can justify the abandonment of one's parents is worth the bother!). This method of assessment was promoted most explicitly by Cheng Yi, who saw it not just as a useful expedient but also as a necessity.

> If you want to go about deciding which Buddhist doctrines to accept by thoroughly investigating them, then you will have already converted to Buddhism even before you're able to complete your investigations. Examine them only on the basis of their practical manifestations. [Ask yourself,] if they proposed instructions like these, then what were they thinking or feeling? Surely it's difficult to accept what they were thinking or feeling without accepting their manifestations in practice. If there's a particular state of thought or feeling then there will be particular practical manifestations. . . . So the better way to investigate is to determine where they disagree with the sages with regard to practical manifestations. If their

---

[65] *Zhuzi yulei*, juan 126, 3088. For more discussion of these two fleeting acknowledgments of "true emptiness," see Fu, "Chu Hsi on Buddhism," 385–386, and Cai, *Zhuzi dui Fojiao de lijie ji qi xianzhi*, 204–206.

teachings have points on which they agree then of course these will already be in our [Confucian] Way. And if they have points on which they disagree then of course it's not to be accepted. In this way one can stand firm even while using an efficient and easy method.

> 釋氏之說，若欲窮其說而去取之，則其說未能窮，固已化而為佛矣。只且於跡上考之。其設教如是，則其心果如何？固難為取其心，不取其跡。有是心則有是跡。．．．．故不若且於跡上斷定不與聖人合。其言有合處，則吾道固已有。有不合者，固所不取。如是立定，卻省易。[66]

On the view suggested here, Buddhists have a habit of defending their wildest beliefs by making immersion in Buddhist scholastics a precondition for understanding those beliefs. To really determine whether a challenging Buddhist doctrine is true, it seems, one must first become a Buddhist, and that is a lot to ask of an incredulous outsider. Surely we are sometimes warranted in foregoing the finer points of argument and assessing a system of thought by the plausibility of its most notable implications, as when deciding whether or not to debate a well-armed conspiracy theorist. But one of the world's great philosophical traditions should not be dismissed so easily as a conspiracy theory, and by dismissing it Zhu missed an opportunity to put two of the world's most influential metaphysical systems into dialogue.

Even so, there are the makings of a better response in Zhu Xi's extant works. The response runs as follows: Whatever metaphysics the Buddhists may endorse in word or principle, in fact their practices affirm and reinforce a different kind of metaphysics. For example, a Buddhist philosopher may say (as many would) that his or her metaphysics is based on true emptiness rather than stubborn emptiness or, just hypothetically, he or she may even say that *li* is not empty after all. Whatever a given Buddhist's ostensible views, however, Zhu would insist that standard Buddhist practices yield a different understanding of the profound relations between things. This is because the methods of insight that the Buddhists promote do not acquaint us with the life-generative impulses in things, so that we ignore or misidentify the basis for the grand unity between ourselves and others. As we saw in the previous section of this chapter, Zhu worries that meditation without reverence gives us no special access to the larger world

---

[66] Zhu Xi and Lü Zuqian 呂祖謙, *Jin si lu jijie* 近思錄集解 (Collected Explanations of *Reflection on Things At Hand*), ed. Zhang Boxing 張伯行 (Taipei: Shijie shuju, 1983), *juan* 19, no. 9 (13.9). Also translated in Graham, *Two Chinese Philosophers*, 88.

and instead engages in a kind of frictionless spinning of introspective wheels. Even if one believes that we have certain profound connections to others, one will not see these connections grounded in ceaseless life production, nor will these connections have a gripping, transformative effect. Accordingly, they treat the world as empty in the sense of being illusory or "stubbornly empty" even as they endorse a more profound and value-laden conception of emptiness as "true emptiness." The book of Buddhism, so to speak, proclaims one sort of insight on the cover, but the insight one gains from reading it is not as advertised.

I find two types of evidence for this reading. First, if we look carefully at Zhu's first set of remarks on true emptiness, we see that he dismisses it in part by noting that the Buddhists' more robust sense of emptiness—presumably one that recognizes our interconnectedness as living creatures—does them little good because "they don't at all concern themselves with heaven, earth, and the four directions, only with understanding a single heartmind" (但是它都不管天地四方，只是理會一箇心).[67] The strong suggestion is that whatever they discover about the ultimate nature of things will be determined by what they find in the tranquil state of their own heartminds, which does little to attune our moral sensibilities to the pattern (*li*) of life generativity that we share with others. The second type of evidence is broader and more thematic. In other criticisms of Buddhist metaphysics, Zhu does not hesitate to distinguish between the Buddhists' abstract doctrines and how they actually see and understand the world in practice. In the introduction to this chapter I mentioned Zhu's claim that the Buddhist practice of "examining the heartmind" (*guan xin* 觀心) treats the heartmind as though it were divided into two, simply by virtue of the fact that examination is an active, agential process but the heartmind under examination is supposed to be a passive object.[68] The truth-value of this claim does not depend on there being a Buddhist authority who declares in favor of heartmind dualism, and indeed we would be hard-pressed to find such an authority. Zhu makes a similar move when he says that Buddhists separate heartmind from *li*, presumably because their methods of discovery reveal only the contents of their own contingent psychology rather than the underlying sources of life generativity. Zhu is, however, careful to say that this difference from Confucians (who link *li* to heartmind) is unintentional (*fei gu yu* 非固欲) and a consequence of

---

[67] *Zhuzi yulei, juan* 126, 3013.
[68] Zhu, "Guanxin shuo." See also John Jorgensen's discussion of this essay in his chapter in this volume.

the different perspectives that they adopt (*jianchu butong* 見處不同).⁶⁹ In short, Zhu thinks that when it comes to Buddhist doctrine, one must take care to distinguish between what views they endorse about the nature of things and what they discover about the nature of things using their own methods of apprehension. If the differences between the two methods are profound, it should come as no surprise the resultant discoveries differ substantially as well.

2.5 Conclusion

What I hope to have shown is that several of Zhu Xi's most powerful arguments against Buddhism are best understood as objections not to Buddhism's explicit doctrines, but rather to the implicit presuppositions of those doctrines and concomitant practices. We have seen that he regards Buddhist aspirations to achieve enlightenment and salvation through non-attachment as contravening what should be our more basic commitments to being good and ethical people, not because he thinks that Buddhists reject other-directed care and concern in principle, but because non-attachment itself is incompatible with being good. Goodness is a matter of participating in and contributing to human relationships, which requires that we care more about some people than others, privileging their interests over that of others. Ethical norms are also grounded in life generativity and not in ends that transcend life. And special attachments are also the more authentic, natural, and effective way of developing other-directed concern, making other-directed virtues possible within the space of a single lifetime rather than goals that hinge on speculative theories about sustained improvement across many lives. With regard to the Buddhist doctrine of emptiness—one of the chief points of metaphysical contention between Zhu and the Buddhists—Zhu recognizes that Buddhists take the doctrine to be more profound than the mere thesis that all things are illusory or nonexistent. Indeed, he even allows that some Buddhists endorse an interpretation of the doctrine, the implications of which come near to Zhu's own metaphysics, a metaphysics that recognizes the fundamental interconnectedness and unity of things. But he thinks they lack the spiritual resources and the larger philosophical framework necessary to appreciate the unity of things, having embraced meditation to the neglect of reverential attention and having ruled out life production as the basis of

---

⁶⁹ *Zhuzi yulei, juan* 126, 3015–3016.

that unity. Finally, and relatedly, we have seen that Zhu thinks Buddhist methods of mental discipline, in the absence of reverential concern, do not equip Buddhists to be responsive to considerations of the world outside their own contingent heartminds, however much they may believe a Buddhist should respond to such considerations.

These more charitable interpretations of Zhu's critique cast the history of Buddhism and Zhu Xi's Confucianism in a different light. If it were the case that Zhu's criticisms were directed at a poor imitation or strawman version of Buddhism, then the lines of influence between Buddhism and Zhu Xi would arguably be mediated by a fictional notion of Buddhist thought, a construction of convenience that well-served his own agenda but made only superficial contact with Buddhism as a religious and philosophical tradition. This would be consistent with the view that Buddhist thought itself had little genuine influence on what became (after the Song) Confucian orthodoxy. Instead, this chapter shows that Zhu was not engaged merely with a fictional notion of Buddhism. Rather, insofar as he succeeded in distinguishing his position from those actually held and presupposed by Buddhists, his views and the arguments he advanced in support of them were developed in direct response to Buddhist thought. By the same token, a more precise and nuanced understanding of Zhu's criticisms shows that he, for his part, participated in a genuine, shared dialogue with his Buddhist adversaries. And perhaps most importantly, this dialogue took place at multiple levels, probing the connections between doctrines, presuppositions, and day-to-day practices in ways that stand apart from the more conceptual and scholastic disputes we associate with philosophy in medieval Europe and beyond.[70]

---

[70] I am indebted to Stephen Angle, Philip J. Ivanhoe, John Jorgensen, Dan Lusthaus, John Makeham, Bryan Van Norden, and Brook A. Ziporyn for their substantial and enlightening feedback on earlier drafts of this chapter.

CHAPTER 3 | Buddhism and Zhu Xi's Epistemology of Discernment

STEPHEN C. ANGLE

THERE ARE AT least superficial reasons for thinking that Zhu Xi's epistemology[1] is significantly influenced by Chinese Buddhism. For one thing, in his youth Zhu studied with Kaishan Daoqian 開善道謙 (d.u.), a leading disciple of the most influential Chan teacher of the era, Dahui Zonggao 大慧宗杲 (1089–1163).[2] For another, his discussions of epistemology lean heavily on terms like "genuine knowing" (*zhen zhi* 真知) that also figure significantly in Buddhist discussions. As is well-known, subsequent critics of the Daoxue movement,[3] with which Zhu was centrally

---

The meetings and intensive discussions made possible by the "Buddhist Roots of Neo-Confucianism" project have been examples of collaborative scholarship at its best. I have learned a great deal and trust that this essay is much better than it would have been without the sustained input of all participants. I must single out John Makeham for having the inspiration and leadership skills that made it happen. In addition, our work on the "Buddhist Roots" project has overlapped with the period that Justin Tiwald and I co-wrote *Neo-Confucianism: A Philosophical Introduction*, and so everything that I say here is doubly indebted to work with Justin; indeed, much of Section 3.4 on Zhu Xi derives directly from an understanding of Zhu Xi that we worked out together.

[1] Although borrowing the term "epistemology" from the history of Western philosophy, I use it simply to mean "theories related to knowing," where "knowing" is intended very broadly. As we will see, Zhu Xi's theories of knowing (*zhi* 知) emphasize the cultivation of a kind of discernment-in-action rather than the status of cognitive beliefs (as is more common in many strands of the Western tradition).

[2] See, for example, Zhu's "Ji Kaishan Qian Chanshi wen" 祭開善謙禪師文 (Sacrificial Essay for Chan Master Kaishan Qian), in *Zhu Xi ji* 朱熹集 (Collected Works of Zhu Xi) eds. Guo Qi 郭齊 and Yin Bo 尹波 (Chengdu: Sichuan jiaoyu chubanshe, 1996), vol. 9, 5698. I owe this reference, and much that I have learned about Zhu's relations with his contemporary Buddhists, to the published work, unpublished conference presentations, and generosity in correspondence of Ari Borrell. On Zhu's relations with Daoqian and Zonggao, see also John Jorgensen's chapter in this volume.

[3] The breadth and definition of the "Daoxue" (literally, Learning of the Way) movement changes over time. Initially a loose fellowship that was often at odds with the court in the Northern and

associated, regularly accused it of being strongly colored by Buddhism. Finally, modern scholars have also drawn similar connections, whether of a general nature or more focused, on Zhu Xi and epistemology.[4]

This chapter explores the relation between Buddhism and Zhu's epistemology in three steps. First, I will spell out the four layers of Buddhist–Confucian interactions that collectively shape the ways in which Zhu was influenced by and reacted to Buddhism. Second, I will summarize distinct Chinese Buddhist approaches to the question of "knowing" (*zhi* 知) and look in particular at the roles played in these different approaches by epistemic terms and categories that will eventually be important to Zhu Xi. Finally, I will spell out the rough parameters of what I call Zhu's epistemology of discernment so that we can look for specific ways in which Zhu is appropriating and, more explicitly, rejecting particular aspects of Buddhist epistemic thinking. My conclusion is that despite the many layers of Buddhist influence on both Daoxue in general and Zhu Xi in particular, Zhu correctly understood his epistemology to be a rejection of Dahui's radical Chan approach. More generally, Zhu Xi's epistemology does not co-opt the Buddhist structure seen, for example, in the Buddhist Zongmi, but is importantly different, responding to a distinct discourse context, which, while getting some of its underlying shape from the shared discourse, has quite distinct concerns and goals.[5]

Southern Song, by the Yuan and Ming dynasties it was used in official discourse to designate Cheng-Zhu orthodoxy. Many scholars equate one or another meaning of Daoxue with "Neo-Confucianism," though I prefer to reserve this latter term for a broader group, including critics of Daoxue. For discussion, see Stephen C. Angle and Justin Tiwald, *Neo-Confucianism: A Philosophical Introduction* (Oxford: Polity, 2017), chap. 1. See also John Makeham's discussion in the Introduction to this volume.

[4] See Philip J. Ivanhoe, *Ethics in the Confucian Tradition: The Thought of Mengzi and Wang Yangming* (Indianapolis and Cambridge: Hackett, 2002); and Peter N. Gregory, *Tsung-mi and the Sinification of Buddhism* (Honolulu: University of Hawaii Press, 2002).

[5] I thus believe that John Jorgenson overstates what his evidence shows when he concludes, in his chapter in this volume, that "Daoxue, especially that of Zhu Xi, formulated a kind of Confucian 'Northern Chan.'" For a stance that bears some similarities to mine, see Broughton's dissent from the significance of structural parallels between Zongmi and Zhu Xi, in Jeffrey Lyle Broughton, *Zongmi on Chan* (New York: Columbia University Press, 2009), 20. Douglas Berger's recent *Encounters of Mind: Luminosity and Personhood in Indian and Chinese Thought* (Albany: SUNY Press, 2015) emphasizes many continuities between Sinitic Buddhist views of the "luminous mind" and those of Neo-Confucians like Zhu Xi, but he specifically notes a crucial way that Zhu Xi's epistemology differs from the Buddhists: "Neo-Confucian philosophers remain faithful to the roots of their tradition in an important way, for awareness [*zhi* 知] can really only be found in physical bodies and its qualities depend on the specific circumstances of those bodies." See Berger, *Encounters of Mind*, 159.

3.1 Four Layers

As has already been explained in the Introduction to this volume, scholars have long debated the relationship between Sinitic Buddhism and Neo-Confucianism, with positions ranging from those minimizing or even denying significant influence of Buddhism on Neo-Confucianism, to those viewing both Buddhism and Neo-Confucianism as emerging from shared *problematiques*, to those emphasizing the creativity of Buddhism and the appropriation of these frameworks by Neo-Confucianism. The argument of the present chapter is that such generalizations are over-simplified in two different ways. First, as I will argue in the balance of this section, the interactions among various forms of Sinitic Buddhism and various forms of Confucianism and Neo-Confucianism need to be analytically distinguished into (at least) four layers; once we make these distinctions, we can begin to identify the kernels of truth in most of the above generalizations. Second, even with these four layers in mind, it is still not the case that Buddhism ever influences Neo-Confucianism—or even a given Neo-Confucian thinker, such as Zhu Xi—*en bloc*. Rather, we must attend to more specific questions and contexts. I take this latter point to be one of the central contributions of the present volume, the chapters of which argue for somewhat different conclusions with regard to different sets of issues. This is not to say that we are all, in the end, entirely in agreement about the complex relations between Buddhism and Zhu Xi's thought, but there is more agreement than may be obvious at first, because Zhu makes different use of Buddhist terms, models, and arguments in different areas of his philosophizing. I argue here that the resemblances between his epistemic thinking and that of relevant Sinitic Buddhists is more superficial than real, but this conclusion is not meant to apply (at least, without detailed analysis and argument) to other areas.

Let us now take a brief journey through the four layers of Buddhist–Confucian relations. The growth and change of Buddhism in China includes many aspects, from initial efforts at translation and explication, to the maturation of translations and sophisticated scholastic engagement with the translated texts, to the composition of apocryphal sutras, and the eventual emergence of Sinitic schools of Buddhist thought and practice. For present purposes, all of this diversity and change count as a single layer of Buddhist–Confucian interaction. This first layer focuses on what happened within the texts and traditions of Buddhism in China. I have in mind major trends like the emerging centrality of "buddha-nature," the role given to a metaphysical "heartmind," and the attention paid to holism and intersubjectivity. There are of course detailed histories associated with each of these developments, and none of them can be seen simply or primarily as the influence of Confucianism on Buddhism; among other things, it is often other aspects of Chinese intellectual traditions that are playing more of a formative role.[6] But my focus with this first, capacious layer—an analytical rather than purely chronological concept—is on developments within Buddhism in response to its new environment. For our purposes, the main significance of this layer is that these developments within Buddhism set the stage for more fluid engagement between the Sinified strands of Buddhism and native Chinese traditions.

The second layer is the gradual articulation of a shared Confucian–Buddhist–Daoist intellectual discourse in the Tang dynasty. What I mean is that a range of key terms, phrases, and texts become common property of Tang dynasty thinkers with many different formal or informal affiliations. Both monks and lay Buddhists contribute to this process, as do literati with varying degrees of identification with the Confucian tradition, not to mention scholars and practitioners explicitly associated with Daoism. A key dimension to the emergence of this shared discourse is the engagement of Buddhists and Daoists with texts like the *Yi jing* 易經 and *Zhongyong* 中庸, and even with still-more-explicitly Confucian texts like *Mengzi* 孟子. It is also fascinating to see the ways in which loaded phrases like "fully explore Pattern and fully realize nature 窮理盡性"—originally from the *Shuo gua* 說掛 commentary to the *Yi jing*—come to be deployed in many different ways.[7] There is some debate over how we should characterize this discourse. Some call it "syncretistic,"[8] but David Tien draws on recent scholarship in religious studies to argue that it is better to speak of repertoires and resources rather than (essentialized) religions that are combined in a syncretism.[9] Uniquely situated individuals

---

[6] For example, Ziporyn convincingly portrays Huayan and Tiantai Buddhism as partly shaped by their engagement with the lengthy Chinese concern with "coherence" in both ironic and non-ironic varieties. See Brook A. Ziporyn, *Beyond Oneness and Difference: Li and Coherence in Chinese Buddhist Thought and Its Antecedents* (Albany: SUNY Press, 2013).

[7] Charles Hartman, *Han Yu and the T'ang Search for Unity* (Princeton, NJ: Princeton University Press, 1986), 192.

[8] T. H. Barrett, *Li Ao: Buddhist, Taoist, Or Neo-Confucian?* (Oxford: Oxford University Press, 1992), 136–137.

[9] David W. Tien, "Discursive Resources and Collapsing Polarities: The Religious Thought of Tang Dynasty Scholar-Officials" (PhD diss., University of Michigan, 2009). Tien's sources include Robert Hymes, *Way and Byway: Taoism, Local Religion, and Models of Divinity in Sung and Modern China* (Berkeley: University of California Press, 2002); Ann Swidler, *Talk of Love: How Culture Matters* (Chicago, IL: University of Chicago Press, 2001); and Robert F. Campany, "On the Very Idea of Religions (in the Modern West and in Early Medieval China)," *History of Religions* 42, no. 4 (2003): 287–319.

build and wield their own repertoires from shared resources. Seunghak Koh offers a window on the process, analyzing the ways that lay Buddhist Li Tongxuan 李通玄 (635–730) shaped the Huayan tradition in the direction of taking seriously native texts.[10] Barrett's study of Li Ao 李翱 (772–841) is another nice illustration of this process, this time from a more Confucian perspective. Barrett emphasizes Li's situatedness and need to communicate with particular audiences, writing that for the decade and a half prior to composing his most famous work, Li was "dominated by a search for patronage in a dangerous world amongst men whose intellectual interests were colored much more by Buddhism and Daoism than by a concern for the type of Confucianism espoused by Li himself."[11] At the same time, Li also hoped to combat some features of what I am calling the "shared discourse," by reversing the existing polysemy and establishing true (original, supposedly) meanings.[12]

The dynamic shaping of a shared discourse does not end with the Tang; consider, for example, the commentaries on the *Zhongyong* by Song dynasty Tiantai monk Gushan Zhiyuan 孤山智圓 (976–1022) and the Chan monk Mingjiao Qisong 明教契嵩 (1007–1072).[13] But as we turn to the Northern Song, a distinctive third layer needs to be added to the picture: namely, the explicit engagement with Buddhism by early advocates of Daoxue, especially the Cheng brothers and their students. This layer of Buddhist–Confucian encounter would not have been possible without the prior two layers. When we observe that early Daoxue figures both appropriate key ideas, terms, and interpretations from Buddhism and yet simultaneously criticize Buddhism, I propose that we see this as early Daoxue Confucianism, itself having been shaped by layers one and two, now simultaneously (in layer three) engaging in self-conscious reflection on the varying commitments, both theoretical and practical, of diverse approaches to Confucianism and Buddhism. The results of these reflections are themselves varied. We need to keep clearly in mind that neither "Confucianism" (or "Daoxue Confucianism") nor "Buddhism"

---

[10] Sunghak Koh, "Li Tongxuan's (635–730) Thought and His Place in the Huayan Tradition of Chinese Buddhism" (PhD diss., UCLA, 2011).
[11] Barrett, *Li Ao*, 82.
[12] Barrett, *Li Ao*, 136.
[13] For the important role of Zhiyuan, see the Introduction to this volume, as well as the references cited therein. For Qisong, in addition to the sources cited in the Introduction, see also Shiling Xiang, "Between Mind and Trace—A Research into the Theories on Xin 心 (Mind) of Early Song Confucianism and Buddhism," *Frontiers of Philosophy in China* 6 (2011): 173–192; Elizabeth Morrison, *Power of Patriarchs: Qisong and Lineage in Chinese Buddhism* (Boston, MA: Brill, 2010).

represent single, well-defined bodies of theory. Depending on the topic and on whether the focus is on Buddhist practice, scripture, or treatise, a given Daoxue thinker might criticize, endorse, or silently (and often unconsciously, thanks to the pre-existing shared discourse) adopt a Buddhist position.

Layer three is multifaceted, but of particular importance for our purposes are two strands: the ambiguous role of Cheng Yi 程頤 (1033–1107)—one of the main founders of Daoxue—and the more unambiguously positive rapprochement with Buddhism in Cheng's second generation students Yang Shi 楊時 (1053–1135) and Zhang Jiucheng 張九成 (1092–1159). Looking first at Cheng Yi, one key issue concerns the degree to which knowing can be an exclusively internal process. Cheng Yi was explicit that there is a difference between Confucian and Buddhist views. For example, he said that Confucian "sages base themselves on the cosmos, while the Buddhists base themselves on the heartmind" (聖人本天，釋氏本心).[14] But just how external or objective does knowing have to be? In the terms popular at the time, must it involve "sensory knowing" (*wenjian zhi zhi* 聞見之知), or can it be entirely "virtuous-nature knowing" (*dexing zhi zhi* 德性之知)?[15] Cheng Yi famously emphasized the role in human moral development of the "investigation of things" (*gewu* 格物). In one passage, the examples of *gewu* that he lists—reflecting on book learning, handling things and affairs, and so on—all sound like external matters that would have been categorized as sensory knowing. That is, the activity that Cheng is calling for would seem to rely on a discrimination between external object and a knowing, reflecting subject.

And yet if we look further at what Cheng Yi and his brother Cheng Hao 程顥 (1032–1085) say, we will see that things are not so straightforward, in two distinct ways.[16] First, the Chengs sometimes assert that one must investigate multiple instances of Pattern (*li* 理), and sometimes say that the Pattern of one single thing or event will suffice.[17] Second and even more

---

[14] Cheng Hao 程顥 and Cheng Yi, *Henan Cheng shi yishu* 河南程氏遺書 (The Extant Works of the Chengs of Henan). I cite this text as follows: "YS" plus the *juan* number/page number from Cheng Hao and Cheng Yi, *Er Cheng ji* 二程集 (Collected Works of the Cheng Brothers) (Beijing: Zhonghua shuju, 1981), YS 21b/274.
[15] For more context of this debate, see Angle and Tiwald, *Neo-Confucianism*, chap. 6.
[16] I draw here on the insightful analysis of Ari Borrell, "*Ko-Wu* or *Kung-an*? Practice, Realization, and Teaching in the Thought of Chang Chiu-Ch'eng," in *Buddhism in the Sung*, eds. Peter N. Gregory and Daniel A. Getz Jr. (Honolulu: University of Hawaii Press, 1999), 62–108.
[17] Here are two contrasting statements by Cheng Yi: "Even Yan Hui would not have been able to investigate only a single thing and thoroughly grasp the myriad Patterns. One must investigate one item today and another tomorrow. When one has practiced this extensively, there will naturally occur a thorough understanding like a sudden release" (若只格一物便通眾理，雖顏子亦不敢如此道。須是今日格一件，明日又格一件，積習既多，然後脫然自有貫通處。). YS 18/189;

consequentially, it is ambiguous whether the investigation of things is primarily focused on "things" that are external to or internal to the self. At one point, one of the Chengs[18] is asked, "Does the investigation of things refer to external things or to distinct things in the nature?" He replies:

> It makes no difference. Whatever is before the eye is a thing, and all things have Pattern. For example, that by which fire is hot, that by which water is cold, and even including the relations between ruler and minister or between father and son: all are Pattern.
>
> 問：「格物是外物，是性分中物？」曰：「不拘。凡眼前無非是物，物物皆有理。如火之所以熱，水之所以寒，至於君臣父子間皆是理。」[19]

Although the examples here look like external things or affairs, we now see that the Chengs allow for a very different kind of inward-oriented practice, either focused on the one single Pattern that is our nature, or even focused on distinct things and Patterns within the nature, as suggested by this last passage.[20]

If the Chengs are ambiguous about whether external, sensory knowing must be part of the investigation of things, several of their most influential followers are not. For Yang Shi and Zhang Jiucheng, the only kind of knowing that really matters is strictly internal. Yang particularly emphasized the role of "quiet sitting" in helping one to "embody with the heartmind [the state] before the feelings . . . are aroused; then the

---

translation from Borrell, "Ko-Wu," 66, modified; and "To investigate things in order to exhaustively attain Pattern does not mean that it is necessary to investigate all things in the world. One has only to fully investigate the Pattern in one thing or one event, and the Pattern in other things and events can be then be inferred. . . . Pattern can be exhaustively attained [in this way] because all things share the same Pattern" (格物窮理，非是要盡窮天下之物，但於一事上窮盡，其他可以類推。. . . 所以能窮者，只為萬物皆是一理。). YS 15/156; trans. from Borrell, "Ko-Wu," 67, modified.

[18] In the Cheng brothers' recorded sayings, some passages or whole chapters are identified with one or another brother, but in other sections, which brother is the speaker is left unclear.

[19] YS 2A/247; translation from A. C. Graham, *Two Chinese Philosophers* (La Salle: Open Court, 1992), 75, slightly modified.

[20] To forestall the possibility that readers will take the inner-oriented kind of investigation of things to be solely associated with Cheng Hao, here is a passage unambiguously identified with Cheng Yi: "To learn them from what is outside, and grasp them within, is called 'understanding.' To grasp them from what is within, and connect them with outside things, is called 'sincerity.' Sincerity and understanding are one" (自其外者學之，而得於內者，謂之明。自其內者得之，而兼於外者，謂之誠。誠與明一也。). YS 25/317; translation from Graham, *Two Chinese Philosophers*, 75, slightly modified.

meaning of equilibrium will appear of itself."[21] Zhang Jiucheng, who was Yang's student and also a close correspondent and political ally of Dahui (the leading Chan Buddhist teacher of the era), adjusted Yang's teachings by removing the emphasis on "quiet sitting," but the internal focus of knowing is equally explicit.[22] For Zhang, the key is to be ever vigilant and watchful over one's "unseen and unheard" inner nature; he repeatedly uses the classical phrase "cautious and apprehensive" to express this idea. For example:

> If a gentleman wishes to seek the essence of the *Zhongyong*, he must get the taste of it through being cautious over what is unseen and apprehensive over what is unheard. This is the basis for knowing equilibrium. If one cannot hold to this method . . . it is as if one were to eat and drink all day yet never know the taste. To know the taste of it you will have to become thoroughly immersed and drenched in what is unseen and unheard.
>
> 君子欲求中庸要，當於戒慎不睹恐懼不聞中。得味則識中之本矣。若夫不能守此法...是猶終日飲食而不知味也。味乎當優游涌游於不睹不聞時可也。[23]

Elsewhere he says that the important types of knowing all come down to "being cautious over what is unseen and apprehensive over what is unheard. . . . If one does not practice this, it will be like duckweed adrift on the water, drifting with the wind to the north or south; where will one anchor oneself?" (戒慎不睹恐懼不聞。...學者不於此入，則泛然如萍之在水，逢風南北，有何所寄泊乎。).[24] Junghwan Lee nicely sums up Zhang's exclusive focus on inner "nature knowing": "Within Zhang's framework, neither moral judgments nor practical knowledge belong to the realm of ordinary human knowledge, but must arise as the spontaneous manifestation of one's nature."[25] Zhang was well aware of certain similarities between his views and those of his contemporary Buddhists (like Dahui), writing at one point that "Buddhists are suspiciously near

---

[21] Quoted in Borrell, "*Ko-Wu*," 68.
[22] Borrell suggests a parallel to Dahui's resistance to silent illumination Chan. See Borrell, "*Ko-Wu*," 7.
[23] Zhang, *Zhongyong shuo* 中庸說 (Explaining the *Zhongyong*), *Sibu congkan* 四部叢刊 edition, 1:6b–7a. Translation from Borrell, "*Ko-Wu*," 70, modified.
[24] Zhang, *Zhongyong shuo* 3:11a–b. Translation based on Junghwan Lee, "A Groundwork for Normative Unity: Zhu Xi's Reformulation of the 'Learning of the Way' Tradition" (PhD diss., Harvard University, 2008), 105, modified.
[25] Lee, "A Groundwork for Normative Unity," 104.

to [getting things right]" (释氏疑近之矣). However, this insight ends up leading the Buddhists astray because they take the wrong view about what constitutes the inner nature, such that they "lack the great functions to flourish" (無敷榮之大用).[26] By this, he means that Buddhists take the moral vitality of the inner nature to be a delusion, and therefore suppress its inherent tendency to be manifest through moral action.[27] In short, layer three is a complex and contested mix of positions, as Daoxue thinkers work to make explicit the relation of their teachings to what they understand as Buddhism.

Layer four, finally, is Zhu Xi's own experience with Buddhism. As I noted at the outset, he studied with the Chan monk Daoqian and corresponded with Daoqian's teacher Dahui. Through these connections Zhu had at least indirect access, and often direct access, to key Buddhist texts and ideas. A review of Zhu's language in *Zhuzi yulei* 朱子語類 (Topically Arranged Conversations of Master Zhu) shows many instances of Zhu quoting or simply employing Buddhist terms, similes, or examples.[28] One of the main contentions in this chapter, however, is that it is wrong to think that Zhu's own extended encounter with Buddhism is what makes his thought look so Buddhist—whether superficially so, as I will argue in the case of his epistemic thought, and perhaps more deeply so in other areas. His own experiences play a minor role: The main action is in the previous three layers.[29] Finally, it has been plausibly argued that Zhu Xi was concerned that, as John Jorgenson puts it elsewhere in this volume, "Dahui was undermining support among the educated gentry for Daoxue or more broadly for Confucianism." I agree that this provides Zhu with a motive to criticize Buddhism. I want to insist, however, that we also pay attention to the details of Zhu's philosophical reasoning. As I show in this chapter, an important reason that Zhu is concerned about Buddhist influence is that he has principled, philosophical reasons to believe that key aspects of Buddhist teachings are wrong and indeed pernicious. He is not simply

---

[26] Quoted in Lee, "A Groundwork for Normative Unity," 125–126.
[27] Given that Zhang found Dahui to be an activist-oriented political ally, it is likely that he saw Dahui's version of Buddhism as less prone to this failing than more traditional forms of Buddhism.
[28] For some details, see John Jorgenson's chapter in this volume.
[29] In conversation, Dan Lusthaus dissented from this stance, arguing instead that Zhu's personal commitment to Buddhism ran deeper than I acknowledge, and that once Zhu officially abandoned Buddhism, he suffered from a kind of "convert's guilt" that colors his writing and thought, and largely explains his many criticisms of Buddhism (even while he retains essentially Buddhist views in many areas). I believe that the whole body of evidence is better explained along the lines I offer in the present chapter; and see also Justin Tiwald's chapter in this volume, which unpacks the philosophical motivations behind Zhu's many criticisms of Buddhism.

defending his turf: He takes himself to be defending the moral and psychological health of his compatriots and his society.

Before moving on I should make clear that these layers are not meant always to be chronologically distinct, and sometimes the same rhetorical action may be interpretable in more than one way. Also, the specific way that I have formulated the layers is aimed at understanding Zhu Xi: With another target, the layers would be somewhat different. Still, I claim that the general distinction into four layers is both true to our evidence and analytically useful when it comes to understanding Zhu Xi's epistemology of discernment.

3.2 Chinese Buddhist Approaches to Knowing

The central goal of all forms of Buddhism is soteriological, not epistemic. That is, rather than learning something or knowing something, what we need is to awaken, be enlightened, transform. Nonetheless, Buddhist schools engage in extensive discussion of knowing, understanding, perception, and the like. It is helpful to think about these uses of epistemic language as falling into three types: the problematic, the useful, and the genuine. I will begin by sketching these three categories before looking in more depth at three examples of Chinese Buddhist epistemology in which we can see these various ideas of knowing in context.

Regular, empirical, conceptually articulated perceiving is often seen as a problem. To rely on it is to assume a mistaken view of our reality that must be overcome for enlightenment to be possible. For example, the hugely influential *Treatise on Giving Rise to Faith in the Great Vehicle* (*Dasheng qixin lun* 大乘起信論) reads as follows:

> When cultivating calming, one resides in a quiet place, sits erect and sets one's mind straight without dwelling on the breath ... and does not dwell on visual or auditory perceptions (*juezhi* 覺知). One removes all concepts in the thought-moment they arise.
>
> 若修止者，住於靜處端坐正意，不依氣息 ... 乃至不依見聞覺知。一切諸想隨念皆除。[30]

---

[30] T32.1666, 582a16-19. The translations from the *Dasheng qixin lun* in this chapter are drawn from the pre-copyedited manuscript of the forthcoming annotated translation by John Jorgensen, Dan Lusthaus, John Makeham, and Mark Strange, *Treatise on Giving Rise to Faith in the Great Vehicle* (New York: Oxford University Press).

Second, we also see the view that conceptually articulated knowing is a useful part of the process of awakening. For Indian and early Chinese Yogācāra philosophers, in particular, sophisticated logical and epistemic theories were seen as instrumental to ultimate enlightenment.[31] The idea that various kinds of knowing or understanding can be useful—can serve as *upāya*, expedient means—is quite common. For example, the *Dasheng qixin lun* makes the point that knowing one's capacity for enlightenment is like knowing the capacity of wood to burn: "If there is no-one who knows this, then people will not resort to the necessary means [to ignite the wood], and it is impossible that the wood will be able burn by itself" (若無人知，不假方便能自燒木，無有是處。).[32]

Finally, many theorists use one or more terms to express ideas of genuine, unproblematic knowing. In the *Dasheng qixin lun* this is sometimes indicated simply with *zhi* 知, as in "which only buddhas can know" (唯如來能知).[33] We also find special terms used to mark genuine knowing, such as "truly know" (*shizhi* 實知) in the *Dasheng qixin lun* and "genuine knowing" (*zhenzhi* 真知) in other texts.[34] For example, in the *Platform Sutra* we are told that when there are "no objects that one knows [conceptually, as being distinct from one another], that is called 'genuine knowing'" (無一物可知，是名真知).[35] The use of "genuine knowing" in this regard is a nice example of the first layer discussed above, since this term comes from the Daoist classic *Zhuangzi* 莊子.[36] It will also be relevant to our later discussion of Zhu Xi to keep in mind that the term "*jue* 覺" is often used by Chinese Buddhists in the sense of "awakened," and thus as a synonym for "enlightened" (*wu* 悟), as when the *Dasheng qixin lun* asserts that we are all "inherently awake" (*benjue* 本覺).[37] "*Jue*" is also frequently used to mean "sense" or "perceive," and in these cases it is not "genuine" but merely useful or even problematic.

With these three ways of thinking about "knowing" in mind, let us turn now to more detailed examination of their uses in specific contexts. The *Buddha-nature Treatise* (*Foxing lun* 佛性論) is an interesting example of

---

[31] Lin Chen-kuo, "Truth and Method in the Saṃdhinirmocana Sūtra," *Journal of Chinese Philosophy* 37, no. 2 (2010): 261–275.
[32] T32.1666, 578c5-6.
[33] T32.1666, 578c3.
[34] T32.1666, 579b13-14. "Why? It means that this is because they know that, in accordance with what is real, all sentient beings, and they themselves, are true suchness, uniform and without differences" (此以何義？謂如實知一切眾生及與己身真如平等無別異故。).
[35] T48.2008, 356b23.
[36] See *Zhuangzi* 6.
[37] T32.1666, 576b1a24-15.

relying on the idea of *upāya* or expedient means, according to which many teachings can be seen as not wholly or absolutely true, but soteriologically useful.[38] As Sallie King stresses, the *Buddha-nature Treatise* opens with the words, "Why did the Buddha speak of buddha-nature?" (佛何因緣說於佛性).[39] Employing semantic ascent allows the text's author to bracket questions of the ontology of buddha-nature and to focus instead on the positive effects that the idea can have on us. And when the author turns to a more careful consideration of what buddha-nature "is," it turns out to be more accurately described as something we "do": a potential all people have that can be realized only via soteriological action. King writes that the reality of our buddha-nature "is known by its functions: purification of the [deluded] nature, liberation, and the cultivation of all virtues."[40] She expresses a similar idea thus:

> The identity between person and Buddha is constituted by their shared Buddha nature; this identity serves to encourage practice by virtue of its optimism. The difference between person and Buddha also is constituted by Buddha nature—the degree to which each *makes real* in practice his or her own Buddha nature. . . . You are Buddha, but you are not Buddha unless you practice.[41]

The text makes clear that buddha-nature neither "exists" (*you* 有) nor "nonexists" (*wu* 無). King argues, therefore, that when the text says that buddha-nature most assuredly inherently exists (*ben you* 本有), the author is seeking a way of signaling the conceptual insufficiency of both existence and nonexistence to capture the status of buddha-nature.[42] Unlike trees or stones, buddha-nature "is not a thing in the world. Rather, as a term, it serves to affirm the potential of all sentient being to realize Buddhahood."[43]

We might wonder what our basis is for such an affirmation—a kind of knowing—of buddha-nature. Where does this optimism come from? And what, after all, does it mean to know and realize buddhahood? By analyzing the text's use of positive terms like *nirvāna* and *dharmakāya*

---

[38] There is considerable scholarly debate over how central the *Buddha-nature Treatise* is to the discourse over buddha-nature in China. I use the text here as a way of introducing one of the distinctive Buddhist approaches to knowing, which I think it does quite nicely, whether or not this formulation of that view was historically influential.
[39] T31.1610, 787a8; Sallie B. King, *Buddha Nature* (Albany: SUNY Press, 1991), 29, modified.
[40] King, *Buddha Nature*, 48.
[41] King, *Buddha Nature*, 82.
[42] King translates *ben you* as "aboriginally exists"; I have modified this to "inherently exists."
[43] King, *Buddha Nature*, 34.

(Dharma-body and truth-body, which refer here to the fruition of buddha-nature),[44] King argues that the text's stance is "pragmatic": We know that buddha-nature "inherently exists" and thus we should be optimistic about our prospects for spiritual progress *because it works*. The text says:

> If the *dharmakāya* were nonexistent, then correct practices should be in vain. Taking right views as the foremost practice, and including in addition such good dharmas as the precepts, concentration, and wisdom, the correct practices that one cultivates are not empty or fruitless. Because these correct practices do yield fruit, we know (*zhi*) that *dharmakāya* is not nonexistent.
>
> 若法身無者。則諸正行皆應空失。以正見為先行。攝戒定慧等善法故。所修正行不空無果。由此正行能得果故。故知法身非無。[45]

The pragmatic approach is connected to the idea that one's actual, conditioned "faithful joy" in engaging in Buddhist practice is a crucial cause of one's attaining buddhahood; as King says, one "intentionally engag[es] in specific acts chosen because they promise to lead one to the desired goal, acts tested by tradition and found to be effective to that end."[46] This does not mean that we have to accept that buddha-nature is only a "metaphor for the validity of the Buddha Way"; as King also emphasizes, buddha-nature is simultaneously seen as the "true cause nature" that is "completed" by practice.[47] Still, the text resists reifying this "nature" in an ontological fashion. King convincingly shows that we are given neither a monism nor a dualism, but a "nondualism," which denies that things are separate and also refuses to reduce them to any single principle. In the end, then, we know buddha-nature through implementing the practice that Buddhist tradition has "promised" will be effective.

Influential Chan (and Huayan) master Guifeng Zongmi 圭峰宗密 (780–841) also avoids reifying the nature as a distinct, self-existing entity and, of course, he too accepts the idea that Buddhist teachings make important use of the idea of *upāya*. Zongmi, however, differs from the *Buddha-nature Treatise* in endeavoring to provide a more substantive account of fundamental knowing. In Zongmi's day there was a wide range of approaches to both Buddhist doctrine and Buddhist practice.

---

[44] King, *Buddha Nature*, 61.
[45] T31.1610, 804a19-21; King, *Buddha Nature*, 66, modified.
[46] King, *Buddha Nature*, 127.
[47] King, *Buddha Nature*, 67 and 127.

Zongmi saw himself as both developing the Huayan doctrinal tradition and intervening in Chan theory and practice. He was worried about some of the more radical developments within Chan, which, it seemed to him, erased the distinction between the ground of the nature and its myriad manifestations. As a result, according to such views, there is only one kind of functioning; "greed, anger, and folly, the performance of good and bad actions and the experiencing of their pleasurable and painful consequences, are all, in their entirety, buddha-nature."[48] (We will look at an example of such "radical" Chan approaches to knowing a little later.) To the contrary, Zongmi holds that while the intrinsic reality and the manifest functioning (*ti* 體 and *yong* 用)[49] of buddha-nature are "different aspects of the same reality, they are nevertheless different," and this difference "is important, because the essence [*ti*] . . . is the basis on which the experience of enlightenment is to be validated."[50] In keeping with the *tathāgatagarbha* tradition, Zongmi believes that the nature itself can be characterized as having various positive qualities (such as "permanence," "steadfastness," "bliss," and "purity");[51] apprehending this nature is thus crucial for genuine enlightenment, whereas the radicals risk mistaking their arbitrary, conditioned feelings for actual enlightenment.

What, then, can we say about the nature and on what basis can we ascribe to it positive qualities? The key idea is *zhi* 知, a term I have generally translated as "know" or "understand," but which in this context I will follow Gregory in translating as "awareness."[52] Zongmi writes that the most profound teaching:

> . . . propounds that all sentient beings without exception have the empty, tranquil, true mind. From time without beginning it is the intrinsically pure, effulgent, unobscured, clear, and bright ever-present awareness. It abides forever and will never perish, on into the infinite future. It is termed the buddha-nature; it is also termed *tathāgatagarbha* and mind ground (*xindi*).

---

[48] Quoted in Gregory, *Tsung-mi*, 237, modified.
[49] I follow John Makeham in taking *ti* 體 here to be short for *benti* 本體, and translate it as "intrinsic reality." For extensive discussion of the Buddhist background to the important pair of concepts *ti* and *yong*, see Brook A. Ziporyn's and Makeham's chapters in this volume.
[50] Gregory, *Tsung-mi*, 237.
[51] Gregory, *Tsung-mi*, 219–220.
[52] In addition to Gregory's astute analysis, I have also benefitted from Araki Kengo 荒木見悟, *Fojiao yu Rujiao* 佛教與儒教 (Buddhism and Confucianism), trans. Liao Zhaoheng 廖肇亨 (Taipei: Lianjing chubanshe, 2008), especially section 2.3, which also contains considerable discussion of the earlier sources for Zongmi's idea of awareness in the Heze Chan tradition.

... 此教說一切眾生皆有空寂真心。無始本來性自清淨明明不昧了了常知。盡未來際常住不滅。名為佛性。亦名如來藏。亦名心地。[53]

This "awareness" is not any specific wisdom, nor one's awareness or knowledge of anything in particular, but rather the "underlying ground of consciousness that is always present in all sentient life . . . [,] the noetic ground of both delusion and enlightenment."[54] In keeping with the general positive orientation of Chinese Buddhism, awareness is not merely empty but also suffused with excellences: pure, unobscured, ever-present, and so on. Not only that, but nature-as-awareness can also be seen as the ground or source (though not physical cause) of all things. Phenomenal appearances are interdependent, conditioned by all other appearances, but underlying all these appearances is awareness itself.[55] There is actually an additional level of complexity: Zongmi says that the intrinsic reality (*ti*) of the true mind has, in turn, both intrinsic reality (tranquility) and function (awareness). Awareness, though, is simultaneously the intrinsic reality that corresponds to the "functioning-in-accord-with-conditions" that is our actual psycho-physical functioning.[56] So awareness is to be contrasted with the sudden experience of enlightenment (which Zongmi calls "*zhi* 智," among other things), since awareness, as intrinsic reality, is always present.[57] Zongmi therefore speaks of this intrinsic reality as "inherently awakened genuine knowing" (本覺真知) in some places.[58] The sudden experience of enlightenment, in contrast, is an explicit experience of this awareness.

This requires some unpacking. The excellent, ever-present awareness—that is, the *tathāgatagarbha* or buddha-nature—is typically hidden, because as actually instantiated in humans, "it appears covered over by their defilements."[59] "Defilement" refers to all our delusions, biases, and attachments; once we are rid of them then we see that buddha-nature was here with us all along. Note that both awareness and delusion are processes rather than things: We should not imagine one thing covered

---

[53] Quoted in Gregory, *Tsung-mi*, 217; *Chanyuan zhuquan ji duxu* 禪源諸詮集都序 (Preface to the Collected Writings on the Chan Source), T48.2015, 404b27-c3.
[54] Gregory, *Tsung-mi*, 218.
[55] Gregory, *Tsung-mi*, 242.
[56] Gregory, *Tsung-mi*, 239–240. This structure bears a close resemblance to the *Dasheng qixin lun*'s model of suchness adapting to phenomenal conditions; see John Makeham's chapter in this volume.
[57] Araki, *Fojiao yu rujiao*, 135.
[58] Araki, *Fojiao yu rujiao*, 134 and 140.
[59] Gregory, *Tsung-mi*, 309.

up by another, but rather, one subtle process that is obscured by another, more "noisy" one. Zongmi therefore believes that it is possible to perceive the buddha-nature directly when one is in a condition of "no thought" (*wu nian* 無念), which means not a mindless somnambulism but rather a moment of non-conceptual, holistic experience. Here it is important to remember the two-tiered structure of "intrinsic reality"–"manifest function" pairs that I introduced in the previous paragraph. The deepest intrinsic reality, referred to above as tranquility, is an eternal state (not a process). Its functioning is awareness. But awareness itself can be thought of as the intrinsic reality corresponding to our everyday, conditioned functioning. The frequently employed metaphor of wetness (intrinsic reality) and waves (function) can help us here. Relative to our everyday experience (i.e., waves), awareness is an eternal state (i.e., wetness itself). But the sudden enlightenment experience is an experience of awareness as the function corresponding to tranquility itself: Directly perceiving buddha-nature is like experiencing wetness.

According to Zongmi, the sudden insight or enlightenment that one gains through such perception then further ramifies throughout one's psychology in the subsequent process of cultivation. In this way we can understand how Zongmi takes the distinction between nature/intrinsic reality/awareness, on the one hand, and actual feelings, on the other, to enable him to speak of enlightenment experiences being validated or grounded, unlike the radical Chanists who conflate nature and feelings. Zongmi's idea is that the initial ("sudden") enlightenment experience allows one to see the truth and thus to guide subsequent ("gradual") practice, which is also needed because sudden insight does not automatically transform one's dispositions and actualized feelings.[60]

Zongmi clearly puts forward a view on which awareness—a very particular kind of knowing that at least on the surface has very little in common with everyday, empirical knowing—is to be sought and is critically important to our ultimate awakening. Awareness is not a mere means, but is instead constitutive of buddha-nature and buddhahood. As Araki emphasizes, many were critical of Zongmi's view, to the extent that an eleventh-century monk parodied Zongmi's view by saying,

---

[60] A central question for many Chinese Buddhists was whether enlightenment was a "sudden" or "gradual" affair; Zongmi's influential view was that it required sudden insight followed by gradual—quite traditional—cultivation thereafter. One explanation for this was that the sudden enlightenment enabled one to stop creating new karmic seeds in the *ālayavijñāna*, but one still needed gradually to remove all the seeds that were already present at the moment of enlightenment. Gregory, *Tsung-mi*, 193–195.

"the single word '*zhi* 知' is the source of myriad misfortunes."[61] One example of this criticism comes from the Tiantai thinker Siming Zhili 四明知禮 (960–1028), who charged that Zongmi's "awareness" is somehow supposed to indicate "pure suchness" and has no connection to any action.[62] Zhu Xi's contemporary Dahui also expresses some skepticism about Zongmi's view of knowing, although defenders of Zongmi will be quick to point out that there are important ways in which these critics have misunderstood him.[63] Be this as it may, neither the *Buddha-nature Treatise*'s approach nor Zongmi's proved to be most influential. Instead, it is precisely the "radical Chan" view criticized by Zongmi that won the day, a version of which we can see in Dahui. I therefore turn now to our final case study of Chinese Buddhist epistemology, the influential teaching of Mazu Daoyi 馬祖道一 (709–788) and Hongzhou 洪州 Chan.

Mazu Daoyi is a good example of Chan Buddhism's developing in precisely the direction criticized by Zongmi. There is nothing special that one needs to come to perceive or know; Mazu announces, "If you want to know the Way directly, then the ordinary mind is the Way. . . . Now all these are just the Way: walking, abiding, sitting, lying, responding to situations, and dealing with things (若欲直會其道，平常心是道。. . . 只如今行住坐臥，應機接物，盡是道。)."[64] Recall that the *Dasheng qixin lun* speaks of a state in which one ceases to dwell on (empirical, conceptually articulated) perception. In apparent contrast, Mazu says:

> Now seeing, hearing, listening, and sensing are fundamentally your inherent nature, which is also called inherent heartmind. It is not that there is a buddha[-nature] other than this heartmind. This heartmind always already exists and exists right now, without depending on intentional creation and action; it is always already pure and is pure right now, without waiting for cleaning and wiping.
>
> 今見聞覺知，元是汝本性，亦名本心。更不離此心別有佛，此心本有今有，不假造作；本淨今淨，不待瑩拭。[65]

---

[61] Araki, *Fojiao yu Rujiao*, 152.
[62] Araki, *Fojiao yu Rujiao*, 151.
[63] Araki, *Fojiao yu Rujiao*, 155–158.
[64] Mazu Daoyi, "Appendix: Annotated Translation of Mazu Daoyi's Discourses," translated in Jinhua Jia, *The Hongzhou School of Chan Buddhism in Eighth- Through Tenth-Century China* (Albany: SUNY Press, 2006), 123.
[65] Mazu, "Annotated Translation," 122; translation modified.

Mazu does not use the term "inherently awakened" (*benjue* 本覺), but he is clearly in this tradition. The crucial thing for him is simply recognizing one's enlightenment: Since all along we have been awakened, there is nothing new that we need to learn or see in order to leave delusion behind.

A common Chan trope can help us understand what is going on.[66] Our eyes can see, but they cannot see themselves. To see, one "just does it": One does not first examine one's eyes and figure out how to see. Indeed, such an examination is impossible. In the same way, enlightenment has been with us all along, inherent to our nature/heartmind, built in to the way we are. So we cannot get outside of ourselves and come to "know" what we are; all we can do is be ourselves. A similar train of thought leads Mazu to reject cultivation of the Way:

> "The Way does not belong to cultivation. If you speak of any attainment through cultivation, whatever is accomplished through cultivation will again decay, just the same as the Śrāvaka (Hearer).[67] If you speak of no-cultivation, then you will be the same as an ordinary man."
>
> [Someone] asked, "What kind of knowledge should one have in order to understand the Way?"
>
> The Master replied, "Self-nature is always already perfectly complete. So long as one is not hindered either by good or evil things, he is called a man who cultivates the Way. Grasping good and rejecting evil, contemplating emptiness and entering concentration—all these belong to intentional creation and action."

> 「道不屬修，即言修得，修成還壞，即同聲聞。若言不修，即同凡夫。」云：「作何見解，即得達道？」師云：「自性本來具足，但於善惡事上不滯，喚作修道人，取善捨惡，觀空入定，即屬造作。」[68]

Having rejected traditional modes of cultivation, Mazu helps to develop the practice of "encounter dialogue" as a means to inspire students to change their perspective and realize that they are already enlightened.[69]

In one way, Mazu and Zongmi are not so different: both accept the idea of inherent awakening, as explicated in the *Dasheng qixin lun*. As the

---

[66] Thanks to Brook A. Ziporyn for pointing out this connection.
[67] "Śrāvaka" refers to disciples of Buddha who, according to tradition, "heard" his teachings and thus were able to attain enlightenment for themselves; most Chinese Buddhists, like Mahāyāna Buddhists generally, view this as a lesser attainment, which Mazu here attributes to its reliance on learning something through explicit cultivation.
[68] Mazu, "Annotated Translation," 126.
[69] Jia, *The Hongzhou School*, 79–82.

contemporary scholar Jia Jianhua emphasizes, we should also not exaggerate the iconoclasm of Mazu: He did read and write texts, and he gave sermons that are full of scriptural references.[70] However, whereas Zongmi recognized the traditional three criteria for truth—scriptural precedent, rational defense, and personal realization—Mazu claimed to heed only the third of these, as we have seen. For Mazu, there is no special kind of knowing that one can seek or attain: One's "ordinary mind" is perfect in its original state, and all one has to do is to shift perspectives so that one realizes this. Despite his fairly conventional practice, therefore, Mazu's teachings can easily be seen as opening the door to an iconoclastic or even antinomian practice of precisely the kind that worried Zongmi.

To sum up this section, we have seen three different attitudes toward "knowing": a primarily pragmatic approach (in the *Buddha-nature Treatise*), an approach emphasizing a deep and genuine knowing (albeit seemingly disconnected from everyday knowing, in Zongmi), and an approach that validates everyday perceptual experience (in Mazu). Zhu Xi is undoubtedly aware of much of this; not only did he personally study a version of the radical Mazu approach (with Daoqian), but he was also subsequently critical of radical Chan in terms that at least resonate with Zongmi's views.[71] Nonetheless, as we now turn to Zhu's epistemic views themselves, I will argue that such similarities mask important differences.

3.3 Zhu Xi's Epistemology of Discernment

By the mid-twelfth century when Zhu Xi was coming of age, the mainstream view within Daoxue was that learning was primarily an inward affair aimed at virtuous-nature knowing (though the term "virtuous-nature knowing" was not always used explicitly). Zhu initially shared this view but came to see it as philosophically problematic and rejected the possibility of directly accessing the nature.[72] As a result, he rejected the distinction between sensory knowing and nature knowing. Asked whether there is such a thing as sensory knowing, Zhu is unambiguous:

---

[70] Jia, *The Hongzhou School*, 79.

[71] See the discussion, in Justin Tiwald's chapter in this volume, of Chan conflation of everyday functioning with "nature" near the end of Tiwald's Section 2.5.

[72] For extensive discussion on what is often called Zhu's "New Doctrine of Centrality and Harmony" (中和新說), see Chen Lai 陳來, *Zhuzi zhexue yanjiu* 朱子哲學研究 (Research into Zhu Xi's Philosophy) (Shanghai: Huadong Shifan Daxue chubanshe, 2000), 157–163; Qian Mu 錢穆, *Zhuzi xin xue'an* 朱子新學案 (Master Zhu: New Studies), 3rd ed. (Taipei: Sanmin shuju, 1989), vol. 2, 123–182; and Hoyt Cleveland Tillman, *Confucian Discourse and Chu Hsi's Ascendancy* (Honolulu: University of Hawaii, 1992), 59–64.

There is only one kind of knowing! The only issue is whether it is genuine (*zhen*) or not. This is the only difference at issue. It is definitely not the case that [after we have sensory knowing] we later have another kind of knowing.

知，只是一樣知，但有真不真，爭這些子，不是後來又別有一項知。[73]

Discussing Zhang Zai's 張載 (1020–1077) assertion that we must avoid allowing sensory knowing to "handcuff" our heartminds, Zhu argues:

In order to be able to learn, we must possess senses of seeing and hearing. How can we possibly do without them? We work hard with our senses until we achieve a wide and far-reaching penetration. Ordinarily, when we study something by relying on senses, a single affair leads us only to know a single principle.[74] However, when we reach the stage of a general penetration, all Pattern becomes one.

如今人理會學，須是有見聞，豈能舍此？先是於見聞上做工夫到，然後脫然貫通。蓋尋常見聞，一事只知得一箇道理，若到貫通，便都是一理。[75]

Even though Zhu Xi only mentions Zhang Zai here by name, he was well aware that Cheng Yi had insisted on, if anything, a stronger distinction between these two purported types of knowing; out of respect, Zhu does not criticize Cheng explicitly.[76] He shows no such restraint for those of the Chengs' students who further pursued a single-minded focus on nature knowing, characterizing Zhang Jiucheng's writings as "outwardly Confucian but secretly Buddhist; . . . his purpose is to confuse the world and lull men to sleep so that they enter the Buddhist school and cannot extricate themselves from it even if they want to."[77]

---

[73] Zhu Xi, *Zhuzi yulei* 朱子語類 (Topically Arranged Conversations of Master Zhu), comp. Li Jingde 黎靖德 (fl. 1263), (Beijing: Zhonghua shuju, 1986), *juan* 34, 1255. Translation from Ying-shih Yu, "Morality and Knowledge in Chu Hsi's Philosophical System," in *Chu Hsi and Neo-Confucianism*, ed. Wing-tsit Chan (Honolulu: University of Hawaii Press, 1986), 242, slightly modified.
[74] "Principle" here is *daoli* 道理; in this context, Zhu is referring to a single, codifiable rule or principle. In terms of the distinctions I develop later in the chapter, this is "Type One" knowing.
[75] *Zhuzi yulei, juan* 98, 2519; translation from Yu, "Morality and Knowledge," 242, significantly modified.
[76] Yu, "Morality and Knowledge," 243.
[77] Cited in Borrell, "*Ko-Wu*," 62.

Zhu's picture of knowing—a continuous process, reliant on the senses, which could eventually lead to a kind of breakthrough and consequently to "genuine" knowing—is of course quite consistent with some of what the Chengs said, and indeed bears resemblances to some aspects of other Northern Song Neo-Confucians. Still, Zhu's mature picture has a systematicity and sophistication that is lacking in his forbearers. We can see this most clearly by focusing on the three different types of knowing that Zhu Xi identifies. In so doing, I also bring into the discussion two other important epistemic terms, both with significant roots in Chinese Buddhism: *jue* 覺 (awakening to) and *zhijue* 知覺 (discernment). Because the terminology and details can get confusing, let me begin with a schematic overview of Zhu's understanding of knowing. To be clear, Zhu never makes it explicit that there are three types of knowing; these are analytical categories developed by Justin Tiwald and myself. According to this analysis, however, we can see in Zhu's many discussions three distinct types of knowing:

Type One: One knows a rule to which things should conform.
Type Two: One sees an isolated instance of how things should be and cannot help but follow it.
Type Three: One awakens to the underlying reason or basis why things are as they are, and responds aptly to whatever situation one encounters.

Knowing of any of these types may be sufficient, in a given case, to lead one to act well, but with Types Two or Three, one's apt responses become more automatic and their scope increasingly broad. Fully knowing in the Type-Three sense—which Zhu describes in a variety of ways, as we will see—is a central characteristic of a sage. As I explain below, knowing does not necessarily develop in a Type One → Type Two → Type Three succession; in different ways, both Types One and Two can be useful in the process of developing Type Three.

The most basic and shallow kind of knowing is to know a rule for a given type of circumstance. Knowing that one should be filial to one's parents, or that one should not eat an extra piece of chocolate cake, are possible examples of such rules. Knowing the rule means that one can say it and knows at least generally how to apply it. Zhu Xi calls such rules "the rule to which [a thing or affair] should conform" (其所當然之則). This type of knowing is common but also problematic, because all too often one "knows" a rule in this sense but fails to follow it. In a well-known passage, Zhu talks about the ways in which merely "knowing an affair" to be right or wrong is unreliable; one can know it to be wrong (知此事不是), and yet suddenly start thinking about doing it, or even do it without really being aware (不知不覺) of doing so.[78] To be sure, someone who knows the rule can sometimes get himself or herself to follow it, but Zhu agrees with earlier Daoxue thinkers that this kind of merely conscientious behavior is worrisome.

Type Two is typically expressed as "seeing an instance of how things should be and being unable not to do it" (見其所當然而不容已). This seems not to depend on antecedent understanding of any rules; it is rather an instance of brute clarity, whereby one sees-and-responds to a particular situation. Zhu says:

> People today who have not "seen how things should be and been unable not to do it," just judge what to do based on their own preferences of the moment. [In contrast,] when someone genuinely sees that it is something that "I ought to do," then there will naturally be that which he or she cannot stop doing. For example, a minister must be loyal: so long as one sees this and is not just mouthing the words, then in acting as a minister one cannot avoid being loyal.
>
> 今人未嘗看見「當然而不容已」者，只是就上較量一箇好惡爾。如真見得這底是我合當為，則自有所不可已者矣。如為臣而必忠，非是謾說如此，蓋為臣不可以不忠。[79]

Lacking Type Two knowing, Zhu is saying, there is no objectivity or reliability to one's judgments. Sometimes, however, one sees a situation in such a way that the reaction is automatic, which he calls "genuinely" (*zhen* 真) seeing it. What is happening in such a case? Consider this exchange:

> Someone asked: "How is it that Pattern is 'unable to stop'?"
>
> Master Zhu replied: "Pattern's normativity naturally is unable to stop. Mencius understood this most clearly, and thus said, 'Among babes in arms, there is none that does not know to love its parents. When they grow older, there is none that does not know to revere its elder brothers.' Naturally these are places at which one cannot stop."

---

[78] *Zhuzi yulei*, juan 13, 228; translated in *Learning to Be a Sage*, trans. Daniel K. Gardner (Berkeley: University of California Press, 1990), 184.

[79] *Zhuzi yulei*, juan 18, 414. Thanks to Chi-keung Chan for help in understanding Zhu's point here.

> 或問:「理之不容已者如何?」曰:「理之所當為者,自不容已。孟子最發明此處。如曰:『孩提之童,無不知愛其親;及其長也,無不知敬其兄。』自是有住不得處。」 [80]

"Pattern's normativity is naturally unable to stop": The idea is that there is a deep, structured dynamism to the cosmos that generates all life in unending fashion.[81] Type Two knowing takes place when we are able to get a glimpse of this, but it falls short of Type Three knowing because it does not flow from a broadly inclusive grasp of Pattern's interconnections. Certain situations are ripe for these brief and bounded, but still "genuine," experiences of Pattern; Zhu insists that they are open to anyone, at any level of cultivation. In addition to the few we have already cited, a final passage that often comes up is Mencius' famous claim that anyone, upon suddenly seeing a baby about to fall into a well, would respond with alarm and compassion. I speculate—although Zhu does not make this clear—that the situations in which Type Two knowing happens most readily are those in which distracting, potentially biasing factors are simply not present, or else are temporarily eliminated by emphasizing the immediacy of the knowing, as in the baby–well case.[82] After all, the Pattern is always there to be seen and to motivate response, so what is at issue here is under what circumstances—short of the full, sagely

---

[80] *Zhuzi yulei, juan* 18, 414; Zhu is quoting *Mencius* 7A:15; translation of *Mencius* from *Readings in Classical Chinese Philosophy*, 2nd ed., eds. Philip J. Ivanhoe and Bryan W. Van Norden (Indianapolis: Hackett, 2005), 175.

[81] Here is another passage, also from *Zhuzi yulei, juan* 18, 413–414, in which the connection of "unable to stop" to the whole functioning of the cosmos is made:

> Someone asked: "When you wrote that 'The changes of heaven, earth, ghosts, and spirits; the apt responses of birds, beasts, flowers and trees—none can avoid seeing an instance of how things should be and being unable not to do it,' what did you mean by 'be unable not to do it?'" Zhu replied: "Spring gives life and autumn kills: this is unavoidable. At the acme of *yin*, *yang* is born. Even if behind your back someone tried to interfere, how could it be avoided!"

> 問:「或問云:『天地鬼神之變,鳥獸草木之宜,莫不有以見其所當然而不容已。』所謂『不容已』,是如何?」曰:「春生了便秋殺,他住不得。陰極了,陽便生。如人在背後,只管來相趲,如何住得!」

[82] It is thus important to note the reaction that one cannot help but make in the baby–well case is simply the initial response of alarm and compassion, which—because of the immediacy of the reaction—Mencius says is "not for the sake of being on good terms with the child's parents, and it is not for the sake of winning praise from neighbors and friends." Once one begins to take such factors into account, one may not in the end move to save the baby, or may do it for such further reasons. Thanks to John Makeham for pressing me on this point.

sensitivity that characterizes Type Three—one is able to fluidly see-and-respond.⁸³

There are two strands within Zhu Xi's writings that lead to the conclusion that in addition to "knowing" of Types One and Two, there is also a third, most valuable type. The first revolves around the verb *jue*, which means "awaken to" or "be sensitive to." As we have seen, for Chinese Buddhists *jue* is an important term that often refers to the awakening that the Buddha experienced and which Buddhists seek for all sentient beings. Early Daoxue Confucians like the Cheng brothers use *jue* repeatedly to mean "awaken," both when speaking critically of Buddhist ideas of "awakening," and to refer to a Confucian kind of "awakening." As they note, there is a passage in *Mencius* that speaks of awakening; the Chengs are insistent, therefore, that "awakening" is a legitimate Confucian notion and refers to something different from the Buddhist idea.⁸⁴ Cheng Yi also explains the difference between "knowing" and "awakening" as follows: "Knowing is to know this affair; awakening is to awaken to this Pattern" (知者知此事也。覺者覺此理也。).⁸⁵ Cheng Yi himself does

---

⁸³ As noted at the outset of this section, Zhu does not explicitly distinguish the three levels from one another, and there are occasional moments in which it is not clear which type of knowing Zhu is best interpreted as talking about—or even whether we might need to add a further category. For example, Confucius' famous spiritual autobiography in *Analects* 2.4 says, "At forty, I was not confused" (四十而不惑), while "At fifty, I knew the cosmic decree" (五十知天命). Being "not confused" seems relevant to knowing, and "knowing the cosmic decree" is obviously relevant. But how do these fit into my schema? In Zhu's commentary, he says that being "not confused" means that one understands affairs without hesitation—like the unstoppable way in which bamboo welcomes a sharp knife—but this still is only at the level of "seeing affairs" (*jian shi* 見事) (*Zhuzi yulei, juan* 23, 556). Actually "knowing" the cosmic mandate, on the other hand, is to "see Pattern" (*jian li* 見理). "Knowing the cosmic decree," in other words, is Type Three knowing. What about being "not confused"? In its connection to "affairs" it sounds like Type One, and indeed, Zhu Xi goes on to invoke Cheng Yi's distinction between "knowing this affair" (知此事) and "awakening to this Pattern" (覺此理). But his emphasis on the unstoppable way in which such knowing proceeds resonates strongly with Type Two. I am tempted by Justin Tiwald's suggestion, in conversation, that being "not confused" falls somewhere between Type Two and Type Three: Confucius at this age is beginning to generalize and has a certain degree of confidence because his generalizations are based on those specific moments of Type Two clarity, but he still has not grasped the whole in its entirety. Still, it is hard to be confident. Perhaps the best conclusion is to recognize that as Zhu Xi strives to interpret a vast array of disparate classical statements using the categories of his own philosophical understanding, sometimes the fit is imperfect.

⁸⁴ *Jue* does not feature very significantly in classical Confucian epistemic discourse, but there is *Mencius* 5A.7: "Heaven, in giving birth to the people, directs those who first become wise (*zhi*) to awaken (*jue*) those who will later become wise. 天之生此民也，使先知覺後知，使先覺後覺也" (translation from translation of *Mencius* from *Mengzi: With Selections From Traditional Commentaries*, trans. Bryan Van Norden [Indianapolis: Hackett, 2008], 127). In more than one place, the Chengs make explicit this Confucian pedigree for *jue*; for example, YS 14/142.

⁸⁵ Cheng Hao and Cheng Yi, *Er Cheng cui yan* 二程粹言 (The Pure Words of the Two Chengs), *Er Cheng ji*, A/1180.

not offer more explanation of the difference, but Zhu Xi approvingly invokes the further gloss of one of Cheng Yi's students. According to this explanation, when one knows the respect of a minister or the filiality of a son, then this is "knowing this affair." When one knows *that by which* ministers are respectful or sons filial, however, that is "awakening to this Pattern" (覺此理).[86] In a related context, Zhu himself says that "at first one is simply loyal or filial, and then later one comes to know *that by which* one is filial and *that by which* one is loyal, and one cannot be budged" (初時也只忠孝，後來便知所以孝，所以忠，移動不得).[87] It is an interesting question whether merely "knowing this affair" refers to Type One or to Type Two knowing. On one hand, the use of "this," connecting it to a particular situation, suggests that it is Type Two; on the other hand, the statement that only when one has moved to the "awakening" level is one invulnerable to being "budged" suggests that the contrast is with the unreliable Type One. In either case, "awakening to this Pattern" offers a different and deeper kind of understanding.

Both of the last passages connect awakening to the rather cryptic idea of grasping "that by which [one is filial, loyal, and so on]." Pursuing this second strand of evidence will help us better understand how Type Three knowing works. In what is probably his best-known statement on the meaning of Pattern, Zhu says: "As far as things in the cosmos go, we can be certain that each has a reason by which it is as it is, and a rule to which it should conform. This is what is meant by Pattern" (至於天下之物、則必各有所以然之故、與其所當然之則。所謂理也。).[88] We have already seen that when one knows only the relevant rule, this is mere Type One knowing. As Zhu develops the idea of understanding the "reason by which it is as it is"—which is the same as the "that by which" mentioned above—we will see that it is significantly more important. In a key passage, Zhu explains as follows:

> [Compared with the rule to which it should conform,] the "reason by which it is as it is" takes it up one level. For example, that by which a lord is humane: the lord is the ruler while the people and territory are his concern. He naturally employs humane love. If we think about this relationship without

---

[86] *Zhuzi yulei, juan* 17, 384.
[87] *Zhuzi yulei, juan* 23, 555.
[88] *Daxue huowen* 15a:3, in *Sishu daquan* 四書大全 (Complete Four Books), Japanese edition of 1626 based on Yongle edition of 1415; translation from Gardner, *Learning to Be a Sage*, 90, slightly modified.

humane love, it just does not work. This is not to say that a lord cannot help but use humane love; it's rather that to do so matches with Pattern.

所以然之故，即是更上面一層。如君之所以仁，蓋君是箇主腦，人民土地皆屬它管，它自是用仁愛。試不仁愛看，便行不得。非是說為君了，不得已用仁愛，自是理合如此。[89]

There are bad rulers who are governed by their selfish desires and fail to employ humane love, but Zhu is saying that reflection on the organic, structural relationship between a ruler and his people reveals that the relationship works only when the ruler is motivated by humane love. Zhu adds several more examples in the passage, all of which make the point that no matter whether one is talking about human relations or patterns in nature, it is the affirmation of birth and life that leads to things fitting together in meaningful fashion, each aspect playing its role. When Zhu talks of going up a level, he is saying that one needs to put a given matter into the special context provided by Pattern. When one learns to do that—to view each individual thing as fitting together thanks to the value we accord to life—then one has the flexible Type Three knowing that can make sense of any stimulus. This is to grasp the "reason by which" things are as they are.[90]

In light of this understanding of the three types of knowing, it makes sense that Zhu repurposes the Buddhist term "*zhijue*"—a compound of "know" and "awaken" that often means perceptual awareness in a Buddhist context—as a general term for the various kinds of knowing activity of our heartmind.[91] Just as "know (*zhi*)" itself can refer to any of the three types, so can *zhijue*.[92] The English verb "discern" does a good job of capturing

---

[89] *Zhuzi yulei*, juan 17, 383.

[90] Zhu uses a variety of terms to refer to this type of knowing, including "genuine knowing 真知," the "discernment 知覺 of the Way heartmind 道心," "eventual awakening 久而後有覺," and "knowing the cosmic mandate 知天命," among others.

[91] Among Zhu's key predecessors, the Cheng brothers do not use *zhijue* in Zhu's capacious way, but instead only in the earlier Buddhist sense (see, for example, Cheng Yi's use of the term in YS 18/201), but in a much-quoted passage, Zhang Zai anticipates Zhu quite closely: "To the combination of nature and *zhijue*, we give the name 'heartmind'" (合性與知覺，有心之名。). Zhang Zai, *Zheng meng* 正蒙 (Correcting the Unenlightened); cited as: ZM juan number/page number from Zhang Zai 張載, *Zhang Zai ji* 張載集 (Collected Works of Zhang Zai) (Beijing: Zhonghua shuju, 1978). ZM 1/9. As for Zhu Xi himself, he says things like, "That which has *zhijue* we call the heartmind" (有知覺謂之心), *Zhuzi yulei*, juan 140, 3340, and "Our heartmind is our *zhijue*, that which is the master of our body and which responds to things and affairs" (心者人之知覺，主於身而應事物者也。). *Zhu Xi ji*, juan 65, 3436.

[92] For example: "The Way heartmind is when one discerns the Pattern of the Way; the human heartmind is when one discerns sound, sight, odor, and flavor" (道心是知覺得道理底，人心是知覺得聲色臭味底。). *Zhuzi yulei*, juan 78, 2010.

the meaning of *zhijue* because of the way that "discern" foregrounds the process of making distinctions and connections among things. This is important because Zhu Xi insists that humaneness is not simply something one "feels (*jue*)." Zhu criticizes the views of the Cheng brothers' student Xie Liangzuo 謝良佐 (1050–1120)—which Araki calls a type of "perceptionism"—for conflating *jue* and humaneness: "The problem with Xie Liangzuo lies in his taking feeling (*jue*) to be humaneness. If one does this, then even pricking one's thigh with a needle, and finding it painful, would also be called 'humaneness.' This is greatly mistaken!" (上蔡之病，患在以覺為仁。但以覺為仁，只將針來刺股上，才覺得痛，亦可謂之仁矣。此大不然也。).[93] Zhu does associate certain feelings with humaneness, but he insists that there is a particular structure and normativity to humaneness, not just a brute reaction to pain.[94] Nor is it the case that discernment (知覺) as a whole is equivalent to humaneness. In response to the question, "Is discernment the same as humaneness?," Zhu replies: "There is humaneness and after that there is discernment" (問：「知覺是仁否？」曰：「仁然後有知覺。」).[95] I take this to mean that humaneness, as one way to refer to the whole of Pattern, is conceptually prior to any specific instance of discernment, even though—as we will see in a moment—specific moments of discernment are that whereby specific aspects of Pattern are made live to us.[96]

For Zhu Xi, knowing and discerning are active processes. He says that "knowing something is our heartmind's being stimulated" (知之者，心之感也。).[97] In a crucial passage, Zhu tells us it is through the actual process of discerning that we come to possess Pattern in its local specificity and activate our specific emotions: "The heartmind's discerning is that whereby we possess this Pattern and activate this emotion" (心之知覺，即所以具此理而行此情者也。).[98] In other words, the world becomes intelligible, normative, and motivational for us precisely through our discerning of it.

---

[93] *Zhuzi yulei*, juan 20, 479. For a defense of Xie's understanding of *ren* in terms of *jue* (translated as "sensitivity"), see Thomas W. Selover, *Hsieh Liang-Tso and the Analects of Confucius* (New York: Oxford University Press, 2005).
[94] For more on the feelings associated with humaneness, see *Zhuzi yulei*, juan 6, 110, and the discussion of "cordial and harmonious intentions" (溫和底意思), feelings of love and sympathy, and so on.
[95] *Zhuzi yulei*, juan 20, 476–477.
[96] For some related analysis, see Brook A. Ziporyn's chapter in this volume.
[97] *Zhu Xi ji*, juan 67, 3513; quoted in Fuji Michiaki 藤井倫明, *Zhu Xi sixiang jiegou tansuo* 朱熹思想結構探索 (Research on the Structure of Zhu Xi's Thought) (Taipei: Taida chuban zhongxin, 2011), 168.
[98] *Zhu Xi ji*, juan 55, 2754; quoted in Fuji Michiaki, *Zhu Xi sixiang jiegou tansuo*, 172.

Zhu makes the same point in more concrete fashion when commenting on *Mencius* 1A.7. In this passage, we read that upon seeing an ox being led to a ritual sacrifice, King Xuan felt pity for it, ordered that it be spared, and that a sheep be found and sacrificed in the ox's place. Mencius' conversation with the king about what this incident reveals is complex, but for our purposes the key has to do with why the king was able to bear sending some unseen sheep to be sacrificed, when he could not bear to have the ox sacrificed. Zhu Xi says: "Having seen the ox, this heartmind was already manifest and could not be suppressed, while not yet having seen the sheep, its Pattern had not yet taken form and there were no [emotions] to hinder him" (然見牛則此心已發而不可遏，未見羊則其理未形而無所妨。).[99] Since Pattern never actually "takes form," what this must mean is that specific configurations of Pattern are "possessed" (*ju* 具) or become live to us only as our heartminds actually respond to a stimulus and produce emotions in reaction.

The nature is a kind of metaphysical structuring that is with us, and indeed present in every aspect of the universe, at all times. Because it is metaphysical and only implicitly or potentially sensible, Zhu Xi says that the heartmind can metaphorically be thought of as having empty space within it. However, we should not take the metaphor of "space" too literally.[100] After all, Zhu is quite explicitly metaphorical in passages like this: "The nature is like the heartmind's field, filling all the emptiness, all is simply Pattern" (性如心之田地，充此中虛，莫非是理而已。). The nature is a metaphorical field, poised to blossom with emotional reactions when the time is right. I have elsewhere endorsed the idea that the heartmind is really a process whereby nature and emotion are unified, which fits well with the present idea that actual discerning is what leads to the most full-blooded "possession" of specific Pattern.[101]

So far, I have argued that Zhu Xi recognizes three distinct types of knowing, and that Types Two and Three involve active discernment whereby the Pattern with which all things are inherently equipped comes

---

[99] Zhu Xi, *Mengzi jizhu* 孟子集注 (Collected Commentaries on Mencius), 1A.7/254, in *Sishu zhangju jizhu* 四書章句集注 (Section and Sentence Commentaries and Collected Annotations on the Four Books) (Beijing: Zhonghua shuju, 1983).

[100] Although I am drawing on Curie Virág, "Emotions and Human Agency in the Thought of Zhu Xi," *Journal of Sung-Yuan Studies* 37 (2007): 49–88, especially 80, I believe that she may be taking the special metaphor somewhat too literally.

[101] See the discussion of Zhu's appropriation of Zhang Zai's phrase "the heartmind unites nature and emotion" (心統性情), in Angle and Tiwald, *Neo-Confucianism: A Philosophical Introduction*, chap. 4.

to be specifically present to us and to be motivating. It remains now to say something about how we cultivate these deeper types of knowing, and to emphasize that even as one moves toward the holistic state that Zhu Xi characterizes as "genuine knowing," distinctions and structure remain vital to this best kind of discernment.

As already emphasized at the outset of this section, Zhu Xi sees the various types of knowing and discernment as continuous with one another. His basic picture is that beginning with whatever Type One knowing of rules one has acquired, as well as with the Type Two moments of brute clarity that one has experienced, one then engages in a process of learning that systematically relates these dimensions of knowing to classic texts, exemplary models, and other dimensions of one's experience. Zhu Xi refers to this process, which depends on both distinguishing between things and between self and other, as well as on coming to see connection among things and thus softening the self–other boundary, by various classically derived terms such as "investigation of things" (*gewu* 格物) and "reaching knowing" (*zhi zhi* 致知). He also uses more specific technical terms like "inferring via analogy" (*tui* 推)[102] and "explicating" (*lun* 論), as in "explicate that by which [it is as it is]" (論其所以然矣).[103]

A particularly telling example comes in one of Zhu's many discussions of the baby–well thought experiment from *Mencius* 2A.6. He writes: "As for a baby falling into a well, this is something that all people can perceive; when one is able analogically to extend to clarity this 'beginning' that has manifested to one, then that is [genuine] clarity" (蓋赤子入井，人所共見，能於此發端處推明，便是明。).[104] In other words, by adopting techniques like analogical extension and applying them to raw materials such as the Type Two knowing experienced upon seeing a baby about to fall into a well, we can hope to reach full-blown Type Three knowing. Here is one more passage in which Zhu offers a powerful metaphor for this extended work:

> For cosmic Pattern is never in all the ages extinguished in any human being; no matter how it is covered over or confined, cosmic Pattern is always constantly there just as ever, emerging from within self-centered desire at every moment without cease—it is just that human beings are not aware of it. It is

---

[102] As in "analogically extend to that by which [something is as it is]" (推其所以然處; 推原其所以然), recalling that "that by which" refers to Type Three knowing.
[103] See *Zhuzi yulei*, *juan* 23,553, *juan* 32, 816, and *juan* 18, 414, respectively.
[104] *Zhuzi yulei*, *juan* 14, 264.

exactly like a bright pearl or a large shell partly covered in turbid sand and gravel, successively flashing forth here and there. Just recognize and gather these successive flashes of the Way and its principles (*daoli*) right where they appear, joining them together until they gradually become an integral whole.

蓋天理在人，恆萬古而不泯；任其如何蔽錮，而天理常自若，無時不自私意中發出，但人不自覺。正如明珠大貝，混雜沙礫中，零零星星逐時出來 。但只於這箇道理發見處，當下認取，簇合零星，漸成片段。[105]

Perhaps the most important thing to note here is that Type Three is not just a generalization of the brute experiences of Type Two. Type Three is not having Type Two experiences all the time, but is the distinctive, holistic result of patient, connective work.

We have already seen two important terms that Zhu Xi uses to describe Type Three knowing, namely "awakening (*jue*)" and "genuine knowing (*zhen zhi*)." With a third term for the same state, he makes more explicit the holistic interconnection that characterizes this type of knowing: "unimpeded interconnection" (*huoran guantong* 豁然貫通). Zhu associates these various categories in passages like this one:

The "awaken" in "The first awakened awaken the later awakened" is the awakening of self-enlightenment, much like when the *Great Learning* speaks of the "investigation of things and extension of knowing [leading to] unimpeded interpenetration."

「先覺後覺」之「覺」，是自悟之覺，似大學說格物、致知豁然貫通處。[106]

At the same time, in another passage he suggests that the categories of "genuine knowing" and "awakening" may not completely overlap:

[A questioner] asked: "Are the 'knowing' of 'genuine knowing' and the 'awakening' of 'after a long time he awakened' the same?" [Zhu] replied: "In

---

[105] *Zhuzi yulei*, juan 117, 2808. As Dan Lusthaus has emphasized to me in conversation, this image resonates in several ways with common Buddhist tropes, although we have not been able to find an exact source for it. Most likely this represents the kind of cultural common property that emerges in the second layer of Confucian-Daoist-Buddhist interactions, as discussed in Section 3.2. In his chapter in this volume, John Jorgensen traces the pearl metaphor to the *Mahāparinirvāṇa-sūtra* (Nirvana Sutra).
[106] *Zhuzi yulei*, juan 58, 1363.

general they are similar; it is just that each refers to something different. Genuine knowing is genuinely being thus-and-so; it is not merely hearing someone say it and having that count as knowing. As for awakening, that is one's heartmind suddenly being enlightened and knowing that Pattern of the Way is thus-and-so."

又問:「『真知』之『知』與『久而後有覺』之『覺』字,同否?」曰:「大略也相似,只是各自所指不同。真知是知得真箇如此,不只是聽得人說,便喚做知。覺,則是忽然心中自有所覺悟,曉得道理是如此。」[107]

In the terms I have been using, Zhu is saying that "genuine knowing" can apply to Type Two knowing as well as Type Three—it is personal and gets things right—but "awakening" must be related to Type Three, because it is explicitly about seeing interconnections.

In any event, the key point about these holistic states of awakening and unimpeded interconnection, which distinguishes Zhu from Huayan and Chan descriptions of holistic states of enlightenment, is that for the Neo-Confucians, "unimpeded interconnection" is still structured or centered in ways that we can at least partly articulate.[108] This is what Zhu emphasizes when he talks about having a good nature as being akin to being in the center of a room, oriented toward the possible exits.[109] Knowing as unimpeded interconnection means that one is not stuck to a single principle—which Zhu analogizes to being stuck in one corner of a room—but instead, having "seen that the myriad Patterns come together, one can choose and follow that which is perfectly apt" (觀眾理之會,而擇其通者而行。).[110]

---

[107] *Zhuzi yulei*, juan 17, 376.

[108] As Brook A. Ziporyn discusses in his chapter in this volume, there is a sense in which for Tiantai thinkers, holistic enlightenment is structured, which they capture through their reference to the "three thousand." However, Tiantai philosophers simultaneously insist on the symmetrical reversibility of relations not only between any two members of the "three thousand," but also between any of the "three thousand" and *li* itself, which leads to a dramatically different way of thinking about what "knowing"—and especially anything like "genuine knowing"—might be. For Zhu Xi, genuine knowing gets its determinacy precisely from the asymmetrical priority of *li* over *qi*.

[109] For extensive discussion of this idea and references, see Angle and Tiwald, *Neo-Confucianism: A Philosophical Introduction*, chap. 3.

[110] *Zhuzi yulei*, juan 75, 1912. For the reference to being stuck in a corner, see *Zhuzi yulei*, juan 35, 927.

3.4 Conclusion

The goal of this chapter has been to explore the relations between Zhu Xi's theories of knowing and Chinese Buddhism. That there are many sorts of relations is obvious. Zhu had significant interactions with Buddhists of his day. His epistemic theorizing is replete with terms and phrases that are strongly associated with, and in some cases originate from, Buddhist writings. And there are respects in which his theories appear to be structurally parallel with Buddhist theories. Be all this as it may, my thesis is that at least in the area of epistemology, the theoretical differences between Zhu and various Buddhist positions are real and deep, and were well understood by Zhu himself. His criticisms of others for Buddhist leanings—again, limiting my scope to epistemic issues—are to a significant degree substantive, based on an accurate appreciation of real differences, rather than merely rhetorical. (Which is not to deny that such statements often did also have rhetorical dimensions.) To be sure, Neo-Confucian ideas, terminology, practice, and genres of expression were all significantly influenced by Buddhism, as Section 3.2 has sketched, and as other chapters in this volume further substantiate. But when we attend carefully to the philosophical issues at the heart of Zhu's writings, we can see that at least in some cases such as epistemology, similarities of terminology or structure mask deep differences.

In this concluding section of the chapter, my aim is to draw together the evidence for my thesis that has been presented in the previous sections, focusing especially on the relations between Zhu's approach to knowing, on the one hand, and the three Buddhist approaches sketched in Section 3.3. I examine five issues: the structured nature of our deepest knowing; the necessity of cultivation; the continuity between empirical and genuine knowing; the role of inherence; and the role of commitment or faith.

My discussion of Zhu's Type Three knowing emphasized its reliance on structured interconnections. Buddhists, too, make much of the interconnection among seemingly distinct things in the world: This is their central teaching of dependent co-arising, on which basis all the Buddhists examined here conclude that things are "empty" of own-nature. The result is a version of what Ziporyn terms "ironic coherence": a uniting that is made possible through its very unintelligibility. Recall that "awareness" for Zongmi is not awareness (or knowing) of anything in particular; it is unconditioned, unconnected from the coming and going of particular thoughts or events. The central metaphysical category of *li* 理 is thus well-translated for Huayan or Chan Buddhists as "Absolute": It countenances no distinctions, parts, or structure.[111] In contrast, for Zhu Xi, Type Three knowing is precisely an all-encompassing knowing of the ways that things best fit together—that is, discerning the dynamic structuring of the cosmos.[112]

The difference between the views of Mazu and Zhu Xi on the necessity of systematic cultivation in order to achieve the proper type of knowing is easy to see. Zhu stresses the need for extensive "investigation of things," "inferring by analogy," and so on; Mazu says (as quoted above), "The Way does not belong to cultivation. If you speak of any attainment through cultivation, whatever is accomplished through cultivation will again decay." As the contemporary scholar Ari Borrell has emphasized, this difference was very salient to the mature Zhu Xi as well, subsequent to his interactions with Daoqian and based on his knowledge of Dahui's teachings. For example, Borrell contrasts the messages that Zhu and Dahui conveyed to Wang Yingchen 汪應辰 (1118–1176), a cousin of Zhu Xi and a leading disciple of the Daoxue thinker Zhang Jiucheng. Dahui tells Wang that awakening is instantaneous, without intermediate steps. In Zhu's letter to Wang, he criticizes those who advocate jumping quickly to the end of the process, as well as the related idea that broad learning is something distinct from and unrelated to higher learning. Zhu asserts that there is no precipitous point of sudden, complete enlightenment and worries that scholars waiting for such a single moment of validation will linger forever in doubt. Instead, they must patiently work at finding connections, within and without the self, which will lead to Type Three knowing.[113]

It might seem, in contrast, that while Zhu's views are clearly different from those in the Mazu tradition, he more closely resembles Zongmi. As we saw earlier, Zongmi believes that cultivation is necessary, albeit of principal importance only after one has achieved a sudden burst of genuine "awareness." As Araki Kengo has shown, however, Zhu took on this

---

[111] See Brook A. Ziporyn, *Beyond Oneness and Difference: Li and Coherence in Chinese Buddhist Thought and Its Antecedents* (Albany: SUNY Press, 2013), 259 and 268; and Gregory, *Tsung-mi*, 6n8. Araki Kengo also argues that "emptiness" is crucial even to the less-radical "Northern Chan" of Shen Xiu, and that this idea finds no parallel in Zhu Xi. Araki, *Fojiao yu Rujiao*, 372.

[112] Thus Zhu endorses Cheng Yi's statement that "There is nothing in the world more substantial than Pattern" (天下無實於理者), YS 3/66. According to Zhu, "All Buddhists talk about is 'emptiness,' Daoists speak only of 'nothingness,' none of them understanding that nothing is more substantial than Pattern" (釋氏便只是說『空』, 老氏便只是說『無』, 卻不知道莫實於理。). *Zhu Xi ji, juan* 95, 2426.

[113] Many thanks to Ari Borrell for sharing with me his analysis of these letters. For Dahui's letters to Wang, see *Dahui yu lu* 大慧語錄 (Record of Dahui), T47.1998A, 930a22-33a24. For Zhu's letter, see *Zhu Xi ji, juan* 30, 1262–1286.

view explicitly, arguing that the "enlightenment" in Zongmi's scheme is problematically disconnected from the gradual cultivation of discernment of real value in the world. Zhu writes, "The way the ancients engaged in learning was solely rising up from below, one firm step at a time, gradually removing [self-centeredness], until human desire naturally was gone and cosmic Pattern naturally was clear. They had nothing like this contrived practice according to which one first needs [to experience] unimpeded enlightenment, and after that [engage in] gradual cultivation" (然觀古人為學，只是升高自下，步步踏實，漸次解剝，人欲自去，天理自明。無似此一般作捺紐捏底功夫，必要豁然頓悟，然後漸次修行也。).[114]

Is there a continuity between empirical and genuine knowing? While Mazu clearly differs from Zhu by rejecting cultivation, he seems more similar to Zhu on the issue of continuity. After all, as quoted above, Mazu says that the "ordinary heartmind is the Way. . . . Now all these are just the Way: walking, abiding, sitting, lying, responding to situations, and dealing with things." This looks at least a bit like Zhu's own stress on finding value in everyday situations. But for Zhu, Type Three discernment (or genuine knowing) is something we achieve, not something that we simply have to realize that we already have. A key difference between Zhu and both Mazu and Zongmi, despite the differences between the two Buddhists, lies in the issue of what can be said to be inherent in us. Zongmi, recall, writes: "all sentient beings without exception have the empty, tranquil, true heartmind. From time without beginning it is the intrinsically pure, effulgent, unobscured, clear, and bright ever-present awareness." This awareness (*zhi* 知) is inherently present. In his own way, Mazu implies the same thing: "Now seeing, hearing, listening, and sensing are fundamentally your inherent nature, which is also called inherent heartmind. It is not that there is a buddha-nature other than this heartmind. This heartmind inherently exists and exists at present, without depending on intentional creation and action; it is inherently pure and is pure at present, without waiting for cleaning and wiping." Present day, actual, everyday perceptual activity is one's inherent heartmind. Mazu does not use the term "inherent knowing (*benzhi* 本知)," but it is widely used within Chan Buddhism.

In striking contrast, Zhu Xi does not use the term "inherent knowing" even once.[115] Indeed, I have not found it in any Neo-Confucian text prior

---

[114] *Zhu Xi ji*, juan 55, 2788; cf. Araki, *Fojiao yu Rujiao*, 373.

[115] At least, it does not appear in the *Yulei* or the *Wenji*, nor anywhere else that I have been able to discover.

to the late-Ming writings of Wang Longxi 王龍谿 (1498–1583)—a philosopher and an era in which a new level of inter-relations among Confucian, Buddhist, and other discourses had been attained. Of course, Zhu Xi is happy to talk about the "inherent heartmind," and here he might sound like Mazu. However, he has no choice but to use the term "inherent heartmind," because it appears in *Mencius*.[116] The question is, what does he mean by it? The evidence shows that Zhu takes it to be equivalent to "nature." Consider the following passage discussing the "human heartmind (*renxin* 人心)" and the "Way heartmind (*daoxin* 道心)," and consider the distinction that appears between the *daoxin* and the *benxin* (inherent heartmind):

> No one is without physical form, and thus even the most wise cannot be without a human heartmind (*renxin*). Similarly, no one is without a nature (*xing*), and thus even the most foolish cannot be without a Way heartmind (*daoxin*). The two are mixed together in the few square inches [of one's physical heart] and if one does not know how to rule them, then [the heartmind's] precariousness will be ever greater, its elusive subtlety ever more elusive, and the impartiality of cosmic Pattern will lack the ability to defeat the self-centeredness of human desire. If one carefully discriminates, then one can distinguish between the two so that they are not mixed, and if one is undivided, then one can preserve the correctness of the inherent heartmind (*benxin*) without wavering. Pursuing matters thusly without the slightest interruption, one necessarily ensures that the Way heartmind is always the ruler of the self and the human heartmind always obeys.
>
> 人莫不有是形，故雖上智不能無人心；亦莫不有是性，故雖下愚不能無道心。二者雜於方寸之間而不知所以治之，則危者愈危、微者愈微，而天理之公卒無以勝夫人欲之私矣。精則察夫二者之間而不雜也，一則守其本心之正而不離也，從事於斯無少閒斷，必使道心常爲一身之主，而人心每聽命焉。[117]

---

[116] See the reference in *Mencius* 6A.10 to "losing one's original heartmind 失其本心."
[117] This is from Zhu's Preface to his commentary on the *Zhongyong* (中庸章句序); see *Sishu zhangju jizhu*, 14; cf. Ian Johnston and Wang Ping, trans., *Daxue & Zhongyong: Bilingual Edition* (Hong Kong: Chinese University of Hong Kong Press, 2012), 401. Throughout the passage Zhu is alluding to a famous passage from the *Book of History*: "The human heartmind is precarious; the Way heartmind is subtle. Be discriminating; be undivided; that you may sincerely hold fast to the center" (人心惟危。道心惟微。惟精惟一。允執厥中。). Translation adapted from James Legge, *The Shoo King*, vol. 3, *The Chinese Classics* (Taipei: Southern Materials Center, 1985), 61–62.

On my reading of this passage, *daoxin* and *benxin* are ontologically quite different. Despite the fact that "even the most foolish cannot be without a Way heartmind (*daoxin*)" and the link between this and our nature, still, *daoxin* is when we perfectly follow the "the correctness of the inherent heartmind (*benxin*)" (i.e., nature), and even the most foolish have flashes of this—for example, when seeing a baby about to fall into a well. Even the most foolish, that is, can have moments of Type Two brute clarity. Only when the *daoxin* is the master of the self, though, have we achieved Type Three knowing. In short, *daoxin* represents an actual, experiential state of self, whereas *benxin* is simply another name for the nature.

Up to this point I have said nothing about the *Buddha-nature Treatise* and the role of faith, commitment, or confidence that we find there. Does this find any resonance in Zhu Xi? In fact, a central theme of Araki Kengo's interpretation of Zhu is emphasizing the role of some kind of confidence or faith. Araki says that Zhu posits a kind of confidence in the "onward flow of the cosmos, the production and reproduction of things, the development of history, and the continuing roles of cultural forms."[118] I think that this is quite perceptive, so long as we understand the modality of "faith" properly, and it might not be all that different from what King finds at the heart of the *Buddha-nature Treatise*.[119] For Araki's Zhu, at least, a key is that we have empirical feedback that reinforces our confidence; this is not a Kierkegaardian leap. In short, it is here that I tentatively see more overlap, rather than in the other more apparent parallels.

Returning for a final time to my main argument, we have seen good reason to conclude that Zhu Xi's epistemology is importantly different from the Buddhism that he studied as a youth. Once we look carefully at the details of Zhu's position, we are able to see the differences from influential Buddhist theorists like Zongmi and Mazu. To some degree, this conclusion may give comfort to those scholars who minimize the significance of Buddhism to the development of Neo-Confucianism. For two reasons, though, I caution against leaping to any such general lessons. First, the influence of the four layers of Buddhist–Confucian interactions upon Zhu—even on his epistemology—is apparent in many of his words and metaphors, even if in the particular area I have studied, it does not determine the philosophy that he articulates with these words and metaphors. Second, it is crucial to my method here that we examine the concepts and

---

[118] Araki, *Fojiao yu Rujiao*, 279.
[119] Faith in something like this sense is also central to the Buddhist *Dasheng qixin lun* treatise; for more on this crucial text, see John Makeham's chapter in this volume.

arguments of particular areas of philosophy in detail. I believe that this method can be generalized and applied in other areas, but my substantive conclusion concerning epistemology cannot. Each of the other chapters in this volume—as well as future scholarship on the Buddhist roots of Zhu Xi's thought—needs to be judged on a case-by-case basis. The ultimate picture will surely be one in which Zhu has strong, substantive connections to Buddhist teachings in some areas and not in others, all of this built on a foundation of deep, layered interactions over many centuries.

CHAPTER 4 | The *Ti-Yong* 體用 Model and Its Discontents

Models of Ambiguous Priority in Chinese Buddhism and Zhu Xi's Neo-Confucianism

BROOK A. ZIPORYN

THIS CHAPTER EXPLORES the structural peculiarities of three different metaphysical models: those found in Huayan Buddhism, in Tiantai Buddhism, and in Zhu Xi's Neo-Confucianism. Each of these models involves a distinctive conception of the relation between one and many, between prior and posterior, between foundational and derivative, between formless and formed, between unperceived and perceived, between indeterminate and determinate, between center and periphery. All three models touch on the issues listed above, and all three regard the relations listed as largely parallel if not ultimately synonymous (viz., the center is the one is the prior is the foundational is the formless is the unperceived, and so on). Moreover, as John Makeham's contribution to this volume amply illustrates, Zhu Xi borrows a huge portion of his metaphysical structural assumptions from a template developed in the Buddhist schools, especially the *ti-yong* 體用 model. Nevertheless, as Stephen Angle's chapter in this volume discusses in depth, the levels of influence and interchange encoded in the shared use of borrowed tropes and images, and even general structural principles, is susceptible to a highly complex dialectic in this period of Chinese intellectual history. Hence, we should expect huge swaths of shared vocabulary and concern that nonetheless are tweaked at decisive points by apparently small but, to the thinkers themselves, decisively important differences in emphasis and torque. These differences and their consequences are what I want to explore here.

Although Tiantai, Huayan and Zhu Xi all deploy the *ti-yong* model as a crucial component of their metaphysics, in certain key places they deploy it to different purposes, restricted or expanded to different ranges of application at different levels of their discussions, leading to subtle structural differences, which for them amounted to large philosophical consequences. I think they were right to see large philosophical consequences implied by these tweaks, and it is this that I will try to clarify in the pages that follow.

The first model we will discuss comes in two forms, which I term "the classic *ti-yong* model," and its "radicalized" modified version. The classic *ti-yong* model is found in a few motifs scattered through early Chinese Buddhism and here and there in non-Buddhist thinkers like Wang Bi 王弼 (226–249). The radicalized *ti-yong* model derives mainly from the Huayan Buddhist development of this classic model.

The "classic *ti-yong* model" prioritizes *ti* over *yong*, and maintains that priority as primary, such that the contents of *ti* and *yong* are always different and opposed; *ti* is one and unseen, *yong* is many and seen, and *yong* is always dependent on *ti* but not vice versa.

The radicalized Huayan modification collapses *ti* and *yong*, making them fully *coextensive* and sharing the same contents, but still distinguished structurally by a conceptual priority of *ti* over *yong,* the latter always being dependent on the former in a way the former is not dependent on the latter. Huayan employs this model globally; that is, it is the key explanatory model on all levels and is applied to well-nigh all aspects of doctrine. In particular, it is applied equally to the individual psychic level and the universal metaphysical levels of explanation. That is, the relation between the mind and its mental acts, the relation between the individual consciousness and its own experiences, conceptions, emotions, and so forth, is a *ti-yong* relation; and the Li-*shi* 理事relation, between the sole ultimate reality and its multiple manifestations, is *also* a *ti-yong* relation. Indeed, ultimately these are one and the same, because all things are functions as *shi* whose *ti* is Li, and the activity of any individual mind is itself a *yong* which is the *shi* whose *ti* is Li, the one universal inter-reflective *ti* that is the sole real Li of all *shi*.

This "one" is however a weird kind of one, also legitimately describable as a "none," and it is this special Buddhist peculiarity that allows the "radical" Huayan modification of the *ti-yong* paradigm. For in this case the *ti* is Emptiness (*kong* 空), conceived not as the passive blank cutting off of all activities but as the active enabling of all activities—Emptiness as the enabling of all beings. It is blank like a mirror, not blank like a white wall: the reflectivity that embraces all forms rather than excluding all forms. It is this that is directly active in any individual thing's activity and awareness, the formless essence pervading each thing that allows it to move and perceive and think and ultimately to be interpenetrating, inter-reflecting, with all other things. The Huayan model is straightforward and elegant: *Ti* is Li, *yong* is *shi*, and these two have the specific Buddhist relation of interpenetration and coextensivity: Form is emptiness, emptiness is form, so Li is *shi, shi* is Li. *However, the conceptual priority of Li and ti remains in spite of their eternal mutual immanence and coextensivity.* The terms denoting this relation, this final irreversibility and asymmetry of dependence even of two terms regarded as coextensive, go all the way back to the first works of the Dushun 杜順 (557–640) corpus laying the groundwork of Huayan thought. It is the distinction between *suoyi* 所依 and *nengyi* 能依, between that which is relied upon and that which relies.[1] Though coextensive, the *ti* and the *yong* are marked by a one-way dependence relation, a conceptual priority of *ti* over *yong*. This brilliant and hugely influential move is possible here because *ti* is Emptiness itself.[2]

The second model is the Tiantai Buddhist model. The third model is Zhu Xi's own innovation. Both continue to employ the modified *ti-yong* model unproblematically on the individual psychic level, albeit with important adjustments in each case.[3] In the Tiantai case, the modified use of *ti-yong* at the psychic level is accomplished through the doctrine that the deluded mind itself transforms into and thereby entails in itself the conditions of possibility of the Three Thousand objects of its possible experience,[4] and

---

[1] *Huayan fajie xuanjing* 華嚴法界玄鏡 (Profound Mirror of the Dharma-realm), T45.1883, 674a-b.
[2] The same model is applied forcefully at the purely individual psychic level not only in Huayan itself but in early Southern Chan, which closely follows Huayan here. For example, this model is front and center in the claim attributed to Huineng 慧能 (638–713) in the *Platform Sutra* (*Liu zu tan jing* 六祖壇經), T48.2007, 338c20: "Suchness is the *ti* of thoughts, thoughts are the *yong* of Suchness" (真如是念之體，念是真如之用。). This still stands as the premise of the further development of Southern Chan, which dumps *ti* altogether, inasmuch as it is phenomenologically unavailable, and collapses *ti* into *yong*. In the Huineng model, *ti* is wholly present in *yong*; in the later model *ti* is wholly present *only* in *yong*, in each *yong*, and has no other form of existence, such that any specific idea of *ti* as opposed to *yong*, any fixed *ti*, any role at all for *ti* within any theoretical account, drops out of discussion entirely. For example, Linji says, "if you grab hold of it, you then use it, but don't attach any name to it," i.e., no *ti* is named; it just functions. See *Linji Huizhao Chan shi yulu* 臨濟慧照禪師語錄 (Record of Chan Master Linji Huizhao), T47.1985, 498a10.
[3] In the Tiantai case, however, this was mainly only after importing this model from Huayan via the work of Zhanran 湛然 (711–782) in the Tang dynasty.
[4] The "three thousand" is a way of saying "everything," but it is really something a bit more than that. As Zhiyi himself points out, any number would be an equally accurate possible way to talk about the totality of all things, from none to infinity. This number, "three thousand," is concocted specifically with meditational practice in mind. For details, see Brook A. Ziporyn, "Tiantai Buddhism," *The Stanford Encyclopedia of Philosophy* (Spring 2017), ed. Edward N. Zalta, https://plato.stanford.edu/archives/spr2017/entries/buddhism-tiantai/.

thus in that sense "creates" them. Since it is deluded, and thus committed to a false sense of subject-object dualism, it is necessarily apparently distinguished from them. But for that very reason it is inseparable from them, and this inseparability is ultimately analyzed into a dialectical identity with them as they appear. In this way Tiantai presents the necessary inter-identity between deluded mind and whatever is putatively outside of and opposed to deluded mind, for which the *ti-yong* description can then be used in certain contexts. We will see this in unpacking Zhanran's description of the individual mind/world relation: "All mental and physical phenomena are experienced only as aspects of the [deluded] mind, and it is just these phenomena that we refer to as that mind's transformations, which nonetheless are all identical to that mind. It is just this transformation of the states of the mind that is the creation [of all these mental and physical phenomena], which means the experienced temporal *yong* are just the *ti* itself" (心之色心，即心名變，變即是造，造謂體用),[5] a conception we will explore in detail below with an expanded gloss of this passage.

In Zhu Xi's case, the modification of *ti-yong* at the individual psychic level is accomplished through a careful adaptation of the dicta of Zhang Zai 張載 (1020–1077), "Mind is the controlling unifier of the Nature and the emotions" (心統性情) and "Mind has no opposite" (惟心無對)—singled out by Zhu Xi as superior to anything the Cheng brothers ever said on the subject of the individual mind.[6] Zhu Xi usually describes this as a straight *ti-yong* relation between the Nature and the emotions, owing much to the Huayan-derived Chan model, with the Nature as the *ti* and the emotions as the *yong* and the former phenomenologically available *only* as the latter. Zhu Xi, however, adds an innovative third term, the mind itself as the unity of the two, which controls their relation.

In many contexts, both Zhu Xi and Tiantai strongly resist applying the classic or radicalized *ti-yong* model directly or straightforwardly to the universal level. The global metaphysical relation between Li and *shi* in the Tiantai case and between Li and *qi* in the Zhu Xi case are ultimately not straightforward classic *ti-yong* relations, or are highly modified versions to which the *ti-yong* model is applied grudgingly and with many qualifiers.

---

[5] Zhanran, *Shi bu er men* 十不二門 (Ten Gateways of Non-duality), T46.1927, 703a.
[6] Zhu Xi says, "Only mind has no opposite," and "Mind combines the nature and the emotions"—even the Cheng brothers have no statement as insightful as these two dicta [of Zhang Zai's]" (「惟心無對」。「心統性情」。二程却無一句似此切。). *Zhuzi yulei* 朱子語類 (Topically Arranged Conversations of Master Zhu), comp. Li Jingde 黎靖德 (fl. 1263), (Beijing: Zhonghua shuju, 1986), *juan* 98, 2513.

They are rather models of center-periphery, of two extremes unified by a center point that paradoxically combines the two extremes, a broader category also very pervasive in Chinese thought. Indeed, we may think of the *ti-yong* model as one particular type of center-periphery model, but one that in some periods of Chinese intellectual history, perhaps due to the brilliance and elegance of the radicalized Huayan version, temporarily eclipsed other forms of the center-periphery model.

In the Tiantai case, the *ti-yong* pair does occur in the works of Zhiyi 智顗 (538–597) in places where he speaks of the general ontological condition of things, but very rarely and unsystematically, and is specifically applied to the inner structure of Li itself, i.e., to the relation among the "Three Truths" (Emptiness, Provisional Positing, Middle),[7] rather than to the relation between Li and events: The Third Truth, the Middle (*zhong* 中), is presented as *ti* in contrast to the other two truths, i.e., of Emptiness and Provisional Positing (*kong* 空, *jia* 假), as *yong*.[8] That is, the *ti-yong* model is emphatically subordinated to the center-periphery model, making both phenomenal reality *and its coextensive negation* the *yong*, with the enabling Middle as the *ti*, rather than phenomenal reality as *yong* and its coextensive enabling negation as *ti* as we shall see in Huayan. We will trace the intricacies and consequences of this seemingly small distinction

---

[7] The Three Truths are Zhiyi's innovation: To the Madhyamaka Two Truths of "Conventional Truth" (ordinary speech, Buddhist practical terms, everyday reality) and "Ultimate Truth" ("Emptiness," i.e., lack of self-nature, of all the above), he adds a third truth, "The Middle," which signifies the ultimate synonymity of the first two truths, relegating even the distinction between them to conventional truth, but also thereby signifying the non-dualism between any two extremes, and the unconditional nature of all entities insofar as they therefore pervade their apparent opposites.

[8] *Miaofa lianhua jing xuanyi* 妙法蓮華經玄義 (The Profound Doctrine of the *Lotus Sutra*) T33.1716, 742c:

> If we focus upon the fact that the [Track of the True Nature, which is Center] is neither moving nor emerging, then we can say [the substance of the One Vehicle] neither travels nor fails to travel. But if we focus on the fact that [the two peripheral extremes of] the Track of Contemplation and Reflection [which is *kong*, Emptiness] and the Track of Dependent Completion [which is *jia*, Provisional Positing] can move and emerge, then it is called traveling. But [since the Center is inseparable from and ultimately identical to the two extremes,] precisely the motion and emerging is non-moving and non-emerging, and precisely the non-moving and non-emerging is moving and emerging. Precisely the function is what we mean when we talk about the *ti* [of the One Vehicle], so the motion and emergence are neither moving nor emerging. Precisely the *ti* is what is described as the function (*yong*), so the non-emergence and non-motion is emerging and moving. It's just that the *ti* and *yong* are not two and yet two.
> 若取真性不動不出，則非運非不運。若取觀照資成能動能出，則名為運。秖動出即不動出，即不動出是動出。即用而論體，動出是不動出。即體而論用，即不動出是動出。體用不二而二耳。

below. Later Tiantai writers, starting with Zhanran, on the contrary, adopt from Huayan the *ti-yong* terminology, sometimes even directly equating *ti* with Li and *yong* with *shi*. But the fit is not a tidy one. Tiantai writers are then forced to rewrite and qualify its usage, and to distinguish it from the classic *ti-yong* model in which *ti* just is Li and *yong* just is *shi*, where *ti* is one and *yong* are many, where Li is one and *shi* are many and so on.

In middle age, Zhu Xi pulls away from the *ti-yong* model for the global metaphysical level—that is, the Taiji/*yin-yang* (*qi*) relation—saying that he had formerly applied it directly to that relation but that "this way of putting it definitely has something wrong with it" (其言固有病); he nevertheless continues to use the model in the very same passage, but with reservations and modifications.[9] These modifications provide us with the deepest insights into his metaphysical vision and how it both builds upon and differs from both Tiantai and Huayan Buddhist conceptions.

The three models have very different ways of conceiving the relation of the central term to its peripheral terms, and thus although all three claim some sort of pre-existent grounding of all events in something prior, either temporally or conceptually, to those events, they do so in different ways. None resembles the kind of conceptual priority we would find in a Platonic or Aristotelian system or their derivatives, because of differences, primarily, in the conceptions of oneness and difference, the one-many relation, which is perhaps the main determinant of resulting differences in the conception of the precise structure of metaphysical priority.

---

[9] *Zhu Xi ji* 朱熹集 (Collected Works of Zhu Xi), eds. Guo Qi 郭齊 and Yin Bo 尹波 (Chengdu: Sichuan jiaoyu chubanshe, 1996), *juan* 45, 2154:

> I formerly regarded the Supreme Pivot (*taiji*) as the *ti* and motion and stillness as its *yong*, but this way of putting the matter is definitely defective. Later I changed it to say, "The Supreme Pivot is the original wondrousness, while motion and stillness are the mechanism it rides." This gets close to covering it. Your recent communication raises doubts about the use of *ti yong*, and quite rightly, but the reasons for your doubts seem to be different from those that led me to change the passage. Speaking generally, The Supreme Pivot contains both motion and stillness, and thus in this sense can be spoken of as their original body (*benti*). It is thus permissible to say that the Supreme Pivot has both motion and stillness, speaking in terms of its flowing forth. But if you say that the Supreme Pivot is itself motion or stillness, you make what is above form and what is below form indistinguishable, which renders the claim that "the *Change* has the Supreme Pivot" superfluous.
>
> 熹向以太極爲體，動靜爲用，其言固有病，後已改之曰「太極者，本然之妙也；動靜者，所乘之機也」，此則庶幾近之。來喻疑於體用之云甚當，但所以疑之之說則與熹之所以改之之意又若不相似然。蓋謂太極含動靜則可，以本體而言也。謂太極有動靜則可，以流行而言也。若謂太極便是動靜，則是形而上下者不可分，而「易有太極」之言亦贅矣。

For an alternative interpretation of this passage, which argues for Zhu Xi's ongoing commitment to the Huayan version of the *ti-yong* paradigm, see John Makeham's chapter in this volume.

4.1 The Classic *Ti-Yong* Model and Its Huayan Radicalization

The basic position of the Huayan school, as it develops in the thought of Dushun, Zhiyan 智儼 (602–668), Fazang 法藏 (643–712), Chengguan 澄觀 (738–839) and Zongmi 宗密 (780–841), proposes that all phenomena are grounded in, rooted in, derived from, ultimately coextensive with, the originally "pure" (i.e., indeterminate, but infinitely determinable) Suchness, also called the buddha-nature or Dharma-nature. All things owe their phenomenal existence to that purity in the sense of its lack of any definite characteristics (viewed as obstructions and thus as defilements), but are not as such "contained in" that Suchness that is the buddha-nature. Indeed, it is held that it is precisely the lack of these specific determinate multiple phenomena in the buddha-nature (or Dharma-nature) itself that makes their arising possible, as images appear in a mirror only because the mirror itself is devoid of any definite images of its own, thereby enabling it to produce any image at all, when the external conditions for doing so are right. As Fazang beautifully puts it:

> The Perfectly Complete Nature, although it becomes defiled or pure as it follows conditions, yet it never loses the purity of its self-nature. Indeed, it is just because it never loses the purity of its self-nature that it is able to follow conditions and become defiled or pure. It is like a bright mirror showing defiled or pure things: although it manifests purity or defilement, it never loses the purity of the mirror's brightness. Indeed, it is precisely because it never loses the purity of the mirror's brightness that it is able to manifest all the marks of purity and defilement. It is through its manifesting of defilement and purity that we know that the mirror's brightness is pure, and it is because the mirror's brightness is pure that we know it can manifest defilement and purity. Thus the two meanings really refer to one and the same Nature. The mirror's brightness is not increased when it manifests pure things, nor dirtied when it manifests defiled things. Not only is it not dirtied—this manifestation of defiled things is actually what shows the purity of the mirror's brightness. You should know that it works just the same way with Suchness. It is not only that the purity of the unmoving nature becomes all defiled and pure things, but precisely this becoming defiled and pure things is what shows the purity of the Nature. Not only is there no need to eliminate defiled and pure things to perceive the purity of the nature, rather it is only because of the purity of the nature that it becomes defiled or pure. Thus the two aspects are completely

absorbed into each other, one nature not two—how could they contradict each other?

且如圓成，雖復隨緣成於染淨，而恒不失自性清淨。秪由不失自性清淨故，能隨緣成染淨也。猶如明鏡現於染淨：雖現染淨，而恒不失鏡之明淨。秪由不失　鏡明淨故，方能現染淨之相。以現染淨知鏡明淨，以鏡明淨知現染淨。是故二義唯是一性；雖現淨法不增鏡明，雖現染法不污鏡淨。非直不污，亦乃由此反顯鏡之明淨。當知真如道理亦爾。非直不動性淨成於染淨，亦乃由成染淨方顯性淨。非直不壞染淨明於性淨，亦乃由性淨故方成染淨。是故二義全體相收一性無二；豈相違耶？[10]

Although Fazang does not here use the *nengyi* 能依 (that which depends), *suoyi* 所依 (that upon which it depends) terminology found in Dushun's writings, it seems fair to see a similar structure in this passage, marked by a one-way dependence relationship between the imageless but image-enabling "brightness" and the "images." Huayan starts with the straightforward assumption that the conditional (finite, limited) is the determinate (that "determination is negation," as Spinoza put it), and thus the unconditional (infinite, illimitable) can only be the indeterminate. The Buddhist indeterminate, however, is not a blank, which would still be determinate as something definite (i.e., pure white or black space that excludes all other colors), but rather is blank in the way that a mirror's brightness is blank, and hence neither inclusive of determinations nor exclusive of them; indeed, it is what enables and in a sense produces all determinations.[11] This idea was a commonplace in Chinese Buddhism at least from the time of Sengzhao 僧肇 (384–414), who declares in his essay "Treatise on the Unknowability of *Prajñā*": "If we took the lack of all characteristics as being a definite lack of any characteristics, then the lack of characteristics would ipso facto be a determinate characteristic" (若以無相為無相，無相即為相).[12] True indeterminacy cannot be indeterminacy to the exclusion

---

[10] Fazang, *Huayan yicheng jiaoyi fenqi zhang* 華嚴一乘教義分齊章 (Essay on the Classified Meaning of the Teaching of the One Vehicle of the Flower Garland Sutra), T45.1866, 499b.

[11] The metaphor cannot be taken literally, insofar as we generally conceive of a mirror as accepting determinations that come from outside itself, and therefore as passive. The point is to indicate an intuitive sense of the relevant non-duality between determination and indetermination, drawing on an empirical example. Once this non-duality is grasped, it is also applied to the "inside-outside" duality, and thus to the "active-passive" duality, and at that point the metaphor has to be amended or dropped.

[12] Sengzhao, *Bore wuzhi lun* 般若無知論 (Treatise on the Unknowability of *Prajñā*), T45.1858, 154b.

of all determinacy, but must rather be the enabling and allowing of all and any determinacies.

On the basis of this insight, Huayan offers a vision of the coextensivity and yet asymmetry between the determinate and the indeterminate. When looking at any given image, the brightness of the mirror and the image are coextensive, and never separate. All of the image is the brightness, and conversely we also see no brightness that is not some image. And yet there remains a clear structural asymmetry between them, having to do with dependence: The brightness is what enables the image to exist, while the images are only what allows the brightness to manifest itself concretely. And the brightness is always the same in the sense of being indistinguishable in one case and in another, while the images are each different and changing. So although any given image is entirely brightness, with nothing extra added, and all brightness is manifest as images, still brightness is brightness, and is primary, is one, is permanent, while images are images, and are secondary, multiple, and impermanent. This implies a specific structure of both: (1) continuity (or even identity); and (2) contrast between the two levels.

In fact, this Huayan model is a Buddhist modification of the classic *ti-yong* structure, and it is in Huayan thought that this trope achieves perhaps its most extensive developments and applications.[13] The basic metaphor of the *ti-yong* model, insofar as it exists at all before Buddhist transformation, is that of a plant, with a root and branches.[14] The root is the *ti*, while

---

[13] It is notably lacking in Tiantai until Zhanran adopts it from Huayan usages and even then uses it quite sparingly. Zhiyi usually employs the much more intricate and convoluted categories of *ben* 本 and *ji* 跡, with *ti* and *yong* appearing only as two of the five categories used in *xuanyi* 玄義 (profound doctrine) commentaries to various sutras, i.e., *ming* 名, *ti* 體, *zong* 宗, *yong* 用, *jiao* 教: explanation of the name of the sutra, its "essence" (*ti*), its main source, its function, and its place in the classification of teachings.

[14] Although it is already used in Wang Bi, *Dao de jing zhu* 道德經注 (Annotated Classic of the Way and its Virtue), chapter 38, there it is a final trope in a much more complex exegesis involving a distinction between the verbal "use" of Non-Being, as in *Dao de jing* chapter 11 and the "embodiment" of Non-Being taken as the pinnacle of sagehood, exemplified by Confucius and described in the first line of chapter 38 of *Dao de jing*, "The highest Virtue does not have Virtue" (*shang de bu de* 上德不德). Unlike the "use" (*yong*) of Non-Being described in chapter 11, Wang interprets this to mean that those who "embody" sagehood, such as Confucius, do not know or speak of it, do not utilize it at all. This is then assimilated to the root-branch plant model and the Mother-Sons metaphor of *Dao de jing* chapter 52. The mutual exclusivity of the contents of *ti* and *yong* is here initially derived from a contrast between praxis and theory, or embodiment and objectification. Wang rather brilliantly brings this into the orbit of the more traditional root and branch metaphor, a commonplace of pre-Qin writings stressing proper sequence, prioritization and one-way dependence, in a way that stresses the one-many aspect and the negation aspect. So we may regard this whole cluster of ideas brought together into the classic *ti-yong* model to be Wang's work.

the branches are the *yong*. This has certain features that made it highly useful to Buddhist thought, above all to Huayan Buddhist thought. The classic *ti-yong* structure, on this model, implies both strong *contrast* and strong *continuity* between *ti* and *yong*.

Strong *contrast* is intrinsic to the model, in that: (1) the *ti* is independent, the *yong* is dependent, just as the branches are dependent on the root; (2) the *ti* is in some sense one and the *yong* is in some sense many, just as the root is one and the branches are many; (3) the *ti* is in some sense unmoving and the branches are in some sense active, again just like a root and its branches; and (4) in some sense the *ti* is hidden and the *yong* are visible, again like a root and its branches (the root is underground). This fourth category can present as any kind of sharp decrease of degree of definiteness between the two levels: either relatively hidden and exposed (levels of relative obviousness or knowability), or absolutely hidden and exposed (indeterminacy and determinacy per se, nothingness and being, and so on), as in the universal metaphysical usage in both Wang Bi's *Dao de jing* commentary and subsequently in Huayan. Indeed, the unmovingness and hiddenness of *ti* amount in the first instance to indeterminacy itself as opposed to determinacy.[15]

Strong *continuity* is, however, implied in that: 5) *ti* is the source or basis of *yong*, like the root of a plant and its branches; and 6) these remain inseparable, again like a root and its branches. This indivisible totality of living interconnection is sometimes pushed so far as to suggest that nothing can be definitively localized as pertaining only to one part rather than to another.[16] This in turn starts to come close to the claims about some sense of identity between *ti* and *yong* in the radicalized version, where

---

[15] In Wang Bi's case, also as subjective realization in practice as opposed to objectification in theory; the case is modeled on his Confucius as one who has "embodied" Non-Being and therefore does not speak of it, as opposed to the Daoists who merely "use" (*yong*) it and therefore always speak of it.

[16] The kind of continuity, and even the weak but non-negligible sense of identity, that pertain to the living connection of root and branches as the *ti* and the *yong* in the classical (pre-Huayan) *ti-yong* model can be understood from Cheng Yi's famous metaphors of a tree and its comparison to a system of roads. I use this only as a heuristic here, since of course this comes long after the advent of the Huayan model historically, and Cheng does not explicitly use the *ti-yong* language in this passage. In a famously difficult passage quoted by Zhu Xi and Lü Zuxian 呂祖謙 (1137–1181) in the *Jin si lu* 近思錄 (Record of Reflection on Things at Hand) (Taipei: Taiwan shangwu yinshuguan, 1996), 19, Cheng Yi 程頤 (1033–1107) says:

> Though in a state of total desolate emptiness, all the images of all things are already present. The [quiescent] state before responsive activation is not really earlier, the [determinate] state after responsive activation is not really later. It is like a hundred foot tall tree, all one continuity from root and trunk to branches and leaves. You cannot say that the formless and indeterminate [lower part—the non-articulated trunk and root] must await someone to bring back to it and arrange into it the [diverse] things on the top part [i.e., the branches and

they are: 6) coextensive, stressing in either case the oneness in spite of the above contrasts.

There is one more item we could add to this list: 7) The *ti* is in the middle, a "Center," while the *yong* are spread out to the periphery, again like a root and its branches.[17] A center between two extremes, however,

> leaves]. When something is made to enter into a network of roads and tracks, since they are after all roads and tracks, it is all one road-track.
>
> 沖漠無朕，萬象森然已具，未應不是先，已應不是後。如百尺之木，自根本 至枝葉，皆是一貫，不可道上面一段事，無形無兆，卻待人鏃安排引入來. 教入途 轍。既是途轍，卻隻是一個途轍。

Here, although one part is leafy and other is not, and they are spatially separated and non-coextensive, both are parts of an inseparable *living* whole, and thus in a certain sense we can say that the root and the branches are "the same thing," as we might say "this is the same road as the one beginning in Minnesota" while standing in Louisiana and pointing to a section of Highway 61. The reason given for this in the Cheng Yi passage is *indivisible continuity of growth and life and activity*, as illustrated in the images of the tree and the system of roads. The idea seems to be simply that the root and the branches are not two different things, so if the branches are multiple and the leaves are leafy, I can legitimately point to the root and say, "*This, this thing right here*, is multiple, is leafy." I should not regard the multiplicity and leafiness as something that has to be deliberately arranged or added externally to the singularity and leaflessness of the root and trunk: They are the root and trunk themselves; they are what the root and trunk themselves are doing. The leaves are not supplements or additions to the root: Rather, what you call the leaves is just a partial designation for what is really root-trunk-branches-leaves, and root equally merely a partial designation for the selfsame root-trunk-branches-leaves. Similarly, if I am on a road, since the nature of a road is to open one point in space to another, to be a way of moving from one to another, I shouldn't call one of the places I reach one road and another place I reach thereby a whole different road; the various parts of the road, as interconnected aspects of a single enabler of journey to all its points, are all one indivisible whole. So if one part of the road is painted red, I should be able to point to another, non-red, part of the road, and say, "This thing right here has redness painted on it." (See Zhou Xiaoping's short film, "Hi, I'm China," https://www.youtube.com/watch?v=KJsep3Jj4ck&lc=z130xzc5cpepenb2f23qwrhjskvqc13wf04. The English says, "This is China's road; while this is also China's road . . . ," not "This is a road in China; this is another road in China." See the effect of removing tense and articles and number from a language!) In this metaphor, which lays bare some of the structural features of the classical *ti-yong* model (although the terms are not explicitly used), the implication is that the nature of the whole in question is what allows for the claim of intensified identity between the two opposite aspects: If it were a genuinely static object, it could perhaps be legitimately divided into parts with separable characteristics of their own. But since a road is only a road if its parts are unseparated, and a living being is only a living being if its parts are unseparated, its parts cannot be considered separate entities at all; as separated, they are no longer the same things as they are when they are parts of this kind of whole. The integration of parts pertains to the essence of all characteristics of each part, and thus what appears to be true of any part is really only true of the whole, the sole real entity that can serve as a referent or possessor of qualities here, which means that in one sense what is true of any part is equally true of every other part.

[17] See my *Beyond Oneness and Difference: Li and Coherence in Chinese Buddhist Thought and Its Antecedents* (Albany: SUNY Press, 2013), 137–157. In the earliest usages, in Wang Bi's commentary to *Dao de jing* chapter 38 for example, when the trope is just taking shape on the basis of a contrast to the usage of *yong* in *Dao de jing* chapter 11, the sharp sense of contrast between *ti* and *yong*, evident in items 3, 4, 5, and 6 above (*ti* as one, hidden, central, quiescent, as opposed to *yong* as many, visible, peripheral, active) is strongly emphasized, along with the sense of continuity evident in items 1 and 2 (causal basis and inseparability).

has some peculiar qualities when it comes to continuity and contrast: The odd thing about this item is that it is difficult to tally it up to the "contrast" side or to the "continuity" side. It is both contrast and continuity, and in an immediate sense: The center is the exclusion of the two opposed extremes, by definition belonging to neither of them, and yet it is also the point of contact, intersection, overlap between the two extremes, as the center of a circle is a part of every radius of the circle, even those that end in diametrically opposite points on the periphery of the circle. It is what is both inseparable from both extremes and yet contained completely in neither extreme. It is in that peculiar sense both immanent to them and transcendent of them. Moreover, on the contrast side, it has another weird property: It is contrasted to both the extremes as extremes, but it also enables *their* contrast with one another. So it is a double contrast and a double continuity, all in one: It contrasts to both, it foments contrast between both, but it is also a part of both, and the ground that enables them to be what they are (i.e., contrasted).

We can thus see how the center-periphery trope does much of the contrast-and-continuity work of the *ti-yong* model, but in a different way. We should also note again that *ti-yong can* be construed as an instance of center-periphery, or vice versa. What I think we find in the Huayan development of the trope is a radicalization of items 1 through 6, ending in complete coextensivity of *ti* and *yong*, but preserving both their contrast and their continuity—to such an extent that the Center model is dispensed with altogether, for it seems as if its effects have been achieved already through other means. As we shall see, this is only partly true: Not all of the effects of the Center have been duplicated by the radicalized *ti-yong* model.

Let us then explore this radicalized Huayan *ti-yong* model. Emptiness, Li, is *ti*: It is indeterminacy as such, quiescence as such, oneness in the special sense of noneness, which is therefore indivisible (this is its main feature in Du Shun's dialectics), and therefore unchanging in any time or place. In an important way, this can indeed also be described as a kind of Center, as the (exclusive) Mean, the Middle Way, the unconditioned—for it is neither without characteristics nor with characters, neither indeterminate nor determinate, neither being nor non-being, neither blank nor full: It is the mirror's reflectivity, the emptiness that is always manifesting as all beings, so it has the characteristics of the joining of opposites. In contrast, phenomena, *shi*, are determinacies as such, changing, multiple, dispersed. As such, they are not this center, but are the one-sided peripheral items, which the center unites and grounds. The *ti-yong* model already makes the determinacies dependent upon and inseparable from indeterminacy.

This is easily accommodated and indeed given a robust intuitive expression in the Huayan indeterminate as a mirror-indeterminacy as opposed to blank-indeterminacy: The images in a mirror are produced by that mirror and always remain inseparable from it. The mirror is quiescent, one, and "hidden" (i.e., always discovered only secondarily, after first seeing through the manifest image), while the images are moving, many, definite. The mirror is unconditioned, eternal, omnipresent, and so forth, and hence is Suchness, is Nirvanic, is the Buddha-mind, free of suffering, while the images are conditioned and transient, and hence suffering.

Now just because this is mirror-indeterminacy and not blank-indeterminacy, the two levels interfuse: Since reflectivity is indivisible, it is fully present in each instance, in each image. The image is nothing but reflectivity, reflectivity is completely images (including the silvery image of mirroriness, since there is no blank: It is always reflecting something, even if it is only definite spaces between definite images). There is no reflectivity outside images, no images outside reflectivity—hence no oneness outside manyness, no quiescence outside motion, no permanence outside impermanence, no unconditionality outside the conditional. It is because the *ti* here is the specific kind of *ti* it is, reflectivity, that it does not remain inertly apart from its functions. The water-wave model works exactly the same way, if we stipulate that we are referring only to a body of water that in entirely engulfed in waves: the water is all waves, the waves are all water. There, instead of reflectivity, we have wetness, fluidity keeping the two levels from being in any way divisible or separable, ensuring that they are thoroughly interfused. Whatever is present in the *ti* is also present in the *yong*, and vice versa.

Nonetheless, the relation of irreversible causal priority intrinsic to the *ti-yong* model is in no way effaced. In fact it remains essential: the waves depend on the wetness of the water, but the wetness in no way depends on the waves. The images depend on the mirror's brightness to exist, but the brightness does not depend on the images to exist, but only to be known or manifested. Note that this means the Huayan writers *can* claim reversibility of *ti* and *yong* at the phenomenal level, but when they are doing so they are actually shifting the reference from Li to *shi* in the two cases. Wave A may be *ti* to Wave B as its *yong*, and Wave B may also be *ti* to Wave A as its *yong*. But what this actually means is simply that Li is always *ti*, and *shi* is always *yong,* and the two are always coextensive, but structurally *yong* always depends on *ti* and *shi* always depends on *yong*. Wave A, considered as water, is *ti* to Wave B considered as wave. Wave B considered as water is *ti* to Wave A considered as wave. Since both are always entirely wave and entirely water, we can shift the description *ad libitum*. But in all cases, water is *ti* and wave is *yong*, Li is *ti* and *shi* is *yong*. That relation of one-way dependence never changes.

It is because of the precise nature of the *ti*, the kind of *ti* it is (bright reflectivity or fluid wetness, not inertness or opacity), that the contrasts, though very real, are also subsumed by the continuity: The diversity and motion of the branches are also present in the oneness and quiescence of the root, because the very nature of a mirror is to reflect and the nature of water is to be wet and hence unrestricted to any one shape.

Let us now return to the status of item 7) above, the aspect of "Center" entailed in the *ti-yong* model. In the Huayan case, the *ti* in question (pure bright reflectivity of the mirror, pure wetness of the water) is indeed in a certain sense a "center" in that it is a perfect union of opposite extremes: It is pure being and pure non-being, pure blank and pure fullness, pure indeterminacy and pure determinacy. But while this could well be conceived as the ground for its ability to serve as *ti* to various *yong*, it does not thereby make it stand as a center to the various specific *yong* that depend upon it, nor to structure them as various pairs of opposites around a particular center, but stands as a center only to the two aspects of affirmation and negation of *yong* as such and in general (i.e., being or not being *yong*: The *ti* in this case "is" in one sense the *yong* but in another sense "is not" the *yong*). Indeed, the *yong* are collapsed into the *ti*, and the *ti* into the *yong*, so that the *ti* does not serve as the center of the *yong*, but rather is just itself a center between what are in the pre-radicalized version the *ti* and the *yong*, which are in that earlier model inseparable but contrasted, not coextensive. In the classical model, the *ti* is the hidden, the indeterminate, the one, the "nonbeing," while the *yong* are the manifest, the determinate, the many, the beings. In the Huayan model, the *ti* is both determinate and indeterminate (and likewise is one and many, nonbeing and being, and so on), and is coextensive with the *yong*, and therefore the *yong* is also both. *Ti* as mirror-like Emptiness is all things and it is no thing, and in that sense alone it is a Center between being something and being nothing. But this being Center is not contrasted to extremes that it also connects. It does not stand beyond and between opposites, unifying them, and in that sense also participating in the extremes, as we described for the center-periphery model above and will explore in more detail below. This is because all those diverse and opposed things, the extremes, are part of the arrayed manifold, the moving diversity, the manifest, the phenomenal, which is simply one half of what it, this *ti* itself, is (since it is itself one-many and so forth). Centrality pertains to the *ti*'s own constitution, its own double nature, rather than being the relation it has with the things it grounds.

We can perhaps begin to glimpse here why Tiantai writers will gleefully critique the Huayan conception as "the exclusive Center/Middle" (*danzhong* 但中), as belonging to the Separate Teaching (*biejiao* 別教),[18] although this should become clearer once we consider the Tiantai alternative. What I want to stress here concerns simply the relation of the *ti-yong* model to the notion of Centrality per se. In the Huayan model, although the *ti* is still in some weak sense the center, just as the root stands in the center between the spreading branching, the importance of centrality as such is much downplayed in this usage. The main result of this downplaying of the Center is that the various functions are not necessarily thought of *dyadically, contrastively*—at least there is nothing in the model that especially encourages such an association. On the plus side, this allows perhaps a freer set of conceptualizations: *Yong* do not need to be forced into any preconceived demand that everything must turn out to be ultimately dyadic. We can have a more empirically derived and diverse array of possible functions, of all functions whatever they are—and in fact this is just how Huayan tends to speak of function, as a blanket "everything" (一切) rather than, say, the more internally structured term preferred by Tiantai, "the Three Thousand" (三千), which enfolds some specific dyadic contrasts and paradoxes. *Ti-yong* encourages a stress on the foundational-yet-coextensive nature rather than the "central" relation of its key term to its peripheral terms—or perhaps we should say, in *ti-yong* the *ti* is loosely central only as a side effect of its foundational character; as a result, the elements it grounds, even when coextensive with them, have no necessary structural relation to its centrality except that which derives from its being a ground or foundation per se. It is not because it is a center that it grounds its functions (which are not dyads), but rather because it grounds its functions that it is *in some loose sense* their center. In the alternate models to be considered below, this is reversed: Whatever weak sense of foundation is attributed to the central term is a side effect of its centrality, and

---

[18] Tiantai thinkers distinguish between two different sense of "Middle": "the exclusive Middle" (*danzhong* 但中), which excludes the two extremes and stands above them, and "the non-exclusive Middle" (*bu danzhong* 不但中), which includes the two extremes and is immanent in them, indeed even identical to them. In the fourfold scheme most often used in "classifying teachings" (*panjiao* 判教)—Tripitaka Teaching (*zangjiao* 藏教), Shared Teaching (*tongjiao* 通教), Separate Teaching (*biejiao*), Perfect Teaching (*yuanjiao*)—these conceptions belong respectively to the "Separate Teaching" (*biejiao* 別教) and the "Perfect Teaching" (*yuanjiao* 圓教). Needless to say, this scheme is hierarchical: The Separate Teaching is considered less complete and less perfectly accurate than the Perfect Teaching, although it is also a true and useful heuristic.

the derivative terms are derivative precisely insofar as they are dyadically related to the center. These models will each involve a different sense of ambiguous conceptual priority.

4.2 The Tiantai Model of the Center and Its Expressions as Affirmation and Negation: Here-Now Presence as Filtering Down of Prior Omnipresence and Omnitemporality

A very different model of ambiguous logical and temporal priority is found within another school of Chinese Buddhism, the Tiantai model, which does not map neatly onto a classic *ti-yong* structure, but allows for an ambiguity with respect to priority in a different sense. The Tiantai view of the relation between Li and *shi* holds neither that Li is one and *shi* are many, nor, as in Huayan, that Li is indeterminate (as a mirror's reflectivity is indeterminate, and is hence also the enabling of all determination) and *shi* are determinate (as mirror-images are determinate, composed entirely of the brightness of the mirror's reflectivity, and thus also enabled to transcend their own determinacy, transforming into any other determinacy). Hence the subsequent turnaround where the determinate and the indeterminate end up being interfused and inseparable, and even in a sense "identical," in the Tiantai case does *not* maintain the irreversible structural *dependence* priority that we still find in the Huayan model. It is not the case that Li is root from which *shi* emerges, and it is not the case that *shi* "arise from" Li.

The classic descriptions for the two alternate models, employed in debates between the two schools, are "All Things Arise from the Omnipresent Nature" (*xingqi* 性起) for Huayan and "All Things Are Inherently Entailed in the Omnipresent Nature" (*xingju* 性具) for Tiantai. It is often difficult to distinguish between these two positions, partially because of the lack of number, of articles, and of grammatical distinguishers in the Chinese language. We can make the difference more simply discernible in English. A sentence like, say, "Each and every dharma is precisely Li" (一切諸法一一即理), or any variant thereof, can mean either "Each dharma is identical to the one Li (= the Omnipresent Nature), inasmuch as they are all functions of that one substance, *yong* of that one *ti*, completely coextensive with it" (the Huayan view), or "Each dharma is precisely *a* Li (i.e., *an* Omnipresent Nature)—that is, each determination as such (chair, table, greed, anger, delusion) is eternal, omnipresent, unconditional (all the characteristics that a Li is supposed to have) is the substance of all other things, and all other things are its functions; each is the *ti* of all *yong*, and since *ti* and *yong* are coextensive and identical, each dharma is the *ti* that is identical to all other dharmas as its *yong*, and vice versa." That is the Tiantai view.

The distinction cannot be gleaned by looking at isolated Chinese sentences, in which this ambiguity is almost unavoidable—leading to the strident use of the tendentious term "Three Thousand" (*sanqian* 三千) in later Tiantai writings as an attempt to clarify that this is meant in the sense that entails irreducible plurality, inter-nested dyadic contrasts, and intersubsumption of bias and completeness, of the dyadically contrasted opposites of delusion and enlightenment. Rather, we must take in the entire system of thought of the two schools and interpret accordingly. The Tiantai view, using the word *ju* 具, holds that there is no phenomenon which is not also *a* Li, an alternate name for the buddha-nature, an Omnipresent determinate-indeterminate which pervades and grounds all other phenomena. This means it is not just "buddhahood" that is the nature, which is why we call that nature the buddha-nature. Rather, cup is also the nature (i.e., omnipresent, unconditional, determinate-cupness as indeterminate and indeterminate as determinate-cupness), and thus we can just as legitimately speak of the Cup-Nature, or the Frog-Nature, or the Greed-Nature, or the Key-of-A-Flat-Minor-Nature as the enabling ground of all phenomena. The nature is not any one nature of all things in the universe; there are infinite alternate natures of the universe. An individual determinate thing is not merely a function of the buddha-nature, which is coextensive and ultimately (*in a sense*) identical with it because of the strange double-natured properties of the Huayan idea of buddha-nature indicated above. An individual determination of any thing is the all-pervasive unconditional Nature itself. In an attempt to distinguish these two positions, both of which equally can read into the vast majority of statements made to describe either one of them, Zhili 知禮 (960–1028) stresses, "The so-called one Nature, although one, is not any fixed or definite one" (一性等者，性雖是一而無定一之性).[19] But this is still quite easily understood in the Huayan sense: It could mean "The Nature is not any one definite thing, just as the reflectivity of the mirror is not any one color—it is a oneness that is really a noneness," rather than his intended meaning as I give in the translation. Hence we find Zhili later in the same work trying to clarify

---

[19] *Shi bu'er men zhiyao chao* 十不二門指要鈔 (The Gist of [Zhanran's] *Ten Gateways of Nonduality*), T46.1928, 710a.

unmistakably: "The Nature itself, does not mean some single nature: it is Three Thousand Nature(s)" (又此性體非謂一性，蓋三千性也).[20] The Nature is importantly both one and many, with neither of these determinations being more primary than the other. This does not mean "It is the one Nature *shared by* all the Three Thousand." In that case, it would still be *a* single nature, which is just what Zhili is denying here. The use of the plural in English is thus our most effective way of getting this point across intuitively, perhaps, or a strange locution like, "It is the Three Thousand-fold Nature(s)," singular. We will have to understand in what sense the Nature, which is the *ti*, is both one and many, even when considered without reference to the *shi*, which is the *yong*. This sense is to be found in the Tiantai doctrine of the Three Truths, which are a synonym for the Nature, for Li, for *ti*. It is Three Thousand alternate Lis, each of which subsumes all other Lis.

Now this Three Thousand-fold Alternately Natured Nature is still the *ti* to the *yong*, which is all empirical phenomena, and the *ti-yong* relation between them is still one of total coextensivity and identity. Moreover, it is still true that there is a kind of priority of *ti* over *yong* here. Indeed, as Zhanran says and as Zhili often quotes, "All of the functions are phenomena only because they are inherently available as Li" (並由理具，方有事用.[21] That certainly *sounds* like a straight dependence relationship, easily understood as a classic *ti-yong* relation, with Li as *ti* and *shi* as *yong*—but it *is not,* and this is where the confusion comes in. So what is this alternate Tiantai model of Li and *shi* that still allows Tiantai writers to make claims that superficially sound so Huayan? Let me attempt an explanation here.

---

[20] The rest of the passage (T46.1928, 712c) makes it clear why this is important for Tiantai notions of inter-subjective *ganying* between buddhas and sentient beings, between delusion and enlightenment, and thus for the entire soteriological project:

Everyone knows that "all things have no difference in terms of their nature," but the following line, that each of them therefore pervades all places, requires deep thought. If we just call all the external [matter] being absorbed into the internal [mind] "non-dual," [as the Shanwai exegetes do], how limited it is! How then do they interpret the sentence, "all things pervade all places"? Not to mention the way they make everything reducible to one side [of each pair of opposites] in each of the remaining nine gates, completely ruining the overall structure of argument.

次明若生若佛各自遍融。又此性體非謂一性，蓋三千性也。以佛具三千方攝心生，生具三千方融心佛。心具三千，豈隔生佛？若心無佛性，豈能攝佛？佛無生性，何能攝生？故性體無殊之語有誰不知，一切咸遍之言須思深致。他解唯論融外歸內名不二者，一何局哉！一切咸遍，如何銷之？況餘九門皆歸一邊，全傷大體。

[21] For example, T46.1928, 711a.

4.3 Divergence of Tiantai and Huayan Views of Determination

The Tiantai view, like the final Huayan view, holds that the contents of Li and *shi* are in a certain sense coextensive, that any determination at all, any real or imagined thing, is readable as either Li or *shi*. But the conception of *what a determination is* differs in Huayan and in Tiantai. In Huayan, to be determinate is like being an image in a mirror or like being a wave: It is to be wholly mirror or wholly wetness, and yet also wholly image or wholly wave-shape. That is, it is to be wholly indeterminate (Li) and wholly determinate (*shi*). To be determinate is really to be determinate-and-indeterminate, and determinacy is possible *only* if it is also indeterminate in this way. But the relationship between these two equally necessary and all-pervasive aspects has a specific structure: The determinate is dependent upon the indeterminate.

The Tiantai view also holds that the determinate is always also indeterminate, and vice versa. So the two schools can both claim that to be determinate as such is really to be determinate-indeterminate. But the Tiantai view does *not* involve the one-way dependence relation between the indeterminate and the determinate Rather, it has a "horizontal" view of their relation: They are not compared to root and branch, not *ti* and *yong* (in the classic-model sense), not basis and expression, not wetness and wave, but rather they are alternate one-sided interpretations of the same totality comprised of two opposites, the determinate-indeterminate. If anything, both determinacy and indeterminacy are *yong*, and both determinacy and indeterminacy (but unified as determinacy-indeterminacy) are *ti*. Neither determinacy nor indeterminacy is more fundamental than the other, neither causes the other, neither is the basis of the other unilaterally. The determinate-indeterminate (which is the *ti*) can always be read in two different ways, either as determinate or as indeterminate (i.e., as either of two diametrically opposed *yong*). The shift in description from determinate (*jia* 假) to indeterminate (*kong* 空) is not from the independent (*ti*) to the dependent aspect (*yong*); it is *simply* an aspect shift, implying no priority of one over the other, even logically or conceptually. *Both* of these, determinacy and indeterminacy, are Li, are *ti*; both apply equally to the prior or independent level, and thus both apply to the posterior level as well; *both* of them are *yong*, phenomenal events. Symmetry applies on both levels, top to bottom.

This conception is perhaps a little trickier to grasp than the relatively straightforward Huayan case. What is this counterintuitive relation between determination and indeterminacy? First, as we saw above, starting with Sengzhao, it is a shared insight of most Chinese Buddhist schools that indeterminacy cannot be determinate blankness, the exclusion of all characteristics. The Huayan solution to this problem was to make "reflectivity" stand for indeterminacy, the indeterminacy of a mirror. The danger of this being taken as a determinate something—e.g., as brightness as opposed to images—was handled by collapsing the two, so that all the brightness was images and all the images was brightness. The indeterminate has no content of its own, not even that of blankness: It is just the enabling aspect of all the determinate, and their interdetermination.

To later Tiantai critics, however, the one-way dependence of this relation still makes the brightness, the reflectivity, the wetness something determinate in another, subtler sense. To them, this was a misunderstanding of what it means to be truly indeterminate. In Tiantai, to be determinate is to be indeterminate in the sense of *ambiguous*, which also accounts for all the effects and qualities of "reflectivity," and the like (light is not *just* the light, it is *also* wholly the image, and the mirror, and so on; by the same token, image is not *just* image, but also wholly readable as nothing but light, and so on)[22] but eliminates the one-way dependence relationship between determinate and indeterminate. Rather, the two terms are seen to be

---

[22] Compare Zhiyi's usage of the mirror metaphor in *Mohe zhiguan* 摩訶止觀 (The Great Calming and Contemplation), T46.1911, 8c28-9a4, with that of Fazang (cited above):

> We should understand that each moment of experience is precisely emptiness, precisely provisional positing, precisely the Center. It is at once ultimate emptiness, the storehouse of the Tathāgata [provisional positing of determinate multiplicity], and the ultimate reality [the Center]. These are not three although three, three although not three, not united or separated and yet united and separated, not non-united and not non-separated, not to be described as the same or different and yet both same and different. It is like a bright mirror: the brightness is Emptiness, the images are Provisional Positing, the Mirror is the Center. These are neither one nor distinct, and yet both their unity and their distinction are clearly present. They are not one, not two, not there, and yet they do not exclude oneness, twoness, threeness.

> 當知一念即空、即假、即中，並畢竟空，並如來藏，並實相；非三而三、三而不三、非合非散、而合而散、非合非散、非非散、不可一異而一異。譬如明鏡:明喻即空，像喻即假，鏡喻即中；不合、不散，合散宛然。不一、二、三；二、三無妨。

> The focus is on the ambiguity of the image rather than the paradoxical qualities of the brightness. I can always point to any image in the mirror and say, "This is formless light," or "this is a particular formed image" or "this is mirroring"—the last being the constant co-presence of formless light and the specific formed image, the paradoxical Center *in addition to* the two extremes. The point is the ambiguity among these three views, their constant synonymity and their constant difference. (My interpretation, stressing the simultaneity of the image and the light, follows that of Keguan 可觀 [1092–1182] in his *Shanjia yiyuan* 山家義苑 [Compendium of Home Mountain Doctrines], X57.956, 76c.)

strict *synonyms*. To be determinate (*jia*) is to be ambiguous (*kong*) and to be ambiguous is to be determinate.

Any determinacy itself (not the coextensive grounding of any determinacy) can be considered in two alternate ways: as omnipresent eternal unconditional buddha-nature or as a temporal phenomenon. That is, as Li or as *shi*, as *ti* or as *yong*. But in *either* case, the determinacy is also an indeterminacy, and it is always also ambiguous. The question is, how can a determination be considered as unconditional buddha-nature? For as we touched on above, determination is negation: Determination per se is conditional, since negation is synonymous with a condition (to say that something is in any way negated means "there are some cases, times or places to which this does not pertain" which means the same as "it is conditional"). Huayan answers by saying, "a determination can be 'identical' to the unconditioned just as an image is coextensive with the reflectivity or brightness of a mirror." Tiantai answers that in this Huayan understanding, it is not the determination as such that is unconditional, but merely the unconditional to which it is necessarily in a weak sense identical, i.e., on which it depends, and with which it is coextensive.

Tiantai offers another solution, which can be redescribed in the following way. Determination (negation itself) is indeed negation, that is, limitation. Determination is created by termini, by ends, by limits; it is a function of boundaries. These boundaries must also be determinate for the determination they accomplish to be determination. Now, "it is determinate" is generally taken to mean, on some level, "it cannot be both what it is and something else; it excludes what it is not." Enormously paradoxical consequences result if we try to evade this intuitive definition on every level. In some sense or other, to be determinate is to exclude, and exclusion is accomplished by boundaries of some sort. But boundaries themselves can never be simply determinate in the sense of mutually exclusive with all that they are not. Instead, to be a boundary is to be an interface. That is, to be a boundary is to be both of the two bounded things and neither of the two bounded things: to be their interface, which can belong to neither, and yet must belong to both; to be what contrasts them, and contrasted to both of them, and yet also to be identical to both, inside and outside both. It is, in short, a *Center*. Determination per se is paradoxical, both transcendental and immanent. It involves being both inside and outside a set of boundaries because determination is a function of the separation of things, and the separations (boundaries, interfaces) of things are precisely *Center*.

It is this doubleness that pertains intrinsically to Centrality that defines buddha-nature as what is everywhere and nowhere, the Unconditional that is the union of the conditional (the two divided determinate items) and the unconditional (the boundary that is at once within both of these definitionally contradictory things), thereby both immanence and transcendent. This means that this very boundary is both inside and outside, and the determination it defines is both inside and outside that boundary. In other words, that determination itself is omnipresent and eternal (if we apply the same logic to the boundaries between putative moments in time). It is unconditional and omnipresent and yet, or therefore, determinate, and is determinate yet, or therefore, unconditional and omnipresent.

Hence from the Tiantai point of view, to consider a determination to be buddha-nature means simply to consider it as omnipresent and omnitemporal, while to consider it as temporal phenomenon is to consider it as manifest in a particular time and place as opposed to other times and places. To consider it as buddha-nature is to consider it as unconditioned, and hence as pervading all times and places, and therefore to be the end of suffering, to be buddhahood itself. To consider it as phenomenon is to consider it as conditional, finite, limited, and suffering. In effect, this means that conditionality and determinacy are no longer synonyms, as they are in the Huayan view, and in the commonsensical view. Nor are unconditioned and indeterminacy synonyms in this Tiantai view. Rather, determinacy as such (which *any* starting point has to be, even to do the work of function as a starting point, including even "indeterminacy" as such, including even both-determinacy-and-indeterminacy as such, and so on) turns out to be both inextricable *and* impossible. Whatever is or is not is determinacy, but determinacy depends on boundaries, and boundaries are incoherent, cannot be determinately one thing at the exclusion of all others: They are Centers. So to be determinate is to be an inside-that-is-contrasted-to-an-outside-which-however-is-not-outside-it. To be determinate is to be Empty is to be Center, which is the unconditioned, but only because it is at once both Empty and Determinate (*kong* and *jia*), and neither Empty nor Determinate. Provisional is conditional, Emptiness is unconditional, but Provisional and Empty are opposites that are also synonyms, not merely opposites that are also applied to all the same things.

So it is not just that everything that is conditional (*shi* 事) is also unconditional (Li 理), that every wave is also entirely wetness and vice versa, albeit with an inviolable conceptual priority, a one-way dependence relation between them, as in Huayan. Rather, conditionality per se really means conditional-unconditional. Unconditionality per se really means unconditional-conditional. That is the Three Truths in a nutshell. Indeed, the idea that externality (having an outside) is itself internal to the being-determinate of any determination or entity is the crux of Tiantai ontology, in the formula of the Three Truths.[23] It applies perfectly univocally to both the buddha-nature per se, the mind, or to any cup, dog, blueness or other specific entity. What pervades the universe, and is coextensive with all particular entities as water is to wave, is not just Emptiness and is not just Mind, not just Li as such: It is *any determination considered as the Three Truths*, i.e., *as Li*. Those are names for what can also be called Matter, or Being, or Dog, or Fish, or Table, or Humming Furious Greenness.

4.3.1 Nature-Entailment As Supplement to Nature-Origination

In one sense, this claim is not so much a rejection of the nature-origination view as its supplement, taken up from the opposite side, the side of the conditional. First, on the ontological level, it accepts the "empty mirror" account of the relation between determinate and indeterminate, but reads it differently: The presence of "external conditions" (*waiyuan* 外緣) as genuinely external is regarded as incoherent with respect to the buddha-nature, which is by definition unconditional and thus necessarily unexcludable from any possible entity. This is just the reverse way of saying that nothing is actually excludable from *any* determinate conditional entity, because determination per se is indetermination, because boundaries cannot definitively exclude anything. Because strictly speaking, no conditional thing has an "outside," the alleged Unconditioned (brightness, wetness, whatever) can also be outside of none of them, which means that it too has no outside. This is because it is also really determinate, or if you like, because that to which it is supposed to be external, the determinate and conditional, turned out not to be so, and thus no conditions affecting it can be considered external to it. The dust, the objects confronting the mirror, the external factors, the deluded thoughts of sentient beings, must also be buddha-nature. Even their externality and deludedness per se (their regarding of themselves as outside the buddha-nature), if those are in any way determinate (which they must be even to be named as having the activity of blocking or obstructing buddha-nature) must be buddha-nature.

This is really just a claim about where the division between one thing and another is to be posited, what is to be named what, and the

---

[23] This "absolute-as-relative-as-absolute" or "unconditional-as-conditional-as-unconditional" is what "absolute" or "unconditional" or Nirvanic or buddhahood (in Tiantai terms, the Center 中) amounts to.

inseparability of the parts of a whole. Mirror-plus-external-object—indeterminate openness plus the limited determinations contributed by deluded conceptions of sentient beings—is one inseparable whole, and it is this whole that produces all specific dharmas. Both Huayan and Tiantai accept the claim that buddha-nature is the absolute, the unconditioned, which therefore must be strictly omnipresent in all possible states. But for Tiantai this all-inclusiveness means that buddha-nature must be non-external even to the delusions that seem to obstruct it. Hence Tiantai writers call this totality of unstained openness *and* delusion the buddha-nature, and say all determinations are "inherently included" (*xingju* 性具) in this whole (indeterminacy plus delusion). The Huayan writers call only the openness per se the buddha-nature. For them, the entire buddha-nature ("vertically") enables the production of each concrete determination and always remains coextensive with it; but each determination is also determined ("horizontally") by all the other concrete determinations enabled by the buddha-nature. In their horizontal relations, when they lose sight of the buddha-nature that enables them all, these can give rise to deluded thoughts and karma, and thus come to posit and believe in illusory objects, which they seek or avoid. When that happens, these karmic actions of seeking and avoiding become definite impediments to the realization of the buddha-nature, impeding its full manifestation. These deluded determinate conditions can still coherently be said to have arisen from the buddha-nature: They arise from it precisely because it is so pure, because it does not hold to any particular nature, as we already saw in the Fazang quotation above. But once they have arisen, they can genuinely obstruct the apprehension of the indeterminacy that is always enabling them, insofar as to-be-determinate-that-manifests-indetermination is not the same thing as to-be-the-indeterminate-that-is-manifested-in-determination, and so this does not change the basic externality that pertains to them. This means that in Tiantai the contrast to the obstructing objects must itself be part of the mirror, and so its being impinged upon by external things is also something inherent to its own nature, as are whatever specific delusions in the minds of sentient beings have conditioned the appearance of precisely these forms and no others. Not only that there are delusions, but the contents of these delusions, whatever these delusions hold to be true, are all unconditional in just the same way, for all that is required to be unconditional is to be determinate in any way, insofar as that always involves inescapable but impossible (i.e., Central) boundaries. Not only the deluded mentations that imagine false images, but also the false images so imagined, are the whole truth and nothing but the truth.

4.3.2 The Sense in Which Tiantai Centrality Can Be Said to Pre-exist and to Enable the Extremes

The above exegesis should allow us to see what is meant by the weird claim that "the One Nature is Three Thousand different One Natures; the one Li is Three Thousand different Lis." Whatever exists necessarily has the characteristics that make it qualify as the Nature: eternity and omnipresence. Whatever determination appears to anyone in any way is a Li, whatever determination appears to anyone is a *ti*. Every experience of every sentient being is a *xing*, a Li, a *ti*. As Zhili says:

> The term Nature means Unchanging. It means that the *ti* of each thing has the Four Meritorious Properties of Permanence, Bliss, Selfhood and Purity, and is never altered. We must understand that all four Properties apply to each dharma, such that even all the way down to each and every one of the causes and effects, environment and organisms of all the purgatories, every one without exception is itself Permanent, is Blissful, is Self, is Pure. This is what the *Lotus Sutra* means when it says, "The phenomenal characteristics of the mundane world are all eternal."

所言性者，不變為義。謂四德之體無遷易故。須知此四遍一切法，下至地獄依正因果，一一無非常樂我淨。「世間相常斯」之謂也。[24]

Here the idea of the Center is crucial. This can be seen clearly if we consider the full quotation from which the "foundationalist-*ti-yong*-sounding" claim above—about how *shi-yong* are possible only because there is, priorly, inherence in the *ti*—was taken. The passage comes from Zhanran's commentary to Zhiyi's *Mohe zhiguan*. The topic here is a meditation technique known as "contemplation of the mind" (*guanxin* 觀心), concerned only with the phenomenal level of mind. After having delineated three senses in which mind may be said to "create" all dharmas,[25] Zhanran says:

> All of these function (*yong*) as phenomena only because they are inherently available as Li. Now if we want to practice the contemplation, all we attend

---

[24] *Jin guangming jing wenju ji* 金光明經文句記 (Notes on [Zhiyi's] *Commentary on the Words and Phrases of the* Suvarṇaprabhāsa-sūtra), T39.1786, 90c.
[25] The three senses are: (1) considered as Li, the Center as the Three Truths, implying omnipresence and unconditionality, it inherently includes what is not itself; (2) past karma as intentionality produces present and future effects, as well as enabling present effects; and (3) buddhas and bodhisattvas produce upayic lures that the minds of sentient beings reproduce in their own experience.

to is this omnipresent availability as Li. That means that all determinations are, all at once, negated as determinate, all are established as determinate, and all are the entire omnipresent all-there-is of the Dharma-realm. Each one then freely integrates, however it may turn, whatever other determinations may appear, whether ultimate and provisional.

並由理具方有事用。今欲修觀，但觀理具。俱破、俱立，俱是法界；任運攝得權實所現。[26]

To say of any determinate here-now X that it is Li is to say that it is identical to the Three Truths, which just means to say of it three things: X is not (definitely) X, X is (somehow) X, and X is everything. The "everything," the Center that denotes omnipresence, is specifically the interchangeability of "X is not X" and "X is X," due to the ambiguous (i.e., "Central") quality of boundaries, which are definitional to all determinacy qua determinacy. It means both that the putative boundary between determinate things is a Center of two determinate extremes, enabling and establishing them, uniting them and distinguishing them, ensuring both that they negate one another and that this negation of each other is precisely what establishes both of them, and yet showing that they do not actually negate each other, since they somehow coexist precisely as this interface, this Center, without which they cannot exist. In fact, the determinate thing defined by such constitutively ambiguous boundaries is itself ambiguous, and is itself a Center, both itself and its outside, and indeed a kind of interface of all the things that precede it and follow it, all its premises and conclusions, all its causes and effects, which stand on either side of it as the two extremes it both excludes and includes.

The conceptual priority is here not the result of a foundation and derivative relationship, as in the radicalized Huayan *ti-yong* model, made merely conceptual and ambiguous by the fact that the foundation in question happens to be non-inert, non-obstructive, actively interpenetrative either as the formless reflective light of a mirror or the lubricity of water's wetness. Rather, it is the ambiguous priority of the kind that a Center has over the two dyadic extremes that it enables. If we think of the extremes to which a pendulum swings in relation to the center-point of that swing range, the extremes qua extremes do not pre-exist the Center, but in a certain weird way the Center does pre-exist the extremes, in that the oscillation may be anywhere from zero to very minute to very huge,

---

[26] Zhanran, *Shi bu er men zhiyao chao*, T46.1928, 293a.

but the one thing that will be constant throughout will be this zero-point of the Center. If the pendulum is not moving at all, it is there at the Center. If it moves slightly, producing extremes A and B, the center is still there. If it moves more robustly, or in a more complex three-dimensional orbit, producing the extremes C and D, the center is still there exactly as before. If it becomes a vortex, or a vortex of vortices, producing hugely complex internested hierarchies of dyadic opposites, the center remains exactly where and what it was in the previous cases. In all cases, it unites, relates, enables, regulates, defines, and establishes whatever extremes there may be. It is still, while they are moving. It is one, while they are many. It is enduring, while they are transient. It is not directly manifest, while they are directly manifest. Its existence can be known only from observing them. And yet they are inseparable from it, and in an important way it permeates and pervades them (wherever we are seeing the extremes we are seeing the Center in action). All these things could also be said about the *ti* relation to *yong*. As should be quite evident now, however, the two models are quite importantly different in their structures and implications.

So what then, on this Centrality-Periphery model, do the Tiantai writers mean when they say, "Only because it is already inherently present in Li does it function as *shi*"? *Not* that a particular *shi* arises because it is already present in Li; rather that it *does not arise at all*. Not that a determination—say, this cup with all its characteristics—arises because anything at all can arise from the formlessness of a mirror's light or a water's wetness, which obstructs nothing; but also not because there was also an identical set of determinations in some spectral eternal realm of Li. Rather, because it is one and the same determination that we are now calling Li and now calling *shi*. The cupness-just-as-it-is is omnipresent and omnitemporal; that is why it is also here and now.

Initially, we cannot reverse *this* relation and say it is omnipresent and omnitemporal because it is here and now, because omnipresence and omnitemporality *include* being here and now. It is not the *basis* of its arising, but the *whole* of which it is a part. However, this is merely the first step. On closer examination, we discover that each part is also intersubsumptive with all other parts, and is thus itself inseparably the whole, so that there is finally a sense of reversibility, or perhaps synonymity, even here: Its being here-and-now is finally synonymous with its being everywhere, alternate descriptions of the same fact. The relation is horizontal rather than vertical. Seeing this cup here and now, in my ordinary deluded experience, is seeing the eternal omnipresent cup, the cup which is the Li of cupness. I am not seeing an expression or it, or a result of it, or the manifestation of it: I am seeing *it*. I am seeing the Li itself with my eyes. I am seeing it where it really is. It is really in this time and this place.

To see it merely as *yong* or as *shi* simply means that I am indeed already seeing the omnipresent *ti* or *Li* that is right here, but that I am not *also* seeing it *everywhere else*. I am seeing it here, where it has always been, but I am not seeing it being here in the past and future, and I am not seeing it being everywhere else. Why? Because of my particular set of attachments and delusions, my karma, which *filters out* all the other instances of its presence, narrowing them down to just this one. Why is it appearing as if here and now only? The Huayan answer has to be, it is arising from Suchness (the Omnipresent Formless Buddha-nature, and so on), and it is directly from Suchness that it gets its arising: It is the *yong* of the *ti* which is Suchness. That is the "vertical" explanation of its causality.[27] The supplemental horizontal explanation in Huayan will be that it is shaped by the totality of other conditions, a single univocal set of them, all with the same status as provisionally real but ultimately unreal, in the universe. The horizontal explanation will be the traditional Buddhist karmic explanation of predictable and univocal causal process, with all its moral-epistemological entailments basically unchanged. Each thing is vertically the open unconditional totality, but these individual versions of the totality are enabled and not prevented by the totality to interfere with and condition and attach to each other in ways that obstruct their apprehension of this totality in themselves and others, and this ignorance in turn exacerbates this alienation and suffering.

In contrast, the Tiantai story about arising *has no vertical dimension.* Arising is a *narrowing down* of what is already there, and is always only spoken of as pertaining to the experience of some specific sentient being or beings. So to explain it, we must explain the arising of the perception of motion or change in a sentient being, which is the arising of mental action chopping up a non-arising reality of infinite alternate omnipresences. The arising of *that* action, which is necessarily subjective, is only horizontal, and alternately explainable in "Three Thousand" different ways, none of which is merely true or merely false, and each of these Three Thousand different causal stories manifests internally to this specific mental event. The mental event orients itself by implicitly positing its own story about where it came from, about which sort of othernesses in time and space it stands surrounded by. It generally posits its own past in terms of either prior

---

[27] See Peter N. Gregory, *Tsung-mi and the Sinification of Buddhism* (Honolulu: University of Hawaii Press, 1991), 232.

conditions (previous moment causes subsequent moment of experience), the conceived conjunction of subject and object (eye comes into contact with object), or conceptual contrast against a negation (long versus short). But its implicit explanation of self-proclaimed arising is not like a single univocal causal account, even on the horizontal level. In Tiantai there is no vertical causality, but even on the horizontal level the explanation for why a particular experience seems to arise at a particular time and place and not elsewhere is not univocal: It is to be sought not in a single birds-eye story about the causes and conditions that actually pertain to modifying the mirror-like indeterminacy and producing this particular image, as in Huayan's horizontal dimension, but rather in an infinite number of subjective causal accounts at once, literally any way any sentient being perceives it at any time (thus we are here typically given layered and reversibly inter-nested explanations of any issue, with each perspective on the matter reconsidered from within another perspective and vice versa), and then the intersubsumption of these alternate subjective explanations. These are the infinite alternate sets of conventional truths that result from Three Truth theory, in contrast to the *single* set of conventional truths that result from Two Truths theory (Huayan and all other Mahāyāna Buddhism).

Let me try to explain this more concretely.[28] I see cupness only here—even though it is everywhere—because of my particular karmic story. I think of it a certain way. But that certain way is not self-containable, any more than any other determinate thing. *Its* boundaries too, the "way's" boundaries, turn out to be paradoxical and porous, due to the incoherent nature of what a boundary is, on which all determination depends. That is why this single explanation, this story I tell myself about myself, always falls apart and starts bleeding into other explanations, other horizontal causal stories. Once I see all possible explanations as versions of my original idiotic self-serving explanation, I see that it is all and none of these that account for the arising of the mental event that made me experience a flash of greenness only here-and-now, constrained within these particular boundaries, rather than everywhere at once and all of the time, in the form of both itself and everything opposed to it. This cupness does not arise: Rather, its other instances are suppressed by my ignorance. This cupness does not depend on indeterminacy any more than indeterminacy depends on cupness, for these are synonyms: The indeterminacy of the cup is just a one-sided way of describing the omnipresence of cupness, its presence *as* every other determinacy, just as the cupness is

---

[28] For a fuller explanation of the derivation of Tiantai epistemology, the reader is invited to consult my "Tiantai Buddhism," especially section 1.3, "From Two Truths to Three Truths."

a one-sided way of describing the indeterminacy. They are both one-sided ways of describing the omnipresence; that is, *kong* and *jia* are one-sided ways of describing *zhong* 中. Another sentient being may agree with me about the presence of the cup right here and not everywhere else because she, to that extent, has similar karma with mine. The causes of her suppression of all the other presences of the omnipresent cupness are part of her present self-accepted implicit karmic story, while mine are part of mine. (Needless to say, these stories differ and interpenetrate in the same way—they too will end up being omnipresent and mutually interpervasive, insofar as they were determinate at all, and determinate is constitutively incoherent.) Yet we are both seeing the same omnipresent cupness, which is unconditional and thus present *as* something or other (in both of these two cases, as something nameable and agreeable-upon as "cup") everywhere.

Among these alternate explanations of the arising of this cup will be the one given by buddhas and bodhisattvas who see me seeing it: For them, it arises as part of their own compassionate *upāya*, and when I see them seeing me seeing it, when I think of them thinking about me thinking about the cup, I also experience this alternate causal account. That means the cup must be there just as it is: It is an expression of buddhahood, of compassion, of upayic wisdom. That is now (one of the) explanation(s) for why it has arisen in this time and place, even though it has always been everywhere.

Putting these two types of explanations together, we see the significance of the Three Truths. The seeming to arise is a necessary aspect of the non-arising, the omnipresence, for Provisional Positing is a necessary dimension of the Center's being the Center. Indeed, in the final analysis, looking back at the arising of the here-now version of an eternal omnipresent determination, I cannot say even that it is a simple unambiguous fact that it ever arose: That too is ambiguous; in one sense it can be said to have arisen but in another not to have arisen at all. For even the act of filtering down is not a positive addition to reality, but itself an eternal quality that is filtered down by that act of filtering, positing itself. This is as far down as we can go: Our intrinsic belief in the determinate nature of each mental event is the primal starting point and primal ignorance to which Tiantai practice is directed. In a sort of *cogito*-esque way, this mental determination is undoubtable; what ensues in practice is that this undoubtable reality is supplemented by conviction of its coterminous impossibility, and that is all the "prior" omnipresence really amounts to, seen finally to have always been both a here-now event of filtering out all the other instances and forms of that determination and the omnipresence of that determination as internally possible only as this prior omnipresence and its provisional contrasting of itself to all that it is not, without which that determination cannot be established as determinate. That is, it is not that it is first omnipresent and then arises in some particular time and place; being omnipresent (Center) and arising in a particular place (Provisional Positing) and not being distinguishable from where it is not (Emptiness) are synonyms, and *all three* belong to Li, to what it is to be omnipresent.

To view any given thing as omnipresent is to view it, as Zhanran says above, as "at once negated, established, and omnipresent" (*jupuo juli jufajie* 俱破俱立俱法界), as three alternate descriptions of the same fact. I have tried to explain this at length elsewhere in two related ways: as an *asness* relation, and as the way this relation is expressed in the setup/punchline structure. That is, X is omnipresent not as X, but as all other things, as non-X, which are X appearing as non-X. Omnipresence itself must posit X in some here-and-now (this being, presumably, the only way to establish it as distinct from other things, as determinate at all) and also as the superseding of the illusion of its limitedness to that particular here-and-now; there is no other way for X to be omnipresent, while the same is true for Y and Z and so on. So ultimately omnipresence itself posits its own illusion and the superseding of its illusion. When sentient beings are experiencing delusion, they are just experiencing the first half of a two-step process, necessary to that process. When the rest of the process is seen by the originally deluded sentient being, he or she no longer sees his or her past delusion only as delusion; he or she also sees it as *upāya*, and as an expression of buddhahood, hence also as non-arising, as omnipresent, as the active presence of buddhahood itself.

So omnipresence posits its own delusions about itself as the only way to be omnipresent, but this is still not vertical causality. First, it is single-plane omnipresence, more/less, whole/part at stake here, rather than two distinct levels. Hence, Zhanran will say, ordinary experience of separate, bounded, finite things and moments is not an illusion but rather is "a small portion of Conventional Truth" (*shidi shaofen* 世諦少分).[29] But more importantly, the deluded sentient being's initial understanding that what he or she is experiencing is just real divisions in the world, or that it is the result of his or her own deluded karma, is on an even footing with the subsequent view that it is omnipresence itself that posits its own limitations. Indeed, *these* two views interpenetrate in Li, neither is given priority, for as the *Lotus Sutra* is taken to establish, it is only by being an illusion that it serves as an *upāya* that it is part of buddhahood, as well as vice versa.

---

[29] Zhanran, *Zhiguan yili* 止觀義例 (Examples of the Doctrine in [Zhiyi's] *Great Calming and Contemplation*), T46.1913, 451c.

4.3.3 Schematic Approach to the Different Models

Here too, then, the claim that all dharmas are originally present in the nature is not a claim that there are mutually exclusive, fully determinate entities existing in the pre-manifest state and waiting to be given a phenomenal form—as for example in Plato's theory of forms, or in another sense in Kant's transcendental forms, or his notion of intelligible character, where something with some determinate characteristics of some kind is waiting behind empirical reality to be given an opportunity to transfer, unchanged, from that state or form to this, from an a priori to an a posteriori form.[30] In the Tiantai Three Truths claim, however, that determinacy is indeterminacy and vice versa, that local coherence is global incoherence,[31] that provisional positing is Emptiness, and indeed even that provisional positing is the Center, and that the Center is a provisional posit, and that Emptiness is the Center, and that the Center is empty.[32] This means that any determinacy is at once fully determinately itself and at the same time inherently always something beyond itself, beyond any given determinacy, and that it is only able to be determinate in any sense at all because it is not fully determinate (it is a specific image because it is formless light, just as in Huayan), but not-being-determinate is itself a determination (formless light, the empty mirror, is itself a specific image).

---

[30] In Plato's case, *more* determinate than their manifestation; in Kant's case, determinate in a different respect—as form, as norm, as universal rule for unifying particulars of sensory intuition—but equally determinate: The necessary law of causality, just as it is as an a priori form, is exactly what I know phenomenally when I recognize an instance of causality empirically.

[31] That is, when all factors are taken into consideration, the original way any thing appears is no longer unambiguously present.

[32] As Zhiyi writes of the mirror metaphor in *Mohe zhiguan*, T46.1911, 55b15-18:

> Insofar as one is empty, all are empty: there is no provisional positing or centrality that is not empty. This is the contemplation of Emptiness as the encompassing term. Insofar as one is provisionally posited, all are provisionally posited: there is no emptiness or centrality that is not provisionally posited. This is the contemplation of Provisional Positing as the encompassing term. Insofar as one in central, all are central: there is no Emptiness or Provisional Positing that is not central. This is the contemplation of Centrality as the encompassing term.

一空一切空無假中而不空。總空觀也。一假一切假無空中而不假。總假觀也。一中一切中無空假而不中。總中觀也。

Note that we could also translate this to mean "there is nothing provisionally posited that is not also central," and so on. But the ambiguity between the adjective "empty" and the abstract noun "Emptiness" is deliberate and crucial here. The concrete and the abstract cannot be cleanly separated here. The three terms are synonyms, three senses with a single reference, so it is essential that there is both a difference between them and an identity, just as synonyms necessarily differ from each other (in stressing some particular aspect), and yet refer to the same thing.

Indeed, in all these Chinese cases, we must note a stark contrast to the doctrines of innate ideas or pre-existing determinate norms or structures in Western thinkers. In Plato, for example, pre-existence is not a result of inseparability of the two realms, and hence the impossibility of either existing independently of the other, *but just the reverse*: Pre-existence is taken to mean that the multiply determinate pre-empirical reality can exist and be known independently of the appearance of the forms of that pre-empirical reality in space and time. Kant's case is different, inasmuch as transcendental forms cannot be known without first being instantiated in sensible intuitions of space and time; but the reason they cannot be known is not because they lack determinacy, nor because they are themselves interdependent with sensible intuitions, of which they are in themselves entirely independent. In short, in all the Chinese cases, pre-existence of the non-empirical is an entailment of inseparability of the empirical and non-empirical, not of the independence of the pre-empirical realm, and a marker of the inseparability of every element within empirical reality from every other element, *and* of every element of non-empirical reality with every other element of non-empirical reality.

In Tiantai, however, the mutual inclusion and identity relationship between any two *shi* entities is not as in Huayan. The Huayan case can be represented as follows:

A = X (*shi-li, yong-ti*) ←----------→ B = X (*shi-li, yong-ti*),
Therefore A = B

Therefore A is the *ti* of B (because A is X, and we already know that X is the *ti* of B) and "reversibly" B is the *ti* of A (because B is X, and we already know X is the *ti* of A).

In Tiantai, however, it is as follows:

A = A + B (3000 as Li, as *ti*, and hence *including* also 3000 as *shi*, as *yong*) ↔
B = A + B (3000 as Li, as *ti*, and hence *including* also 3000 as *shi*, as *yong*)
Therefore A = B

Therefore, if we apply *ti-yong* language, A is the *ti* of B (it is A + B, the 3000, that serve as the *ti* of B), and reversibly, B is the *ti* of A (it is A + B, the 3000, that serve as the *ti* of A).

4.3.4 Reversible *Ti-Yong* and the Tiantai Center

This contrast might become clearer if we examine the redescription from usually non *ti-yong* language in Zhiyi to *ti-yong* language in Zhanran. The *locus classicus* of this doctrine of mutual inclusion, the identity of one moment of thought and the Three Thousand aspects of reality, is a famous passage of the *Mohe zhiguan*, where Zhiyi says:

> One mind inherently possesses the ten dharma-realms, and each of the dharma-realms possesses the ten dharma-realms again, making a hundred dharma-realms. Each dharma-realm inherently possesses thirty aspects of existence, and thus the hundred dharma-realms inherently possess a total of three thousand aspects of existence. These three thousand reside in any single moment of sentience. If there were no sentience, that would be one thing, but as soon as there is the least sentience, even the smallest moment of it, it immediately possesses these three thousand. We should not say sentience exists first and that all known phenomena later, nor that all known phenomena are first and sentience of them comes later. It is like the characteristics of change in an object [generation, persistence, decay, destruction]: if the thing were prior to characteristics, the thing would not be changed by them, and if the characteristics were prior to the thing, the thing would also not be changed. Neither prior nor posterior is permissible here. When we speak of the thing, we refer to just the process of change of the characteristics, and when we speak of the process of change of the characteristics, we refer to just the thing. The mind is also like this. If all dharmas were produced by the mind, this would be a vertical relationship of priority. If the mind simultaneously encompassed all dharmas, this would be a horizontal relationship of coexistence. Neither of these is permissible—rather, the mind is precisely all dharmas, and all dharmas are precisely the mind.

> 夫一心具十法界，一法界又具十法界:百法界。一界具三十種世間，百法界即具三千種世間。此三千在一念心。若無心而已；介爾有心，即具三千。亦不言一心在前，一切法在後；亦不言一切法在前，一心在後。例如八相遷物:物在相前，物不被遷；相在物前，亦不被遷--前亦不可後亦不可。秖物論相遷，秖相遷論物，今心亦如是。若從一心生一切法者，此則是縱。若心一時含一切法者，此即是橫。縱亦不可，橫亦不可。秖心是一切法；一切法是心故。[33]

The topic here is the phenomenal individual psychic level, not the relation between Li and *shi* as such: Mind in this passage is emphatically phenomenal mind, a here-now moment of mentation, arising from the interaction of sense-object and sense-organ, rather than mind as a synonym for the

---

[33] *Mohe zhiguan,* T46.1911, 54a5-16.

pure mirror-like reflectivity of the *ti* in the Huayan *ti-yong* model. Note that there is no *ti-yong* language at all here, as this is with Zhiyi, written at a time before that model enters the mainstream of Tiantai discourse. Zhiyi tells us that the mind, as a particular entity, does not "contain" all things, nor does it really "produce" them; rather, it *is* them. Any moment of sentience *is* all the objects of sentience, and all other ways of sensing them. The noetic and noematic aspects of a single act of consciousness are compared to a thing and its characteristics—as we might say that a red box right here is nothing but redness and boxness and right-hereness (and so on). The entity and its characteristics are the same thing described in two different ways, unitarily or severally. Their relationship is like that given by the Huayan *ti* and *yong* at the universal metaphysical level: Coextensive, collapsed into the other. Whatever is mind is its objects, whatever is its objects is mind. But in Tiantai this is said not at the universal level, but at the direct phenomenological level, the individual psychic level: This ambiguity of mind and matter is what is to be noticed as characterizing every particular experience. They are in a reversible relationship, where just as I can say with equal legitimacy either that the thing is reducible to its characteristics, or the characteristics are reducible to the thing, I can say that all mind is its objects, or all objects are the mind.

It is here, on the inter-phenomenal level, that we see something close to the Huayan coextensive *ti-yong*, but now applied reversibly, and *it is this reversibility, rather than one of the two aspects of the coextensive ti-yong, that describes Li*. This is true in Huayan too, inasmuch as the Center/buddha-nature (Li) is revealed ultimately only as the interpervasion of all *shi*. But as mentioned above, the reversibility in Huayan is really still always Li as *ti* and *shi* as *yong*, simply switching the aspects in the two alternate descriptions. In Tiantai, each determination is reversible both in Li and in *shi*, the latter initially as a small portion of the former, or a single side of what is delineated by the former qua Center. In Tiantai it is weakly *ti* because it is strongly Center, rather than being weakly center because it is strongly *ti*. Significantly, it is not just any characteristics that Zhiyi gives as identical to the entity itself: It is the characteristics of the process of change, or arising and perishing, the history of the entity's generation and destruction. The thing is the thing's life-death process, the thing's temporal career in its transition from not-being-X to being-X to not-being-X. Transition here is impermanence, which is the most immediate manifestation of conditionality, which is simply the necessary relation to otherness. The internal characteristics of a thing with which its being is reversibly reducible are thus its relations to othernesses—its intrinsic inclusion, in its very essence, of what is not itself. It is not accidental but necessary for any determinate thing to have an outside. Having an outside is essential—and hence internal—to all determination. Having precisely *this* outside is essential—and hence internal—to being precisely *this* thing. A thing is nothing but its characteristics, and its characteristics are nothing but the thing, but all those characteristics are the internality of its own externality. A thing is nothing but its own otherness.

Here is Zhanran's summation of the situation, again emphatically at the individual psychic level (translated according to the explanation by Zhili):

> All dharmas without exception are of the nature of mind, but any all-inclusive nature is ipso facto no specific nature, and thus it is the Three Thousand, all present there unchanged. We must understand that the [phenomenal, momentary] mind, [is shown through the meditative process to be inseparable from the eternal, omnipresent] minds and bodies [of all beings, including their partial appearance as the initially apparently external objects of that phenomenal mind's experience, related to it just as in Zhiyi's metaphor of the thing and its marks of transformation above], so even as it goes through the transformation of states [which are its experiencing of putatively external objects], these are just the mind itself. It is just this transformation that is called the "creation" of all dharmas of its experience, which means the experienced temporal *yong* [Three Thousand] are just the *ti* [Three Thousand] itself. It is truly for this reason that each of those contents is neither matter nor mind, and yet is matter as opposed to mind and mind as opposed to matter, and yet is also only matter, and is also only mind. Thus merely be looking at one's own present moment of experience one sees oneself, sees all others, sees all sentient beings, sees all buddhas. Since even the sentient beinghood and buddhahood of others is thus the same as one's own [single phenenomenal moment of] mentation, how much more so one's own sentient beinghood and buddhahood?
>
> 一切諸法無非心性，一性無性。三千宛然。當知心之色心，即心名變，變名為造，造謂體用。是則非色非心而色而心，唯色唯心良由於此。故知但識一念，遍見己他生佛。他生他佛尚與心同，況己心生佛寧乖一念？³⁴

Here we see how *ti-yong* is grafted onto Zhiyi's *ti-yong*-free exposition above, and how that model is thereby apparently but not ultimately

---

³⁴ Zhanran, *Shi bu er men* 十不二門 (Ten Gateways of Non-duality), T46.1927, 703a.

modified. What is key to note is, first, that the oneness of the Nature and the noneness of the Nature and the multiplicity of the Nature(s) are all synonyms here, the Three Truths restated. The Three Truths are Li, that is the Nature, which is the Nature of mind but also the Nature of any other thing. This Li is what will be described as the *ti,* but it is not the noneness alone (as in Fazang's trope of pure unchanging imageless reflectivity alone) nor even just the noneness and its coextensive muchness (imageless reflectivity necessarily always expressed as multiple images), as it was in the Huayan "exclusive Center." Rather, it is first *one specific determinate nature*: This is not the imagelessness here (reflectivity), but rather *the characteristic of mentalness*, which is one *specific, partial, determinate, conditional* characteristic. As Zhili likes to stress, this could equally well be "the nature of materiality" *se'xing* 色性, rather than "the nature of mentalness" *xinxing* 心性. We might have said, "All dharmas without exception are of the nature of *matter, are instances of the characteristic of materiality*, i.e., *are material*. But any all-inclusive nature is ipso facto no specific nature, therefore. . . ." "Mind" is not the universal *indeterminate* formlessness here; it is a particular *determinate* characteristic, *this* single moment of experience qua a single mentation. When everything is seen as having the characteristic of "being mental as opposed to material," then "mental" loses its original meaning, which was based on its boundaries excluding the material as non-mental. That is why Zhanran goes on to say, "one nature is no nature," and that this is all Three Thousand Natures.

Let us note also that, according to Zhili, the first usage of "mind" here refers to the momentary, temporal, deluded, phenomenal mind, while the phrase "mind and body," which the first is claimed to be identical to, refers to all minds and bodies available phenomenally in space and time *and* those very same minds and bodies re-seen as each eternal and omnipresent, of which the temporal version is a small *portion*. It is seeing the co-extensivity of this single temporal moment of mentation and all other possible objects of experience that establishes an immediate experience of the untenability of their mutual exclusivity: "This mentation" and "that chair it is seeing" claim to be either/or entities, since they are determinate, but the fact that what we are experiencing is simultaneously "this mentation" and "that chair" shows that this cannot be so. This lived co-extensivity of allegedly mutually exclusive determinates is why whatever this phenomenal moment of mentation perceives, it nonetheless is *also* perceiving itself, and this is the manifestation in direct experience of its being at once self and other, and therefore omnipresent and eternal.

Further, it is through their identity with this one phenomenon (this moment of mentation) now demonstrated to be eternal—and not with a prior eternal formlessness (reflectivity as *ti*, and so on)—that each and every one of the Three Thousand experienced phenomena is also seen to be uncontainable in any particular time and place, and thus Three Thousand alternate names for the Nature, Three Thousand alternate Lis.[35]

---

[35] Tiantai master Zhili explains this passage in *Shi bu er men zhiyao chao*, T46.1928, 710b):

> The first *xin* refers to any random moment of experience. The *zhi* is a grammatical auxiliary. *Se xin* refers to the Three Thousand as Properties of the Nature. The Integrated Teaching understands that the Nature, not being Principle-Only, is the Nature as Entailing the Three Thousand. This Nature perfectly intermelds, pervading and entering all that coexists in this moment of experience. This "mind as all minds and all matters" means that precisely this moment of experience alone is all three thousand minds and matters, like the "eight characteristics" of an object so that there is no before or after, just as is described in the passage on the mind's entailment of the Three Thousand in the *Mohezhi guan*. Each and every one of these three thousand mental events and material things is eternally unchangeable, and that is why they are called the Nature. This sentence describes the whole and the parts with respect of Ultimate Principle: the originally entailed Three Thousand are the parts, while the one moment of experience is the whole. It is because the Three Thousand are just one Nature that any one moment of experience can serve as the whole that includes them all.
>
> The next line, "so even as it goes through the transformation of states [which are the experiencing of its experiences of putatively external objects], these are just the mind itself," refers to the above-mentioned moment of experience that is comprised of and entails the Three Thousand in its process of following pure or defiled conditions, transforming but not transforming, creating various states but not thereby creating anything anew, thereby able to become any of those Three Thousand events or characteristics as they exist in temporal phenomenal reality. Although the term "transformation" is used in both the Integrated and the Separated Teachings, and the term "creation" is used in all four teachings, their usage here such that precisely the entailing mind is itself its transformations and this transformation is all that is meant by creation is possible only in the Integrated Teaching, not in the other three teachings.
>
> These two lines describe the whole and the parts within phenomenal reality: the transforming and created Three Thousand are the parts, the one moment of experience is the whole. This is also because the Three Thousand are one Nature and thus can all reduce to any given moment of experience.
>
> "The experienced temporal *yong* [Three Thousand] are just the *ti* [Three Thousand] itself" indicates that in the above described transformation and creation of all dharmas, it is the entire *ti* that gives rise to each *yong*. Because the previous mentioned moment of experience entails all the mental and material things, and transforms into and creates them according to conditions, all the mental and material things within phenomenal reality have the Three Thousand as they are within the Nature as their *ti*, with the Three Thousand as they are when arising within phenomenal reality as their *yong*. Thus the entire Principle-*ti* gives rise to each phenomenal *yong*. Only thus do we see the meaning of "following conditions" in the Integrated Teaching.
>
> 初言心者，趣舉刹那也。之者，語助也。色心者，性德三千也。圓家明性既非但理，乃具三千之性也，此性圓融遍入同居刹那心中，此心之色心乃祇心是三千色心，如物之八相更無前後，即同《止觀》心具之義，亦向心性之義。三千色心一不可改，故名為性，此一句約理明總別，本具三千為別，刹那一念為總，以三千同一性故，故總在一念也。即心名變等者，即上具三千之心，隨染淨緣不變而變、非造而造，能成修中

In his interpretation of this passage, Zhili emphasizes that this cannot be taken simply to mean the mind is Li, and that Li is one, whereas phenomena created by the mind are *shi*, and *shi* are many. Rather, both mind and experienced phenomena are here both Li and *shi*, and Li and *shi* each separately are both one and many.[36] That means simply that each and every phenomenon is all-pervasive and eternal, and that all other experiences are seen, on examination, to be one-sided, narrowed-down experiences of each of them *as* something else. The eternal Three Thousand are the *ti* here, the phenomenal Three Thousand are the *yong*, but they are really just one and the same Three Thousand.

We could utter a sentence that sounds almost identical to that last sentence to describe the Huayan *ti-yong* model (just alternate ways of describing the wave, as wetness or as wave): The eternal Li is all the phenomena, the phenomena are the eternal Li, just as the wave is the wetness and the wetness is the wave. But there the unity is the wetness and the multiplicity is the wave—the radicalized classical *ti-yong* model. Here on the Tiantai side, *"ti"* is borrowed to mean the eternity and omnipresence of any determination, i.e., that determination seen as Li, i.e., as the Three Truths, that is, as determinacy-indeterminacy—as provisional positing which is also present as Emptiness, which is also present as the other two being identical to each other—that is, as the Center. It is this Centrality that is meant by omnipresence, and it is this alone that makes any given dharma the *ti*.

三千事相，變雖兼別、造雖通四，今即具心名變、此變名造，則唯屬圓不通三教。此二句則事中總別，變造三千為別，剎那一念為總，亦以三千同一性故，故咸趣一念也。造謂體用者，指上變造即全體起用，故因前心具色心隨緣變造，修中色心乃以性中三千為體，修起三千為用，則全理體起於事用，方是圓教隨緣之義。

[36] Zhili, *Shi bu er men zhiyao chao*, T46.1928, 708c:

> The previous parts spoke of all phenomena as not losing their own character as the parts; now we show how they all together reduce to any one moment of experience as the whole comprised of them. They are always themselves without losing their own character, and yet also always together reduced to any one moment of experience. All dharmas as inherently entailed in the Nature are such that the whole and part are completely encompassing of each other, and the same is true of all phenomena as conditionally arising. It does not mean that the phenomenal events are the parts and the Principle is the whole. You should also know that both as events and as principles, it is a phenomenal moment of experience that serves as the whole, since sentient beings exist within phenomena and have not yet awakened to Principle, and thus use this to manifest the wondrous principles in accordance with the deluded aggregate of mind.

> 前約諸法不失自體為別，今明諸法同趣剎那為總，終日不失終日同趣，性具諸法總別相收，緣起諸法總別亦爾，非謂約事論別、以理為總。又復應知，若事若理，皆以事中一念為總，以眾生在事未悟理故，以依陰心顯妙理故。

So the claim of inherent inclusion, the pre-existence of all determinacies prior to their manifestation in a particular time and place, is really just a claim about the nature of determinacy itself. It means simply that what is prior to any given determinacy cannot be thought of as the definitive exclusion of that newly arisen determinacy, for that would mean that that exclusion of X was itself fully determinate, continently boundaried, in at least this one way. The pre-existence of X does not mean something could be *known* about X prior to its manifestation in some time and space. It means that *once it has appeared in time and space*, the times prior to and after its appearance must be viewed as nonexclusive of it, as all of one piece as it. Given the inseparability (due to the incoherence, i.e., Centrality, of boundaries) of being-so-determined and not-yet-being-so-determined, each is really both. The *ti* is an omnipresence not merely of being-indeterminate-as-being-determined as in Huayan, but of being-indeterminate-as-being-*so*-determined.

Yet we also see here clearly that entailment does not actually mean the presence of fully-formed determinations in the mind, on the model of "innate ideas," or some sort of non-physical realities like Plato's ideas. There really are no purely non-physical realities in the Tiantai world: Physicality is rather a narrowed down one-sided view of something that is always both physical and mental. As in Zhu Xi, pre-existence does not mean there could exist knowledge of something prior to some kind of physical manifestation of it, for there would be no one to do this knowing; both Tiantai and Zhu Xi deny that there could exist any purely non-physical, purely non-temporal, purely non-spatial knowers—a key point for all truly atheist epistemologies! The point in Tiantai is that the phenomenal mind is precisely the putatively external dharmas that are contrasted to it, and the dharmas are none other than that mind itself. This also means precisely that neither could mind "alone" produce all dharmas nor could the totality of all dharmas alone produce the mind: For it is impossible for either to be "alone." But then, further, in another sense each one alone can produce the other: Precisely because each one alone is entirely unintelligible, what is referred to when I say "mind" or "the totality of non-mind dharmas" is actually always the whole comprised of both, or the whole readable as either; because each "alone" can only really *mean* "the whole, including both parts." Mind means mind-and-dharmas, dharmas means mind-and-dharmas, so either mind alone or dharmas alone can provide all mind and all dharmas. The issue is again inseparability, indivisibility, such that really what we are denoting when we say "mind" is also the dharmas, and vice versa; they are two ways of looking at the same thing.

4.3.5 Why It Matters: Inherent Evil in Tiantai and *Ti-Yong* as Center-Periphery

This position also has a special soteriological implication important to Tiantai writers: that all evils and delusions are themselves not only ineradicable from the buddha-nature, but that each of them *is* the buddha-nature from which nothing can be eradicated. As Zhili says in maximally explicit mode, "The entire *ti* of every here-and-now evil deed or cognition is the same evil as omnipresent, unconditional Nature: thus each of the twelve links in the chain of samsaric causation, each of the five aggregates of clinging, is like space: eternally dwelling, pervading all times and places" (修惡全體是性惡故。十二因緣及以五陰。一一如空常住周遍 。).[37] That is, part of what is at stake in the Tiantai claim discussed here is the soteriological idea that delusions and evils are not to be eliminated to reach the pristine purity of the original nature, but rather that each and every one of them can itself function *as* that nature, i.e., as unconditioned, omnipresent, omnipotent, appearing in and as all other phenomena. Zhanran makes this very explicit:

> [For sentient beings] the Three Thousand at the stage of [mere identity to buddhahood in terms of] Li[38] are all to be called Ignorance, while the same Three Thousand, upon attaining buddhahood [when this identity is realized in *shi*], are all to be called eternal and blissful. The Three Thousand do not change in the least, so the Ignorance is precisely the Enlightenment. Each of the Three Thousand is eternal; each is *ti*, each is *yong*.
>
> 三千在理同名無明，三千果成咸稱常樂。三千無改無明即明，三千並常俱體俱用。[39]

The deluded world of the sentient being is the Three Thousand; the enlightened world of the buddhas is the same Three Thousand. To

---

[37] *Guanyin yi shu ji* 觀音義疏記 (Notes on [Zhiyi's] *Elucidation of the Meaning of the Avalokiteśvara*), T34.1729, 936c.

[38] Many apologies to newcomers to Tiantai for this confusing terminology! When Zhanran says "Li," here, he actually means precisely *shi*!!!! Li here means when their interpervasion and eternity and so on is merely potential, the first of Zhiyi's "six identities" (六即), namely, identity with Li (理即), which is the ordinary experience of sentient beings. Zhanran knows this is amusingly reversible. Hence he dwells on it in the *Jin'gang pi* 金剛錍 (The Adamantine Scalpel), T46.1932, 784c24: "You must understand that sentient beings have only Li [their buddhahood, etc.], whereas the buddhas put it into practice in actual here-now experiences; and conversely sentient beings have only here-now experiences, whereas the buddhas realize [all of these] as Li" (應知眾生但理諸佛得事。眾生但事諸佛證理。)! Zhanran means Li here in the first sense.

[39] *Shi bu er men*, T46.1927, 703c.

understand the full thrust of this claim we must remind ourselves that "the Three Thousand" explicitly includes among its members both the deluded sentient being and the enlightened buddhas themselves. Hence each includes the others' Three Thousand—that is, each way of viewing the cosmos includes a view of every other view of the cosmos—and these are still all the same Three Thousand, the same cosmos. This is so only because of what "the same" means in Tiantai: one corner of the Three Truths, hence also "different" and "omnipresent into whatever is different from it."

Zhili's explanation clarifies the radical meaning of this position precisely in terms of the Tiantai understanding of *ti* and *yong*:

Each and every one of the Three Thousand worldly phenomena is eternal. These Three Thousand considered as pre-existing Li are all named *ti*, and these same Three Thousand considered as phenomenal transformations are all named *yong*. Thus Zhanran says, each is *ti*, each is *yong*. The first two lines here show that the cause and the effect each possess all Three Thousand; the third line shows that the Three Thousand of the cause and the Three Thousand of the effect are one and the same Three Thousand, because none of them are altered. The fourth line shows that all of the Three Thousand of causes and effects can give rise to functions. Before buddhahood, each of the Three Thousand gives rise to defiled functions, while after buddhahood, each of the same Three Thousand gives rise to pure functions. This fourth line delineates the Perfect Teaching most explicitly. Why? Because the terms *ti* and *yong* are originally a way of asserting full mutual identity. So whenever we say that all dharmas are identical to Li, this "identical" is legitimate only if it is the entire *yong* without exception that is precisely the *ti*.

三千世間一一常住，理具三千俱名為體，變造三千俱名為用，故云俱體俱用。此四句中，初二明因果各具三千，三明因果三千祇一三千，以無改故，四明因果三千之體俱能起用，則因中三千起於染用，果上三千起於淨用，此第四句明圓最顯。何者？夫體用之名本相即之義，故凡言諸法即理者，全用即體方可言即。[40]

Ti-yong in its radicalized Huayan sense is still a crucial premise for this usage, because of its implication of total coextensivity and identity, combined with a certain sense of categorical priority of *ti* over *yong*.

---

[40] *Shi bu er men zhiyao chao*, T46.1928, 715b.

Indeed, the identity is more thoroughgoing, but at the same time the categorical priority is also more thoroughgoing. The one-way dependence relation that still divided the alleged identity between the determinate and the indeterminate in Huayan is here eliminated. Only one of the contrastive elements is retained: quiescence versus activity. *Ti* is still quiescent and eternal as opposed to the transience of *yong*, though these two are now also seen as coextensive on a meta-level, as just described in the previous few paragraphs. But the other key contrastive elements of the classical *ti-yong* model—*ti* as one/*yong* as many, *ti* as indeterminate/*yong* as determinate, *ti* as *suoyi*/*yong* as *nengyi*—are eliminated in Tiantai. These crucial contrastive elements are moved into the nature of *ti* itself, and also into the nature of *yong* itself. *Ti* is self-contrasted as one and many, *yong* is also self-contrasted as one and many. The two "contrastive" elements, dependence and quiescence, are retained but altered: They are now understood on the model of whole and part. Thus the *ti* has conceptual priority in the sense in which whole is conceptually prior to part, and where omnipresence is conceived as a function of Centrality. The Center is conceptually prior to its peripheral elements, and pervades them. The *ti* is thus quiescent in the sense that it pervades all times and places, and cannot shift from one position to another or ever be absent in some and present in others. It is not quiescent or one in the sense of being Emptiness as contrasted to Provisional Positing, for it is both. In other words, the contrastive elements are reconceived on the Center-periphery model: a contrast between center and periphery, which also enables a contrast of the more normal *ti-yong* kind between the diverse peripheries. The normal *ti-yong* kind of dependence pertains, but reversibly, to the relation between any one Li and all the other Li, and any one *shi* and all the other *shi*—and indeed to any one Li and all *shi*, and to any one *shi* and all Li. As Zhili says, "The Three Thousand of deluded sentient beings and the Three Thousand of the Buddhas are one and the same 'secret treasury,' and each and every one of those Three Thousand is fully endowed with the Three Truths. All of them together occupy any single moment of experience" (眾生三千諸佛三千同一祕藏是故一一皆具三諦。此等法門同居一念).[41] Thus, although Tiantai masters after Zhanran freely used the originally Huayan *ti-yong* terminology, they were able to do so only by radically altering and qualifying its meanings.

---

[41] *Guanyin xuanyi ji* 觀音玄義記 (Notes on [Zhiyi's] *Profound Doctrine of [the] Avalokiteśvara [Chapter of the Lotus Sutra]*), T34.1727, 912c.

4.4 Zhu Xi on Li's Pre-existence of *Qi*

Let us now turn to Zhu Xi. How does he build his own usage of *ti-yong* in relation to the two Buddhist versions we have examined, and how does this relate to his claim that Li, in some sense but not in every sense, pre-exists *qi*? As we shall see, Zhu Xi's case lies interestingly right between the two Buddhist cases. As with Huayan, he admits full conceptual priority of a singled-out metaphysical entity which is characterized by absolute disjunction and absolute co-extensivity with all physical manifestations (Taiji). As with Tiantai, the reason he gives for this special wondrousness is derived from considerations of its *Centrality*. This Centrality is considered to be synonymous with the actual effectivity of the Li that stands above and within all manifest existence (also Taiji). This Centrality is given primary expression in its capacity to enable and unite dyadic *oppositions*, and derives from that neither-one-nor-many asness relation between a *multitude* of Li (each of which is also the entire Taiji). In this way, Zhu Xi brings the two models together. Let us see how.

> Someone asked: "Is it that there must first exist a certain Li before there can be a certain sort of *qi*"?
>
> Zhu Xi answered: "Basically neither is prior to nor posterior to the other. But if you insist on searching out the origin, you must say that the Li is first. But Li is also not some separate thing; it exists here within this *qi*. Without this *qi*, the Li has no other place that can carry it. *Qi* refers to metal, wood, water and fire, while Li means benevolence, rightness, ritual and wisdom."
>
> 或問：「必有是理，然後有是氣，如何？」曰：「此本無先後之可言。然必欲推其所從來，則須說先有是理。然理又非別為一物，即存乎是氣之中；無是氣，則是理亦無掛搭處。氣則為金木水火，理則為仁義禮智。」[42]

Again:

> Someone asked about the theory that Li precedes *qi*. [Zhu Xi] said, "One cannot say that. Can we know that, as things appear at present, Li precedes *qi*, or *qi* precedes Li? Neither can be found out. But if we speculate on it, it seems that this *qi* always moves in dependence on this Li, and wherever this *qi* gathers, Li is also present. Now *qi* can solidify and thereby create

---

[42] *Zhuzi yulei, juan* 1, 3.

things, while Li has no sentiment or intention, no plan, no calculation, no creation. But wherever *qi* solidifies, Li is within it. It is something like the plants and animals and people in the world; none is born without a root; and it is certain that nothing grows in unplanted land from no seed. But all of that [root-branch stuff] is a matter of *qi*. As for Li, it is just a realm (世界) of its own, pure and open, without form or trace. It cannot create, whereas *qi* can ferment and solidify to generate things. But wherever this *qi* is, Li is within it."

或問先有理後有氣之說。曰:「不消如此說。而今知得他合下是先有理,後有氣邪;後有理,先有氣邪?皆不可得而推究。然以意度之,則疑此氣是依傍這理行。及此氣之聚,則理亦在焉。蓋氣則能凝結造作,理却無情意,無計度,無造作。只此氣凝聚處,理便在其中。且如天地間人物草木禽獸,其生也,莫不有種,定不會無種子白地生出一箇物事,這箇都是氣。若理,則只是箇淨潔空闊底世界,無形迹,他却不會造作;氣則能醞釀凝聚生物也。但有此氣,則理便在其中。」[43]

We all know many more examples of this kind of hedging and prevarication on Zhu Xi's part. He seems to be saying that Li and *qi* are always co-present and inseparable, but then again, if forced to speculate about the question at all, one has to conclude that in some unspecified sense Li has some priority, a sense that seems to imply that it is somehow in one sense priority and in another sense not. I believe this can be simply resolved. The key is the equivocation between *singular and plural*, inherent in the Chinese language when left unmodified. When Li is mentioned without modification, it may denote either Li per se, and any given specific Li, or possibly both. This is further complicated by the fact that Zhu Xi's metaphysics specifically stipulates that in one sense there is only one Li everywhere in the universe (the Taiji), but that in another sense each thing has its own specific distinct Li—these being two ways of viewing a neither-one-nor-different asness relation inherent to the nature of Li, to be explored in a moment. With these premises in mind, I think we can locate a fairly straightforward position in Zhu Xi: (1) In a temporal sense, Li and *qi* never exist without each other, so there is no Li existing alone in the universe without *some qi*. In that sense there is no priority, no temporal priority of Li per se over *qi* per se. (2) However, in all states Li has a certain conceptual priority, to be

---

[43] *Zhuzi yulei*, juan 1, 3–4.

specified below. (3) But in the case of any *specific* Li, the specific Li always literally precedes its instantiation in *qi* even temporally—*for it is already retrospectively found to be present in and as any other previous Li.*

Although Zhu will say in some passages that Li can exist before and after Heaven and Earth exist, this is not the same as saying it can exist before or after *qi* exists. Heaven and Earth are a specific arrangement of *qi*. They are *yin* and *yang* already divided. Li existing in inchoate undivided *qi*, before and after Heaven and Earth (or any particular Heaven and Earth cycle) is really just Li existing in an extreme macro-form of *yin qi*, really not conceptually different from the way the Li of life, of springtime, of Benevolence (*ren* 仁), exists unexpressed in the depths of winter before the solstice, a necessary phase of dormancy.[44] We may pause here to consider the fact that Zhu Xi was a careful and appreciative reader of

---

[44] *Zhuzi yulei, juan* 1, 4:

> Someone commented: "There must be a certain Li for there to be a certain sort of *qi*, but it seems like this does not allow for a separation of before and after."
>
> [Zhu Xi] answered: "The main point is that Li must be prior. But that doesn't mean we can say today there is a certain Li and tomorrow we finally get the corresponding sort of *qi*. But there still has to be a kind of priority between them. If for some reason heaven and earth with all their mountains and rivers were to disappear, there would still after all be their Li here."
>
> 問：「有是理便有是氣，似不可分先後？」曰：「要之，也先有理。只不可說是今日有是理，明日却有是氣；也須有先後。且如萬一山河大地都陷了，畢竟理却只在這裏。」
>
> Xu asked, "Before heaven and earth have divided, do all the different things of the subaltern world already exist?"
>
> [Zhu Xi] replied: "It's just that there is the Li of all of them already. For heaven and earth may be producing things for hundreds of thousands of years, but in all times it's just these particular things and no others."
>
> 徐問：「天地未判時，下面許多都已有否？」曰：「只是都有此理，天地生物千萬年，古今只不離許多物。」

Cf. *Zhuzi yulei, juan* 1, 7:

> "At the beginning of heaven and earth, when all was mixed in primal chaos and undivided, I think there was nothing but the two elements fire and water. The dregs of the water became the earth. For even now we can climb up to the high places and see that the mountains are in the shape of the waves like all kinds of water. We just don't know when they coagulated. At first they were most soft, and only later became hardened."
>
> Someone asked: "I wonder if it might be as waves arise and stir up sand?"
>
> [Zhu Xi] answered: "Yes. The most turbid part of the water became the earth, while the clearest part of the fire became the wind and thunder and lightning and the sun and stars and the like."
>
> 「天地始初混沌未分時，想只有水火二者。水之滓腳便成地。今登高而望，羣山皆為波浪之狀，便是水泛如此。只不知因甚麼時凝了。初間極軟，後來方凝得硬。」

Zhang Zai, and although he does not by any means accept everything Zhang has to say, he is emphatic in pointing out where he disagrees with him. I am assuming that Zhu basically accepts Zhang's account of what *qi* is and how it behaves, and Zhang's key point about the impossibility of *qi*'s literal non-existence. Among later Neo-Confucians, Zhang Zai was perhaps the accepted authority on what *qi* is, although they may have regarded him to have been badly confused about Li. Zhang's conception of *qi* is designed specifically to exclude the very idea of *qi* ever not existing. Very explicitly and emphatically, *qi* in its most indeterminate, vacuous state is still *qi*, and is to be sharply distinguished from the heretical notion of "non-being," which the Sages never talked about and which Zhang considers to be both incoherent and pernicious. I think Zhu probably accepted this view of *qi*, while sharply disagreeing with Zhang about the status of Li in relation to it.[45] So, on my reading, contrary to appearances, Zhu Xi does *not* admit the existence of Li without any *qi* existing, even as a possibility, at any actual moment of time, either past or future. If he thought there definitely was a time when Li existed and *qi* per se did not, it is hard to understand why he would feel the need to prevaricate on this issue at all, let alone so persistently and insistently. Admittedly, it is possible that he is merely prevaricating out of empirical humility—that he is really unsure, not having been there (and no mind could be there to know it, since minds are *qi*), although he thinks

---

問:「想得如潮水湧起沙相似?」曰:「然。水之極濁便成地,火之極清便成風霆雷電日星之屬。」

Clearly, *qi* exists before heaven and earth are divided.

[45] See for example *Zhuzi yulei, juan* 99, 2532–2541; see especially 2534, where Zhu Xi is asked about the claim that Taixu 太虛, the Great Vacuity, is *qi*. Zhu Xi had already stated that really Taixu should be identical to the Wuji 無極 of Zhou Dunyi 周敦頤 (1017–1073), and thus is really Li, not *qi*. But what he says is, "他亦指理," which I take to mean that, although this is *qi*, it is *also* Li in its unexpressed state, or as present in that vacuous state of *qi* before heaven and earth take shape. That is, *qi* and Li are *always* together, and "the Great Vacuity" refers to the state of *both* in the *qi* that is completely vacuous, before heaven and earth are divided, before there are any determinate things at all. Zhu Xi is quite critical of Zhang in these pages, especially on 2538: "When Zhang Zai says the Great Vacuity is precisely *qi*, he is referring to Li as the Vacuity; that seems not to be taking it as something in the realm of form." Zhu said, "Even if he is referring to the Vacuity as Li, how can he cram it together with *qi* in one place?"「橫渠云『太虛即氣』,乃是指理為虛,似非形而下。」曰:「縱指理為虛,亦如何夾氣作一處?」This *could* be read as saying Zhang should not have considered Li and *qi* mixed together as one when speaking of the Great Vacuity as *qi*, and I think this mixing is just what Zhu objects to—*not* because they are not in fact mixed and always co-present, but because Zhang mixes up his categories when he speaks in this way of Taixu as *qi*, thereby directly equating Li and *qi*. This is Zhu's objection to Zhang. But Zhang's idea that *qi* is something to which a straightforward "being" or "non-being" is inapplicable is never anywhere questioned by Zhu Xi, which I think he would have to if he thought that *qi* could ever be wholly nonexistent.

it possible and consistent with the nature of the Li-*qi* relation.⁴⁶ I do not rule that possibility out (and it would mean reading his reservations about Zhang Zai more harshly, which is indeed possible), but I think we have a simpler explanation for the prevarication that does not involve Zhu's taking the odd and problematic stand that Li could ever exist without *qi*. That position is not what Zhu is claiming when he does feel the need to affirm pre-existence of Li as one leg of his paradox. The issue is rather the sense in which, in spite of the constant co-presence of Li and *qi* in all actual instances, Li is nevertheless *also* in some sense "prior" (*xian* 先). As suggested above, I think this is true in two senses: (1) Li as such is conceptually but not temporally prior to *qi* as such, with a dependence relation that is not a simple classical or radicalized *ti-yong* relation but the *ti-yong-plus* relation that is a center-periphery relation; but also in that (2) *any particular Li* is prior *temporally* to *its* manifestation as a *particular* configuration of *qi*. ⁴⁷

We saw in the Huayan radicalization of the *ti-yong* model how Li and *shi* can be inseparable, coextensive, beginninglessly and endlessly so, but still retain a structural relation of one-way dependence between them. Is the Huayanesque *ti-yong* model what Zhu Xi also means when he says Li and *qi* are inseparable, always existing together, but that there is also some sense in which Li is "prior"? In one sense, yes, but not completely. Although he also still speaks of the Taiji as the *benti*, he is at pains to avoid the straightforward *ti-yong* relation uninflectedly. Indeed, when reporting how his views on the Li-*qi* relation changed radically around the age of 40, Zhu relates that he had previously mistakenly applied a straight *ti-yong* structure to Li and *qi*, as quoted at the beginning of this chapter.⁴⁸ This suggests that he has an alternate model in hand after that time, one that still

---

⁴⁶ If so, being faithful to Confucius' dictum at *Analects* 2.17: "To regard what you know as what you know and what you don't know as what you don't know—that is knowledge" (知之為知之，不知為不知， 是知也。).

⁴⁷ For example, "When we speak of the Nature of Heaven and Earth, we are speaking exclusively with reference to Li. When we speak of the *qi*-constitution Nature, we are speaking of the same thing but with regard to Li and *qi* mixed together. Before there is this *qi*-[constitution] there is already this Nature. When [this] *qi*-[constitution] ceases to exist, the Nature will constantly be there." (論天地之性，則專指理言；論氣質之性，則以理與氣雜而言之。未有此氣，已有此性。氣有不存，而性却常在。), *Zhuzi yulei*, *juan* 4, 67 and passim. "*Qi*" in the last phrase really means the "this *qi*" 此氣 of the previous phrase.

⁴⁸ Quoted already above in the Introduction to this chapter: "I formerly regarded the Supreme Pivot (*taiji*) as the *ti* and motion and stillness as its *yong*, but this way of putting the matter is definitely defective" (熹向以太極爲體，動靜爲用，其言固有病，後已改之曰「太極者，本然之妙也；動靜者，所乘之機也」，此則庶幾近之。), *Zhu Xi ji*, *juan* 45, 2154.

admits of an ambiguity when it comes to priority, but in a rather different sense. What is this new model?

We saw one alternative in the Tiantai model of whole as unconditional and part as conditional, where the unconditional is precisely the Center, taken to mean non-one-sidedness to either presence or absence, and hence omnipresent asness. Here it is Centrality itself that stands for something roughly describable as *ti*, that makes phenomenal appearances depend on its prior existence. It is not central because *ti*; it is *ti* because central. It is *ti* only to the extent of, and in the manner of, uniting opposites—in the Tiantai case, the opposites of presence and absence, inside and outside, this and that. Thus in a certain sense the Center is the overlapping of the two radii, and must contain the both of the two extremes (it belongs to both X and non-X), while in another sense it is opposed to the extremes (it belongs to neither X nor non-X). As the overlap of the two it is the whole that contains all the opposed determinations. As belonging to neither, it is transcendent, standing beyond all determinations. The Li pre-exists the *shi* as the Center pre-exists the two extremes, as the whole pre-exists the part. In another sense the two extremes and the Center are coeval. It seems that Zhu Xi's modification of *ti-yong* as applied to the Li-*qi* relation shares this trait: The Taiji is fundamental and prior because it is a Center, a union of opposites that contains them but also transcends them. But in this case the opposites are designated in a precise way that derives from traditional Confucian ethics and its philosophy of nature: motion and rest, *yang* and *yin*.

Zhu gives his most comprehensive account of the macro-structure involved here in the opening passage of his commentary to Zhou Dunyi's "Taiji tu shuo" 太極圖說 (Explanation of the Supreme Pivot Diagram). The problem there is precisely the relation between the Supreme Pivot (*taiji*) and the motion and stillness that produce *yang* and *yin*. Here is Zhou's text and Zhu's commentary:

> Zhou Dunyi: The most formless of all is yet the Supreme Pivot of all! The motion of the Supreme Pivot generates *yang*. When this motion reaches its ultimate it pivots into stillness, and this stillness generates *yin*. When the stillness reaches its ultimate it pivots back to motion. Alternate motion and stillness thus serve as the root of one another, separating into *yin* and *yang*, thereby establishing the two modes.
>
> 周敦頤:無極而太極。太極動而生陽，動極而靜，靜而生陰。靜極復動。一動一靜，互為其根；分陰分陽，兩儀立焉。

Zhu Xi: "The workings of Heaven above have not even sound or smell" and yet it is genuinely the axis, the hinge, the pivot of all creation and transformation, the root and foundation of all manner of existences. Thus he says, "The most formless of all is yet the Supreme Pivot of all!" He does not mean that outside of the Supreme Pivot there is something else which is the least formless of all. The motion and stillness of the Supreme Pivot is the flow of the Heavenly Mandate. This is what the *Yi* describes when it says, "The alternation of *yin* and *yang* is called the Way." Now True Integration (*cheng* 誠) is the root of the sage and is the end and new beginning of each thing; that is just what here is called "the Way." Its motion is the unobstructed going forth of the True Integration, [what the *Yi* calls] "the Good which is its continuation," "that which all things depend on to begin to exist." Its stillness is the reversion of the True Integration, [what the *Yi* calls] "human nature as its completion," "all things making straight their own natures and destinies." Motion goes still at its extreme, stillness returns to motion at its extreme, motion and stillness alternating and serving as the root of one another—this is why the life and mandate of Heaven flow on without cease. The motion generates *yang*, the stillness generates *yin*, separating *yin* and *yang* so that the two modes are established—that is why their individual roles and identities are fixed and unchanging. *In sum, the Supreme Pivot is the inherent original paradoxical numinosity at the root of all things,*[49] *and motion and stillness are the triggers of transition in which it is carried.* The Supreme Pivot is "the

---

[49] *Miao* is a word with that literally means "minute, hard to see," but is already used for the unmanifest and unnamed aspect of Dao in the first chapter of the *Dao de jing,* and picked up in the "Xici zhuan" 繫辭傳 (Great Commentary) of the *Book of Change* as a demythologizing replacement word for *shen* 神, the pre-philosophical notion of "spirit": "Spirit is just a word devised to speak of the numinousness of all things" (神也者妙萬物而為言也). We should perhaps then also think here of all the other remarks about *shen* in the "Xici zhuan": It is what arrives without traveling, accomplishes without working, what shows no sign of the process yet does the job "miraculously." It is also "the unfathomableness of *yin* and *yang*" (or "what is not fathomable in terms of *yin* and *yang*"): All of these point to what is not palpable or formed, what is beyond dichotomous thinking, and yet what is most powerful and efficacious. We should think here also of Zhou Dunyi's own cryptic remark: "What moves without being still and is still without moving is things. What moves without moving and is still without being still is spirit." The latter applies quite neatly to the Supreme Pivot and its relation to *yin* and *yang* as stillness and motion, whether on Zhou's own interpretation (where the Axis is perhaps itself moving and still) or on Zhu Xi's reading (where it is not). We might also note the significance of the term *miao* in Tiantai—the greater part of its main theoretical work, Zhiyi's *Miaofa lianhua jing xuanyi,* is several hundred pages of exegesis of this one character. Its basic definition there fits right into this discussion. It means "what cannot be conceived" (*bu ke siyi* 不可思議). Things are the dyadic, the divided. The numinousness is what is at the same time one thing and another, inherently paradoxical, beyond sensory apprehension but also beyond determination as one thing

Way that is above form," while motion and stillness are "its tools that are endowed with form."

朱熹:上天之載，無聲無臭，而實造化之樞紐，品彙之根柢也。故曰：「無極而太極。」非太極之外，復有無極也。太極之有動靜，是天命之流行也，所謂「一陰一陽之謂道」。誠者，聖人之本，物之終始，而命之道也。其動也，誠之通也，繼之者善，萬物之所資以始也；其靜也，誠之復也，成之者性，萬物各正其性命也。動極而靜，靜極復動，一動一靜，互為其根，命之所以流行而不已也；動而生陽，靜而生陰，分陰分陽，兩儀立焉，分之所以一定而不移也。蓋太極者，本然之妙也；動靜者，所乘之機也。太極，形而上之道也；陰陽，形而下之器也。[50]

The crucial line here, indicating Zhu Xi's deliberate and self-conscious post-midlife-crisis revision of his earlier ti-yong undersanding of the Taiji/yin-yang relation (which is also the global Li-qi relation) is, "In sum, the Supreme Pivot is the inherent original paradoxical numinousness at the root of all things, and motion and stillness are the triggers of transition in which it is carried." Whalen Lai deserves great credit for focusing on this substitution of ji (trigger, incipient reversal) for yong (function) as the key to Zhu Xi's mature metaphysics, although I disagree with almost all the

---

or another, as either of any two opposites. It is, of course, the Center between them, enabling and uniting and relating them. See for example the explanation given by Zhu Xi's student Cai Jitong 蔡季通, *Zhuzi yulei, juan* 5, 84:

"The master's *Taiji tu jie* says, 'motion and stillness are the triggers that carry it.' Cai Jitong was very intelligent, and could see what was meant there, and said that this phrase is where the master is at his most precise and insightful. For it basically means that while the Supreme Pivot is Li, and is above form, and *yin* and *yang* are *qi*, and thus below form, although Li has no form of its own, the *qi* reveals these specific traces of it. Since the *qi* has motion and rest, how could the Li it carries be said to be devoid of motion and rest?" He also quoted the "Motion and Rest Chapter" of Zhou Dunyi's *Tongshu* in this connection: 'What moves without being still or is still without moving is a *thing*. What moves without moving and is still without being still is spirit (*shen*). To move without moving or be still without being still is not to be devoid of motion and rest. Things are obstructed, but spirit is the numinousness of all things.' Motion and stillness are the triggers that carry it!"

「先生《太極圖解》云：『動靜者，所乘之機也。』蔡季通聰明，看得這般處出，謂先生下此語最精。蓋太極是理，形而上者；陰陽是氣，形而下者。然理無形，而氣却有迹。氣既有動靜，則所載之理亦安得謂之無動靜！」又舉《通書．動靜篇》云：「『動而無靜，靜而無動，物也；動而無動，靜而無靜，神也。動而無動，靜而無靜，非不動不靜也。物則不通，神妙萬物。』動靜者，所乘之機也。」

[50] Zhu Xi, "Taiji tu shuo jie" 太極圖說解 (Explanation of the Taiji Diagram Essay), *Zhouzi quanshu* 周子全書 (Complete Writings of Zhou Dunyi), comp. Dong Rong 董榕 (1711–1760), ed. Hu Baoquan 胡寶瑔 (1694–1763), *Guoxue jiben congshu* 國學基本叢書 edition (Taipei: Shangwu yinshuguan, 1964), 4–7 passim.

conclusions he draws in his analysis of Zhu Xi's "turn."⁵¹ What we can agree on is that the Li-*qi* relation is not straightforwardly a "substance-functioning" relation. It is a "numinousness carried in triggers of transition" relation. The key is to understand the idea of *triggering reversal* in Zhu Xi's metaphysics. What does reversal have to do with the Taiji, with the Supreme Pivot?

Taiji, the Supreme Pivot, is intrinsically *paradoxical*, and this is what makes it appropriate to describe it as numinous (*miao*). That is what the first line of Zhou's text has told us: It is nowhere and everywhere, the least and the most, it is most absent and most present, it is most formless and yet the decisive pivotal element of all things. It is the source of their production, the principle of their formation, and the standard of harmonious flourishing, but always by virtue of precisely its absence, its formlessness, its non-assertion and non-control, by being unfindable as any one specific element or thing. But these familiar paradoxes, which also pertain to the Dao of the *Dao de jing*, are so not for the Daoist reasons pertaining to the formlessness and namelessness of the undifferentiated unhewn (*pu* 樸, *wuming* 無名) as opposed to formed named and valued objects of desire cut out from that background (*qi* 器, *ming* 名), nor for the similar Huayan reasons (the formlessness of the brightness enables, negates, and co-extends the forms), but for the specifically Confucian reason derived from the "Great Commentary" to the *Book of Change:* the Taiji, the pivot and interface between *yin* and *yang*. This is the center point between the two extremes of motion and rest, the point of transition between them, which is also the point of connection between them. A pivot between two extremes is also paradoxical in the ways just mentioned, but also in a different and additional way: It participates in both of the two extremes, it unifies them, it defines them, and yet it must also be above them, beyond them, contained in neither of them.

The key to understanding the structure here is the figure of the axis, the center. I have written about this at length elsewhere, borrowing Qian Mu's 錢穆 metaphor of a swinging pendulum.⁵² Qian's metaphor, in fact, comes from a long and thoughtful engagement with precisely Zhu Xi's idea of the Supreme Pivot and its relation to the two extremes of *yin* and *yang*.

---

⁵¹ Whalen Lai, "How the Principle Rides on the Ether: Chu Hsi's Non-Buddhistic Resolution of Nature and Emotion," *Journal of Chinese Philosophy* 11, no. 1 (1984): 31–65.

⁵² Qian Mu, *Hushang xiansi lu* 湖上閒思錄 (Lakeside Reflections) (Taipei: Dongda tushu gongsi, 1988), 42–44. See also my earlier discussion of the pendulum in this chapter.

The Supreme Pivot is undivided, "wondrous" (*miao* 妙), which means paradoxical, more than one thing at once, not limited to the boundaries of any one side of a dyad of opposites—a usage deriving from the *Yijing* on *miao* 妙 and *shen* 神. Zhu Xi makes clear just what he means by the numinous in his extravagant praise for Zhang Zai's dicta, "It is the co-present twoness that makes it inconceivable" (兩在故不測) and "it is the [simultaneous] twoness that causes change" (兩故化)[53]—this being the key to

---

[53] See *Zhuzi yulei, juan* 98, 2511–2514:

> Someone asked about Zhang Zai's dictum, "Because of the Oneness, it is spiritual."
> Zhu Xi said, "Oneness means a single principle of Li, but it has its two ends, and thus it functions in different ways. It is like the *yin* and the *yang*: within *yin* there is *yang* and within *yang* there is *yin*, so when each reaches its extreme it produces the other, and this is why they can spiritually transform infinitely."

> 或問「一故神」。曰:「一是一箇道理,却有兩端,用處不同。譬如陰陽:陰中有陽,陽中有陰;陽極生陰,陰極生陽,所以神化無窮。」

> Someone asked about "Because of the Oneness, it is spiritual."
> [Zhu Xi] replied: "Zhang Zai put it extremely well here; you must read this very attentively and carefully.... Zhang Zai himself added a commentary to this line, saying, 'Because twoness is present in it, it is unfathomable.' It is just this one thing, and yet it proceeds everywhere amongst all things and events—for example, *yin* and *yang*, contraction and expansion, coming and going, rising and falling, even in all the hundreds and thousands of different events, none are not just this one thing. This is what he means by saying 'Because twoness is present in it, it is unfathomable.' For 'Because of the twoness, it transforms,' he adds the comment, '"Pushing forth the activity in the One." Nothing in the world that is solitary can transform; it is only twoness that can produce change. For example, only when there is one *yin* and one *yang* can the ten thousand things be produced through transformation. But although these are two things, the essence of them is how they push the activity through this Oneness between them. This explanation is extremely insightful, you must read it very carefully."

> 問「一故神」。曰:「橫渠說得極好,須當子細看。...『一故神』,橫渠親注云:『兩在故不測。』只是這一物,却周行乎事物之間。如所謂陰陽、屈伸、往來、上下,以至於行乎什伯千萬之中,無非這一箇物事,所以謂『兩在故不測』。『兩故化』,注云:『推行乎一。』凡天下之事,一不能化,惟兩而後能化。且如一陰一陽,始能化生萬物。雖是兩箇,要之亦是推行乎此一爾。此說得極精,須當與他子細看。」

> Lin asked, "What's the principle behind Zhang Zai's statement, 'Because of the Oneness, it is spiritual'?"
> Zhu Xi said, "The Twoness is that whereby there is activity pushed forth in the One. Zhang Zai's whole dictum is, 'Because of the Oneness, it is spiritual, but because there is twoness in it, it is unfathomable. Because of the twoness it transforms, pushing forth activity in the One.' This means that it is because these two are present that the One exists. This is also the meaning of 'If the two were not established, the One would not appear. If the One did not appear, the function of the two would just about cease.' For example, an event has a before and after; so that as soon as the beginning appears, one can already anticipate that there will also be an end. This is what is meant by necessary twoness. So if there is the cold of winter, the heat of summer is also present within it, if there is day, there is also the night present within it. Thus is the Oneness lodged within them."

his entire account of how change occurs,[54] while this wondrousness, this numinousness, is completely identical with that seemingly exclusive "one state" that it occupies, whether *yin* or *yang*. Although it is in one sense the undermining opposite of any state, it is also completely coextensive and immanent to that state, present *as* that state. As Zhu Xi says, "When in the state of *yin*, it is entirely *yin*; when in the state of *yang*, it is entirely *yang*."[55]

林問：「『一故神，兩故化』，此理如何？」曰：「兩所以推行乎一也。張子言：『一故神，兩在故不測；兩故化，推行於一。』謂此兩在，故一存也。『兩不立，則一不可見；一不可見，則兩之用或幾乎息矣』，亦此意也。如事有先後，才有先，便思量到末後一段，此便是兩。如寒，則暑便在其中；晝，則夜便在其中；便有一寓焉。」

[Zhu Xi further commenting on this passage from Zhang Zai said]: "This One is in *yang* and also in *yin*. Without this One, the two would be unable to produce activity in it. The two are just this growth and shrinkage, which is just what transformation and the proceeding of activity mean." He also said, "This dictum of Zhang Zai is extremely insightful and precise, which is why Li Tong, my teacher, said, 'Previously I couldn't understand this passage, and I sat up all night in my chair thinking it over, personally going into it with my own body—only then could I see the idea clearly and stably. Every time we truly understand a principle it should be like this.'"

「是在陽又在陰，無這一，則兩便不能以推行。兩便即是這箇消長，又是化，又是推行之意。」又曰：「橫渠此語極精。見李先生說云：『舊理會此段不得，終夜椅上坐思量，以身去裏面體，方見得平穩。每看道理處皆如此。』」

[54] Cited in *Zhu Xi ji*, juan 51, 2493, to explain this passage:

Sudden, qualitative changing over is what is meant by *bian*—as when *yin* changes over into *yang*, soft changes over into hard, cold changes over into warmth. When *yang* transforms (*hua*) into *yin*, it advances to its ultimate and then returns and thus retreats. When *yin* changes over (*bian*) into *yang*, the retreat reaches its extreme and thus becomes advance. Thus it is said, "Transformation and changing over is the image of advance and retreat." *Yang* transforming into *yin* and *yin* changing over into *yang* is what is meant by "transformation and changing over." What makes them transform and change over is Dao. Dao is the original numinousness, while transformation and changing over are the triggers that carry it. Thus in the transformation and changing over of *yin* and *yang* the Dao is never and nowhere absent. Because the twoness is there, it is unfathomable. Thus it said, "He who knows the Dao of transformation and changing over knows what spirit (*shen*) does!" Can it be understood thus? [Zhu Xi said], "Yes it can!"

突然改換者，變也；陰變為陽，柔變為剛，寒變為暖是也。陽化為陰，是進極而回，故為退、陰變為陽，則退極而上，故為進。故曰：「變化者，進退之象也。」陽化為陰、陰變為陽者，變化也。所以變化者，道也。道者，本然之妙，變化者所乘之機。故陰變陽化而道無不在，兩在故不測。故曰：「知變化之道者，其知神之所為乎」，不審可作如此看否？亦得之。

Everything up to the last three characters is perhaps Zhu Xi recounting the question of his interlocutor, Dong Shuzhong, while the last three characters are his approving comment on this presentation.

[55] *Zhu Xi ji*, juan 51, 2493: "When he says 'Twoness is present," it may be in *yin* and it may be in *yang*, but when it is in *yin* it is entirely *yin*, when it is in *yang* it is entirely *yang*" (言「兩在」者，或在陰，或在陽，在陰時全體都是陰，在陽時全體都是陽。).

The Center is the paradoxical place that is One yet Two, omnipresent yet nowhere, unmoving and yet unstill, and participating in motion and rest yet beyond motion and rest. Zhu Xi explicitly calls it an axis or hinge (*shuniu* 樞紐), a center point around which two extremes oscillate. The two extremes are non-paradoxical, "simply located" (i.e., determinate and restricted within their own boundaries), one-sided, in flux, dependent on the central axis. But they are the dynamic "carriers" of that axis, that center. As Qian puts it, the two extremes in the pendulum swing are only what they are, only identifiable, only determinate, if they *turn back*, toward each other: Any motion, any tendency, any process going "its own way," in its own direction, infinitely without turning back, never actually becomes knowable or determinate as any particular thing; it is perpetually unfinished, unclosed, uncircumscribed, undescribed. So motion stays motion only because of its relation to ceasing to be motion (its defining boundary), only in relation to stillness. Stillness likewise is only stillness in relation to motion, by turning back toward motion. The transition point, the center of gravity, the holding together of these two extremes, which makes them determinate, which makes them themselves, which allows them to be and to continue to be, is the Center, the axis. Qian gives examples of health and sickness, peace and war, sleep and wakefulness, etc.; each is able to maintain itself only by never going *too far* from the other. Herein lies also its normative dimension: It sets the limits beyond which a thing cannot go and still remain coherent with the whole, which is what is required for it to exist and continue. The Center is manifest in any thing as this pullback against going too far, the centripetal force drawing it back toward the opposite.

But the claim here is that this entails an important sense in which the Center is really prior to and transcendent to the extremes. While it may seem natural for us to speak of them as mutually dependent, there is also some justification to the claim that the Center is not constituted by the extremes; rather, the extremes are constituted by the Center. For the Center is the enabler of the whole swing of the motion between the two extremes. It is the enabler of the being of the whole as a whole, and thus of the parts being the parts of that whole, for the dynamic and holistic model of a swinging pendulum implies that the parts (the two extremes of the swing) are only anything if they are parts of this whole (the swing). The two opposed motions of a pendulum swing do not exist outside of the pendulum swing. It is not a whole that is composed of parts; it is a whole that is temporally simultaneous with its parts, but with an identifiable and fairly straightforward sort of priority over those parts. We do not have the construction of a whole from pre-existing parts; we have only virtual parts that are aspects or functions of the whole, that are inconceivable and impossible without the whole, which is only identifiable through the grasp of a Center, even though that Center too is merely virtual (i.e., the pendulum never rests there, it is not marked in space by any visible form). We may say that each part is impossible without the other parts, indeed that "each is the root of the other." But that provides no explanation of either part—each is enabled by what it itself enables, and neither can be prior. Hence we must speak separately, and in a different sense, of the Center as the enabler of both extremes and, what is the same, of their necessary relation to each other. The Center is the relation of each part to the other, and it is thus in that sense prior to either part, though temporally simultaneous. The model here is not building up from atomistic pre-existing units, but rather a kind of *mitosis*. But even if the entire swinging pendulum is eternal, we still have a reason to speak separately of the Center as the explanatory principle of the whole and of all of its parts.

The whole enables the parts, and the Center enables the whole. Is it then itself precisely the whole? Yes and no. It is what makes the parts the parts by making whole the whole, and is alone what we name when we identify the whole. We call the vortex by the name of its identifiable vertex, which is what it reads *as* from outside. In that sense it is the whole that makes the parts the parts. Is it a specific part of the whole? Yes and no. The pendulum never comes to rest in the Center, and yet the Center is what is most evident in its motions, continually and everywhere expressed in either of the extremes, and in the relations of the extremes to each other, their copotentiality to become each other and thus form a whole that sustainably continues the swing. It is nowhere and everywhere. It is nothing and everything. It is the most absent and yet the omnipresent axis. And this is just what Zhu Xi says about the Taiji in relation to *yin* and *yang*. It must be prior, it must be transcendent, it must be elevated above them and it must not be mistaken for them. Li is not *qi*, Li is prior to *qi*. And yet it is always coexistent with them, always present only as manifested in them, always immanent to them.

Specifically, it manifests as their triggers of transition, their boundaries, which are what make them what they are. Zhu Xi explains the idea of a "trigger of transition" with a mechanical example of a pedal:

> Zhou Quiqing asked about the line, "Motion and stillness are the triggers of transition in which it is carried."

Zhu Xi said, "*Ji* 機 means a mechanical stop-start switch. You step on the pedal when the thing is moving, and the stillness comes; you step on the pedal when its still, and motion comes."

周貴卿問「動靜者,所乘之機」。曰:「機,是關捩子。踏著動底機,便挑撥得那靜底;踏著靜底機,便挑撥得那動底。」[56]

The motion and stillness of *qi* are the triggers of reversal that manifest the Taiji, the original numinous paradoxicality of the Supreme Pivot. For we now see that Taiji is literally a *pivot*: it acts on any state as *the trigger of its reversal*. That is, it "rides on" and "attaches to" and "is carried by" *qi*, but it is "on" them in the manner of a triggering mechanism that reverses them: The touch of the Taiji is what reverses the state of *qi*, brings it back into contact with its opposite; it is what joins the two extremes into a balanced productive totality. It is carried by *qi*, hence always immanent in *qi* and sharing its state; but it is that in any state which *reverses* that state:

> Someone asked: "[What does it mean], 'motion and stillness are the triggers that carry it'?"
>
> Zhu Xi answered, The Supreme Pivot is Li, whereas motion and stillness are *qi*. When *qi* proceeds, Li also proceeds. The two are always together as mutually dependent and never separated from one another. The Supreme Pivot is like a man and motion and stillness are like the horse upon which he rides. Wherever the horse goes, the man also goes. For any single motion or stillness, there is none in which the numinousness of the Supreme Pivot is not present in it. This is what I meant by 'the trigger that carries it.' For this ultimate formless [Supreme Pivot] is precisely what allows the two [*yin* and *yang*] and the Five Elemental Phases of *qi* to 'numinously combine' (*miaohe*)."

問:「動靜者,所乘之機。」曰:「太極理也,動靜氣也。氣行則理亦行,二者常相依而未嘗相離也。太極猶人,動靜猶馬;馬所以載人,人所以乘馬。馬之一出一入,人亦與之一出一入。蓋一動一靜,而太極之妙未嘗不在焉。此所謂『所乘之機』,無極、二五所以『妙合而凝』也。」[57]

---

[56] *Zhuzi yulei, juan* 94, 2376.

[57] *Zhuzi yulei, juan* 94, 2376. That it is the specifically dyadic pairs and their reversal is what matters here can be seen by a further gloss Zhu Xi offers on the same page: "Motion and stillness

The Supreme Pivot rides on the *qi*, is carried on it, is dependent on it for its activity, but is also in control of it, like the man on the horse. Li is never apart from *qi*, and is always there doing whatever *qi* is doing. Its "control" resides in its "numinousness" (i.e., its union of opposites, its paradoxicality, its identity to the least present of all, Wuji), which resides in its "unifying"—*all of these are combined in the idea of pivot as the trigger of reversal*. The reversal is the shaping of the contour that gives them their proper boundaries, their proper measures, which makes them parts of the whole, which makes them what they are, makes them identifiably and conceivably this or that.

On the other hand, numinous means inconceivable, beyond the defined and exclusive character of motion or of stillness: It is that in each thing by which the opposite thing is also present, for it is both and it is neither. Hence it is what is "unseen" in that thing or state, "the least palpably present of all," and yet what allows it to exist as that state, on the holistic premise that existing as that state is only possible when it is coherent with other states, with opposite states.

The above could be said, *mutatis mutandis*, by either a Huayan or a Tiantai writer. A Huayan writer would mean: "The entire indivisible Li is present completely in any *shi*, just as the indivisible quality of wetness is wholly present with nothing left out in any wave, or the undivided bright reflectiveness of the mirror is completely present and identical with any image." The Tiantai writer would mean, "It is the entire Three Thousand acting and manifesting itself *as* this one of the Three Thousand which always arises together with the remaining 2999 as its background."

Zhu Xi means the same thing, but in in a derivative and importantly tweaked way: He means that, as in Zhou Dunyi's diagram (fig. 4.1), the

---

are the triggers that carry it. Triggers are the incipient triggers of *qi* itself. As the *Odes* says, 'Riding upon the triggers of the atmosphere (*qi*) to enter and exit'" (「動靜者，所乘之機。」機，言氣機也。詩云:「出入乘氣機。」). This is further clarified elsewhere (*Zhuzi yulei, juan* 94, 2370) by a student's summary:

"... The Supreme Pivot is simply Li. Li cannot be itself described as moving or still. But 'when it moves it produces *yang*, when it is still it produces *yin*'—that means that Li is lodged in *qi*, which cannot be devoid of the reversing triggers of motion and stillness. 'Carry' here means something like how cargo is carried in a vehicle. The motion and stillness of Li referred to here are how it is carried on *qi*: without realizing it, motion comes to an end and then stillness begins, and then stillness ends and motion begins again." Zhu Xi said, "That's right."

「...太極只是理，理不可以動靜言，惟『動而生陽，靜而生陰』，理寓於氣，不能無動靜所乘之機。乘，如乘載之『乘』，其動靜者，乃乘載在氣上，不覺動了靜，靜了又動。」曰:「然。」

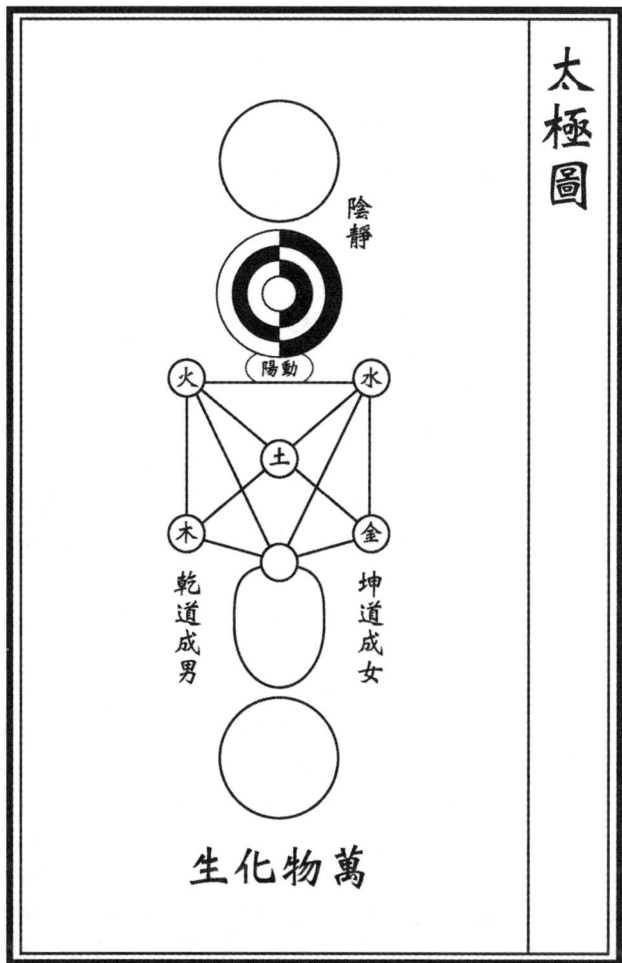

FIGURE 4.1 *Zhou Dunyi's Taiji Diagram*
CREDIT: Drawn by John Makeham based on Zhu Zhen 朱震 (1072–1138), *Hanshang Yizhuan* 漢上易傳 (Zhu Zhen's Commentary to the *Book of Change*), *Chizao Tang Siku quanshu cuiyao* 摘藻堂四庫全書薈要 (Essentials of The Complete Collection of the Four Treasuries from the Chizao Hall).

top circle and the small center of the lower circle remain the same in each instance, performing the same function, no matter whether the contents of the circle are wood, metal, earth, fire, water, or plain *yin* and *yang*. It is coextensive with them, and yet is also what unites them in this particular structure as a union of opposites around a center, making them interface with each other, turn back to each other, change into each other. This is what changes the behavior of a thing—hence although seemingly completely coextensive with it, it is also that which can undermine and control it and regulate it into coherence with whatever is outside it, like the repeated circles in the diagram. This is true of the human mind as well, which is why it can regulate and control itself, an extremely important advance for Zhu Xi's moral psychology. And this is how the two extremes interface and thereby unite. All of these are combined in the notion of the Center and beautifully illustrated by the circle in the diagram on which Zhu Xi is commenting.

More specifically, the *ji* 機 in question here are undoubtedly what are manifested and carried by what the Zhou Dunyi text refers to as the extreme points, or *ultimates, at which reversal occurs*. The word Zhou uses for that reversal point is *ji* 極, the same as the name of word used for the Taiji, which is the numinousness. The nature is Taiji, the Supreme Pivot, manifest as the limit (also *ji* 極), the standard (also *ji* 極). For the limits of a thing are what define it as what it is, providing the proper measure that allows it to form a harmonious part of the whole, and this is the normative standard by which it is to be regulated. The Taiji, the Supreme Pivot, is the roofbeam, the hinge, the center point of the pendulum between motion and stillness, *yin* and *yang*. As such, it is Center, it is Balance, it is expressed as Harmony of opposing dyads (e.g., as joy and anger, happiness and sorrow), as connection and interface, as integrater, as Coherence that is also endlessly productive and reproductive (*sheng sheng bu xi* 生生不息). That is Li. But it is also the specific Li of each thing: its specific turning-around point, its proper measure and limits, the standard that defines it, the Li as "why it is so" (*suoyiran zhi li* 所以然之理), and the Li as "how it should be" (*dangran zhi li* 當然之理) of each thing. That Li in both senses is just *ji* 極, the turning around point which is the trigger of reversal *ji* 機, which is what carries the numinous wondrous paradoxicality of the Center, the Taiji 太極. Thus are all definite things produced, carved out, boundaried, while also containing their ability to go beyond their boundaries into their opposites, to mate and produce further.

This interpretation can help us better understand the nature of this production and reproduction Zhu Xi speaks of. For the process of production here is given a general character rooted in boundary and boundary-overstepping, in Centrality and dynamic holism that combines and reverses opposites, which touches on the sexual reproduction of living beings but is not limited to it. *Yin-yang* is sexual but also more than sexual, and in the same way *sheng* (production, generation) is here life and also more than life. It does not mean that there is some preference for living beings over non-living beings, and that this really defines the reason things are as they are, or that the universe intends to produce living beings. The process of production and reproduction spoken of by Zhu Xi is not some sort of folk-Schopenhauerian "will to life"[58] or a Bergsonian *élan vital*, a will to life that is the secret purpose behind the production of non-living things. The reason for this qualification lies in the meaning of the Chinese word *sheng* 生. Consider the following explanations from Zhu Xi:

> Someone asked, "I have seen that in your letter responding to Yu Fangshu you consider even dry and withered things to have Productive Compossibility. But I don't see what Productive Compossibilities there are in dried and withered things, or in tiles and shards."
>
> [Zhu Xi] replied, "Consider the medicines made from rhubarb and from aconitum. These are dried and withered, but the rhubarb medicine cannot be used in place of aconitum, and aconitum cannot be used in place of rhubarb."
>
> "'Dried and withered things also have the Nature'—what does this mean?"
>
> "It means they should also be said to have this Productive Compossibility. Thus [Cheng Hao] said, 'In the whole world there are no things outside the Nature.' Then walking on the street he said, 'The bricks of the steps have the Productive Compossibility of the bricks of the steps.' Sitting down he said, 'The bamboo chair has the Productive Compossibility of a bamboo chair. Dried and withered things can be said to lack the intention to produce (*shengyi* 生意), but not the Compossibility of Production (*shengli* 生理).[59] For example, rotten wood cannot be used, and can only be put to the flame. This is what it means to say it has no impulse of production. But even so, burning a given kind of wood produces a given kind of smoke, each one different from the others. This is because the Productive Compossibility of each is thus.'"
>
> "Do dry and withered things have Productive Compossibility or not?"
>
> "If there is any thing at all, it has its Productive Compossibility. Heaven produced no writing brushes; it was human beings who take rabbit hair and

---

[58] Schopenhauer equivocates on this point. When he is speaking more strictly in delineating his metaphysics, he specifies quite clearly that "the Will" has no specific end, that it is blind in precisely the sense of wanting no particular object, just *wanting*. But in his more popular writings, or when discussing living organisms, or perhaps when he is being less careful, he does speak of a "Will to Life."

[59] Here I take *shengli* 生理 to be an explicit explication of the meaning of the usually abbreviated and general term *li* 理 itself, so I translate them the same way.

make a writing brush out of it. But as there is a brush, there must be the Productive Compossibilities of the brush."

"How do you discern humaneness from rightness in the brush?" "Such a small thing does not bear a division into its humaneness and its rightness."

問:「曾見答余方叔書,以為枯槁有理。不知枯槁瓦礫,如何有理?」曰:「且如大黃、附子,亦是枯槁。然大黃不可為附子,附子不可為大黃。」問:「枯槁之物亦有性,是如何?」曰:『是他合下有此理,故云天下無性外之物。』因行街,云:『階磚便有磚之理。』因坐,云:『竹椅便有竹椅之理。枯槁之物,謂之無生意,則可;謂之無生理,則不可。如朽木無所用。止可付之爨灶,是無生意矣。然燒甚麼木,則是甚麼氣,亦各不同,這是理元如此。』」問:「枯槁有理否?」曰:「才有物,便有理。天不曾生箇筆,人把兔毫來做筆。才有筆,便有理。」又問:「筆上如何分仁義?」曰:「小小底,不消恁地分仁義。」[60]

"Production," *sheng*, does not refer only to what we mean by the English word "life": It means *any transformation, any emergence of a qualitatively distinct entity*. Burning rotten wood *produces* smoke. Neither of these is "alive," but the relation of production is the expression of the Li, which I will venture to define as the Productive Compossibility, of the wood. As the center, Li makes the two extremes possible and *possible together*, and it is "in" either extreme as the possibility of the other extreme coexisting with itself.

Basically, any event that *occurs* is an example of "ceaseless production and reproduction" 生生不息. The rotten wood does not "intend" to produce; it has no living "intention" or "impulse" to produce (*sheng yi* 生意), but it has the potentiality to produce. To exist is to have this potential to produce a certain effect, and requires that this entity was something that could come into existence, could be produced, in tandem with everything else that exists. To have a Li is to be something that can be generated by whatever is already existing, and to participate in this process of ceaseless production and reproduction by virtue of having the capacity to produce something else beyond itself. This is why I translate Li in this way for Zhu Xi. The Song Neo-Confucians often use the term in its everyday sense to mean "possibility," as when they say something could possibly exist with the phrase *you ci li* 有此理, or when something is impossible, *qi you ci*

---

[60] *Zhuzi yulei, juan* 4, 61.

li 豈有此理. This can apply to things like the existence of spirits, or telepathy, or the recitation of Du Fu's poetry by a person in a fever. Those things *can exist* because they *fit in* with what else exists in a way that is consistent both with their being produced by them and by them continuing the process of production within the context of the total matrix of relations that exist, and this interrelation of all beings is considered to be intrinsically productive, even where the "impulse" of production is lacking. Li is a kind of *coherence that is productive*, a way in which things join together so as to continue the process of production and reproduction, and the continuation of the process of creativity, which is the cosmos.

We thus venture to suggest as a translation of Li the term "Productive Compossibility." The "co-" in "compossibility" denotes this possibility of coexistence, a harmonious coherence, and this already implies a kind of *value*. Coexistence is itself a *value*, a kind of unity among produced entities that allows them all to exist without obstructing each other, without excluding each others' production. We see this in the Neo-Confucian tropes of humaneness (*ren* 仁), the most direct manifestation of Li, as primarily manifested in (though not identical to) unbiasedness (*gong* 公) and as sensitivity (*jue* 覺). All of these terms suggest a kind of extension beyond any given boundary to include and connect and respond to whatever else exists, which is also the key characteristic of production and reproduction: non-limitation within a given determinate sphere, the continuation of one thing into something else, the expansion into, and the generation of, otherness. It is growth, but in the sense that also includes any non-living *event* as well, even that of firewood turning into smoke.

Defining Li as "Productive Compossibility" helps us understand one of the most distinctive and puzzling features of Zhu Xi's metaphysics: the simultaneous oneness and manyness of Li. Zhu Xi is very clear that Li is at the same time one Li (the Taiji) of all things, and at the same time is, in its entirety, all the many individual mutually differentiating "principles" and "patterns" and natures of things (*liyi fenshu* 理一分殊). Note well that the *fen* here does *not* mean that only a portion or division of Li is present as the specific principle which is the nature of any individual thing: The entire Li is present *as* the specific principle of production and growth of each thing. For the "compossibility"—i.e., the possibility of coexistence of two items, A and B—would be described in just this way. This reconfiguration of singular and plural is precisely the biggest difference between "possibility" and "compossibility." The "possibility" of A is something entirely different from the "possibility" of B, and the "possibility of the coexistence of A and B" is yet a third thing. But the "compossibility of A with B" is exactly "the compossibility of B with A," which is none other than the compossibility of A and B. Analogously, for Zhu Xi, the Li of a chair is the Li of a table, and this is the same as the Li of the world that has table and chair. And yet the compossibility of A and B can never be reducible to a featureless unarticulated "Oneness": It specifically delineates the possibility of A and the possibility of B as two separate and definite aspects. The possibility of A is the compossibility of A with all other things (abstract and concrete, human and natural); this is different from the possibility of B, which is the compossibility of B with all other things. But the compossibility of A *is* the compossibility of B, while maintaining this specific difference.

Li for Zhu Xi is thus coherence qua compossibility, or to put it more strongly, the copotentiality of production of all things. We can see this quite clearly in Zhu Xi's descriptions of specific Li. For example, speaking of the Li of a chair or a fan, he says:

> Clothing, food, activities are just things, while their Li is Dao. It is impermissible to call the thing the Dao. For example, this chair has four legs, and can be sat on: this is the Li of the chair. If we take away one of the legs, it will be impossible to sit on it, and thus it will have lost the Li of a chair. . . . Or take this fan, which is a thing, but has the Dao, the Li, of a fan. How the fan is made, and how it should be used, is the Li of the fan that is above its form.
>
> 衣食動作只是物，物之理乃道也。將物便喚做道，則不可。且如這箇椅子有四隻脚，可以坐，此椅之理也。若除去一隻脚，坐不得，便失其椅之理矣。....且如這箇扇子，此物也，便有箇扇子底道理。扇子是如此做，合當如此用，此便是形而上之理。[61]

Dao (Li) is how the chair is constructed (it has four legs cohering in a certain way to form a whole) and what can thus be done with it (people can sit on it). These are both obviously coherence: how the pieces fit together, and how it fits in with other entities, i.e., human desires to sit down. It is coherence as productive compossibility, i.e., it is possible for these pieces of wood to coexist with each other and with the world in such a way that the pieces of wood can be put together in this way so as to make possible another thing, the sitting down of a person. Of course this facilitates

---

[61] *Zhuzi yulei*, juan 62, 1296.

human flourishing, production and reproduction, and so on—a little piece of *ren* (humanenss), which is Impartial, which is the Copotentiality of all things. The greater coherence of the chair with the rest of the world—its use, the way it fits together with things that are not chairs nor what the chair depends on—is the direct content of the Li. Li is a double coherence, a second-order coherence necessarily also involving those among human desires that are themselves coherent with each other, i.e., "harmonious," i.e., remaining expressive of the Center,[62] an enabling of further coherences, a compossibility of planks of wood and the human desire to sit which together are productive of a new situation: humans sitting on chairs. These compossibilities precede the chair, and the chair depends on it, in the sense that no chair would occur without this compossibility. Simply to describe it as "coherence" arguably muddles the sense in which it might precede its concrete existence. But by redescribing this sort of coherence as Productive Compossibility and even Productive Copotentiality,[63] we see immediately in what sense it is still the standard idea of coherence

---

[62] Humans are, after all, the finest and most sensitive *qi*, the most balanced and complete representation of Li or Taiji in any concrete entity.

[63] In Zhu Xi, I believe, we see a shift from the immanent model of this kind of Center-as-coherence-making-coherence as immanent vertex to the more transcendent-sounding model of the Center. We may think of this as a shift from Productive Compossibility to Productive Copotentiality. What is the difference? Possibility and potentiality are almost synonyms; but potential implies something a little more determinate and self-standing, something that is real in the world and beyond the world and with a sense of its active readiness to become actual, whereas possibility suggests a mere logical condition of non-contradictoriness. Both are contrasted to actuality and can be spoken of in the absence of actuality—a thing can be possible though not actual, or potential but not actual. But when speaking of an actual thing, we can still ask what made it possible: It is actual because it is possible, and it remains possible even when it is actual. But potential is what it is when it is not actual. Once it becomes actual, it is not also, at the same time, potential. Potential suggests something that is hidden, non-apparent, in sharp contrast to what is actual. So the qualitative ontological jump that Zhu Xi seems to be insisting on, which makes him uneasy with merely speaking in *ti-yong* terms suggesting a continuity or coextensivity of substance, is perhaps well-indicated by the term Copotentiality, suggesting more of a distinct force of its own, as opposed to merely a derivative function of actualities. Considered as a positive force in one of two opposite extremes, the pull toward the balance with the other opposite, then, the Compossibility may be called Productive Copotentiality. As such it is distinct from the actuality of either extreme or indeed of both extremes considered together. The shift in translation is a way to indicate a more positive presence: Li in *yin* is the productive copotentiality of *yang* as Li in *yang* is the productive copotentiality of *yin*. Note that if we were speaking merely of "potentiality," we could say that the potentiality of *yin* is something completely different from, and opposed to, the potentiality of *yang*. But the Productive Copotentiality of *yin* is precisely the Productive Copotentiality of *yang*. They are opposed but also identical, many but also one and the same. This is a key distinguishing mark of Zhu Xi's metaphysics. Productive Copotentiality means these literally serve not only as possible coexistences with each other but as actively grounding each other, indeed actively producing each other, the roots of each other. It is what is always there in a sense "grounding" their actuality, and present in their actuality as the force pulling toward balance, i.e., unobstructed coexistence of opposite qualities.

(internally and externally), but with the extra sense of its place in the total context of all existing and all future things, the role it is able to place among whatever already exists to help maximize the unity of things, the interconnection of things, the production and reproduction of things, the balance of things, the coexistence of maximal things, the maximization of functions, of life, of impartiality, of mutual non-numb sensitivity of one thing to another—in short the impartiality and oneness-in-manyness which is Ren, which is Li.

4.5 *Ti-Yong* in Zhu Xi

We can now see the specific role played by the more familiar *ti-yong* model in Zhu Xi's thinking. In general metaphysics, for the Taiji and *yin-yang* relation, we have the radicalized Huayan *ti-yong* model of immanence and transcendence used but subordinated to the Tiantai Center-periphery model of immanence and transcendence. For moral psychology, we have an application of *ti-yong* that is unique to Zhu Xi, and which we shall address below. But in the horizontal relations between one phenomenal thing and another, we have the *ti* role being played by whichever element is *productive* of the other, serving in that situation as the "carrier" of the Taiji or Li (Productive Copotentiality), i.e., as the agent triggering transition, reversal, production. *Yin* and *yang* are mutually roots of each other, reversibly so. This conception deeply complexifies the *ti-yong* relations of all concrete things, insofar as all are composed of *yin* and *yang*, and thus of combinations of stillness and motion, which are consistently associated by Zhu Xi with *ti* and *yong*, respectively, implying a back and forth reversal of *ti* and *yong* in many instances; in that sense, *yin* and *yang* function as reversible *ti* and *yong* to each other:

> Humaneness is primarily concerned with generation, and thus its *yong* is always in motion, but its *ti* is nevertheless still. Wisdom, on the other hand, is primarily concerned with flowing comprehensively through all events, and even though its *ti* is thus in motion, its *yong* is deeply submerged and densely firm, so its *yong* is never other than still. Although their *ti and yong*, their motion and stillness, are thus, it is not necessary to cling to one side of the matter; it must be contemplated from all sides. . . . If we insist on correlating them to *yin* and *yang*, then humaneness correlates to spring, is

mainly concerned with generation, and thus correlates to *yang* and motion, while wisdom correlates to winter, is mainly concerned with submerged storage, and thus correlates with *yin* and stillness. But *yin* and *yang* and motion and stillness are the roots of one another, and hence they cannot be sought in any fixed formulation. It all depends on the scholar's silent understanding of the matter.

仁主於發生，其用未嘗不動，而其體却靜。知周流於事物，其體雖動，然其用深潛縝密，則其用未嘗不靜。其體用動靜雖如此，却不須執一而論，須循環觀之。... 若必欲以配陰陽，則仁配春，主發生，故配陽動；知配冬，主伏藏，故配陰靜。然陰陽動靜，又各互為其根，不可一定求之也。此亦在學者默而識之。[64]

Here the mutual rootedness of *yin* and *yang* means that stillness and motion are always inseparable, so the *ti* of one is grouped with the *yong* of the other. That the mutual rootedness of *yin* and *yang* is further taken to imply a reversibility of *ti* and *yong* in primary cases—as in the relation between humaneness and rightness—can be seen in the associations stacked up in the citations below, which show how two phenomenal things can be simultaneously *ti* and *yong* to each other, how one thing is thus both *ti* and *yong* in the same dyadic relationship (humaneness is *ti* to rightness as its *yong*, but at the same time rightness is *ti* to humaneness as its *yong*), and how this is linked to the most general case of *yin* and *yang* as such:

> The relation between humaneness and rightness is that of *ti* to *yong*. [And yet] humaneness has its own *ti and yong*, and rightness too has its own *ti* and *yong*.
>
> 仁對義為體、用。仁自有仁之體、用，義又有義之體、用。
>
> Zhao Zhidao asked, "How do we understand humaneness and rightness in terms of *ti* and *yong* and *motion* and *stillness*?"
> Zhu Xi said, "Humaneness is definitely the *ti* and rightness is definitely the *yong*. But humaneness and rightness each has its own *ti* and *yong*, its own motion and stillness. You must experience this for yourself in detail."
>
> 趙致道問：「仁義體用、動靜何如？」曰：「仁固為體，義固為用。然仁義各有體用，各有動靜，自詳細驗之。」

---

[64] *Zhuzi yulei*, juan 32, 823.

Humaneness and rightness are *ti* and *yong* to each other, stillness and rest to each other. The *ti* of humaneness is originally still, but its function flows without cease. The *yong* of rightness is originally in motion, but its *ti* is for each to rest in its own place.

仁義互為體用、動靜。　仁之體本靜，而其用則流行不窮；義之用本動，而其體則各止其所。

Someone asked about, "In humaneness yielding, in rightness firm."

Zhu Xi said, "The *ti* of humaneness is yielding but its *yong* is firm, while conversely, the *ti* of rightness is firm while its *yong* is yielding."

[Dong] Zhu[65] asked, "Is this what is meant by '*Yang* is rooted in *yin* and *yin* is rooted in *yang*' "?

Zhu Xi said, "Yes it is."

問「於仁也柔，於義也剛。」曰：「仁體柔而用剛，義體剛而用柔。」銖曰：「此豈所謂『陽根陰，陰根陽』邪？」曰：「然。」

In his response to Shuchong's[66] doubts, Zhu Xi said, "The *ti* of humaneness is firm while its function is yielding, while conversely, the *ti* of rightness is yielding while its *yong* is firm."

[Fu] Guang[67] sought instruction about the following: "In terms of the motion of the Supreme Pivot we can say that humaneness is firm and rightness is yielding. But in terms of the *yin* and *yang* in individual things, we can say that humaneness is yielding and rightness is firm."

Zhu Xi said, "That's also right. Humaneness has the sense of flowing motion springing forth and transcending limits, but its function is all about kindly yielding. Rightness has the sense of negotiating and following what fits the situation, but its function is all about decisive severing."

先生答叔重疑問曰：「仁體剛而用柔，義體柔而用剛。」廣請曰：「自太極之動言之，則仁為剛，而義為柔；自一物中陰陽言之，則仁之用柔，義之用剛。」曰：「也是如此。仁便有箇流動發越之意，然其用則慈柔；義便有箇商量從宜之義，然其用則決裂。」[68]

---

[65] Dong Zhu 董銖 (b. 1152) was one of Zhu Xi's students.
[66] Shuchong is the style (*zi*) of Dong Zhu.
[67] Fu Guang 輔廣 (d. u.) was one of Zhu Xi's students.
[68] See *Zhuzi yulei, juan* 6, 121.

The *yin* aspect of any existent thing is that thing's *ti* while its *yang* aspect is its *yong*. The Supreme Pivot is not the *ti* to the *yong*, which are *yin-yang*; rather, both *ti* and *yong, the very reversible ti-ing and yong-ing of any two horizontal empirical elements*, are what are enabled by the Supreme Pivot, the Taiji.⁶⁹

As Zhu Xi remarks, in his "diagrammatic" commentary to the "Taiji tu" (see fig. 4.1), that the semicircle to the left, *yin* within *yang*, the Li trigram, is "the motion of *yang*, and that whereby the *yong* of [empty circle, the Wuji/Taiji] proceeds," while the semicircle to the right, *yang* within *yin*, the Kan trigram, is "the stillness of *yin*, and that whereby the *ti* of [empty circle, the Wuji/Taiji] is established."⁷⁰ This suggests that we cannot unilaterally look at the Taiji as *ti* and motion and stillness as *yong*. The Taiji is the *benti* that enables the motion that produces *yang* and the stillness that produces *yin*, but neither mixed with them nor separated from them; it is an *aspect* of the *yin-yang* combination, the circle that is present in their center and brings them together, their enabling Copotentiality which is identical to each specific figure in the diagram but also identical to all the others, and itself beyond any single one of them. Thus the diagram well illustrates that "it is precisely the *yin-yang*, but pointing to their original *ti*" (即陰陽而指其本體).⁷¹ What we are looking at is this same circle we see above, but now with the two trigram figures in it. This new figure can be looked at as an internal mitosis of the original figure, which still preserves

---

⁶⁹ For example, Zhu Xi, *Zhuzi yulei, juan* 94, 2372, says:

> The Taiji naturally includes the principles of both motion and stillness, but we cannot divide *ti* from *yong* on the basis of [the division between] motion and stillness. In general, stillness is Taiji's *ti*, and motion is Taiji's *yong*. But it is like this fan: it is just one thing, the fan; when waved around it is the *yong*, when put down it is the *ti*. The moment it is put down, it is just this one principle; when it is picked up and waved around, it is still just this one principle.
>
> 太極自是涵動靜之理，卻不可以動靜分體用。蓋靜即太極之體也，動即太極之用也。譬如扇子，只是一箇扇子，動搖便是用，放下便是體。才放下時，便只是這一箇道理；及搖動時，亦只是這一箇道理。

The point here is that *ti* and *yong* should not be divided as if they were two separate elements both "included" in the Taiji. Rather, the Taiji is entirely both its own *ti* and its own *yong*, like the fan. In the Taiji's case, the global phenomenon of stillness as such is the *ti* and the global phenomenon of motion is the *yong*, but each is the entire Taiji. In the fan's case, fan-lying-still is the *ti* and fan-waved-around is the *yong*, but each is the entire fan. It is not the case that the Taiji is the *ti* and stillness-and-motion are the *yong*, nor that the fan as such is the *ti* and being put down and being waved around are collectively the *yong*.

⁷⁰ Zhu Xi, "Taiji tu shuo jie" 太極圖說解 (Explanation of the Taiji Diagram Essay), *Zhouzi quanshu* 周子全書 (Complete Writings of Zhou Dunyi), comp. Dong Rong 董榕 (1711–1760), ed. Hu Baoquan 胡寶瑔 (1694–1763), *Guoxue jiben congshu* 國學基本叢書 edition (Taipei: Shangwu yinshuguan, 1964), 3.

⁷¹ *Zhouzi quanshu*, 2.

the entire figure if we care to focus on that aspect: it is there as the circle circumscribing them and also as the circle in the middle. This is what "controls" (*zai* 宰) their relation, the Center which also brings them together inside itself, bringing them into relation so that they form a whole. We can view the whole as the center, or the center as the whole—and yet the center has a special function in bringing about the relation between the sides which makes them the whole, which governs their reversals, which defines their Productive Copotentiality.

It is the Productive Copotentiality of these two aspects that is manifest on the phenomenal level as the *ti-yong* relationship—not just as *ti*, but as *ti* always functioning, and all functions having a *ti*, i.e., the inseparability of motion and rest. As in Tiantai, the *ti-yong* model on that *qi* level is reversible—at the most abstract level (simple *yin* and *yang*), straightforwardly and symmetrically so, but at the "lower" levels of *qi* interaction as well (moving further down the *Taiji tu*), we find Zhu Xi very alert to and interested in aspect-related reversibilities of *ti* and *yong* on many levels, developed with considerable ingenuity. This complexity may be regarded as a result of the initial reversible *ti-yong* relation at the basic level of *qi* existence, the *yin-yang* relation described in the second and third lines of the "Taiji tu shuo" and its exegesis, which give the basic nature of all *qi* as reversibility of *ti* and *yong*.

So in the global sense we should be a bit wary of simply stating that Dao and things, or Li and *qi*, stand straightforwardly in a *ti-yong* relationship for Zhu Xi, but it can be used freely and indeed as a supple indicator of the reversibility relationships of an ontology of universal production and reversal within a dynamically Centered whole. We may see this clearly by reconsidering Zhu Xi's chair example cited above. Dao (Li) is how the chair is constructed (it has four legs cohering in a certain way to form a whole) and what can thus be done with it (people can sit on it) so that it is productive of a new situation, which is itself productive of continued new situations. The Li here is not hidden or obscured; it is out in the open, operating as the obvious function of the chair and the way it is constructed. The Li is not in any way of a continuous substance with the *qi*; it is another level of entity altogether, in no way exchangeable with *qi*. The Li does not grow into *qi* nor does it materially support it. Although this is still a dependence relation, it is not the dependence relation entailed in the *ti-yong* model. The sense in which the chair is dependent on its Li to be a chair is not the sense in which a branch is dependent on its root to be a branch, nor the way in what an image in a mirror is dependent on the coextensive bright reflectivity of the mirror. In all these ways, the relation between the Li of the chair and the physical chair has little in common with a straightforward *ti-yong* relationship. Most of all, the greater coherence of the chair with the rest of the world—its use, the way it fits together with things that are not chairs nor what the chair depends on, so as to produce further situations—is the direct content of the Li, but not of the *ti* in a *ti-yong* relation. On the contrary, that would be part of the *yong*. So for physical things, we seem always to have a complex relation of *ti* and *yong* which stresses reversibility and internesting, where Li cannot be simply equated with *ti* in any unilateral way. The entire *ti-yong* structure in individual material things is rather a way of instantiating Li as Productive Copotentiality, where *ti* is the potentiality and *yong* is the production, but both are included in the Productive Copentiality which is Li.

4.6 Comparisons of Moral Psychology of Huayan, Tiantai, and Zhu Xi

I said above that Zhu Xi's case lies interestingly between Huayan and Tiantai. This is particularly evident in his doctrine of the *ti-yong* structure of the Nature and the emotions, constituting and unified in the mind. In Huayan and later in Chan, mind is indeterminate Li and *ti*, while all determinations of the perceived world are *shi* and *yong*, in the coextensive relationship of wetness and waves, or bright reflectivity and images. In Tiantai, both mind and world are *shi*, and each is directly reversibly the *ti* and *yong* of the other, with this reversibility being the manifestation of Li, the Center. While something similar to this Tiantai structure seems to inform Zhu Xi's description of physical things like chairs and fans, as seen above (though *mutatis mutandis*, since the emphasis is now on production and reproduction as intrinsic value), Zhu's moral psychology takes a somewhat different approach. There, mind is the controlling unifying totality (*tong* 統) of *ti* and *yong*, of the unmanifest Nature (*xing* 性, which is itself *li* 理, *taiji* 太極) and the manifest emotions (*qing* 情)—and even the "human desires" (*renyu* 人慾), which are these same emotions when they have departed too far from the Mean (or Center). For Zhu Xi, the Nature is both Li and *ti*, and the emotions are both *shi* and *yong*, as in the Huayan and Chan cases. But as in Tiantai, this is still the relationship between two phenomena, in this case *qi*-phenomena, two *shi*, rather than directly between Li itself (which just *is* mind in later Huayan and Chan—as also later in Wang Yangming 王陽明 [1472–1529]) and *qi*. This is because for Zhu Xi the human mind is a unique kind of *qi*-phenomenon, one that possesses a uniquely complete manifestation of the Taiji which is the Li of each thing, but which is here simply the Nature of mind, the Heaven-and-Earth nature manifesting through the *qi*-endowment, present as the substance of mind, the ever present but not specifically determinable Center before the emotions emerge (*wei fa zhi zhong* 未發之中). The Nature as embodied in the human mind is both Li and *qi* in a way that the emotions, its functions, are not because it completely reflects the centrality of the Center in the way they do not unless they are perfectly harmonious. Hence there can be no reversibility of the Tiantai kind between *ti* and *yong* here, in spite of the fact that mind and its activities are two phenomena rather than noumena and phenomena. In Tiantai, both mind and its activities (i.e., in this case, all possible and actual experienced worlds) are each both noumena and phenomena. In Zhu Xi, the mind is both Nature and emotions, with Nature as noumena/phenomenon and the emotions as just phenomena unless perfectly harmonious, in which case they can perfectly manifest Li while still being fully phenomenal. This is what makes Zhu Xi a robust moralist with a single moral program, while Tiantai writers employing a similar *ti-yong* structure are not, being rather radical pluralists in moral matters. Finally, different from both the Tiantai and the Zhu Xi models, in Huayan and Chan, and arguably in Wang Yangming as well, the mind is noumena and its activities qua the experienced world are phenomena, but always allowing that this can be redescribed to say mind includes its phenomena and hence is both, and its activities include mind, so they are also both—yet without ever eliminating the one-way dependence relationship we discussed in the section on Huayan in this chapter.

What Zhu Xi gets from Tiantai (or at least has in common with Tiantai) is reversible asness in the one-and-many structure of Li, denying that Li is simply one and *shi* are simply many. This allows both Zhu Xi and Tiantai to affirm the existence of multiple different Li that are nevertheless in some sense all one and the same Li. This goes hand in hand with the dyad-around-a-center model of what Li actually is. Each Li is every other Li as this Li, both one and many Li. In Huayan, properly speaking, there is only one Li, which is no Li at all: Emptiness, which is Mind (wetness, reflectivity). As a result, we see the basis of Zhu's notion of moral practice: Investigation of things as increased clarity of any one Li is simultaneously the means to clarity about the "other" Li that are in a sense also the initial Li itself, manifest *as* these others, and with the Li of the mind that thus knows them, brings them together, actualizes their coherence, realizes their Productive Copotentiality. (We will return to this point in the intercultural comparative considerations at the very end of this chapter.)

The work of moral transformation differs accordingly in the three traditions. In Huayan, it seems to me, the practice of contemplation is the realization of interpenetration itself, often simply as philosophical reflection on its various complex inter-nested vicissitudes, cultivating an expanded and fine-grained beatific vision of the implications of the simple idea of Li-*shi* co-extensivity. The Huayan *ti-yong* model of the mind as the direct *ti* of all experiences would thus be well served by the Chan model of meditation, seen already in Shenhui 神會 (684–758) and Zongmi, but constantly reiterated in Chan texts when they talk about meditation technique at all: "When a moment of experience arises, be aware of it. Once you are aware of it, it is nothing" (念起即覺，覺之即無).[72] This is an artful handling of both the immanence and the transcendence involved in this conception. When any function of the mind arises, that is entirely the substance of mind—the Non-Dwelling nature, the reflectivity of the mirror, the wetness of the water. It is the buddha-nature, awareness, itself. Realizing this requires remembering only that all experience is awareness, and this is just being aware of experience as coming from awareness, and staying within awareness, so that the awareness never changes. This is done by not following the contents of the thought, but attending only to its quality of awareness: Ignore the shape and color of the image, just notice that it is image qua image, which is to say, that it is always pure brightness. That is to make the wave go away, both literally (unelaborated, the karma is not fed to continue) and metaphysically (even just as it is, the image is now known entirely as brightness rather than image). In this way, no image is clung to, and thus even unwholesome images are soon stilled, since it is attachment that stirs up new images. So by affirming even the unwholesome images as entirely buddha-nature, one is freed of their influence immediately, and diminishes their future propensity to arise again.

The Tiantai method boils down to "contemplation of inherence" (*guanju* 觀具). That means noticing each thought that arises, not as a direct manifestation of the awareness that is the buddha-nature, but as boundaried, finite, biased, deluded. This is also a kind of seeing finitude as finitude, image as image, but here this means attending to the way it is situated and defined by its relation to everything that it is not: what preceded it in time, what is outside it in the world, what contrasts to it qualitatively

---

[72] Zongmi, *Chanyuan zhuquanji duxu* 禪源諸詮集都序 (Preface to the Collected Writings on the Chan Source), T48.2015, 403a. For a good discussion of the centrality of this trope in Chan meditation, see Carl Bielefeldt, "Ch'ang-lu Tsung-tse's Tso-ch'an I and the 'Secret' of Zen Meditation," in Peter Gregory, ed., *Traditions of Meditation in Chinese Buddhism*, vol. 4, *Kuroda Institute Studies in East Asian Buddhism* (Honolulu: University of Hawaii Press, 1986), 129–161.

or conceptually. Then these boundaries are seen to be incoherent when closely examined, applying Nāgārjunian dialectical reductions: They are seen to be incoherent, to be literally impossible. But although impossible, they are still appearing. This changes the nature of the object defined by these boundaries, the specific qualitative moment of experience. Now it is seen that it can exist only in this "miraculous, numinous" (*miao* 妙) way, as both inside and outside its boundaries, as the world positing itself as these boundaries. This means to see it as active and responsive everywhere, taking infinite forms, omnipresent and eternal. This is to see the whole *ti* of the Three-thousand-fold devil-nature (*et alia*) subsumed into but inalienably present in the Three-thousand-fold buddha-nature (*et alia*), compassionately acting as the Three-thousand-fold upayic functions, responding dyadically to the same Three-thousand-fold individual karmic situations,[73] the universe seeing and feeling itself in all possible ways. So here too, even an unwholesome experience is used as a vehicle of amelioration, but the process is quite different and the end result is quite different. The unwholesome quality itself is seen to be omnipresent; it is not only let go of but also expanded, and relinquishing attachment to it makes it in a special sense all the more present, but this dual character of absence and omnipresence is precisely what makes it unconditional, both compassionate and nirvanic, and precisely making it so is the goal of practice.

For Zhu Xi, Taiji is immanent in us as our Nature, the *ti* of the emotions that are its *yong*, both contained in and controlled by the mind, which thus always necessarily has contact with and access to both the good Nature (Equilibrium, Center, Copotentiality of all the emotions and of this totality of emotions with all things) and its sometimes not-so-good emotions. The Nature, although quiescent, is fully present in its emotional functions, "as a body uses an arm, as an arm uses a hand uses fingers" (如身使臂，如臂使指).[74] The mind is this bothness of body in arm, arm in fingers—an asness relation. It is this bothness that allows it to be "master" of the emotions, to bring them into contact with the Center which, though manifest, serves as their proper boundary, their standard and measure, their *ji* 極. As emotions arise from the unseen Center, which is this nature in its quiescent state, that nature is filtered through the *qi*-endowment. If that

---

[73] This is because their error is merely one-sidedness, bias, which means each is remedied by some diametrically opposed other bias. Making them all simultaneously available to each other is thought to bring the remedial diametrical opposite to activate as function through a kind of dyadic elective affinity.
[74] *Zhuzi yulei, juan* 117, 2808.

qi-endowment is perfectly clear and balanced, they will emerge in perfect harmony, meaning they will rotate around the Center, like the motion of a pendulum: Anger will not go so far as to be incapable of returning to the center and hence to joy, nor will joy swing so far in the other direction. At their extreme points (*ji* 極), they reverse, and these extremes are precisely the standards (*ji* 極) that carry the nature (*taiji* 太極). That virtual contact with the Center is what allows each of the emotions to be properly controlled, to be brought into harmony. If that *qi*-endowment is not so clear or straight, then a lot of emotions will miss this measure, and become excessive agitations and desires, oriented not toward the unexpressed inner Center, the Equilibrium, but following along with external things. These external things are also *qi*-endowments fully carrying their own immanent Li, which is itself also the entire Taiji; those Li and the Li that is the nature of the mind are neither one-nor-different: They are each the entire Taiji, but "playing its many different roles."

This oneness-and-difference is crucial for Zhu Xi's moral psychology. It is why external things can be a disturbance to my Li (that is, if I follow *only* the Taiji as *their* Li, letting it subsume or subordinate my nature to their Li, which are indeed that Li itself but *as* something quite different—a center, the Center, yes, but the center of different vortices, and necessarily ones that are less complete than the human one). That will make the emotions that arise from my nature lose their proper measure and harmony. But this oneness-and-difference is also what makes moral progress possible. If I can investigate those other Li, rather than following and subordinating myself to them, rather than thinking they in their one-sided form are the sole authoritative standard (even though in a certain sense they are in fact the entire standard itself), then I can join them into a coherence, see their productive compossibility with my own Nature, which encompasses all of them because it is the Taiji as manifest through the most balanced and clear type of *qi*-endowment. To study them until they become coherent with my mind is thus to realize my own nature, and to subordinate them to that larger coherence, that more balanced and productive coherence, which is the Taiji in the form of human nature, as opposed to the Taiji in the form of any individual material thing or set of things.

This process is to be combined with introspecting on my own emergent impulses and finding the ways to make these fragmentary, unbalanced bits and pieces cohere with each other and with the larger coherence of Inherent Cosmic Productive Copotentiality as present in my own Nature. As Zhu Xi says:

Inherent Cosmic Productive Copotentiality (*tianli* 天理) is never in all the ages extinguished in any human being; no matter how it is covered over or confined, Inherent Cosmic Productive Copotentiality is always constantly there just as ever, emerging from within selfish desire at every moment without cease—it is just that human beings are not aware of it. It is exactly like [fragments of] bright pearl or of a large shell mixed in together with sand and gravel, successively flashing forth here and there. Just recognize and gather these scattered pieces of the Network of all Copotentialities (*daoli* 道理) right where they appear, joining the fragments until they gradually become an integral whole. After your own good intentions grow and increase by the day and the month, Inherent Cosmic Productive Copotentiality will naturally become pure and firm in you. What you formerly called selfish desires will naturally retreat and scatter, until finally they no longer sprout up at all.

蓋天理在人，恆萬古而不泯；任其如何蔽錮，而天理常自若，無時不自私意中發出，但人不自覺。正如明珠大貝，混雜沙礫中，零零星星逐時出來 。但只於這箇道理發見處，當下認取，簇合零星，漸成片段。到得自家好底意思日長月益，則天理自然純固；向之所謂私欲者，自然消靡退散，久之不復 萌動矣 。[75]

Sprouts of the full Inherent Cosmic Productive Copotentiality that are Truly Integrated (*cheng* 誠) as my human nature are continually arising, scattered among those bits that are already subordinate to other Centers. All I have to do is gather them together, make them cohere, by attending to them and the way they fit together, and they will come to subsume what were formerly the impulses subordinated to other Centers—for after all, those other centers are just more partial expressions of the Coherence that is more fully expressed as my own Nature, together forming a total network of Inherent Cosmic Productive Copotentiality. So the difference of all Li is what makes things go wrong, and that these are all ultimately also the same Li is what makes moral progress possible.

The one-many asness relation of Li and Taiji is thus crucial to Zhu Xi's solution to the problem of evil. The mind steps in with ways to re-tether them to that equilibrium, that unexpressed Center; remembering it is there, and nourishing it, gathering its scattered unharmonious bits and pieces back into compossible harmonies, with respectful attention (*jing* 敬) and True Integration (*cheng* 誠), with the investigation of things (*gewu* 格物),

---

[75] *Zhuzi yulei, juan* 117, 2808.

which finds the central principles, the compossibilities and copotentials, of all things, especially of sagely actions in the past, but also politics and nature. It also presumably finds the principles of unwholesome moral psychology itself, i.e., the centers that those excessive and inharmonious emotions and desires really do belong to, what makes them productively compossible (namely, the centers in things rather than the center in myself, their natures rather than my Nature, or rather my nature-as-their-natures rather than their-natures-as-my-nature), filling in enough dots to reach a sudden comprehension, where they all cohere with each other and with the Center that is one's own nature, the Unexpressed Equilibrium, now seen as the Inherent Cosmic Productive Copotentiality of all things, *ren*, generation and regeneration, true integration. Thereafter the harmonious connection to the Center becomes effortless. So here, although the Center is immanent in everything as its source and what makes it compossible, seeing this and how it expresses itself, even in evil things, is part of the necessary process of amelioration. Thus we see that for Huayan and for Tiantai and for Zhu Xi, there is a kind of inescapable immanence of the good in all things, and with it an omnipresent pre-existence of a kind. This is what they share. But this goodness and its manner of pre-existence are conceived differently and applied differently in each of the three cases.

4.7 Comparison More Generally

Let us compare Zhu Xi more closely to Huayan. As in Huayan, for Zhu Xi the entire Li is fully present in each *shi*. In Huayan, this Li is both transcendent and immanent: transcendent because it is the negation of all the determinate contents of the *shi*, immanent because it is coextensive with the *shi*, and enables its existence, and is expressed by it. Only an aspect shift is required to shift from referring to one to referring to the other. They are two senses that share the same referent, but the senses have a strict dependence relationship between them. All this is true for Zhu Xi as well. But the Li in Huayan is like the wetness of the water: It is genuinely identical, in its totality, in each thing. In Huayan there is only one Li, though it is a weird one: the absence of any determinate nature, which entails also the absence of any ability to obstruct or exclude any determinate nature. For Zhu Xi the same total Li is also different Li in each particular configuration of *qi*: It is like the circles in the Taiji diagram. Each thing is a circle, and thus each is structured around a center that unites, and triggers the interactions of, its opposed parts, of its *ti* in its quiescent state and its *yong* as active state, and also among its various *yong*. But the circle has different contents in each case, has undergone genuine mitosis and development. It is a constancy of form into which many things can be put, rather than a specific content or contentlessness (the latter being also a kind of specific content). We may say that wetness too represents transcendence and immanence only as relationship and interconnection in Huayan, and this is all that is the same in each case. The Center in Zhu Xi is also transcendence and immanence only because it is interconnection, Copotentiality. But there are two differences: (1) for Zhu Xi the immanence is manifested as *limit*: not as openness but as determinacy and rule and closedness; and (2), for that very reason, the interconnection in question is always dyadic. It is not just that the Taiji itself is in a sense dyadic, though it is: The statement *wuji er taiji*, "the most formless of all and yet the Supreme Pivot of All," is equivalent to the Huayan Emptiness as neither Emptiness nor Being, or simultaneous Emptiness and Being, the Exclusive Mean, which is the One Nature in Huayan. But that which it interconnects, the contents, are also always necessarily dyadic and dialectical, cohering precisely through their mutual limits rather than through their inherent limitlessness, through the normative restrictions of their Productive Copotentiality. This is not the case in Huayan.

In Tiantai, however, there is something similar, where not only the Three Truths but also the Ten Realms have an oppositional, dyadic, dialectical structure: the first three realms (purgatories, hungry ghosts, animals) are opposed by the next three (asuras, humans, gods), all of which are negated by the next two ("Hīnayāna," saints), which are negated by the next (bodhisattva), which is negated and included by the next (buddhahood), and all this is, according to Zhanran, a "synonym" for the Three Truths, whose inner structure is precisely contrasting and identical opposites around a Center. Both Li and *shi* have this dyadically arranged, oppositional structure of mutual limitation and negation. In this structural feature, Zhu Xi shows a Tiantai resemblance. In a broad way, the other distinctive point also has some Tiantai resonances: For the immanence of the Three Truths as each phenomenal thing is also purely in the limits, the defining boundaries, of those things, making them present, thus Provisional, thus Empty, thus Central. But limit is not here conceived of in the sense of *standard*. On the contrary, limitation, and finite determination derived therefrom, is viewed simultaneously as suffering and as compassion, as the positing of determinations and limited views first as deluded karma and also compassionate upayic response to that suffering. Here the two views diverge.

4.7.1 Pre-existence and the Good in Cross-Cultural Perspective

"All things come from the Good" is a claim made, in some form, in certain strands of Western thought as well. But the Good in these three Chinese schools is in no case a crypto-theistic Good à la Plato's description of *nous* as *arche* in the *Phaedo* or *Timeaus* or the Hebrew Bible's *Genesis*, with someone arranging things according to a single conscious plan of what is best, on the model of human consciousness. In the Chinese cases, the model is rather human coherence, *ren* 仁, generation and regeneration, spontaneity and effort combined, as unexpressed equilibrium, as impartiality, as mutual sensitivity of all parts, as the seed of all growth and generation, Productive Copotentiality. In all the Chinese cases, the basic solution to the problem of evil is one or another variation of the Guo Xiang 郭象 (d. 312) solution: Everything is good in its origin, in itself, in its innerness, in its own spontaneous activity. And yet almost everything is messed up. Why? Because of the *mutual interferences* of many things, which are each themselves right. In Tiantai, two wrongs make a right (biases are mutual *upāya*s to each other, restoring the Center); in Zhu Xi and in Huayan, however, *two rights make a wrong* (in Zhu Xi, two different manifestations of the whole Taiji interfere with one another, the mind lets itself be misled by its response to things, and that is the source of wrongness, although both are in their way right; in Huayan, two phenomena, each the entirely of Li—because Li must take infinite shapes—come into conflict, obstructing each other: Two waves crash into each other).

For both Zhu Xi and Huayan, the solution lies in seeing that these were right all along, in a particular sense, and thus not in conflict after all. In the Huayan case, that means seeing the waves as water, and thus intermelding even if they seem to be crashing. In actuality, they merely appeared to be conflicting, because each is the total wetness; they are wetness hitting wetness. In Zhu Xi's case, the less inclusive coherence of the thing must be made coherent with the more inclusive coherence of human nature, manifest in the mind, through investigation of things, and preserving and nourishing the nature. This is also a way of reclaiming their original rightness, but through subordinating them to the greater (more complete) coherence of the human over the non-human, subsuming the non-human Li into nature, seeing that they are one and the same Productive Copotentiality but that this is most comprehensively expressed as the Productive Copotentiality of the human being rather than the Productive Copotentiality of the thing. It is as it should be that there is *qi*, and that *qi* is varied. That is in balance with there being Li itself, as the uppermost two levels of the "Taiji tu" show. There being the Taiji, there must be its motion and rest, alternating and seeding each other, and producing all kinds of variations of things. Since there is Li (and Li is just what there is when everything is gone, "the least present of all"), there must be *qi* in *yin-yang* forms, and so on down the line. So when we say "Everything is Good" here, we must remember two crucial premises. First, the "everything": To be an identifiable thing at all is to be an integration of diverse (dyadically opposed) parts, not a simple substance. It is a coherence, which means many of the elements of a good "thing" may not be good. (Think hexagrams, Wang Bi and so on.) Second premise: Good is not *Phaedo* good, Anaxagoras good, *Timeaus* good, *Genesis* good, monotheism good. It is the statistical, integrated good of each whole qua whole. This is not a micromanaged conscious operation; it is a general detritus-scattering spin of the potter's wheel. Moreover, none of these individual different forms, of whatever quality of *qi*, can exist without being balanced and actualized by their inborn Taiji, their Li, their Productive Copotentiality (with other things, and the copotentiality of its own parts as coherence around a center, conceived usually dyadically). This is like the repeating circles in the "Taiji tu": The Five Phases, the individual things, all are circles, all are Taiji. But when the perfectly good Li hits the as-it-should-be *qi*, a diffraction takes place, and the outputs no longer "accord" with their source. They come from it, but no longer resemble it. We may think here, in the Neo-Confucianism of the Northern Song, of Cheng Hao's metaphor of pure water flowing into both pure and impure streams, or Zhang Zai's vision of the palpable things, including the physicality that sometimes leads to imbalances, on the model of ice cubes forming from the pure water of the Great Vacuity. *Qi* is right, Li is right, but the filtering of Li through *qi* is sometimes not right—i.e., not in accord with the Li at the origin (even with the Li of there being varying *qi*), which is to say the Li of the whole, which is what is "continued" and "completed" (*ji zhi* 繼之, *cheng zhi* 成之) as the Li of human beings, the unexpressed Center (*wei fa zhi zhong* 未發之中), human nature.

We now have a fairly straightforward way to understand how Zhu Xi might say both that there is in one sense a temporal priority between a given Li and its manifestation through *qi* and in another sense there is not. The so-called conceptual priority is an entirely different question. There, we have unambiguous priority in the sense that any *qi* depends on its Li in a way that is in no wise reversible, in spite of their eternal temporal simultaneity. The case is the same as in the Huayan model: *Shi* depends on Li, but Li does not depend on *shi*, as images depend on the light but not vice versa. But that is not a question of "before" and "after," and I believe that when Zhu Xi prevaricates on this issue, he is talking purely about the temporal issue. We must treat these separately.

As for the asymmetrical vertical relation of dependence between Li and *qi*, always referring not to *qi* as a whole, but to a particular determinate manifestation of *qi*, it is simply the relation between the Supreme Pivot and *yin* and *yang*, which carry it as the reversal nodes of motion and stillness.[76] Nor does it imply that Li is something "non-physical" in any robust sense. It is virtual, it is omnipresent, but it is continually stressed that it is not "some other thing." Nor is it recognizable apart from the two extremes.

The Center is the compossibility, the Productive Copotentiality, of the two extremes. That is, the Center is what makes it possible for *yin* and *yang* to coexist. It is the fact that neither of them excludes the other, that the existence of one is not a threat to the other's existence but rather a condition and result of the others' existence. Possibility has slightly unusual properties within a strict holism, in a system that admits of no atomism, where there are no smallest units of which the world is composed, where wholes are not built up by assembling pre-existing parts. To speak of the presence of the Center in *yin* is to speak of *yin*'s compossibility with *yang*. The same applies vice versa. In this sense we can say that the Center is everywhere. *Yin* is itself only possible because it is compossible, and the same is true for *yang*. In a holism, to be possible is to be compossible, and all the diverse individual compossibilities of various things are the same universal compossibility of all the various things.

In the temporal sense, we can say that "this Li" literally precedes "this *qi*" because Li is precisely compossibility. That means "this Li" is always already present before "this *qi*" actually appears: It is present *as* "*that* Li"! That is, the compossibility of previous *qi* manifestations is itself both one with and different from the compossibility of the subsequent *qi* manifestation. For this is the relation of compossibilities, of Li: They

---

[76] I hesitate to call this a simple "logical" or "conceptual" priority in the usual sense, and yet, because it is predicated on a very specific sort of holism, and it might be argued that conceptual priority presupposes an atomism of concepts, at least. One concept simply is not another concept; they are mutually external to each other, so that when an inherence of one concept in another is discovered—which should really mean they are not actually two different concepts at all—it is instead described as the "conceptual priority" of one concept over the other.

are all one compossibility, and yet they are equally the specific different compossibilities of each individual thing, both one and many, both the one Taiji and each Li as that Taiji in its entirety. There is an asness relation of one and many between Li; all Li are different, and yet all Li are one Li. Li is one; the roles it plays are many.

This Productive Copotentiality is identified with *ren* 仁, which is the Coherence of oneself with all things, and simultaneously the Coherence of humaneness with all the other virtues that express and develop it, even when they are apparently opposite to it, like rightness and wisdom. The relation is like that between spring and the other seasons: in one sense summer, autumn and winter are just further developments of spring, the impulse of growth, itself, flourishing, dying, going dormant and being reborn. This is again the pendulum flow. What all of these together make up when properly balanced and coexisting around the Center is Life, Integration, effortless and unceasing generation and regeneration.

This is everywhere, at the root of all generation. It is why things are so, and also how things should be. It is why there is *qi*, and also how it should be. There has always been *qi* and always will be *qi*, even when heaven and earth disappear. There has always been Li and always will be Li, even when heaven and earth disappear. But Li has a certain priority, in that it is why and how *qi* exists, *and* the temporally priorly existing why and how any particular concrete *qi* thing exists. In any individual case, any concrete thing (including heaven and earth), there is *that* Li before there is *that* thing. Before any particular thing appears, the Productive Copotentiality of it is already there. Where? In everything else, precisely because it is a copotentiality with those already existing things. This is the relation between Li and *qi*: not a *ti-yong* relation, but a compossibility-actuality relation, conceived on an axis-extreme model.

Finally, we should stress that Cheng Yi's breakthrough notion that "Productive Compossibility is one but the roles it plays are many" (理一分殊) offers a unique solution to the pre-existence problem that distinguishes it from Platonic pre-existence, as well as from "conceptual" priority. The pre-existence of compossibility of X, even temporally, is not the same as eternal existence of all the Forms prior to the demiurgic formation of the world. In the Platonic case, and even in the derivative but modified Aristotelian case, each Form is a separate entity, a hypostatization precisely of a definition, i.e., of a way of distinguishing one entity from another. It is true that they all somehow depend on the Form of the Good, which suggests that though they are many, they are in some other sense one, just as the instantiations of any Form are many but, in the sense in which they are all instantiations of the same Form, are also one (as in the divided line parable in the *Republic*). But the speculation that a soul freed of a body could know the Forms more clearly could not occur in Zhu Xi, for there are no such minds. Li are therefore not the kinds of things that are knowable by such minds, and this tells us how they differ from Platonic Forms. Their pre-existence is always in *qi*, which is as eternal as Li. The pre-existence of the compossibility (Li) of X, which is the nature of X, resides in the pre-existing nature already actual in Y. It does not require another realm of being that has any existence, accessible to any mind, prior to all *qi*. If Y does not yet exist, that same compossibility exists as the nature of Z. Z might be entirely formless *qi* in a period before or after the presently existing heaven and earth, in which case the compossibility of X will exist only as the uninflected Wuji/Taiji. But the two are in that case still coexisting, even though any given Li always precedes, even in time, its actualization.

In the case of Aristotle too, where matter is pure potentiality, and hence never knowable as such, being nothing in particular, we have form as actuality and as formal cause, coinciding with final and motive causes, resulting in pure individuation of the actuality. So the process of actualization always involves a progression from no identity to exactly one identity, excluding all others. The more perfect a thing is, the more it has actualized just this one form and no others. Form individuates, and even when it is still acting only as not fully realized formal cause, as a thing is growing from potential to actual, it is a force of separation and bordering, of articulation. The one-many asness structure of *li yi fen shu* 理一分殊 form as coherence, Li as coherence of coherences, as compossibility, is entirely lacking. Potential here is not Copotential. For this reason, the Form of Forms, the Actuality of Actualities, God, has to be introduced to reunite them—but the forms are then united only externally: They are still ultimately different from one another, and different from the uniting God.

For Zhu Xi, Li as Productive Compossibility is thus already at once one and many, manifested in *qi* as an actual entity that is more perfect as it is more "one body with all things," i.e., actualizes the coherence with all other Lis, with the Taiji, and as its one is more fully also all the many, all the others, with which it is compossible, and whose compossibility is seen to be the same as its own compossibility. The more one thing is articulated in its determinate Li, as both that by which it is so and how it should be, the more all other Li are also articulated as coherent with it, as its own Productive Copotentiality.[77]

---

[77] And on this particular point we do have a result that resembles the Tiantai result: "Whenever one of the Three Thousand becomes increasingly manifest, so do all the others become increasingly manifest," i.e., the doctrine of *sanqian qizhang* 三千齊彰. Compare Zhili, *Guan wuliang shou fo jing shu miao zong chao* 觀無量壽佛經疏妙宗鈔 (Notes on the Profound Tenets of the Commentary on the Sutra on Contemplation of the Buddha of Immeasurable Life), T37.1751, 200a23-28:

> Moreover, you should realize that the six levels of identity apply not only to our [always present but gradually realized] identity to buddhahood, but to all beings, whether real or unreal: bodhisattvas, Pratyekabuddhas, Śrāvakas, gods, humans and so on, all the way down to every last body and every last mind of even the lowest dung beetle in hell. For all of these we must distinguish all six levels of identity: we are identical to that dung beetle in principle, then in name, and so on, all the way up to our final fully realized ultimate identity with that dung beetle. Since [Zhiyi] is now talking about the founder of the teaching [Śākyamuni], it spells out these levels of our identity only with the Buddha. But because the Ten Realms are all Li, the Omnipresent Nature, such that each of them is the entire universe, and each and every one of them is eternally unchanged, thus in our practice when we proceed to identity not only in principle but also in name and so on, it is not only our identity with the Buddha that is realized: the other nine realms are manifested proportionally at the same time. When we reach the state of fruition, ultimate identity with the Buddha, our identity with all Ten Realms is also ultimate, and all of them are the ultimate. Thus the six identities should be distinguished with respect to the dung beetle as well.

> 又復應知六即之義不專在佛，一切假、實三乘、人、天，下至蛣蜣地獄色心，皆須六即辯其初後:所謂理蛣蜣名字，乃至究竟蛣蜣。今釋教主，故就佛辯。以論十界皆理性故，無非法界，一一不改。故名字去不唯顯佛；九亦同彰。至於果成，十皆究竟。故蛣蜣等皆明六即。

Would Zhu Xi agree? Yes and no. The interesting thing in comparing these schools of thought is working out in what sense yes and in what sense no.

CHAPTER 5 | Monism and the Problem of the Ignorance and Badness in Chinese Buddhism and Zhu Xi's Neo-Confucianism

JOHN MAKEHAM

CONCEPTUAL STRUCTURES DERIVED from the late sixth-century Buddhist text the *Treatise on Giving Rise to Faith in the Great Vehicle* (*Dasheng qixin lun* 大乘起信論) became a shared resource for East Asian philosophers and religious theorists over the course of centuries and continue to do so even today. The most influential of these has been the One Mind Two Gateways (*yi xin er men* 一心二門) paradigm. Variations of this paradigm were central to the development of schools of Sinitic Buddhism, in particular, Huayan and Chan from the seventh centuries onwards (and Tiantai from the eleventh century). This chapter argues that this paradigm was also fundamental to Zhu Xi's 朱熹 (1130–1200) conception of the relationship between pattern (*li* 理) and vital stuff (*qi* 氣).

The chapter consists of three parts. The first part shows how although the *Dasheng qixin lun* subscribes to a substance monism[1] based on the One Mind, it failed to provide a reason to accept ontological monism over ontological dualism. The *Dasheng qixin lun* primarily champions a soteriological goal. It attempts to guide the novice towards this goal by means of a number of strategies. One of its key strategies is via a monism, which

---

I wish to acknowledge the constructive critical feedback on earlier drafts of this chapter provided by my fellow contributors to this volume and by Jason Clower, Anders Sydskjor, and Eyal Aviv. John Jorgensen, Dan Lusthaus, Mark Strange, John Powers, and Keng Ching have also contributed greatly to my understanding of the *Dasheng qixin lun*, a text central to this chapter.

[1] Here substance is understood as something that does not rely on anything else to be what it is.

is deployed to show the pernicious effects of, but also the illusory nature of, ignorance. As I argue, by drawing on analogies that present ignorance as external to suchness, the text leaves itself vulnerable to the charge that it introduces a dualist analogy into a monistic ontology. And in failing to provide a consistent account of the origin of ignorance, the *Dasheng qixin lun* can be construed as also failing to provide a satisfactory account of how badness, evil and suffering arise, thus undermining its own soteriological goal. The second half of this first part examines Huayan master Fazang's 法藏 (643–712) apologist attempt to resolve the problem by arguing that ignorance does not exist.

Beginning with Fazang in the early Tang (618–907) and continuing through to Tiantai masters of the Northern Song (960–1127), a rich diversity of arguments was developed to preserve the monistic ontology yet also to account for the origin of ignorance and badness. These arguments were framed in terms of the relationship between Li 理[2] and *shi* 事 (phenomena), with Li representing suchness, and phenomena representing dharmas. The second part of this chapter analyzes attempts by two groups of Tiantai thinkers to reconcile the origin of badness with a monistic ontology.

The third part of the chapter argues that Zhu Xi was able to reconcile the origin of badness with a monistic ontology in such a way that it provided a more compelling case for affirming the phenomenal world, the life-world, as the ground for ethical practice. I endeavor to show that Zhu Xi's understanding of the *li-qi* relationship is a further development of the rich and complex body of discourse that arose in the Tang and Northern Song about Li 理 and *shi* 事, which had attempted to reconcile the origin of ignorance and/or badness with a monistic ontology. I demonstrate how Zhu's conception of the *li-qi* relationship is isomorphic with the *Dasheng qixin lun*'s One Mind Two Gateways paradigm, articulated within the framework of Zhu's creative interpretation of eleventh-century Neo-Confucian Zhou Dunyi's 周敦頤 (1017–1073) Taiji Diagram and its accompanying essay. I argue that Zhu provided a new solution to the problem of the origin of badness—one that avoided the radical proposals entailed in Buddhist attempts to deal with the issue for over half a millennium.

Throughout these three parts I also develop a second thesis about the role of the *ti-yong* polarity in Zhu's metaphysics, which also links Zhu with the *Dasheng qixin lun*. I show that his understanding of *ti-yong* is consistent

---

[2] In Sinitic Buddhist contexts, when contrasted with *shi* 事, Li 理 is synonymous with suchness (*zhenru* 真如; *tathatā*): reality as it truly is without any conceptual overlay. In order to distinguish this Buddhist usage I capitalize the term as Li.

with the model found in the *Dasheng qixin lun* and as described by various Huayan thinkers. Finally, I emphasize the importance of identifying the Buddhist models Zhu drew on, because they provide new insights into what Zhu Xi was trying to achieve as a philosopher.

5.1 Pattern and Phenomena

5.1.1 The Primary Model of the *Dasheng qixin lun*

As a system of thought that blossomed in China between the fifth and seventh centuries, the Tathāgatagarbha tradition within Mahāyāna Buddhism is particularly associated with a cluster of texts, central to which is the *tathāgatagarbha* (*rulaizang* 如來藏) or buddha-nature (*foxing* 佛性) doctrine. *Tathāgatagarbha* means the repository of a buddha, the potential to achieve buddhahood; and the *tathāgatagarbha* doctrine is the idea that buddha-nature exists within all sentient beings. The doctrine had a profound influence in the development of East Asian Buddhism, but its origins lie in India.

Michael Zimmermann has shown that in India *tathāgatagarbha* was understood in two different ways. The first is a disclosure model, according to which sentient beings inherently possess perfect buddhahood within themselves and that this perfect buddhahood requires no refinement or further development. Being obscured or hidden by adventitious defilements and ignorance, however, sentient beings are unaware of it.[3] "Once these defilements have been cleared away, the buddha-nature can unfold its full potency, and a being that has realized this stage would be called a buddha in the full and unrestricted sense of the word." The second is a

---

[3] The doctrine that "consciousness is intrinsically pure but defiled by adventitious defilements" goes back to early Buddhist groups such as the Mahāsāṅghika. See Alex and Hideko Wayman, *The Lion's Roar of Queen Śrīmālā* (New York: Columbia University Press, 1974), 42. Similarly, early Buddhist suttas in the *Nikāya/Āgama* collection of the Pāli Canon include descriptions of a brightly shining *citta* (mind) that is covered and obscured by defilements such as hatred and delusion. See Edward Conze, *Buddhist Texts Through the Ages* (Delhi: Motilal Banarsidass, 2002), 33. Peter Harvey identifies this radiant mind as "the basis for Mahāyāna talk of the 'Buddha-nature', or enlightenment-potential, in all beings. . . . Even the corrupt person destined for hell thus has a 'brightly shining' *citta* 'covered', so to speak, by the defilements which obscure it." See his *The Selfless Mind: Personality, Consciousness and Nirvana in Early Buddhism* (London: RoutledgeCurzon, 1995/2004), 166–167; David Seyfort Ruegg, *La théorie du tathâgatagarbha et du gotra: études sur la sotériologie et la gnoséologie du bouddhisme* (Paris: École Française d'Extrême Orient,1969), 411 ff.

development model, according to which buddhahood is a potential that needs to be developed before it can be realized.[4] Both models are evident in a number of the texts associated with the Tathāgatagarbha tradition as it developed between the fourth and sixth centuries in China. The motif of defilements' obscuring awareness of the *tathāgatagarbha*, of buddha-nature, was common to all the texts in the Tathāgatagarbha tradition.

By the fifth century, Chinese translations of the *Laṅkāvatāra-sūtra* 楞伽經 (composed in India in the fourth or early fifth century) had begun to reflect the idea that insofar as *tathāgatagarbha* carries potential *tathāgata*-hood (buddhahood), it is the conveyor of suchness (*zhenru* 真如; *tathatā*; reality as it truly is); insofar as it is obscured or concealed, the concealment aspect is reflected in the store consciousness (*ālayavijñāna*; 阿賴耶識),[5] which is the admixture of purity and defilements produced by ignorance. For example, Guṇabhadra's (394–468) distinction between *rulaizang* 如來藏 and *shizang* 識藏, as presented in his translation of the *Laṅkāvatāra-sūtra*, can be understood to mean that the term *zang* in the compound *rulaizang* (*tathāgatagarbha*) indicates *tathāgatagarbha* is covered over, concealed purity, but the focus is on what is concealed (the purity); whereas the *shizang* (*ālayavijñāna*) shifts the focus to the concealing, since the *ālaya* (store, container) is the gathering point for the afflictions (*kleśa*) produced by ignorance that are doing the covering. This can be made clearer using the following analogy. *Tathāgatagarbha* is employed to put emphasis on the gold in the mountain (the goal), *ālayavijñāna* shifts the focus to the mountain that contains the gold (the mining task), and ignorance is the mountain itself (where we start, pickaxe in hand, knowing that our mountain contains the sought-after gold). The implication is that the work needs to be done mentally, in the *ālayavijñāna*, where our cognitive functions are jumbled.[6]

The main import of this relationship is that, on the one hand, the *tathāgatagarbha* (functionally equivalent to suchness) provides the ontological grounding for the *ālayavijñāna*, and on the other hand, *ālayavijñāna* represents the adventitious defilements that cover over or

---

[4] Zimmermann, "The Process of Awakening in Early Texts on Buddha-Nature in India," in Chen-kuo Lin and Michael Radich, eds., *A Distant Mirror: Articulating Indic Ideas in Sixth and Seventh Century Chinese Buddhism* (Hamburg: Hamburg University Press, 2014), 515–517.
[5] This consciousness (one of eight or nine identified by Buddhists) retains the impressions of past experiences and "perfumes" new experiences on the basis of that previous conditioning.
[6] *Lengqie abaduoluo bao jing* 楞伽阿跋多羅寶經, T16.670, 510c1-10 passim; translation dated 443.

obscure realization of the *tathāgatagarbha*.⁷ Later in the sixth century, the idea of an intrinsically pure mind (*zixing qingjing xin* 自性清淨心; *prakṛti-pariśuddha-citta*)—a very old concept—came to be associated with the disclosure model of the *tathāgatagarbha*, and referred to by the term "inherent awakening" (*benjue* 本覺) in the *Dasheng qixin lun*.

The *Dasheng qixin lun* has no attested Sanskrit counterpart. It purports to be a translation of an Indian text but the weight of modern scholarly opinion is that it is a work of Chinese not Indian provenance. Dating from sixth-century China, the treatise seemed to resolve disparities between competing forms of Buddhist doctrine and practice, providing a model for later schools to harmonize teachings and sustain the idea that there was only one doctrine, or Dharma. Conceptual structures derived from the *Dasheng qixin lun* became a shared resource for East Asian philosophers and religious theorists over the course of centuries. It played a formative role in shaping the doctrines and practices of the major schools of Sinitic Buddhism: Chan, Tiantai, Huayan, and to a lesser extent Pure Land.

The *Dasheng qixin lun* presents the mind or the so-called One Mind, as the ultimate source of reality. The One Mind has two modalities or aspects, which the text calls gateways, and each of these contain all dharmas, conditioned and unconditioned:⁸

> There are two gateways based on the doctrine (dharma) of One Mind. What are they? The first is the gateway of the mind as suchness. The second is the

---

⁷ Lü Cheng 呂澂, "*Qixin yu Chan – duiyu Dasheng qixin lun laili de tantao*" 起信與禪 – 對於大乘起信論來歷的探討 (The *Dasheng qixin lun* and Chan: An Investigation into the Historical Origins of the *Dasheng qixin lun*), reprinted in *Xiandai fojiao xueshu congkan* 現代佛教學術叢刊 (Modern Buddhist Scholarship Series), vol. 35, ed. Zhang Mantao 張曼濤 (Taipei: Dasheng wenhua chubanshe, 1978), 302, goes so far as to propose that the extant Sanskrit version of *Laṅkāvatāra-sūtra* (and also reflected in the Chinese translation by Guṇabhadra)—a text that blends Yogācāra and Tathāgatagarbha ideas—actually identifies the *tathāgatagarbha* with the *ālayavijñāna*. In more recent decades, scholars such as Takasaki Jikidō and Peter N. Gregory have followed up with similar assessments. See Takasaki, *A Study on the Ratnagotravibhāga (Uttaratantra): Being a Treatise on the Tathāgatagarbha Theory of Mahāyāna Buddhism* (Rome: Istituto Italiano per il Medio ed Estremo Oriente, 1966), 53. In referring to the term *tathāgatagarbha*, Peter N. Gregory writes: "Although the original Sanskrit term can mean both the 'embryo' or 'womb' of the Tathāgata, by rendering *garbha* as *zang* 藏 ('repository' or 'treasury') the Chinese translation emphasizes the latter meaning. This translation made it easier for the Chinese Buddhist exegetes to identify the *tathāgatagarbha* with the *ālayavijñāna* ('store consciousness'), which was translated into Chinese as *zangshi* 藏識. The identification of the two found scriptural justification in the *Laṅkāvatāra-sūtra*." See his "The Three Truths in Huayan Buddhism," in *Avataṃsaka Buddhism in East Asia: Huayan, Kegon, Flower Ornament Buddhism: Origins and Adaptation of a Visual Culture*, eds. Robert Gimello, Frédéric Girard, and Imre Hamar (Wiesbaden: Harrassowitz Verlag, 2012), 90n6.

⁸ "Conditioned dharmas" refers to existence that is subject to determination by the laws of cause and effect.

gateway of the mind as arising and ceasing. The two gateways each contain all phenomena (dharmas).

依一心法，有二種門。云何為二？一者、心真如門，二者、心生滅門。是二種門，皆各總攝一切法。⁹

The gateway of the mind as suchness (*xin zhenru men* 心真如門) is the true mind—unchanging, eternal, and pure. The gateway of the mind as arising and ceasing (*xin shengmie men* 心生滅門) is cyclic existence (*saṃsāra*) in which the mind's propensity to awaken struggles against the mental and physical behaviors that arise from the mind's defilement by ignorance. Both the mind as suchness and the arising and ceasing mind are ultimately the One Mind but, because ignorance obscures realization of the One Mind, deluded beings create false perceptions and so become mired in suffering. The arising and ceasing mind then generates misguided perceptual distinctions, which in turn provide new conditions for the ongoing defilement of the mind and for the suffering caused by taking the wrong sorts of actions.

The mind as suchness is quiescent, unchanging, unconditioned, and it neither arises nor ceases. It is free of conceptualization and distinction-making. The arising and ceasing mind is identified with the *ālayavijñāna*. It represents the adaptation of *tathāgatagarbha*, the mind of suchness, to phenomenal conditions, to ignorance. Crucially, *tathāgatagarbha/*suchness—the unconditioned—remains constant, unchanged, undiminished, undefiled by these phenomenal conditions (see fig. 5.1).

5.1.2 The Problem of Ignorance and Ontological Dualism

In the *Dasheng qixin lun*, it is due to ignorance (*wuming* 無明) that suchness remains concealed from us:

> How does habituation [by ignorance] give rise to defiled dharmas without interruption? Because it is based on the dharma of suchness, there is ignorance. Because there are the defiled dharmas of ignorance as cause, these then habituate suchness. Because of habituation, there is the false mind. And since there is the false mind, it then habituates ignorance. Because the dharma of

---

⁹ *Dasheng qixin lun*, T32.1666, 576a5-7. All translations from the *Dasheng qixin lun* in this chapter are drawn from the pre-copyedited manuscript of the forthcoming annotated translation by John Jorgensen, Dan Lusthaus, John Makeham, and Mark Strange, *Treatise on Giving Rise to Faith in the Great Vehicle* (New York: Oxford University Press).

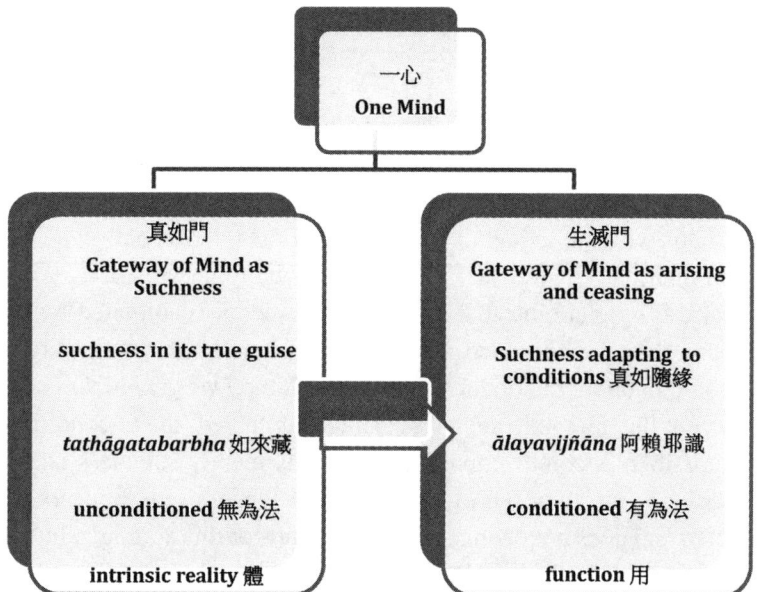

FIGURE 5.1 The *Dasheng qixin lun*'s "One Mind, Two Gateways" Model
CREDIT: This diagram was created by John Makeham.

suchness is not fully discerned, conceiving arises without one being aware of it, presenting false perceptual fields. Because there are the defiled dharmas of false perceptual fields as conditions, these then habituate the false mind, so that conceiving and attachments generate all kinds of karmic action and one experiences all the sufferings of body and mind.

云何熏習起染法不斷？所謂以依真如法故有於無明，以有無明染法因故即熏習真如；以熏習故則有妄心，以有妄心即熏習無明。不了真如法故，不覺念起現妄境界。以有妄境界染法緣故，即熏習妄心，令其念著造種種業，受於一切身心等苦。[10]

Like suchness, ignorance is without origin; it is simply a given.[11] According to the above passage, suchness somehow comes to be habituated by ignorance. This leads to false mind, which in turn habituates ignorance, enhancing

---

[10] T32.1666, 578a23-27.
[11] "Because the *tathāgatagarbha* has no starting point, the characteristics of ignorance also have no beginning...." 以如來藏無前際故，無明之相亦無有始 . . . 。(T32.1666, 580b1-2). "Because all sentient beings have been habituated by ignorance from beginningless time...." 一切眾生從無始來，皆因無明所熏習 . . . 。(T32.1666, 582c22-23). This understanding of ignorance may seem to be drawing on the concept of "fundamental ignorance" (無明住地; *avidyāvāsabhūmi*). The concept features centrally in the *Śrīmālā-sūtra*:

its power to delude the mind and so suchness is unable to be fully discerned. The unawakened mind then generates false perceptual distinctions, which in turn provide new conditions for the ongoing defilement of the false mind and for the suffering caused by taking the wrong sorts of actions.

The *Dasheng qixin lun* here stands apart from other texts associated with the Tathāgatagarbha tradition—not to mention placing it fundamentally at odds with the Indian understanding of the relation between unconditioned dharmas (*wuwei fa* 無為法) and conditioned dharmas (*youwei fa* 有為法)—by claiming that suchness is somehow habituated by ignorance, that the unconditioned is acted upon casually by the conditioned. Later commentators maintained that although the *Dasheng qixin lun* asks us to accept that although suchness can be habituated (the unconditioned, per impossible, becomes conditioned), this is merely suchness adapting to conditions (*sui yuan* 隨緣) and, in fact, suchness only appears to be habituated and does not change at all.[12] Support for this apologist interpretation is readily found in the *Dasheng qixin lun*'s own analogy of the wind and the ocean. Even though the wind stirs up the phenomenal appearance of waves and motion, the wet nature of the ocean is not affected and does not change, whether the wind blows or does not blow:

> Since all the characteristics of the mind and consciousness are ignorance,[13] the characteristic of ignorance is not separate from the nature of awakening.

The enlightened cognition of the Tathāgata severs severe afflictions more numerous that the sands of the Ganges. All [severe afflictions] are established on the basis of fundamental ignorance. All severe afflictions arise by taking fundamental ignorance as their cause and condition. World-honored one, the momentary mind is momentarily associated with these active afflictions. World-honored one, the mind is not associated with beginningless, fundamental ignorance.

如是過恒沙等上煩惱，如來菩提智所斷。一切皆依無明住地之所建立。一切上煩惱起皆因無明住地緣無明住地。世尊。於此起煩惱，剎那心剎那相應。世尊。心不相應無始無明住地。(T12.353, 220b24-c1)

Each moment of mind ceases as soon as it arises, providing an opportunity to become aware of our afflictions. What is much harder to discern, however, is fundamental ignorance (*wuming zhudi* 無明住地), which is the basis for momentary mental afflictions, yet is itself not momentary but rather unchanging and unconditioned. Unlike the concept of fundamental ignorance as featured in *Śrīmālā-sūtra*, however, in the *Dasheng qixin lun*, ignorance operates at the level of momentary expressions of cognitive functioning: "This is explained as beginningless ignorance because thought-moment after thought-moment have followed one another in a continuous flow from the very beginning and [sentient beings] have never been free from conceiving.'" 以從本來念念相續未曾離念故，說無始無明。(T32.1666, 576c1).

[12] See, for example, Tanyan 曇延 (516–588), *Qixin lun yishu* 起信論義疏 (Explaining the Meaning of the *Qixin lun*), X45.755, 159b6-22.

[13] Early commentators here interpret "the mind" to refer to the seventh consciousness and "consciousnesses" to refer to the first six consciousnesses.

It is neither destructible nor indestructible.[14] This is because, just as the water of the ocean is moved in waves due to the wind, the characteristics of water and the characteristics of wind are not separate from one another. It is not in the nature of water to move; and if wind stops, the characteristic of motion ceases, but the wetness is not destroyed.

以一切心識之相皆是無明，無明之相，不離覺性，非可壞，非不可壞。如大海水因風波動，水相風相不相捨離，而水非動性，若風止滅動相則滅，濕性不壞故。[15]

Even though the deluded mind is stirred into erroneous distinction making, in fact its self-nature—inherent enlightenment, suchness—is constant and unchanged. Only ignorance prevents us from realizing this.

Yet if the mind is inherently enlightened how can there be ignorance that leads to the mind's becoming deluded? If the only game in town is the ocean, where does the wind come from?[16] There is no room for the ontological independence of both the ocean and the wind in a monistic ontology. The *Dasheng qixin lun* does not present a clear solution to the problem of ontological dualism and or even address the attendant problem of the origin of suffering and badness, which in turn arises from the problem of the origin of ignorance.[17]

5.1.3 Fazang's Solution

Huayan master and influential commentator on the *Dasheng qixin lun*, Fazang 法藏 (643–712), dealt with the problem of ontological dualism by denying that ignorance has its own intrinsic reality, its own self-nature:

> My interlocutor asked: "Why is that when previously you explained [the idea that Mahāyāna's] intrinsic reality is great [because it] permeates all

---

[14] Because the characteristic of ignorance is never apart from suchness, it is indestructible. Because the characteristic of ignorance has no self-nature, it is not indestructible.
[15] T32.1666, 576c11-13.
[16] This is how the problem was conceived by influential traditional commentators. The *Dasheng qixin lun* itself, however, can also be seen to provide a solution to the problem of overcoming ignorance. Indeed, the real concern of the *Dasheng Qixin lun* is to demonstrate that ignorance can be overcome. Like suchness, ignorance is seen to be without origin; it is simply a given. Ignorance operates at the level of momentary expressions of cognitive functioning. As the text explains, ignorance amounts to breaking the constancy of the mind into discrete, successive moments. Beginningless ignorance means that this has always happened—there is no point at which mind/thought starts—but that does not entail that one cannot become aware of this and stop the process of erroneous thoughts.
[17] Peter N. Gregory, "Theodicy in the *Awakening of Faith*," *Religious Studies* 22, no. 1 (1986): 63–78, provides an excellent introduction to the topic, analyzed in terms of a similar set of problems associated with theodicy.

dharmas,[18] and does not distinguish between pure and impure [dharmas] or their characteristics and functions, you nevertheless only affirmed that it is good and does not permeate badness?"

I replied: "The principle whereby [Mahāyāna's] intrinsic reality is great is said to be that [suchness] permeates all dharmas without distinguishing [between pure and impure dharmas]. If it were the case that, external to suchness, ignorance were to exist separately as the intrinsic reality of badness then [such a notion] would lead to many errors. . . . It is not possible for ignorance to exist separately from suchness to serve as the intrinsic reality of badness. Nor is it the case that badness and such dharmas can be the characteristics and function of suchness. If they were affirmed to be the characteristics and function of suchness, this would lead to many errors."

問。「何故前明體大中，通一切法，不簡染淨及其相用，唯是其善，不通不善？」答。「體大理曰通諸法。不得簡別。若真如外別有無明為不善體者,有多種過。...真如之外不得別立無明作不善體、不善等法。亦不得作真如相用。若是相用亦有過过。」[19]

Here Fazang simply makes the point that suchness is all permeating, all pervasive. He does not explain why it is not possible for ignorance to exist separately from suchness to serve as the intrinsic reality of badness. Elsewhere, however, he does.

In commenting on the following *Dasheng qixin lun* passage—"Because all the characteristics of mind and consciousnesses is ignorance, the characteristic of ignorance is not separate from the nature of awakening"[20]—he advances the following explanation:

The karmic and other defiled consciousnesses (*xin*)[21] are called cognitive characteristics. Since they are all characteristics of nonawakening, [the *Dasheng qixin lun*] states that "all the characteristics of mind and consciousnesses[22] are ignorance." This remark is not made with respect to the intrinsic reality of the mind. (*xinti* 心體).

---

[18] The *Dasheng qixin lun*, T32.1666, 575c26: "Mahāyāna's intrinsic reality is great because, with respect to all dharmas, suchness is non-discriminating and neither adds nor detracts."
[19] *Dasheng qixin lun bieji* 大乘起信論別記 (Further Notes on *The Dasheng qixin lun*), T44.1847, 288a28-288b2; 288b6-288b8.
[20] T32.1666, 576c10: 以一切心識之相皆是無明，無明之相不離覺性。
[21] In the *Dasheng qixin lun*, mentation (*yi* 意; *manas*), the seventh consciousness, is given five different names, the first of which is karmic consciousness. This refers to the conditioning carried over from experiences in previous lives, which sets the unawakened mind in motion.
[22] As already noted, early commentators understood "the mind" to refer to the seventh consciousness (*xin* 心) and "consciousnesses" (*shi* 識) to refer to the first six consciousnesses.

This, however, presents a further objection. Since it is said that the characteristics of all these is ignorance, then the explanation for the cessation of ignorance would be that there is an additional intrinsic nature separate from that of suchness. This is the objection that there is an intrinsic nature that exists apart from suchness.

The response to this objection is as follows. The characteristic of nonawakening [associated with] these consciousnesses is not separate from the nature of inherent awakening as it accords with defilements. It is for this reason that [the *Dasheng qixin lun*] says: "[The characteristic of ignorance] is not separate from the nature of awakening." The characteristic of ignorance and the nature of inherent awakening are neither the same nor different. Because they are not different [the characteristic of ignorance] is not destructible. Because they are not the same [the characteristic of ignorance] is not indestructible. The sense in which, [because] they are not different, [the characteristic of ignorance] is not destructible explains why ignorance is identical to true understanding. Hence, the *Nirvana Sutra* says: "The nature of true understanding and that of ignorance is non-dual. The nature of this non-duality is true nature."[23] The sense in which, [because] they are not the same, [the characteristic of ignorance] is destructible explains why ignorance ceases but the nature of awakening is not destroyed. The meaning of extinguishing delusion can be understood in the light of this.

業等染心名諸識相。此等皆是不覺之相。故云心識之相皆是無明。非約心體說也。又更轉難云。既言識相皆是無明故，說滅者即應別有體性離於真如。即真妄別體難也。答云:如此諸識不覺之相不離隨染本覺之性。以是故云:「不離覺性。」此無明之相與彼本覺之性非一非異。非異故非可壞。非一故非不可壞。若依非異非可壞義。說無明即明。故涅槃經云:「明與無明其性不二。不二之性即是實性。」若就非一非不可壞義。說無明滅覺性不壞。滅惑之義準此知之。[24]

Although mental activity is associated with ignorance and hence with nonawakening, Fazang interprets the *Dasheng qixin lun* as maintaining that ignorance is not a characteristic of the intrinsic reality of the mind (*xinti* 心體), of suchness.[25] This claim, however, introduces a potential theoretical difficulty: If ignorance is able to cease—as it must if there is to be initial

---

[23] Based on the *Mahāparinirvāṇa-sūtra* (*Da bore niepan jing* 大般涅槃經), T12.374, 410c21-22.
[24] *Dasheng qixin lun yiji*, T44.1846, 260a19-29.
[25] Here he is drawing on views expressed in the *Dasheng qixin lun*, such as "Awakening means that the mind itself [as suchness] is free from conceiving." 所言覺義者，謂心體離念。(T32.1666, 576b12).

awakening—this implies that this is due to the cessation of the intrinsic nature (*tixing* 體性) of ignorance. As such, this would be to acknowledge the existence of "a nature that exists apart from suchness," and so open up the unwelcome problem of the origin of ignorance.

Following the lead of the text of the *Dasheng qixin lun*, Fazang presents ignorance as a characteristic (*xiang* 相), but making it explicit that this means that qua characteristic, ignorance is an appearance devoid of self-nature. Ignorance is indestructible only so long as the deluded mind continues to sustain and support it. This is analogous to the situation where waves (= deluded mind) continue to exist as long as the ocean continues to move in response to the movement of the wind (= ignorance). The sense in which the characteristic of ignorance and the nature of inherent awakening are said not to be different is analogous to the sense in which the wind is never separated from the ocean, the nature of which is wetness. Once the ocean stops moving, however, the waves cease to exist, and it becomes apparent that ignorance and the wetness of the ocean are not the same, since only the ocean has an enduring self-nature. Similarly, ignorance ceases to exist with the realization that one has always been awoken.

In citing the passage from the *Nirvana Sutra*—"The nature of true understanding and of ignorance is non-dual. The nature of this non-duality is true nature"—Fazang is making the point that ultimately there is only one nature, not two. The nature of true understanding and of ignorance is non-dual because there is only one nature. True understanding is the realization that ignorance has no nature.

5.1.4 Li and *Shi* in Glossing Two Gateways

This central idea of the mind's adapting to, according with conditions (delusion and ignorance, phenomenal reality) was also formulated in terms of Li 理 and *shi* 事. Inspired by the idea that the mind of suchness can merge with the mind of arising and ceasing yet still retain its own nature,[26] the Huayan master Dushun 杜順 (557–640) introduced the concept of the non-obstruction of Li and phenomena (*li shi wu ai* 理事無礙), effectively re-inscribing the older "emptiness—material form" (*kong se* 空色) dichotomy.[27] Fazang subsequently identified the non-obstruction of

---

[26] In explaining this, Dushun even identifies the gateway of the mind of suchness and the gateway of the mind arising and ceasing with Li and *shi* respectively. *Huayan wu jiao zhiguan* 華嚴五教止觀 (Calming and Contemplation in the Five Teachings of Huayan), T45.1867, 511b6-7.

[27] See Robert M. Gimello, "Apophatic and Kataphatic Discourse in Mahāyāna: A Chinese View," *Philosophy East and West* 26, no. 2 (April 1976), 122–123. Feng Dawen 馮達文, *Lixing*

Li and phenomena as the characteristic teaching of one of four Buddhist lineage traditions (*zong* 宗)[28] that he recognized: the tradition of "the dependent arising of the *tathāgatagarbha*" (*rulaizang yuanqi zong* 如來藏緣起宗). He describes the main feature of the dependent arising of the *tathāgatagarbha* doctrine as "the seamless merging of Li and phenomena" (*li shi rongtong wu ai* 理事融通無礙):

> Because this lineage tradition accepts that *tathāgatagarbha* accords with conditions to become the *ālayavijñāna*, accordingly, Li pervades phenomena. It also accepts that phenomena arise in dependence on one another, are devoid of self-nature, and are the same as Li. Accordingly, phenomena pervade Li.
>
> 以此宗中許如來藏隨緣成阿賴耶識。此則理徹於事也。亦許依他緣起無性同如。此則事徹於理也。[29]

Here *tathāgatagarbha* as Li 理—synonymous with suchness—responds to conditions to become *ālayavijñāna*, the locus of phenomenal existence (*shi* 事). And just as Li in its *ālayavijñāna*-aspect pervades (*che* 徹) all phenomena, conversely, phenomena—lacking self-nature—pervade and are not separate from Li. Crucially, however, in claiming that phenomena pervade Li, rather than understanding this to imply that the defilements associated with *ālayavijñāna* are somehow able to "infiltrate" the purity of *tathāgatagarbha*, that the conditioned is able to condition the unconditioned, it should be understood to mean that in the locus of phenomenal reality—*ālayavijñāna*—phenomena and suchness merge seamlessly, but suchness remains unchanged.

This point is explained within the context of an expanded five-fold scheme of doctrinal classification of Buddhist teachings proposed by

---

yu juexing: Foxue yu Ruxue luncong 理性與覺性: 佛學與儒學論叢 (Principle as Nature and Awakened Nature: Essays on Buddhism and Confucianism) (Chengdu: Ba-Shu shushe, 2009), 15–18, argues that the Madhyamaka doctrine of "the emptiness of all conditioned phenomena and conditioned origination" (緣起性空) came to be transformed by Chinese Buddhist thinkers as early as Zhu Daosheng 竺道生 (355–434) and later Paramārtha 眞諦 (499–569) into a general principle of emptiness (*kong li* 空理) that itself had a reality and that this understanding came to be represented by the term Li 理 (textual support for which can be found in Daosheng's commentary to the *Vimalakīrtinirdeśa*, T38.1775, 354a11-17), which in turn came to be used as a characterization of buddha-nature. This subsequently led to a new development: the idea that Li, as a shared dharma (*gong fa* 共法), constitutes the nature of sentient beings, and that phenomena (*shi* 事) are the manifestation of this nature.

[28] See the Introduction to this volume.
[29] Fazang, *Dasheng qixin lun yiji*, T44.1846, 243c1-4.

Fazang: the Hīnayāna teaching, the Mahāyāna Elementary Teaching, the Mahāyāna Advanced Teaching, the Mahāyāna Sudden Teaching, and the Mahāyāna Perfect Teaching. He identifies the Elementary Teaching (Weishi [Yogācāra] and Sanlun [Madhyamaka]) with the mildly derogatory term *faxiang* 法相 (dharma characteristics), and the Advanced Teaching (Tathāgatagarbha) with the doctrine of the interfusion of suchness and phenomena ("the gateway in which intrinsic reality and phenomenal characteristics merge" (*ti xiang rongrong men* 體相鎔融門):

> If one were to rely on the Elementary Teaching, only the purport of the arising and ceasing part of the *ālayavijñāna* could be grasped. This is because [this limited understanding] fails to [explain how] arising and ceasing seamlessly merges with true Li. It merely explains that [suchness] is immutable and that it does not create dharmas. And so the *ālaya* [consciousness] is entirely relegated to the interdependent arising associated with phenomenal arising and ceasing.
>
> 若依始教。於阿賴耶識。但得一分生滅之義。以於真理未能融通。但說凝然不作諸法。故就緣起生滅事中建立賴耶。[30]

Fazang relates that the Elementary Teaching explains only how suchness is quiescent. By contrast, the Advanced Teaching, which takes into account the gateway in which intrinsic reality (suchness) and phenomenal appearances merge—the equivalent of the gateway of mind of arising and ceasing in the *Dasheng qixin lun*—is able to account for the non-duality of the unchanging nature of suchness as well as its according with, adapting to, the conditions of phenomenal arising and ceasing.[31] He identifies the Advanced Teaching with such scriptures as the *Dasheng qixin lun*, *Laṅkāvatāra-sūtra* 楞伽經, *Ratnagotravibhāga* 寶性論, and the *Śrīmālā-sūtra* 勝鬘經:

> According to the Advanced Teaching, it is in *ālayavijñāna* that the two parts, Li and phenomena, are able to merge seamlessly. Hence the *Treatise* [*Dasheng qixin lun*] states, "The nonarising and nonceasing [mind] combines with arising and ceasing [mind]. They are neither the same nor different. This is called the *ālaya* consciousness." [This is stated] to

---

[30] *Huayan yisheng jiaoyi fenqi zhang* 華嚴一乘教義分齊章 (Essay on the Classified Meaning of the Teaching of the One Vehicle of the Avataṃsaka), T45.1866, 484c13-16.
[31] T45.1866, 485a20-23.

acknowledge that suchness accords with karmic impressions [*vāsanā*] and that they combine to become this root consciousness [*ālayavijñāna*]. . . .

Question: "Since you claim that suchness is a constant dharma how can you say that it accords with karmic impressions to arise and cease? And given you acknowledge that it arises and ceases how can you also say that it is immutable and constant?"

Answer: "[Although] I have stated that suchness is constant, it is not what is meant by 'constant' in ordinary speech. How so? The Buddha described suchness as immutable because when it accords with conditions to create dharmas it does not lose its self-nature and so is said to be constant. And it is precisely the constant that is not different from the non-constant that is termed 'the inconceivable constant.' . . . Because the Advanced Teaching is concerned with the gateway in which intrinsic reality and phenomenal appearance are merged, it explains that the two parts [suchness/Li and phenomena] are non-dual."

若依終教。於此賴耶識。得理事融通二分義。故論但云不生不滅與生滅和合。非一非異。名阿梨耶識。以許眞如隨熏和合成此本識。... 問：「眞如既言常法。云何得説隨熏起滅。既許起滅。如何復説爲凝然常。」答：「既言眞如常故。非如言所謂常也。何者？聖説眞如爲凝然者。此是隨緣作諸法時。不失自體。故説爲常。是即不異無常之常名不思議常。... 此終教中。約體相鎔融門故。説二分無二之義。」³²

Here Fazang emphasizes the non-dual character of Li (suchness, *tathāgatagarbha*) and phenomena as they merge in "the gateway of intrinsic reality and phenomenal appearance" (*ti xiang rongrong men* 體相鎔融門), another name for the gateway of arising and ceasing (*shengmie men* 生滅門), the *ālayavijñāna*. In particular, he emphasizes that suchness is unchanging "because when [suchness] accords with conditions to create dharmas it does not lose its self-nature and so is said to be constant." In other words, the unconditioned (Li 理) remains unchanged even as it adapts to, accords with conditioned reality (*shi* 事), such that the unconditioned and the conditioned "merge seamlessly as two parts" to be "neither the same nor different."

---

³² *Huayan yisheng jiaoyi fenqi zhang*, T45.1866, 484c24-485a4; 485a9-a15; 485a21-23. Francis Cook, "Fa-tsang's Treatise on the Five Doctrines: An Annotated Translation" (Unpublished Ph.D. diss., University of Wisconsin, 1970), 218, significantly modified.

It is important to note that Fazang ranked the Advanced Teaching as third in a hierarchy of five teachings, with the Perfect Teaching ranked highest.³³ Fazang identified the Perfect Teaching with the doctrine of "the dependent arising of the dharma realm" (*fajie yuanqi* 法界緣起), which he describes in terms of the harmonious identity of each determinate thing with all things and vice versa, in which not only does the whole determine the character of all of its parts but each part determines the character of the whole.³⁴ It was this doctrine that the later tradition also referred to as the "unobstructed interpenetration of all phenomena" (*shi shi wu ai* 事事無礙). In doing so, Fazang accorded the doctrine of non-obstruction of Li and phenomena (*li shi wu ai* 理事無礙) a subordinate status. This did not, however, signal a more broad-based, ongoing subordination of this doctrine. Far from it.

The Huayan master Chengguan 澄觀 (738–839) emphasized the pivotal role of the doctrine of the non-obstruction of Li and phenomena in enabling the doctrine of the non-obstruction of all phenomena to be established. Peter N. Gregory describes how in Huayan theory, *li shi wu ai* provides the ontological basis for *shi shi wu ai* by providing the noetic ground that makes the experience of *shi shi wu ai* possible.³⁵ In turn, the Huayan master Zongmi 宗密 (780–841) elevated the doctrine of the non-obstruction of Li and phenomena (*li shi wu ai* 理事無礙) to become the highest teaching of the Huayan school. Zongmi attached particular importance to the conditioned aspect of the One Mind, which, following Fazang's teacher, Zhiyan 智儼 (602–668), he referred to as nature origination (*xingqi* 性起). "It is precisely this conditioned aspect of the one mind that allows it to act as a creative pattern in the generation of all pure and impure dharmas. . . . Nature origination is thus but another term for the conditioned functioning of the one mind, and, as such, centers on the linkage between the phenomenal realm of pure and impure dharmas

---

³³ See the Introduction to this volume.
³⁴ *Huayan yisheng jiaoyi fenqi zhang*, T45.1866, 485b7-9; 503a17-20; 507c12-15.
³⁵ Peter N. Gregory, *Tsung-mi and the Sinification of Buddhism* (Honolulu: University of Hawaii Press, 2002/1991), 159, 162–165. Taking a slightly different tack, Brook A. Ziporyn, *Beyond Oneness and Difference: Li and Coherence in Chinese Buddhist Thought and Its Antecedents* (Albany: SUNY Press, 2013), 304 argues that Dushun and Fazang attempted to transcend Li altogether in order to privilege *shi shi wu ai* but in fact their attempts to suppress discussion of Li actually served to accord it an implicit role as the fundamental standard of order and coherence. In other words, *shi shi wu ai* by default becomes the only Li there is. This vision—the cosmos of interpenetrating events—is itself Li. It "locks in a definite point of view that excludes other points of view" and it becomes "all the more entrenched for being invisibly embedded in the framing of what defines events, that is to say, what serves as the standard by which to determine what is 'real' and what [is] merely 'appearance.'"

and the absolute realm of suchness."³⁶ Importantly, nature origination privileges the nature (synonymous with the One Mind, suchness, and Li) as the ontological basis for everything else.

5.2 Tiantai Home Mountain vs. Off Mountain Views on Li and *Shi*, Mind and Dharmas

Elsewhere, Gregory identifies Zongmi's understanding of the doctrine of the non-obstruction of Li and phenomena, in particular, as having provided "the doctrinal cornerstone on which the Off Mountain thinkers in the Sung elaborated their understanding of the T'ien-t'ai tradition."³⁷ Identifying the doctrine of *li shi wu ai* with the doctrine of nature origination, and the doctrine of *shi shi wu ai* with the doctrine of nature inclusion (*xingju* 性具) (explained below), the Shanjia 山家/Shanwai 山外 (Home Mountain/Off Mountain) controversy in the Northern Song replicated the tensions between the doctrines of "the dependent arising of the dharma-realm" (that is, the mutual inclusion of all aspects of reality) (*fajie yuanqi* 法界緣起) and nature origination (*xingqi*) that were inherent in the Huayan tradition. This core issue was whether Li should be ontologically privileged over things (*shi* 事), over dharmas, or whether there is a kind of ontological parity between, and indeed intersubsumption of, all dharmas, encapsulated in the idea that every dharma contained all other dharmas.

As described by Brook A. Ziporyn, the leading Shanjia master Zhili 知禮 (960–1024) maintained:

> Li is both a unity and a multiplicity (known respectively as *lizong* 理總 and *libie* 理別), and each phenomenon similarly serves both as a unifier and as one of many items unified in any other phenomenon (known as *shizong* 事總 and *shibie* 事別, respectively), while his opponents, the so-called Shanwai 山外 or "Off-Maintain" school, take Li purely as unity, with diversity accounted for solely by *shi* 事, as in Huayan thought.³⁸

In particular, Home Mountain masters such as Zhili objected to the ontological privileging of Li over phenomena—whereby Li could exist

---

³⁶ Gregory, *Tsung-mi and the Sinification of Buddhism*, 189.
³⁷ Peter N. Gregory, "The Vitality of Buddhism in the Sung," in *Buddhism in the Sung*, eds. Peter N. Gregory and Daniel A. Getz Jr. (Honolulu: University of Hawai'ii, Press, 1999), 9.
³⁸ Ziporyn, *Beyond Oneness and Difference*, 22.

independent of phenomena—that they saw in both Huayan and Off Mountain teachings:

> The term *ti-yong* (intrinsic reality-function) originally has the sense of "mutual identity." Hence, wherever it is stated that all dharmas are identical to Li, "identical" pertains only when all of the functioning is identical to Li. *[Judgments to Propagate and] Aid in Practicing [the Great Calming and Discernment]*[39] states, "According to the *Guangya* dictionary, *ji* 即 means 'to combine.' If this gloss were to be followed, it would still seem that even though two things are conjoined, Li remains separate [from all dharmas]. Now, if we instead seek the [actual] meaning, it is because intrinsic reality [and its function as dharmas] are non-dual, [intrinsic reality and its functioning] are said to be 'identical.' "[40] Hence, it is only the functioning of intrinsic reality in its entirety that is termed non-dual.
>
> The Huayan School promulgates [the doctrine] that a unitary Li accords with conditions to create the differentiated dharmas. Differentiation is the characteristic of ignorance and unadulterated oneness is the characteristic of suchness. When [suchness, the unitary Li] accords with conditions then there is differentiation; when it does not accord with conditions then there is no differentiation. Thus it is known that there are differentiations only when the unitary nature [= suchness] combines with ignorance. This is exactly what "combine" means. It does not mean that [suchness and ignorance] are non-dual in their intrinsic reality. This is because when ignorance is removed there is no differentiation.[41]
>
> Now, our [Tiantai] school promulgates [the doctrine] that the intrinsic reality of the three thousand[42] accords with conditions to give rise to the functioning of the three thousand. And [even if we were to postulate a situation, per impossible] when [suchness, the unitary nature, the unitary Li] does not accord with conditions, the three thousand would remain

---

[39] This a reference to Zhanran's *Zhiguan fuxing chuanhong jue* 止觀輔行傳弘決, a commentary to Zhiyi's 智顗 (538–597) *Mohe zhiguan* 摩訶止觀 (The Great Calming and Contemplation).
[40] Zhanran, *Zhiguan fuxing chuanhong jue*, T46.1912, 149c13-16.
[41] Cf. the *Dasheng qixin lun*, T32.1666, 578b14-15:

> Because ignorance has ceased, the mind has no arising. Because there is no arising, perceptual fields subsequently cease. Because the causes and conditions [of erroneous thoughts and perceptual fields] have both ceased, the characteristics of the mind all end. This is called attaining nirvana and achieving [cognition of how] karmic action spontaneously operates.
>
> 以無明滅故心無有起，以無起故境界隨滅，以因緣俱滅故心相皆盡，名得涅槃成自然業。

[42] The "three thousand" is a formulaic way of referring to all things.

just as clearly distinct. Thus, differentiated dharmas and intrinsic reality are non-dual. This is because when ignorance is removed there are [still] differentiations.[43]

Having investigated the Huayan school's explanation of "identity," its account of the meaning fails to be established. This is because for that school, enlightenment consists in nothing other than suchness, and in order to seek refuge in the one [true] nature that is the buddha-realm it is necessary to remove the nine realms [= conditioned reality].

何者？夫體用之名本相即之義，故凡言諸法即理者，全用即體方可言即。《輔行》云：「即者，《廣雅》云合也。若依此釋，仍似二物相合，其理猶疏。今以義求，體不二故，故名為即」(上皆《輔行》文也)。今謂全體之用方名不二。他宗明一理隨緣作差別法，差別是無明之相，淳一是真如之相，隨緣時則有差別，不隨緣時則無差別，故知一性與無明合方有差別，正是合義，非體不二，以除無明無差別故。今家明三千之體隨緣起三千之用，不隨緣時三千宛爾，故差別法與體不二，以除無明有差別故。驗他宗明即，即義不成，以彼佛果唯一真如，須破九界差別歸佛界一性故。[44]

Here the Huayan school is presented as maintaining that the buddha-realm—suchness, Li, the nature, the absolute—is conceptually distinct from the dharmas created when it encounters conditions; and that it exists even in the complete absence of dharmas.

The Home Mountain masters distinguished themselves from the Off Mountain masters by charging that the latter had adopted the teachings of the Huayan School, which the Home Mountain group referred to as the Separate Teaching,[45] reserving the category of Perfect Teaching to describe their own views. Chi-wah Chan relates that in the context of the Home Mountain/Off Mountain debates:

"Perfect" revealed the all-inclusive character of the T'ien-t'ai teachings, which saw all modes of existence as imbued with Buddhahood, and thus provided a valid Buddhist ground for practice. By contrast, "separate" emphasized the Shan-chia view that the Hua-yen (and by extension, Shan-wai) teachings privileged certain modes of existence over others as the

---

[43] This is because of the teaching "Li includes the three thousand" (理具三千).
[44] Zhili, *Shi bu'er men zhiyao chao* 十不二門指要鈔 (The Gist of [Zhanran's] *Ten Gateways of Non-duality*), T46.1928, 715b10-22.
[45] This term is part of a four-fold taxonomy of teachings originally developed by Zhiyi.

proper focus for practice. The separate teaching identified absolute, pure suchness (*chen-ju*; *tathatā*) as the basis for realizing Buddhahood, whereas the perfect teaching saw all modes of existence, including defiled and deluded ones, as affording access to Buddhahood.[46]

Although critical of the Separate Teaching, Zhili still accords it a place within the Tiantai taxonomy of teachings, even likening it to a medicine that counteracts adventitious afflictions and the resultant karma that are the cause of suffering (the second of the Four Noble Truths):

> The Li advocated by the Separate Teaching is the Middle Way, spoken of in terms of the buddha-nature that lies beyond the realms of rebirth. This nature serves as the support for all dharmas. In regard to the intrinsic reality of this nature, however, the Separate Teaching does not discuss it in terms of nature inclusion. Because it discusses only nature origination, this leads to dharmas *qua* particular entities' not being identical.
>
> 然此教論理則是界外中道佛性。此性為一切法而作依持。但其體不論性具。唯論性起故，使諸法當體不即。[47]

Zhili finds no fault with the Separate Teaching's account of the nature, "the buddha-nature that lies beyond the realms of rebirth" and that "serves as the support for all dharmas." Rather, he directs his criticism at the Separate Teaching's failure to acknowledge that only the doctrine of nature inclusion (*xingju* 性具) provides the means to discern the intrinsic reality of this nature. Nature inclusion is the teaching that all dharmas, all things,

---

[46] Chi-wah Chan, "Chih-li and the Crisis of T'ien-t'ai Buddhism," in Gregory and Getz, *Buddhism in the Sung*, 417.

[47] "Si zhong si di wenda" 四種四諦問答 (Questions and Replies on Four Ways of Understanding the Four Noble Truths), in *Siming zunzhe jiaoxing lu* 四明尊者教行錄 (Record of Zhili's Words and Deeds), T46.1937, 884c19-25. This ecumenical gesture even extends to the *Dasheng qixin lun* itself, as is evident in the following passage from his *Tiantai jiao yu Qixin lun ronghui zhang* 天台教與起信論融會章 (The Fusion of Tiantai Teachings and the *Dasheng qixin lun*):

> The *Treatise* [*Dasheng qixin lun*] takes the One Mind as its main tenet, stating that "This mind includes all mundane and supramundane dharmas." This falls squarely within the gateway of the Perfect Teaching and it also conjoins the other two teachings.
>
> 論以一心為宗。乃云：「總攝世出世法。」此則正在圓門。亦兼餘二。(T46.1937, 871b25-26)

The teachings referred to here are those identified in Zhiyi's fourfold hierarchy of doctrinal classification: the Tripitaka Teaching (藏教), the Common Teaching (通教), the Separate Teaching, and the Perfect Teaching.

including buddhahood, are present in each and every thing and that any dharma includes all other dharmas and is identical with all other dharmas. Everything has this nature of being present in and including every other thing. In contrast, the doctrine of nature arising or nature origination (*xingqi* 性起) favored by Huayan thinkers, such as Zongmi, identifies the nature with the One Mind or the one true dharma realm (*fajie* 法界), which is the origin or basis for the arising of all dharmas—including the phenomenal world. According to this doctrine, phenomena share a common ontological basis but are themselves ultimately empty, lacking self-nature. As expressed in the *Dasheng qixin lun*:

> The mind as suchness is precisely the dharma-gate reality, which is the overarching characteristic of the entire dharma realm.[48] That is to say, the nature of the mind neither arises nor ceases; it is due solely to erroneous thoughts that there are distinctions between every dharma. If one is free from false thoughts, then there are none of the characteristics of perceptual fields. Therefore, all dharmas from the very beginning have been free from the characteristics of language, of naming, and of mental perceptions. They are ultimately uniform, invariant, and indestructible. They are nothing but this One Mind and therefore they are called "suchness."
>
> 心真如者，即是一法界大總相法門體。所謂心性不生不滅，一切諸法唯依妄念而有差別。若離妄念則無一切境界之相。是故一切法從本已來，離言說相、離名字相、離心緣相、畢竟平等、無有變異、不可破壞、唯是一心，故名真如。[49]

The following passage from Zhili's commentary on Zhanran's 湛然 (711–782) *Shi bu'er men* 十不二門 (Ten Gateways of Non-duality) highlights the doctrinal fault line separating the two groups. Zhanran wrote extensive commentaries on the writings of Zhiyi 智顗 (538–597)—de facto founder of Tiantai—and as the key figure in the attempt to revive Tiantai in the eighth century, Zhanran was subsequently identified with Tiantai orthodoxy. The passage also highlights why, despite Fazang's ultimate privileging of the doctrine of *shi shi wu ai*—a doctrine compatible with the philosophical orientation of the Tiantai Home Mountain theorists—Zhili singles out Fazang for criticism, in particular Fazang's claim that the unconditioned (suchness, Li, One Mind, *tathāgatagarbha*) remains unchanged even as

---

[48] The dharma realm, *dharma-dhātu*, denotes the field of sensory and mental experience.
[49] T32.1666, 576a8-18.

it accords with conditions (phenomena) because phenomenal reality is ultimately unreal, having no self-nature.[50] Because Zhanran had adopted Fazang's formulation that suchness is immutable yet is able to accord with conditions, the controversy concerned whether Zhanran had taken a position similar to that advanced by Fazang or whether he was creatively adapting Fazang's formulation. The intensity of this controversy was no doubt heightened by the fact that the imprimatur of Zhanran's interpretive authority was seen to vouchsafe claims to doctrinal legitimacy. In the following passage from his commentary on Zhanran's *Shi bu'er men*, Zhili begins by critically citing Shanwai master Yuanqing's 源清 (d. 999) commentary on *Shi bu'er men*:

> [Yuanqing's views] are contrary to the import of Zhanran's *Zhiguan dayi* and *Jin gang pi*. After citing [Zhanran's] remark, "[that which] accords with conditions without changing is called the nature; [that which] does not change yet accords with conditions is called the mind,"

---

[50] In *Tiantai jiao yu Qixin lun ronghui zhang*, Zhili wrote:

> It was Fazang who first fully utilized the two principles of "according with conditions" and "being immutable" to differentiate the two schools of Dharma-nature and Dharma-characteristics [Fazang, *Huayan yisheng jiaoyi fenqi zhang* 華嚴一乘教義分齊章, T45.1866, 485a21]. Such writings do not appear in Tiantai. On the basis of reason [it can be stated that] "according with conditions" does not constitute the Perfect Teaching. Even his own school [Huayan] judged this doctrine to be the Advanced Teaching—it does not measure up to the [Huayan] Perfect Teaching. It is thus certainly not the case that Tiantai's Perfect Teaching is the same as their Advanced Teaching. It should be understood that whether it be "according with conditions" or "being immutable," they are simply one-sided expedient doctrines and both belong to the Separate Teaching.

> 盛將隨緣以* 凝然二理簡於性相二宗此乃出自賢首。天台未見此文。據理，隨緣未為圓極。彼宗尚自判終教。未及於圓。豈天台之圓同彼之終。須知，若凝然若隨緣，但據帶方便義邊。皆屬別教。(T46.1937, 871c17-21)

*Amending 以 to 與 on the grounds of intelligibility. The mistake is probably a scribal error (due to homophony).

Here Zhili is associating the Advanced Teaching with the thesis that "suchness accords with conditions," which he attributes to the Dharma-nature school (Huayan), and the Elementary Teaching with the view that "suchness is immutable," which he attributes to the Dharma-characteristics school (Yogācāra). (Cf. Fazang's own criticism of the Elementary Teaching, cited above, on the grounds that it "merely explains that suchness is quiescent and that it does not create dharmas.") Fazang himself does not seem to have made the specific distinction between Dharma-nature and Dharma-characteristics. Later, *faxing* 法性 and *faxiang* 法相 came to refer to Huayan and to Xuanzang's Yogācāra, respectively, but Imre Hamar presents evidence demonstrating that although Fazang did use the term *faxiangzong* to critique the Yogācāra teachings introduced by Xuangzang, it was Chengguan who first used *faxingzong* to refer to both Madhyamaka and Tathāgatagarbha teachings. See his "A Huayan Paradigm for the Classification of Mahāyāna Teachings: The Origin and Meaning of Faxiangzong and Faxingzong," in *Reflecting Mirrors: Perspectives on Huayan Buddhism*, ed. Imre Hamar (Wiesbaden: Harrassowitz Verlag, 2007), 220.

[Yuanqing] declared, "The mind is identical to the unchanging nature of suchness."[51]

As for the matter at hand, I think that he would disagree with Jingxi [Zhanran's] thesis. Why? Since Zhanran stated that that which does not change yet accords with conditions is called the mind, clearly this is [simply] a case of a phenomenon[52] that is identical with Li. How could it solely be an explanation of Li? Although according with conditions one-sidedly focuses on the phenomenal, since phenomena are identical with Li, this points to the fact that the mind is that which does not change in its nature. How could [unconditioned] buddha dharmas and [conditioned] sentient dharmas not be identical? And if they are all Li why single out mind alone as unchanging in its nature? Hence *Jin* [*gang*] *pi* says: "Suchness is the myriad dharmas because it accords with conditions; the myriad dharmas are suchness because they do not change." Thus it is known that if we take the myriad dharmas to be identical with Li, then sentient beings and buddhas, as well as subject and object, are all Li because none changes.[53] So how could the mind alone be Li? If one were to make [an argument] based on sentient beings as phenomena[54] then since the inner and the outer, material and mental [dharmas] all accord with conditions, how could it be that the mind alone is not phenomenal?

違《大意》及《金剛錍》。他自引云:「隨緣不變名性，不變隨緣名心。」引畢乃云:「今言心即真如不變性也。」今恐他不許荊谿立義。何者？既云不變隨緣名心，顯是即理之事，那得直作理釋？若云，雖隨緣邊屬事，事即理故，故指心為不變性者。佛法生法豈不即邪？若皆即理，何獨指心名不變性？故《金錍》云:「真如是萬法，由隨緣故，萬法是真如，由不變故。」故知若約萬法即理，則生佛、依正俱理，皆不變故，何獨心是理邪？若據眾生在事，則內外色心俱事，皆隨緣故，何獨心非事邪？[55]

Zhili's opening comments refer to the following passage by Zhanran. If we follow Zhili's understanding, that passage can be translated as follows:

All dharmas are nothing other than the nature of the mind, but one nature is no nature and the three thousand are just as they are. One should understand

---

[51] Yuanqing's comments in *Fahua shi miao bu'er men shi zhu zhi* 法華十妙不二門示珠指 (Pointers That Reveal the Jewels of Huayan's Ten Gateways of Non-duality), X56.926, 319b111057.
[52] The mind. Here the mind represents that which is conditioned, that which is phenomenal and subject to arising and ceasing.
[53] None changes in being identical to any other and each term in these polar pairs entails and includes the other.
[54] An argument along the lines that sentience is associated with phenomena rather than with Li.
[55] Zhili, *Shi bu'er men zhiyao chao*, T46.1928, 709a5-15.

that with respect to the mind *qua* material [dharmas] and mental [dharmas], it is precisely the mind that is said to transform. To transform is called to create, and creating refers to the functioning of intrinsic reality.

一切諸法無非心性，一性無性。三千宛然。當知心之色心，即心名變，變名為造，造謂體用。⁵⁶

As Zhili explains, "one nature is no nature" because even though the nature (Li, suchness) is singular, it has no fixed, determinate nature, thus enabling each and every one of the three thousand material dharmas and mental dharmas to be just as they are. All dharmas are themselves the non-abiding root (*wuzhu ben* 無住本)—or perhaps rhizome, which is both one and many—that transcends any individual dharma to be the root for all other dharmas.⁵⁷ In this passage Zhili is emphasizing that "the mind" could be replaced by any other conditioned phenomena, any one of the myriad dharmas. The mind has no privileged identity with the nature. The nature has a presence in/as all dharmas, one of which happens to be the mind.

Yuanqing, in contrast, treats mind as the true mind, as suchness itself, as Li:

> The [first] "mind" [in Zhanran's phrase *xin zhi se xin* 心之色心] refers to "one nature is no nature." "Material [dharmas] and mental [dharmas]" is identical to "the three thousand just as they are." The word *zhi* 之 means "to go toward" and is not a grammatical particle. This is saying that the whole nature proceeds towards, hence the text says, "goes toward material [dharmas] and mental [dharmas].". . . This is saying that suchness *qua* the nature accords with conditions. This is the meaning of "suchness accords with conditions" in the *Dasheng qixin lun*. [Zhanran's] *Zhiguan dayi* 止觀大意 (Import of Zhiyi's *Great Calming and Contemplation*) says, "[That which] accords with conditions without changing is called the nature; [that which] does not change yet accords with conditions is called the mind." Now, what is referred to as mind [the first "mind" in Zhanran's phrase *xin zhi se xin* 心之色心] is identical with the unchanging nature of suchness.

---

⁵⁶ Zhanran, *Shi bu'er men*, T46.1927, 703a24-26.
⁵⁷ 一性等者，性雖是一而無定一之性，故使三千色心相相宛爾，此則從無住本立一切法。Zhili, *Shi bu'er men zhiyao chao*, T46.1928, 710a6-7. For an extended analysis of Zhili's understanding of this passage by Zhanran and its broader philosophical context, including a discussion of the "non-abiding root" (*wuzhu ben* 無住本), see Ziporyn, *Beyond Oneness and Difference*, 268–293. See also his shorter discussion in his chapter in this volume.

"To go toward material [dharmas] and mental [dharmas] (之色心)" is identical with "according with conditions."

心，即上一性無性也。色心，即上三千宛然也。之，往也，非語助也。謂全性往趣，故云之色心也。... 此則真如性隨緣，起信真如隨緣義也。 止觀大意云:「隨緣不變名性，不變隨緣名心。」今言心即真如性不變也。之色心，即隨緣也。[58]

Whereas Zhili treats mind as nature (= suchness), and dharmas as nature, Yuanqing draws a clear distinction between the mind as suchness, and dharmas or phenomenal entities. For Yuanqing, dharmas arise and cease—having no self-nature—but the mind qua suchness is unchanging.

The next example, also from Zhili's commentary on Zhanran's *Shi bu'er men*, similarly hinges on different interpretive claims over Zhanran's intended meaning in the following passage from Zhanran's *Fahua xuan yi shi qian* 法華玄義釋籤 (Explanation the *Profound Meaning of the Lotus Sutra*):

> If one recognizes that since beginningless time it is none other than dharma-nature that is ignorance, then one will comprehend that at this very moment ignorance is dharma-nature. Together with dharma-nature, ignorance creates dharmas everywhere. This is called defilement. Together with ignorance, dharma-nature responds to the myriad conditions everywhere. This is called purity.

> 若識無始即法性為無明，故可了今無明為法性。法性之與無明遍造諸法，名之為染。無明之與法性遍應眾緣，號之為淨。[59]

Dharma-nature here is the functional equivalent of suchness, of Li, of the absolute. Zhanran identifies dharma-nature as ignorance and ignorance as dharma-nature. Ignorance is part of the truth. The basis for his doing so is the Tiantai doctrine of nature inclusion (*xingju* 性具), according to which all dharmas contain or entail all other dharmas.

Home Mountain and Off Mountain thinkers offered different interpretations of the remainder of this passage, in part because they favored different versions of Zhanran's text. The version used by Off Mountain master Yuanqing lacks the word *yu* 與 in the two phrases 法性之與無明 and 無明之與法性. He objects to the inclusion of this word in

---

[58] Yuanqing, *Shi bu'er men shi zhi zhu* 十不二門示珠指 (Pointers to Reveal Pearls in the *Ten Gates of Non-duality*), X56.926, 319b111057.
[59] Zhanran, *Fahua xuan yi shi qian*, T33.1717, 919a9-12.

the two phrases on the grounds that Zhanran's text would then mean, "the dharma-nature joins with ignorance to create badness" (法性共無明造惡也). Yuanqing explains that according to this reading, "dharma-nature is inherently pure but suddenly ignorance comes from some external source to combine with dharma-nature, giving rise to defiled habituations, which in turn create dharmas" (法性本淨。忽有無明外來共法性和合。便起染習而造諸法也。).[60] To this, Yuanqing responds:

> If [this is read to mean that] the dharma-nature joins with ignorance to create [dharmas] then the next line about pure dharmas should also [be read to mean] that ignorance joins with dharma-nature to respond [to conditions]. As for "[it] responds to the myriad conditions everywhere," surely "responding everywhere" is an effect? Why should the nature of this pure effect [dharma-nature] have to join with ignorance before it can respond [to conditions]? If this were so then there would be neither the means by which to differentiate between defilement and purity nor that by which to distinguish delusion from enlightenment—how ridiculous!
>
> 若是法性與無明共造者下句淨法亦是無明共法性起應。如云:「遍應眾緣」遍應豈非果用。此淨果性如何更與無明共方起應乎。此則染淨不可分、迷悟無以別。誠為可笑。[61]

For Yuanqing, dharma-nature should be able to respond to conditions without having to join with ignorance; otherwise dharma-nature's purity could never be distinguished and one would be forever mired in delusion. Based on Yuanqing's comments, his version of the key passage in Zhanran's text can be translated as follows:

> Dharma-nature goes towards[62] ignorance, creating dharmas everywhere, and this is called defilement. Ignorance goes towards dharma-nature, responding to the myriad conditions everywhere, and this is called purity.
>
> 法性之無明遍造諸法，名之為染。無明之法性遍[63]應眾緣，號之為淨。[64]

---

[60] As will be recalled, this implicit objection to ignorance's having a separate ontological basis and thus presenting a dualism clearly concords with views expressed much earlier by Fazang. This, however, is not the main issue at hand in Yuanqing's following comments.
[61] Yuanqing, *Fahua shi miao bu'er men shi zhu zhi*, X56.926, 322a22779.
[62] Yuanqing glosses *zhi* 之 in this passage as "to go to" rather than as a possessive particle.
[63] Amending *pian* 偏 to *bian* 遍.
[64] *Fahua shi miao bu'er men shi zhu zhi*, X56.926, 315b6260.

Yuanqing explains that even if dharma-nature in its entirety "goes towards" (accords with) ignorance, this serves merely to create defiled dharmas (even though these dharmas, like ignorance, ultimately have no self-nature). Conversely, when ignorance "goes towards" (accords with) dharma-nature, this engenders purity, as ignorance is dispelled.[65]

Zhili, by contrast, defends the version of Zhanran's text that includes the word *yu* 與 in the two phrases 法性之與無明 and 無明之與法性:

> *Yu* 與 means "to lend," "to give"—that is, "to assist." Since dharma-nature and ignorance take turns with one another to constitute the two functions [of defilement and purity], [*yu* 與] has the sense of aiding one another to assist in constituting the two functions such that the weaker lends support to the stronger. If dharma-nature's inner perfuming[66] is weak and the defiled function of ignorance is dominant, then the dharma-nature lends ignorance strength to create defiled dharmas. If ignorance's attachment to mistaken conceptual discrimination is weak and dharma-nature's inner perfuming is dominant, then ignorance lends dharma-nature the strength to give rise to pure responses.
>
> 有則於義更明。何者？夫與者，借與、賜與也，亦助也。法性無明既互翻轉成於兩用，互有借力助成之義，而劣者借力助於彊者。若法性內熏無力、無明染用彊者，則法性與無明力造諸染法。若無明執情無力、法性內熏有力，則無明與法性力起諸淨應。[67]

The two functions are purity and defilement. The reference is to the following passage in the *Dasheng qixin lun*: "The pure dharma of suchness really has no defilements; it is only because of habituation by ignorance that it has defiled characteristics. The defiled dharma of ignorance is really devoid of pure karma, and it is only because of its habituation by suchness that it has a purifying function" (無明染法實無淨業，但以真如而熏習故則有淨用。).[68] For Home Mountain masters, purity and defilement are ultimately identical and can never be separated. Rather, purity and defilement merely assume a different focus depending on whether it is ignorance or dharma-nature that serves as stimulus or response. They are not, however, different from one another nor are they different from the dharmas that emerge in the course of this

---

[65] *Fahua shi miao bu'er men shi zhu zhi*, X56.926, 322a22779; 319b111057.
[66] That is, its capacity to purify ignorance.
[67] Zhili, *Shi bu'er men zhiyao chao*, T46.1928, 716b9-14.
[68] T32.1666, 578a20-21.

relationship.⁶⁹ The relationship between dharma-nature and ignorance, purity and defilement is one of intersubsumption in which neither is privileged over the other. The implication here is that there is no need to remove ignorance in order to realize dharma-nature, because ignorance is dharma-nature, just as much as it is anything and everything else.

And even though Off Mountain thinkers did also subscribe to the Tiantai nature inclusion thesis⁷⁰ (despite Zhili's claims to the contrary), some of these thinkers could be construed as evidencing a distinct bias towards Li over phenomena, such as the following comments by Off Mountain master Zhiyuan 智圓 (976–1022):⁷¹

> It should be understood that even though mentail and material [dharmas] are simultaneously [contemplated], since material [dharmas] arise through creation by the mind, in their entirety they are the mind. Hence, since dharmas in their entirety are the mind, contemplation of the producer is identical to perceiving dharmas. . . . Accordingly, even though contemplating mental and contemplating material [dharmas] are each appropriate [as meditative procedures], both reveal that dharmas are nothing but the mind. Therefore, if one contemplates a single [moment] of mind, this will include everything.
>
> 當知心色雖則同時而色由心造全體是心。故觀能造即見諸法，以諸法全是心故。. . . 是以觀心觀色雖宜樂不同，並了諸法唯心耳。所以若觀一心，即攝一切。⁷²

Everything is a creation of the mind (here to be understood as synonymous with suchness, with Li), and the creations of the mind are nothing other than the mind itself. From the Home Mountain perspective, the offending idea in this account of nature inclusion (where mind is not different from the nature) is that Zhiyuan asks the practitioner of meditative contemplation

---

⁶⁹ In commenting on this passage, Brook A. Ziporyn points out that the stimulus is actually identical to the response, and he draws on the field-focus (ground-figure) model to elucidate the nature of this identity, where the dharma-nature and ignorance wax and wane between the foregrounded figure and its self-identical and inseparable ground. Ziporyn, *Evil and/or/as the Good*, 221.

⁷⁰ Gong Jun 龔雋, "Bei Song Tiantai zong dui *Dasheng qixin lun* yu *Shi bu'er men* de quanshi yu lunzheng" 北宋天台宗對《大乘起信論》與《十不二門》的詮釋與論爭 (Arguments about and Interpretations of the *Dasheng qixin lun* and the *Ten Gateways of Non-duality* in Northern Song Tiantai), *Zhongguo zhexue* no. 3 (2005): 83–94.

⁷¹ Zhiyuan was an influential figure during his own time, both in Buddhist and Confucian circles. See the Introduction to this volume.

⁷² Zhiyuan, *Jin'gang pi xianxing lu* 金剛錍顯性錄 (Record of the *Adamantine Scalpel*'s Revelation of the Nature), X56.935, 523b91685.

to focus on the mind's inclusiveness rather than on individual dharmas. Dharmas in effect become displaced by nature inclusion; phenomena become displaced by Li.

Summarizing the above findings, we can see that the Home Mountain solution to the problem of ontological dualism and the attendant issue of the origin of ignorance is to deconstruct the problem by arguing that badness is goodness and everything in between—including suchness, Li, ignorance, and the rest of the three thousand. Li (理) is phenomena (事) and phenomena are Li; intrinsic reality (體) is function (用) and function is intrinsic reality. And because ignorance is function and is also intrinsic reality, then ignorance is not an external condition, separate from intrinsic reality. This can be characterized as inclusive monism. The Off Mountain position advances a different form of deconstruction by advocating a position strongly reminiscent of Fazang's interpretation of the *Dasheng qixin lun*: denying that ignorance has a self-nature. Once this is realized, the motive force generating karmic activity is removed. And even though the characteristic of ignorance—whence badness and suffering arise—is not different from suchness, it is not the same as suchness. Suchness alone has self-nature. Ignorance has no self-nature. Only Li is has self-nature, not phenomena (*shi*). Only intrinsic reality (*ti*) has self-nature, not function (*yong*). This can be characterized as exclusive monism.

5.3 Zhu Xi's Solution to the Problem of Badness

In introducing the water and wind analogy to account for the origin of ignorance/badness, the author of the *Dasheng qixin lun* introduced a dualist analogy to explain a problem within a monistic ontology. Beginning with Fazang in the early Tang and continuing through to Tiantai masters of the Northern Song, a rich diversity of arguments was developed to preserve a monistic ontology yet also account for the origin of ignorance and badness. Many such accounts were framed in terms of the relationship between Li and phenomena, with Li representing suchness, and phenomena representing dharmas. Zhu Xi, in turn, re-inscribed this relationship between Li and phenomena in terms of *li* 理 (pattern) and *qi* 氣 (vital stuff).

In this section I will first argue that Zhu's conception of the *li-qi* relationship is isomorphic with the *Dasheng qixin lun*'s One Mind Two Gateways paradigm, articulated within the framework of Zhu creative interpretation of eleventh-century Neo-Confucian Zhou Dunyi's 周敦頤

(1017–1073) Taiji 太極 (Supreme Pivot) Diagram. I will then endeavor to show that Zhu Xi's understanding of the *li-qi* relationship is a further articulation of the rich and complex body of discourse developed in the Tang and Northern Song about Li and *shi*, at the heart of which was the attempt to reconcile the origin of badness with a monist ontology. Zhu's position bears close affinities with both (1) the Off Mountain thesis that the locus of badness is in phenomena, not in Li; and (2) the mutual entailment of Li and phenomena in the Home Mountain nature inclusion thesis, as well as its attendant affirmation of the phenomenal world. I view all of this as single family of discourse.

5.3.1 Zhu Xi and Taiji

Zhu advocated an ontological monism, the centerpiece of which is a polarity. This polarity is most fully articulated in Zhu's interpretation of Zhou Dunyi's Taiji Diagram (see fig. 5.2) and its accompanying "Taiji shuo" 太極說 (Essay on Taiji). Although it has long been speculated that Zhou derived the Diagram from Daoist and/or Buddhist sources, there is insufficient evidence to support this claim.[73]

Whereas Zhou Dunyi presents the Diagram as representing a process of cosmogenesis, Zhu explicitly denied this, instead understanding the Diagram to represent an ontology that grounded the nature or human nature (*xing* 性) in pattern (*li* 理). Zhu significantly reinterpreted both the Diagram and the Essay so as to provide a metaphysical framework in which to develop his understanding of the relationship between *li* 理 and *qi* 氣; to provide an ontological foundation for the concept of human nature *ren xing* 人性; and to provide a new solution to the problem of badness that avoided the radical proposals entailed in Buddhist attempts to deal with the issue for over half a millennium.

Taiji on the upper level is represented by ◯. It is beyond characterization hence the blank circle. Taiji is the basis of all phenomenal reality. Taiji is pattern (*li* 理), is the nature (*xing* 性), and is also intrinsic reality (*benti* 本體).[74] Zhu characterizes Taiji or pattern as being above form, in contrast to that which has phenomenal form (*qi* 氣, *yin-yang* 陰陽, *qi* 器). "Taiji is the

---

[73] For a succinct overview of some of the relevant scholarship, see Joseph A. Adler, *Reconstructing the Confucian Dao: Zhu Xi's Appropriation of the Zhou Dunyi* (Albany: SUNY Press, 2014), 153–158. See the Appendix to this chapter for my views on whether Zongmi's "charts" may have been a source for Zhou Dunyi's Taiji Diagram.

[74] Like Taiji, the nature is both transcendent and immanent. See below.

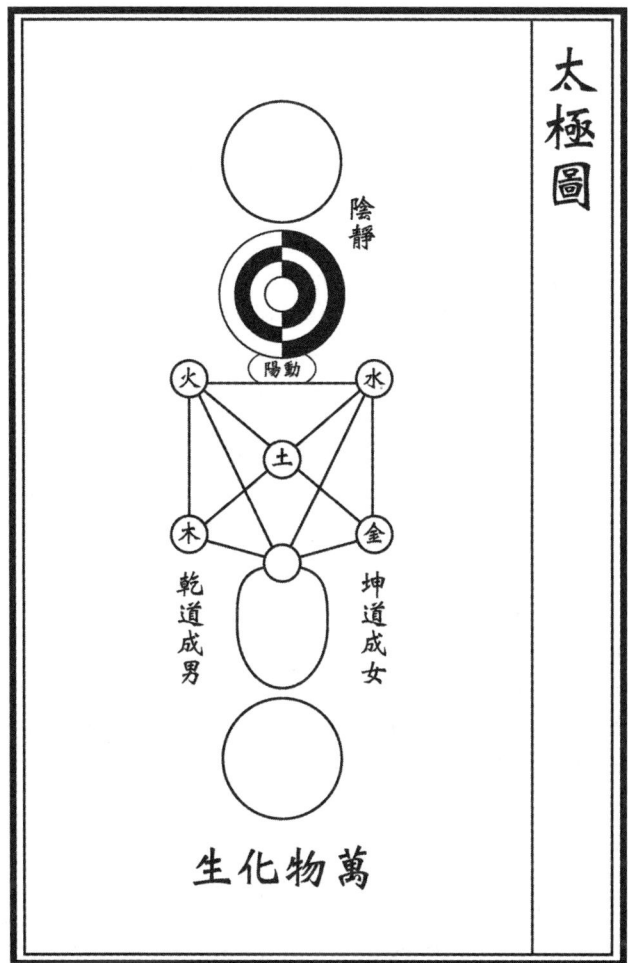

FIGURE 5.2 *Zhou Dunyi's Taiji Diagram*

CREDIT: Drawn by John Makeham based on image by Zhu Zhen 朱震 (1072–1138), *Hanshang Yizhuan* 漢上易傳 (Zhu Zhen's Commentary to the *Book of Change*), *Chizao Tang Siku quanshu cuiyao* 摛藻堂四庫全書薈要 (Essentials of The Complete Collection of the Four Treasuries from the Chizao Hall).

way that is above form; *yin* and *yang* are phenomena within form" (太極，形而上之道也。陰陽，形而下之器也。).⁷⁵

Despite this clear-cut distinction between these two realms or fields, Zhu underscores both the inseparability of what is above form and what is

---

⁷⁵ Zhu Xi, "Taiji tu shuo jie" 太極圖說解 (Explanation of the Taiji Diagram Essay), *Zhouzi quanshu* 周子全書 (Complete Writings of Zhou Dunyi), *Guoxue jiben congshu* 國學基本叢書 (Taipei: Shangwu yinshuguan, 1964), 7.

within the realm of form, and the fact that Taiji (pattern, nature) is not in any way "intermixed" with *yin* and *yang* (and in doing so is strongly reminiscent of Fazang, who in his account of "the seamless merging of pattern and phenomena" [理事融通無礙] sought to rule out any possibility that the defilements associated with *ālayavijñāna* are somehow able to adulterate the purity of *tathāgatagarbha*):

> Although [Taiji] is the intrinsic reality by means of which there is *yang* in movement and *yin* in stillness, it is not possible for it to be separate from *yin* and *yang*. It is precisely in *yin* and *yang* that their intrinsic reality is pointed to. That is to say, their intrinsic reality is not intermixed with *yin* and *yang*.
>
> 所以動而陽、靜而陰之本體，然非有以離乎陰陽也。即陰陽而指其本體。不雜乎陰陽而為言耳。[76]

> When discussing the heaven-and-earth bestowed nature, the reference is exclusively to *li*. When discussing the psychophysical nature, the reference is to the mixing of *li* and *qi*. Before the psychophysical [nature] exists, the [heaven-and-earth bestowed] nature already exists. Although the psychopysical [nature] sometimes does not exist, the [heaven-and-earth bestowed] nature exists constantly. Even though the nature exists within *qi*, *qi* of course is *qi*, and the nature of course is the nature, and they are not mixed into one another.
>
> 論天地之性，則專指理言；論氣質之性，則以理與氣雜而言之。未有此氣，已有此性。氣有不存，而性卻常在。雖其方在氣中，然氣自是氣，性自是性，亦不相夾雜。[77]

> "Does pattern come first or does *qi* come first?"
>
>   [Zhu Xi] replied: "Although pattern has never been separated from *qi*, pattern is that which is above form and *qi* is that which is within form. From the perspective of that which is above and that which is within form, how could there be no priority between them? Pattern is without form whereas *qi* is gross and has dross."
>
> 「先有理，抑先有氣？」曰：「理未嘗離乎氣。然理形而上者，氣形而下者。自形而上下言，豈無先後！理無形，氣便粗，有渣滓。」[78]

Master Zhou referred to [Taiji] as "Wuji" 無極 (Ultimateless) precisely because it has no location or shape. [Taiji] is taken to come before there were

---

[76] Zhu Xi, "Taiji tu jie," *Zhouzi quanshu*, 2.
[77] *Zhuzi yulei* 朱子語類 (Topically Arranged Conversations of Master Zhu), *juan* 4, 67. Comp. Li Jingde 李靖德 (fl. 1263) (Beijing: Zhonghua shuju, 1986).
[78] *Zhuzi yulei*, *juan* 1, 3.

things, and yet it is not established after things [already exist]. Although it is taken to be located beyond *yin* and *yang*, it has always operated within *yin* and *yang*. Although it is taken to interconnect with the whole [of phenomenal existence] and to exist everywhere, it is devoid of any sound, scent, shadow or echo that can be spoken of.

> 周子所以謂之無極，正以其無方所，無形狀。以為在無物之前，而未嘗不立于有物之後，以為在陰陽之外，而未嘗不行乎陰陽之中。以為通貫全體，無乎不在，則又初無聲臭影響之可言也。[79]

Taiji thus both transcends phenomena and *simultaneously* inheres in phenomena, just as suchness/*tathāgatagarbha* transcends phenomena yet also inheres in phenomena, as set out in the *Dasheng qixin lun*. This same idea is repeated widely:

> Someone asked: "In your comments to the 'Pattern, Nature, Mandate' chapter [of Zhou Dunyi's *Penetrating the Book of Change*] you state: 'From root to tip there is the actuality of but a single pattern yet the ten thousand things share in it as their intrinsic reality, and so each of the ten thousand things has the one Taiji.' This being the case, then is Taiji split apart?"[80]
>
> [Zhu] replied: "There has always only ever been one Taiji. Each of the ten thousand things is endowed with it—moreover each is endowed with the whole Taiji. It is like the single moon in the sky. Just because it can be seen everywhere when dispersed in the rivers and lakes, this does not mean that the moon has been split up!
>
> 問：「《理性命章》注云：『自其本而之末，則一理之實而萬物分之以為體，故萬物各有一太極。』如此，則是太極有分裂乎？」曰：「本只是一太極，而萬物各有稟受，又自各全具一太極耳。如月在天只一而已，乃散在江湖，則隨處而見，不可謂月已分也。」[81]

The reason the *Great Learning* talked about the investigation of things but did not talk about exhaustively tracing patterns is because if it were to have talked about exhaustively tracing patterns it would seem to be abstract and elusive. By talking only about the investigation of things, the way that is

---

[79] *Zhu Xi ji* 朱熹集 (Collected Works of Zhu Xi), eds. Guo Qi 郭齊 and Yin Bo 尹波 (Chengdu: Sichuan jiaoyu chubanshe, 1996), *juan* 36, 1575–1576.
[80] Zhu Xi's commentary to *Tongshu* 通書 (Penetrating the *Book of Change*), *Zhou Dunyi ji* 周敦頤集 (Zhou Dunyi's Collected Writings) (Beijing: Zhonghua shuju, 2014/1990), 32.
[81] *Zhuzi yulei, juan* 94, 2409.

above form can thereby simply be sought in the phenomena within form, enabling it to be understood that the two have never been separated.

大學所以說格物，卻不說窮理。蓋說窮理，則似懸空無捉摸處。只說格物，則只就那形而下之器上，便尋那形而上之道，便見得這箇元不相離。[82]

Feiqing[83] asked about the psychophysical nature. [Zhu Xi] replied: "If it were not for the psychophysical then the heavenly ordained nature would have no place to lodge. With respect to people's endowment of *qi*, however, there are differences of purity and degree. Hence, with respect to the impartiality of what heaven ordains[84] there are also differences in degree and density. Crucially, however, [both] must be deemed to be the nature. On one occasion when I had I met with Bingweng[85] he said, 'What [Cheng] Yichuan said about the psychophysical nature is just like what the Buddhist books mean by 'The saltiness in [sea-]water and the glue in paint.'"

Feiqing also asked, "How does Mencius' account of the nature compare with Yichuan's account?"

[Zhu Xi] replied: "They are different. Mencius removed reference [to *qi*] so as talk about the basis of the nature; Yichuan talked about [the nature] together with the psychophysical, his crucial point being that they cannot be separated. Therefore, Master Cheng said, 'To discuss the nature without discussing *qi* is to be deficient; to discuss *qi* without discussing the nature is to be ignorant.'[86] In "Explanation of the Taiji Diagram" I also said, 'Taiji cannot be talked about separated from *yin* and *yang*, nor can it be talked of in terms of being intermixed with *yin* and *yang*.'"[87]

蜚卿問氣質之性。曰：「天命之性，非氣質則無所寓。然人之氣稟有清濁偏正之殊，故天命之正，亦有淺深厚薄之異，要亦不可不謂之性。舊見病翁云：『伊川言氣質之性，正猶佛書所謂水中鹽味，色裏膠清。』」又問：「孟子言性，與伊川如何？」曰：「不同。孟子是剔出而言性之本，伊川是兼氣質而言，要之不可離也，所以程子云：『論性不論氣，不備；論氣不論性，不明。』而某於太極解亦云：『所謂太極者，不離乎陰陽而為言，亦不雜乎陰陽而為言。』」[88]

---

[82] *Zhuzi yulei*, juan 62, 1498.
[83] Tong Boyu 童伯羽 (b. 1144), follower of Zhu Xi.
[84] That which heaven ordains is the nature.
[85] Liu Zihui 劉子翬 (1101–1147) was a former teacher of Zhu Xi. See John Jorgensen's chapter in this volume for more details.
[86] *Er Cheng ji, Yi shu*, 81.
[87] Paraphrase of Zhu's comments at "Explanation of the Taiji Diagram," 1.
[88] *Zhuzi yulei*, juan 4, 67. See also John Jorgensen's discussion of this passage in this volume.

"The saltiness in [sea-]water and the glue in paint" is a line taken from "Mahāsattva Fu's Mind-king Inscription" (Fu dashi xinwang ming 傅大士心王銘) attributed to Fu Xi 傅翕 (497–569): "The saltiness in [sea-]water and the glue in paint are definitely present but we do not see their form. The mind-king is also as such, abiding with the body."[89] Given Zhu Xi's frequent lambasting of the Buddhist concept of mind, in particular the Chan account of mind, it is ironic that the inscription proceeds to emphasize that the mind is the Buddha and the Buddha is the mind. For our purposes, however, the key point is the inseparable inherence of pattern in the constitution of the psychophysical nature and the corresponding link with Taiji and *yin* and *yang*. The inseparable inherence of *li* in the constitution of the psychophysical nature is clearly isomorphic with the *Dasheng qixin lun*'s paradigm of the inherence of suchness or *tathāgatagarbha* in cyclic existence (the gateway of arising and ceasing) to constitute the *ālayavijñāna*.

This is made graphically evident in Zhu's explanation of the Taiji Diagram. In that Diagram, ◉ represents *yin* and *yang*, the two fundamental modes of *qi* 氣 (vital stuff). As Zhu explains, the ○ at the center of ◉ in the second level of the diagram represents Taiji.[90] ◉ is the functional equivalent of the presence of suchness/*tathāgatagarbha* in the arising and ceasing gateway of the mind (= the *ālayavijñāna*) in the *Dasheng qixin lun*. Just as the *ālayavijñāna* is the locus for the co-presence of the unconditioned and conditioned aspects of the One Mind, so too in Zhu Xi's moral psychology the nature is the locus for the coalescence of *li* and *qi* in humans.

In his "Explanation of the Taiji Diagram" Zhou Dunyi sets out a model of cosmogenesis and a creation theory, beginning with Wuji 無極 (Ultimateless), and proceeding to Taiji 太極 (Supreme Pivot),[91] to

---

[89] Included in *Jingde chuandeng lu* 景德傳燈錄 (Record of the Transmission of the Lamp Published in the Jingde Era), T51.2076, 456c26-457a17.

[90] Zhu Xi, "Taiji tu jie," 1.

[91] There is evidence that the opening line in Zhou's original essay, "Essay on Taiji," read *zi Wuji er wei Taiji* 自無極而為太極, which has the sense of "Taiji is created from Wuji." The evidence for this comes from Zhu Xi's "Ji Lianxi zhuan" 記濂溪傳 (A Note on Zhou Lianxi's Biography), where Zhu relates that the *Sichao guoshi* 四朝國史 (State History of the Four Reigns), compiled under the directorship of Hanlin academician Hong Mai 洪邁 (1123–1202), included a biography of Zhou Dunyi (Lianxi) in which the opening line of his Taiji Essay read *zi Wuji er wei Taiji* 自無極而為太極. Zhu's objection to this reading is consistent with his own ontological reading. The matter, however, is more complicated, due to the long-standing political animosity between Hong and Zhu, as Shu Jingnan 束景南 sets out in detail in his *Zhuzi dazhuan* 朱子大全 (Biography of Zhu Xi) (Fuzhou: Fujian chubanshe, 1992), 663–684. (It should be noted that in his account, Shu himself evidences a clear bias in favor of Zhu Xi.) Yet even so, Zhu provides other evidence indicating that at least one version of Zhou's *Tongshu* (which includes the "Essay on Taiji"), extant in Zhu's time, read *Wuji er sheng Taiji* 無極而生太極 ("Wuji generates Taiji"), which again drew Zhu's criticism. This was in the so-called Jiujiang 九江 version of *Tongshu* transmitted by Zhou's

yin 陰 and yang 陽, and to the five phases (wuxing 五行). In stark contrast, Zhu Xi presents Zhou's Taiji Diagram as an ontology rather than a cosmology, explicitly ruling out any notion of entity A's producing an ontologically separate entity B. The following passage is from a letter Zhu wrote in reply to Yang Zizhi 楊子直:

> In saying "Wuji yet Taiji" (無極而太極)[92] and that "Taiji is rooted in Wuji,"[93] it is not the case that following after Wuji, Taiji is separately produced, and that prior to Taiji, Wuji already exists. In talking about the five phases and yin-yang, yin-yang and Taiji, it is not the case that following after Taiji, yin-yang and the five phases are separately produced, and that prior to yin-yang and the five phases, Taiji already exists. Right through to [the way of Qian's] becoming the male and [the way of Kun's] becoming the female, transforming to produce the myriad things, the wonder that is Taiji never even begins not to be present therein. The guiding pattern of this Diagram—the meaning bequeathed by the great [Book of] Change—is diametrically opposed to what Laozi meant by "[All] things are produced from existence, and existence is produced from non-existence"[94] and to treating the process of creation as truly having a beginning and an end.
>
> In your letter [you pointed out that] I had sought to treat them as one,[95] and that is why my interpretation of the Diagram was often obfuscating and missed the point. I had previously presented Taiji as intrinsic reality, and movement and stillness as function. This way of stating things is certainly problematic and so later I changed this to "Taiji is the fundamental wonder, and movement and stillness are the mechanism it rides."[96] This comes near to it. The doubts you raise in your letter about intrinsic reality and function are well taken, but your account of why it is that you have doubts does not entirely correspond with the intention behind the change [in my wording].

---

descendants, which Zhu Xi saw circa 1178. See Zhu's colophon to the Yanping edition of *Tongshu*, in *Zhouzi quanshu*, 209. To complicate matters further, there is more than one Jiujiang version. For an informative, concise study of early editions of *Tongshu*, see Tian Zhizhong 田智忠, "Cong Chongling ben *Tongshu* lun *Tongshu* de zaoqi liuchuan" 從 "舂陵本"《通書》論《通書》的 早期流傳 (The Early Transmission of *Tongshu* from the Perspective of the Chongling Edition), *Zhouyi yanjiu* 117, no. 1 (2013): 49–55.

[92] Here Zhu seems to be warning against reading *er* 而 as consequential. His following comments confirm that he takes the term to be contrastive.

[93] Zhu Xi, "Taiji tu jie," 2.

[94] *Laozi*, *zhang* 40. I have translated this in the sense in which I believe Zhu Xi was adapting it. The original meaning is more likely to be invoking notions of having characteristics (*you* 有) and not having characteristics (*wu* 無), rather than abstract notions of existence and non-existence.

[95] Unify what is above form and what is within form.

[96] Zhu Xi, "Taiji tu shuo jie," 7 passim.

This is because although it is acceptable to say that Taiji contains [the *li* of] movement and stillness (referring to Taiji as intrinsic reality[97]), or that Taiji possesses movement and stillness (referring to the flow of Taiji[98]), if it were said that Taiji *is* movement and stillness then that which is above and that which is within form would be indistinguishable,[99] and so it would also be pointless [for the Attached Statements Commentary] to state "Change has Taiji."[100]

然曰「無極而太極」,「太極本無極」,則非無極之後別生太極而太極之上先有無極也。 又曰五行陰陽,陰陽太極則非太極之後別生二五而二五之上先有太極也。以至於成男成女,化生萬物,而無極之妙蓋未始不在是焉。此一圖之綱領,大易之遺意,與老子所謂物生於有,有生於無,而以造化為真有始終者正南北矣。來諭乃欲一之,所以於此〈圖〉之說,多所乖礙,而不得其理也。熹向以「太極」為體,「動靜」為用,其言固有病,後已改之曰:「太極者,本然之妙也;動靜者,所乘之機也。」此則庶幾近之。來諭疑於體用之云甚當,但所以「疑之」之說,則與熹之所以「改之」之意,又若不相似。然蓋謂「太極含動靜」則可,(以本體而言也)。謂「太極有動靜」則可,(以流行而言也)。若謂「太極便是動靜」,則是形而上下者不可分,而「易有太極」之言亦贅矣。[101]

---

[97] Intrinsic reality (*benti* 本體) and flow (*liuxing* 流行) are synonymous with *ti* and *yong*. Zhu makes a similar comment at "Taiji tu jie," 1.
[98] This refers to "The movement and stillness possessed by Taiji are the flow of what is ordained by heaven, which is what is meant by 'the alternation of *yin* and *yang*'" above. In other words, not only does Taiji enable this alternation; it continues to exist within this process of alternation.
[99] Cf. the ocean analogy in the *Dasheng qixin lun*, which stresses that it is in the inherent nature of the ocean to be wet but it is not in the inherent nature of the ocean to move. Movement is caused externally by the wind.
[100] See *Zhou Yi* 周易 (Book of Change), *Shisan jing zhushu* 十三經注疏 (The Thirteen Classics with annotations and sub-commentaries), comp. Ruan Yuan 阮元 (1764–1849) (Taipei: Yiwen yinshuguan, 1985), 7.28b.
[101] *Zhu Xi ji*, "Da Yang Zizhi" 答楊子直 (Reply to Yang Zizhi), *juan* 45, 2154. Chen Lai 陳來, *Zhuzi shuxin biannian kaozheng* 朱子書信編年考證 (Evidenced-based Examination of Zhu Xi's Letters, Arranged Chronologically) (Beijing: Sanlian, 2007), 89, dates this letter to 1171. Nor is it the case that pattern creates *qi*:

> Whereas *qi* can coalesce and create, *li* is devoid of desire, calculation, creativity. So long as there is a locus where *qi* coalesces, then *li* will be therein. As for the humans, plants and trees, and birds and animals that exist between heaven and earth, their generation involves seeds. It is definitely not the case that something is generated without a seed. In all cases, this is *qi*. As for pattern, it is nothing but a pure, clear, empty world, devoid of traces. Pattern, unlike *qi*, cannot create. *Qi*, however, can ferment and coalesce as living things.
>
> 蓋氣則能凝結造作,理卻無情意,無計度,無造作。只此氣凝聚處,理便在其中。且如天地間人物、草木、鳥獸。其生也,莫不有種,定不會無種子白地生出一箇物事。這箇都是氣。若理,則只是箇潔淨空闊底世界,無形迹,他卻不會造作。氣則能醞釀、凝聚生物也。(*Zhuzi yulei*, *juan* 1, 3)

Zhu's main point here is to clarify the relationship between Taiji, and movement and stillness.[102] In other words, he addresses the problem of how to demarcate the relationship between what is above form and what is within form, while not falling into the trap of ontologically separating them. Having made the point that Taiji is never separate from *yin-yang*, the five phases, male and female, and so forth, Zhu then expresses concern that in his earlier interpretations of the Taiji Diagram, by presenting Taiji as intrinsic reality (*ti*), and movement and stillness (= *yin-yang*) as function (*yong*), he had given the impression that Taiji itself was reducible to movement and stillness.[103] Zhu felt that his earlier formulation could easily be misconstrued as giving the impression that Li itself could take on physical characteristics. Thus, in revising his description of their relation to "Taiji is the fundamental wonder, and movement and stillness are the mechanism it rides," he believes he has avoided the offending reductionism by providing a stark contrast between the (non-physical) abstractness of "fundamental wonder" and the physicality of the "mechanism." As we will see, however, Zhu remained committed to the *ti-yong* paradigm.

As for the correct way to present the relationship between Taiji and movement and stillness, in his "Taiji tu shuo jie" Zhu elaborates as follows:

> The movement and stillness possessed by Taiji are the flow of what is ordained by heaven, which is what is meant by "the alternation of *yin* and *yang*."... When movement reaches its extreme there is stillness and when stillness reaches its extreme, once again there is movement. The alternation of movement and stillness, with each serving as the root for the other, is that whereby what is ordained flows ceaselessly. Through movement, *yang* is produced and through stillness, *yin* is produced. Differentiated as *yin* and

---

Thus when Zhu is cited in *Zhouzi quanshu*, 7, as saying "Taiji gives rise to (*sheng* 生) *yin* and *yang*, and *li* gives rise to *qi*; once *yin* and *yang* are arisen then Taiji is within them, and *li* is also within *qi*" (太極生陰陽，理生氣也。陰陽既生，則太極在其中，理復在氣之內也。) this should not be understood literally, per impossible, to mean that *li* creates *qi*, but rather that it is by virtue of *li* that *qi* is able to transform into all kinds of phenomena. *Qi* relies on *li* to do this but *qi* is not a predicate of *li* or of something more fundamental. It should also be noted that the earliest record of this particular passage is of relatively late provenance: Lü Nan 呂柟 (1479–1542), *Zhuzi chaoshi* 朱子抄釋 (Explanation of Zhu Xi's Writings). See Chen Rongjie (Wing-tsit Chan) 陳榮捷, *Zhuzi xin tansuo* 朱子新探索 (New Explorations of Zhu Xi) (Taipei: Xuesheng shuju, 1988), 243–245.

[102] For an alternative account of the import of this passage, see Brook A. Ziporyn's chapter in this volume.

[103] If Zhu was drawing on a conceptual paradigm already articulated in the *Dasheng qixin lun*, then it is clear why he should have this misgiving: The *Dasheng qixin lun*'s analogy stresses that it is in the nature of the ocean to be wet but it is not in the nature of the ocean to move.

as *yang*, the two modes are therein established. Differentiating them is how they become determinate and stable.

Taiji is the fundamental wonder, and movement and stillness are the mechanism it rides. Taiji is the way that is above form. *Yin* and *yang* are the vessels within form. If viewed from the perspective of the evident,[104] then movement and stillness are not simultaneous, and *yin* and *yang* have different stages, but there is nowhere that Taiji is not located in them. If viewed from the perspective of the subtle,[105] then movement and stillness, *yin* and *yang*, are empty and devoid of characteristics, yet the *li* of movement and stillness, and *yin* and *yang*, are already all included therein. Even if one could push back into the past, one would not see them being initially combined; or if one could draw forth into the future, one would not see them being finally separated. Thus Master Cheng [Yi] stated: "Movement and stillness have no end; *yin* and *yang* have no beginning."[106]

太極之有動靜，是天命之流行也，所謂「一陰一陽之謂道」. . . . 動極而靜，靜極復動。一動一靜，互為其根，命之所以流行而不已也。動而生陽，靜而生陰，分陰分陽，兩儀立焉，分之所以一定而不移也。蓋太極者，本然之妙也；動靜者，所乘之機也。太極，形而上之道也；陰陽，形而下之器也。是以自其著者而觀之，則動靜不同時，陰陽不同位，而太極無不在焉。自其微者而觀之，則沖漠無朕，而動靜陰陽之理，已悉具於其中矣。雖然推之於前，而不見其始之合；引之於後，而不見其終之離也。故程子曰：「動靜無端，陰陽無始」。[107]

Although movement and stillness are "possessed" by Taiji, Taiji is not some entity that alternates between states of movement and stillness. Transcending form, Taiji is devoid of physical characteristics. Only that which can take on phenomenal form, *qi* 氣, can move and be still. *Yin* and *yang* represent two fundamental modes of *qi*: *yang*, its active mode, and *yin*, its quiescent mode. It is *qi* that alternates between these two states:

Within heaven-and-earth there is only the ceaseless circulation between the two extremities of movement and stillness—nothing more. This is called

---

[104] *Yin* and *yang*, *qi*.
[105] Taiji, *li*.
[106] *Er Cheng ji*, 1029.
[107] "Taiji tushuo jie," 6–7.

Change, yet the movement and the stillness of Change necessarily possess therein the patterns that enable movement and stillness. [108]

天地之間只有動靜兩端循環不已，更無餘事。此之謂易而其動其靜則必有所以動靜之理焉。是則所謂太極者也。[109]

Taiji/*li* itself does not move, but Taiji/*li* is that by virtue of which movement and stillness are possible. The key point is that it is only through the alternation of *yin* and *yang*, moment and stillness that Taiji—the unity that is all *li*—is revealed. "Even if one could push back into the past, one would not see them being initially combined; or if one could draw forth into the future, one would not see them being finally separated." Although Zhu cites Cheng Yi 程頤 (1033–1107) to explain this ("Movement and stillness have no end; *yin* and *yang* have no beginning"), the broader context makes it clear that it is not just movement and stillness that are never apart—more pertinently, it is *li* and *qi* that are never apart:

Someone asked about "Movement and stillness are the mechanism that [Taiji] rides."

Master Zhu said: "Taiji is *li*. Movement and stillness are *qi*. When *qi* is active then *li* is also active. Being constantly interdependent they are never apart. Taiji is like a rider and movement and stillness are like a horse. The horse is that by which the rider is carried and the rider is that by which the horse is ridden. Everywhere the horse goes the rider also goes. This is because in every alternation of movement and stillness the wonder that is Taiji never ceases to be present therein. 'The mechanism that it rides' refers that by which Wuji, *yin* and *yang*, and the five phases 'wondrously combine to be consolidated.'"

問：「動靜者所乘之機。」朱子曰：「太極，理也。動靜，氣也。氣行，則理亦行。二者常相依，而未嘗相離也。太極猶人，動靜猶馬。馬所以載人，人所以乘馬。馬之一出一入，人亦與之一出一入。蓋一動一靜，而太極之妙未嘗不在焉。 此所謂『所乘之機』，無極、二五所以『妙合而凝』也。」[110]

All *li* are already included in Taiji (unified *li*), and *qi* is never separate from *li*. (Cf. the passage cited above explaining that *li* and *qi* have never

---

[108] See *Zhou Yi*, 7.28b.
[109] *Zhu Xi ji, juan* 45, 2153.
[110] *Zhuzi yulei, juan* 94, 2370.

been separated.) *Li* and *qi* exist in a relationship of mutual entailment. This understanding is consistent with the understanding of Li and *shi* in the Tiantai Home Mountain nature inclusion thesis.

Despite this, on a number of occasions, Zhu does draw an analytical distinction in which, in some abstracted sense, it can be stated that *li* already exists before *qi*-constituted phenomenal entities, thus (misleadingly) suggesting affinities with the Tiantai Off Mountain understanding of Li and *shi*:

> *Li* and *qi* are most definitely two things. If viewed only from the perspective of phenomena, these two things are a whole that cannot be individually separated out. This, however, does not interfere with their each being a single thing. If viewed from the perspective of unified *li*, even before a particular thing exists, the *li* of that thing already exists. It would, however, only be its *li* that exists—the particular thing would not yet actually exist.
>
> 所謂理與氣，此決是二物。但在物上看，則二物渾淪不可分開各在一處。然不害二物之各為一物也。若在理一看，則未有物而已有物之理，然亦但有其理而已，未嘗實有是物也。[111]

Zhu Xi is making the point that even though a particular *li* may not yet exist in a particular thing by virtue of that *li*'s being combined with *qi*, because unified *li* inherently includes all differentiated *li*—otherwise it would not be unified *li* or Taiji—"even before things exist the *li* of things already exists." One way to understand this statement is to think about the number "one" and a single phenomenal entity. Just as we can talk intelligibly about "one" without having to refer to any particular single entity,[112] so too we can talk about *li* without having to refer to any particular single entity. Crucially, however, abstracted "oneness" will have no meaning until there is an instance of a single entity. In other words, without *qi*, it is quite meaningless to speak of *li*. Zhu was not a substance dualist.

Just as the *Dasheng qixin lun* posited the relationship between the two gateways as a *ti-yong* relationship, and the Tiantai Home Mountain theorists posited the relationship between Li and phenomena as a *ti-yong* relationship, so too Zhu continued to present the relationship

---

[111] *Zhu Xi ji, juan* 46, 2243.
[112] Nor does one have to resort to theories such as Platonic forms or Aristotelian universals in order to be able to do this, as our everyday experience confirms.

between Taiji/*li* and *qi* as a *ti-yong* relationship (despite his earlier reservations):

> What is within form is precisely what is above form. The commentary to the *Book of Change* states: "That which is extremely subtle is pattern." This is referring to what is above form. "That which is extremely apparent is images." This is referring to what is within form. "Intrinsic reality and function are a single source; there is no gap between the apparent and the subtle." Thus whether above form or within form there is only this single normative pattern.
>
> 形而下即形而上者，易傳謂:「至微者理」，即所謂形而上者也。至著者象，即所謂形而下者也。「體用一源，顯微無間」，則雖形而上形而下亦只是此箇義理也。¹¹³

The passages cited are from Cheng Yi's commentary to the *Book of Change*: "That which is extremely subtle is pattern; that which is extremely apparent is images. Intrinsic reality (*ti* 體) and function (*yong* 用) are a single source; there is no gap between the apparent and the subtle" (至微者理也，至著者象也。體用一源，顯微無間。).¹¹⁴   Elsewhere Zhu comments on this passage in more detail:

> From the perspective of pattern, it is precisely within intrinsic reality that function exists. This is what is meant by the "single source." From the perspective of images [i.e., phenomena] it is precisely in the manifest that the subtle [i.e., pattern] is unable to be external. This is what is meant by "no gap."
>
> 蓋自理而言，則即體而用在其中。所謂一源也。自象而言，則即顯而微不能外。所謂無間也。¹¹⁵

---

¹¹³ *Zhu Xi ji*, juan 48, 2333. Chen Lai, *Zhuzi shuxin biannian kaozheng*, 434, dates this letter to 1197. For Cheng Yi's cited comments, see *Zhouyi Chengshi zhuan* 周易程氏傳 (Cheng Yi's annotation of the *Book of Change*) (Beijing: Zhonghua shuju, 2011), 1.
¹¹⁴ Cheng Yi, *Zhouyi Chengshi zhuan*, 1.
¹¹⁵ *Zhu Xi ji*, juan 30, 1279. Cheng Yi already implicitly identifies *xiang* with *shi*:

> As for that which is extremely apparent, nothing can be compared with phenomena; as for that which is extremely subtle, nothing can be compared with principle. Indeed, phenomena and principle are unified, and the subtle and the apparent are a single source.
>
> 至顯者莫如事，至微者莫如理；而事理一致，微顯一源。

Cheng Hao 程顥 and Cheng Yi, *Henan Cheng shi yishu* 河南程氏遺書 (The Extant Works of the Chengs of Henan), *Er Cheng ji* 二程集 (Collected Works of the Cheng Brothers) (Beijing: Zhonghua shuju, 1981), 323.

"Intrinsic reality and function are a single source": from the perspective of pattern, pattern is intrinsic reality, images are function, and the having of images within pattern is the "single source." "There is no gap between the apparent and the subtle": from the perspective of images, images are apparent, pattern is subtle, and the having of pattern within images is the "no gap."

「體用一源」者，自理而觀則理爲體，象爲用，而理中有象是一源也。「顯微無間」者，自象而觀則象爲顯，理爲微，而象中有理是無間也。[116]

"Intrinsic reality and function are a single source." Even though intrinsic reality has no trace, there is already function within it. "There is no gap between the manifest and the subtle" means that wherever there is the manifest then the subtle is included within it. Before heaven and earth exist the ten thousand things are already included. That is, there is function within intrinsic reality. After heaven and earth are established, particular patterns (ci li 此理) will also exist. That is, there is the subtle within the manifest.

「體用一源」，體雖無迹，中已有用。「顯微無間」者，顯中便具微。天地未有，萬物已具，此是體中有用；天地既立，此理亦存，此是顯中有微。[117]

For Zhu Xi, "intrinsic reality and function are a single source" means that unified li or Taiji in its transcendent aspect is inherently imbued with the li of all phenomena, and in its immanent aspect it is immanent in all things. "Before heaven and earth exist the ten thousand things are already included" means that Taiji is inherently imbued with the li of all phenomena—there is no temporal event or causal incident precipitating this, such as Zhu's example of heaven and earth's coming into existence.[118] (Heaven and earth are just one specific configuration of li and qi.) "From the perspective of pattern, it is precisely within intrinsic reality that function exists." This is akin to the idea expressed in the analogy featured in the *Dasheng qixin lun*: wetness embraces all waves. As for "Where there is the manifest then there is the subtle within it," this means that any determinate phenomenon exists by virtue of being endowed with li. This is li or Taiji in its immanent aspect. Function is the function of intrinsic reality. Manifest and subtle respectively refer to the immanent and

---

[116] *Zhu Xi ji*, juan 40, 1889.
[117] *Zhuzi yulei*, juan 67, 1654.
[118] Recall Zhu's reply to Yang Zizhi, cited above, page 312, first paragraph.

transcendent aspects of a single whole that is Taiji. They refer to the two polar perspectives of that whole.

Zhu Xi's understanding of "intrinsic reality and its function are a single source" can be characterized as an expression of immanent transcendence. In Sinitic Buddhist and Neo-Confucian contexts, immanent transcendence is a realist metaphysical view (i.e. not a nominalism). It describes how, on the one hand, the referent wholly lies within the boundaries of a specifiable domain yet, on the other hand, it simultaneously extends beyond the boundaries of that domain.[119] The *Dasheng qixin lun* provides a paradigmatic model: Suchness exists in the gateway of the mind of arising and ceasing (*ālayavijñāna*) while *simultaneously extending beyond* the gateway of the mind of arising and ceasing (suchness qua the unconditioned). (Wetness exists in all waves while simultaneously extends beyond any particular wave.)

Zhu Xi's following comment on a key passage in the "Attached Statements Commentary" on the *Book of Change* (refracted through Zhu's interpretation of the Taiji diagram) makes a similar point:

> [Huan Yuan said]: "Taiji generates two modes and the two modes give rise to the four images." This is a like a mother giving birth to a child, with the child being external to the mother. In the case of the two modes and the five phases, however, the child is within the mother. [Is this correct?]" [Zhu Xi] said "This is indeed so. Within *yin* and *yang*, the five phases, and the ten thousand things—each has the one Taiji.
>
> 「『太極生兩儀，兩儀生四象』，此如母生子，子在母外之義。若兩儀五行，卻是子在母內。」曰：「是如此。陰陽、五行、萬物各有一太極。」[120]

"Taiji generates two modes and the two modes give rise to the four images" is from the Attached Statements Commentary to the *Book of Change*. The "two modes and five phases" refers to the second and third levels of the

---

[119] Robert Cummings Neville defines transcendence as "that to which reference can be made, in any sense of reference, only by denying that the referent lies within the boundaries of a specifiable domain, whatever else is supposed or said about the referent." *Boston Confucianism: Portable Tradition in the Late-Modern World* (Albany: SUNY Press, 2000), 151. For a recent defence of the idea of immanent transcendence in the Chinese philosophical context, see Karl-Heinz Pohl, "'Immanent Transcendence' in the Chinese Tradition: Remarks on a Chinese (and Sinological) Controversy," in *Transcendence, Immanence, and Intercultural Philosophy*, eds. Nahum Brown and William Franke (New York: Palgrave Macmillan, 2016).
[120] *Zhuzi yulei*, juan 94, 2377–2378. Cf. *Zhuzi yulei*, juan 1, 1.

Taiji Diagram. (Here the two modes refer to *yin* and *yang*). In other words, Taiji qua unified *li*, includes all differentiated *li* and hence transcends any particular phenomenon—but by virtue of being imbued in phenomenal entities, Taiji inheres in those entities. The *Dasheng qixin lun* similarly posits suchness as the basis of all phenomena, while simultaneously transcending any particular phenomenon, and also posits suchness as merging seamlessly with phenomena in the gateway of the mind of arising and ceasing, just as the wetness of the ocean inheres in individual waves.

Although the *Dasheng qixin lun* also championed a substance monism, it failed to provide a consistent account of the origin of ignorance. Drawing on analogies that present ignorance as external to suchness complicated matters by introducing a dualist analogy into a monistic ontology. Zhu Xi's *li-qi* polar monism averted dualism by not privileging the ontological (*li, xing er shang* 形而上) over the phenomenal (*qi, xing er xia* 形而下). On the one hand, *li* provides the ontological ground for *qi* qua things to be what they are; on the other hand, *qi* provides the phenomenological ground for *li* to be experienced, to be realized.

This understanding is clearly incompatible with the Off Mountain understanding of the Li-*shi* relationship and underscores the affirmation of phenomenal reality in Zhu's metaphysics, a feature shared in common with the Home Mountain "nature inclusion" thesis. Yet, this does not entail that Zhu's understanding of the *li-qi* relationship is entirely commensurate with the Home Mountain understanding of the Li-*shi* relationship. This is because, for Zhu Xi, *li* and *qi* are not reducible to one another—even when *li* and *qi* are conjoined in things—with *li* pertaining to what transcends form even as it inheres in form, and *qi* pertaining to the phenomenal realm of form. This relationship mirrors the idea of being "neither the same nor different" (*bu yi bu yi* 不一不異) featured in the *Dasheng qixin lun*, where we find a structural parallel in the unconditioned (*tathāgatagarbha* = *li*) remaining unchanged even as it adapts to, accords with, the conditioned reality of phenomenal existence (*ālayavijñāna* = 事) such that the unconditioned and the conditioned merge seamlessly.[121] Zhu Xi held this view in common with Huayan and Tiantai Off Mountain theorists.

Viewed holistically, Zhu's position draws on and extends styles of reasoning developed over centuries of Sinitic Buddhist discourse in response to the One Mind Two Gateways paradigm of the *Dasheng qixin lun*. Significantly, it also develops a view of immanent transcendence that

---

[121] See the related discussions of the non-obstruction of Li and phenomena (*li shi wu ai* 理事無礙).

sublates the two seemingly irreconcilable views animating key aspects of that discourse: the transcendence of exclusive monism and the immanence of inclusive monism.

How, then, did Zhu deal with badness? In order to begin to answer this question we first need to understand his theory of the nature.

5.3.2 The "Heaven-and-Earth-Bestowed Nature" and the "Psychophysical Nature"

The relationship between pattern and phenomena/*qi* was not only central to Zhu Xi's polar monism—it was also central to his account of the nature (*xing* 性). As with Cheng Yi and Zhang Zai 張載 (1020–1077) before him, Zhu drew a conceptual distinction between the psychophysical nature (*qizhi zhi xing* 氣質之性) and the "heaven-and-earth-bestowed nature" (*tiandi zhi xing* 天地之性).[122] Whereas Zhang Zai and Cheng Yi used the distinction to demarcate two different kinds of nature, Zhu used the distinction to refer to the same nature in two different modalities. For Zhu, the "heaven-and-earth-bestowed nature" is pure pattern, and the "psychophysical nature" is pattern as it is manifest in and through *qi*. This distinction represents the nature in its fundamental aspect and in its conditioned, manifest aspect. The locus in which *li* and *qi* merge seamlessly, and in which the heaven-and-earth-bestowed nature remains unchanged, is the psychophysical nature. In the *Dasheng qixin lun*, the locus in which phenomena and suchness merge seamlessly, and in which unconditioned suchness remains unchanged, is the eighth consciousness or *ālayavijñāna* (*alaiye shi* 阿賴耶識), characterized as the gateway of arising and ceasing.

Angus Graham credits Cheng Yi's introduction of "something fundamentally new" into the human nature debate as having led to a "sudden decisive resolution of a controversy which had continued without result for a millennium and a half." Cheng's contribution, according to Graham, was to elevate pattern "to the central place among Confucian concepts" and to reinterpret heaven and the nature as aspects of pattern. Graham regards the "restatement of the problem in terms of *li* was an event comparable with" a Kuhnian paradigm shift.[123]

---

[122] The term *qizhi zhi xing* is derived from Zhang Zai, *Zhangzi quanshu* 張子全書 (Complete Writings of Zhang Zai), *Guoxue jiben congshu* 國學基本叢書 (Taipei: Shangwu yinshuguan, 1964), 42.12a.
[123] A. C. Graham, "What Was New in the Ch'eng-Chu Theory of Human Nature?," in *Studies in Chinese Philosophy and Philosophical Literature* (Singapore: Institute of East Asian Philosophies, National University of Singapore, 1986), 412–413. For an account of how thinkers from pre-Qin

For Zhu Xi, the "heaven-and-earth-bestowed nature" is pure pattern, and the "psychophysical nature" is pattern as it is manifest in and through *qi*. This distinction represents two modalities or aspects of the nature: in its fundamental aspect; and in its manifest aspect. (In Buddhist terms, this distinction might be characterized as the difference between unconditioned and conditioned.) Now, although the nature is nothing but pattern, without *qi* there would be nowhere for pattern to inhere:

> If it were not for the psychophysical then the heavenly endowed nature would have no place to settle. Like a ladleful of water, if there was nothing in which to contain it, there would be nowhere for the water to lodge. Master Cheng said, "to discuss the nature without also discussing *qi* would be incomplete; to discuss *qi* without also discussing the nature would be ignorant. If both were so discussed this would be quite wrong."
> 天命之性，若無氣質，卻無安頓處。且如一勺水，非有物盛之，則水無歸著。程子云:「論性不論氣，不備；論氣不論性，不明，二之則不是。」 [124]

The "heaven-and-earth-bestowed nature"-"psychophysical nature" distinction is another example of isomorphism with the One Mind Two Gateways model, first articulated in the *Dasheng qixin lun*. Furthermore, Zhu's portrayal of the psychophysical nature, which combines *li* and *qi*, mirrors the coalescence of *tathāgatagarbha*-cum-*ālayavijñāna* in the *Dasheng qixin lun* (see figs. 5.3 and 5.4).

As for the relation between *li* and the nature, Zhu explains:

> Someone asked: "The nature is certainly pattern but does it get its name from its endowment in people at birth?"
>
> [Zhu] replied: "'That which continues it is the good and that which completes it is the nature.'[125] When patterns are between heaven and earth[126] there is good alone and nothing that is not good. Only when received by

---

to Tang times developed the idea that the quality of *qi* inherent in the makeup of an individual's inborn nature predetermines the limits on that individual's moral growth and other capabilities, see my *Transmitters and Creators: Chinese Commentators and Commentaries on the Analects* (Cambridge, MA: Harvard University Asia Center, 2003), 97–104.

[124] *Zhuzi yulei*, juan 4, 66; *Er Cheng ji, Yi shu*, 81.

[125] "Attached Statements Commentary," *Zhou Yi*, 7.11a–12a ("The alternating procession of *yin* and *yang* is the way; that which continues this process is goodness, and that which completes this process is the nature.").

[126] Before they are endowed in human nature.

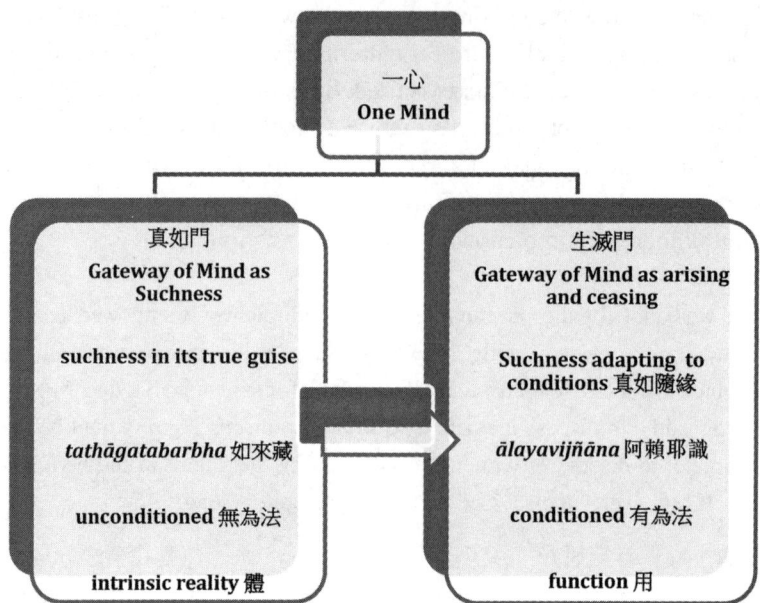

FIGURE 5.3 The *Dasheng qixin lun*'s "One Mind, Two Gateways" Model
CREDIT: This diagram was created by John Makeham.

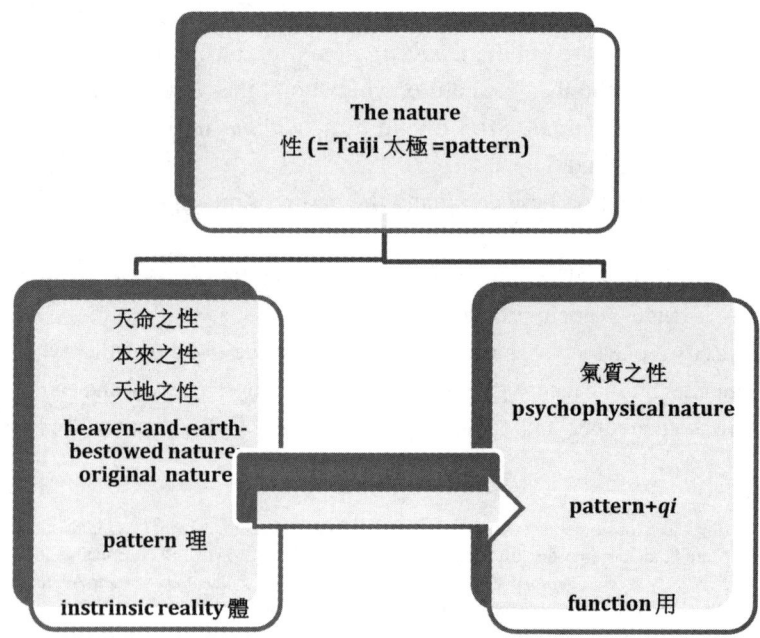

FIGURE 5.4 Zhu Xi's "Heaven-and-Earth-Bestowed Nature"-"Psychophysical Nature" Model
CREDIT: This diagram was created by John Makeham.

living things does pattern start to be called the nature. It is nothing other than this pattern, which with respect to heaven, that is called 'the command,' and with respect to humans, that is called 'the nature.' "

問:「性固是理。然性之得名,是就人生稟得言之否?」曰:「『繼之者善,成之者性。』這箇理在天地間時,只是善,無有不善者。生物得來,方始名曰『性』。只是這理,在天則曰『命』,在人則曰『性』。」 [127]

Before being endowed in individual humans, the nature is nothing but *li*. As we have already noted in the context of Zhu Xi's interpretation of the Taiji Diagram, unified *li* inherently includes all differentiated *li* ("even before things exist the *li* of things already exists") and so we can talk about *li* without having to refer to any particular embodiment of pattern. In the passage above, this is the nature qua pattern in its transcendent aspect. As soon as we speak of humans, however, the nature is no longer exclusively pattern but necessarily is a conjoining of pattern and *qi*.

People have this physical body and when pattern begins to be endowed therein this is called the nature. As soon as one speaks of the nature then this concerns human beings, but because the nature includes the psychophysical it cannot be deemed to be the nature as intrinsic reality. The nature as intrinsic reality is, however, never intermixed [with the psychophysical]. The key thing for people to understand here is that even though the nature as intrinsic reality is never apart from the [psychophysical] nature, it is never intermixed [with the psychophysical].

人有此形氣,則是此理始具於形氣之中,而謂之性。纔是說性,便已涉乎有生,而兼乎氣質不得為性之本體也。然性之本體,亦未嘗雜。要人就此上面見得其本體元未嘗離,亦未嘗雜耳。 [128]

"Even though the nature as intrinsic reality is never apart from the [psychophysical] nature it is never intermixed [with the psychophysical]" clearly echoes Zhu's comment about Taiji and *yin* and *yang*, already cited above. [129]

---

[127] *Zhuzi yulei, juan* 5, 83.
[128] *Zhuzi yulei, juan* 95, 2430.
[129] "Although [Taiji] is the intrinsic reality by means of which there is *yang* in movement and *yin* in stillness, it is not possible for it to be separate from *yin* and *yang*. It is precisely in *yin* and *yang* that their intrinsic reality is pointed to. That is to say, their intrinsic reality is not intermixed with *yin* and *yang*." 所以動而陽、靜而陰之本體,然非有以離乎陰陽也。即陰陽而指其本體。不雜乎陰陽而為言耳。

The nature consists of an endowment of pattern. The nature also consists of *qi*, and it is in the realm of "what is within form," where *li* and *qi* come to be conjoined as our nature, that the conditions that make badness possible are able to arise. Zhu explains:

> Mr Shi's *Collected Commentaries* [*to Zhongyong*]¹³⁰ cites the following: "'That which is inborn is what is meant by the nature.' The nature is *qi* and *qi* is the nature." In my view, this passage first explains that *li* and *qi* are not separate from one another, and then says that even though the psychophysical nature has both good and bad, it was never the case that at birth the nature had these two qualities in opposition. At the outset, the nature is nothing but good. Because the *qi*-endowment is turbid, however, and further because selfish desires contaminate, that which is good transforms into badness. Yet it is not the case that when it is badness there separately exists a good nature. Hence it is said that even though it is badness it must be deemed to be the nature, just as when water is made turbid it must still be deemed to be water.
>
> 石氏集解引「『生之謂性。』 性即氣，氣即性。」一章，竊謂此章先明理與氣不相離，遂言氣質之性雖有善惡。然性中元無此兩物相對而生，其初只是善而已。由氣稟有昏濁，又私慾污染，其善者遂變而為惡。當為惡時，非別有一善性也。故有惡不可不謂之性，濁不可不謂之水之說。¹³¹

The patterns endowed in our nature are, to varying degrees, covered over, obscured by *qi*:

> Someone asked: "The psychophysical has different grades of turbidity—does this mean that there are different degrees of the heavenly endowed nature?"
>
> [Zhu] replied: "It is not the case that there are different degrees. It is like sunlight or moonlight. If one is in an open area—one sees it fully; if one is under the thatched roof of a hut, it will be partly obscured and so one sees it incompletely. It is the psychophysical that is turbid and so it is the psychophysical itself that obscures. It is like being under the thatched roof of a hut.

---

¹³⁰ *Zhongyong jijie* 中庸集解 (Collected Explanations of the *Doctrine of the Mean*), 2 *juan*, compiled by Zhu's contemporary, Shi Zichong 石子重 (fl. 1165–1173). The passage quoted is found at *Er Cheng ji, Yishu*, 10.

¹³¹ *Zhuzi yulei, juan* 4, 58.

問:「氣質有昏濁不同,則天命之性有偏全否?」曰:「非有偏全。謂如日月之光,若在露地,則盡見之;若在蔀屋之下,有所蔽塞,有見有不見。昏濁者是氣昏濁了,故自蔽塞,如在蔀屋之下。」[132]

If one is endowed with pure and clear *qi*, then patterns will readily be manifested as one's nature; if the defilements of turbid *qi* are intense, however, pattern becomes obscured, providing the conditions for selfish desires to predominate and badness to arise. "If [one] has only clear *qi* then [*li*] will not be concealed and will be freely expressed. Where this concealment is limited then the expression of heavenly pattern will predominate. Where this concealment is great then selfish desires will predominate."[133]

Only sages are born with an endowment of *qi* so pure and undefiled that their *qi* provides unmediated access to pattern. Other people have varying qualities of *qi* that impede the realization of pattern. "Only those who are endowed with pure *qi* are sages and worthies. Their patterns are like precious pearls in clear, cold water. Those who are endowed with turbid *qi* are the benighted and the hapless. Their patterns are like pearls in turbid water."[134]

"The natures of all people are good, yet although there are some people who are born good, there are others who are born bad. This is due to differences in endowments of *qi*."[135] If one is endowed with pure and clear *qi*, then pattern will readily be manifested as one's nature; if the defilements of turbid *qi* are intense, however, pattern will be obscured, providing the conditions for selfish desires to predominate and badness to arise. As for our *qi*-endowment, it is a function of natural and cosmic processes beyond our control. As with ignorance in the *Dasheng qixin lun*, it is a simply a given that must be dealt with.[136]

Given this natural "condition," how is this situation to be addressed? How does one exercise moral choice? This is where the mind plays its role.

5.3.3 Of Two Minds

For Zhu Xi, the mind is the seat of cognitive activity and of our capacity for moral decision-making, enabling us to apprehend and to discern the

---

[132] *Zhuzi yulei*, juan 4, 58.
[133] *Zhuzi yulei*, juan 1, 66.
[134] *Zhuzi yulei*, juan 1, 73. On the Chan use of the pearl metaphor, see John Jorgensen's chapter.
[135] *Zhuzi yulei*, juan 1, 69.
[136] Also recalling the *Dasheng qixin lun* is the trope of a pure nature's being obscured by defilements. This, in turn, has roots in the wider body of Tathāgatagarbha literature. Zhu's repeated choice of metaphors such as precious pearls hidden in mud has precedents in those texts.

patterns inherent in our nature, as well as those in the world in which we live and in the cosmos more generally:

> The mind is one. If it is held fast and so preserved then the normative patterns will be evident and this is called the mind of the way. If it is abandoned and becomes lost then the desire for things will be unbridled and this is called the mind of humans. If one retrieves it, starting with the mind of humans, then it will be the mind of the way. If one lets go, starting with the mind of the way, then this will be the mind of humans, and in an instant it will transform into a myriad forms. This is what is meant by, "it leaves and enters at any time and no one knows where it might go."

> 心一也。操而存，則義理明而謂之道心；舍而亡，則物欲肆而謂之人心。自人心而收回，便是道心；自道心而放出，便是人心。頃刻之間，悦惚萬狀，所謂「出入無時，莫知其鄉也。」[137]

> "Preserved," "lost," "leaving and entering" certainly [refer to] the mind of humans. "The subtle"[138] that is intrinsic reality, however, never increases; and even though it is let hold of and lost, it never diminishes. Even though it is said to leave and to enter at any time, it never [ceases] to stand out in our daily existence and cannot be concealed. If it is discerned therein then [one will understand that] the subtleness of the mind of the way has never been anything other than this. If it is not discerned, then [what one discerns will be] the mind of humans and nothing more. Even though the mind of humans is certainly different from the mind of the way, nevertheless [the mind of humans and the mind of the way] cannot be regarded as two things nor sought in two different places.

> 存亡出入固人心也，而惟微之本體，亦未嘗加益；雖捨而亡，然未嘗少損；雖曰出入無時，未嘗不卓然乎日用之間而不可掩也。若於此識得，則道心之微初不外此。不識，則人心而已矣。蓋人心固異道心，又不可做兩物看，不可於兩處求也。[139]

The crucial issue determining the "mind of the way"-"mind of humans" distinction is whether our cognitive choices are impacted by selfish desires:

---

[137] *Zhu Xi ji*, juan 39, 1786. The quotation is a passage attributed to Confucius in *Mencius* 6A.8.
[138] This is a reference to the mind of the way. "Da Yu mo" 大禹謨 (The Counsels of Yu the Great), *Shangshu* 尚書 (Book of Documents), *Shisan jing zhushu*, 4.8b: "The human mind is precarious; the mind of the way is subtle. By being meticulous and focused one will sincerely uphold the mean" (人心惟危，道心惟微，惟精惟一，允執厥中。). I have interpreted this passage in the way I think Zhu Xi intended the passage to be understood, based on a variety of glosses in his preface to the *Zhongyong* and also in *Zhuzi yulei*.
[139] *Zhu Xi ji*, juan 32, 1377.

The mind is one. Insofar as the endowment of heavenly patterns is manifest in all situations it is called the mind of the way. Insofar as the operation [of the mind] is directed at planning and deliberation it is called the mind of humans. It is not always necessarily bad that the operation [of the mind] is directed at planning and deliberation. As for selfish desires, if even by an iota one does not accord with heavenly patterns as they emanate naturally, then this is selfish desire.

蓋心一也，自其天理備具隨處發現而言，則謂之道心；自其有所營為謀慮而言，則謂之人心。夫營為謀慮非皆不善也。便謂之私慾者，蓋只一毫髮不從天理上自然發出,便是私慾。[140]

Zhu remarks that in every word and deed there is a right way and a wrong way to act. The right way conforms to pattern; the wrong way indulges selfish desires. "Even when drinking a cup of tea one must understand what is heavenly pattern and what is human desire."[141] If one's motivation for drinking tea serves to indulge a selfish desire, one will not be drinking tea.

Badness arises due to the constitution of the psychophysical nature, in which *qi* obscures pattern, but its direct cause is selfish desires.[142] Badness does not arise from the heavenly endowed nature.[143] It is, however, the mind, in particular, that determines whether badness is realized and the extent to which it is realized, through awareness of that with which we are innately endowed:

> If the mind is in charge then the emotional responses will be true. If it is guided by the nature's constants, then this cannot be called desire. If the mind is not in charge then the emotional responses will be unrestrained, ensnaring the nature so that it functions solely to serve human desire.

> 心宰則情得正，率乎性之常而不可以欲言矣。心不宰則情流而陷溺其性專爲人欲矣。[144]

If the mind is not in charge then the emotional responses will act on their own. In this way, the mind drifts into human desires and fails to be true. The

---

[140] *Zhu Xi ji, juan* 32, 1376.
[141] *Zhuzi yulei, juan* 3, 963.
[142] As with other Neo-Confucian thinkers, Zhu was concerned with moral badness, not natural badness (natural calamities, etc.).
[143] "The mind has good and bad but the [heavenly endowed] nature is devoid of anything bad. As for the psychophysical nature, it too has what is bad." 心有善惡，性無不善。若論氣質之性，亦有不善。*Zhuzi yulei, juan* 5, 89.
[144] *Zhu Xi ji, juan* 64, 3362.

difference between heavenly pattern and human desire hinges on regulation. In particular, it depends on whether or not the mind is in charge, such that emotional responses are unable to harm it.

惟心不宰而情自動，是以流於人欲而每不得其正也。然則天理人欲之判，中節不中節之分，特在乎心之宰與不宰，而非情能病之。[145]

The mind's numinous awareness is but one, yet there is a difference between the mind of humans and the mind of the way because [this awareness] either issues from the selfishness of the physical body or derives from the impartiality of the [heavenly-]ordained nature. And because that whereby there is awareness differs, [the mind] is either unstable due its precariousness or difficult to discern due its subtleness. Because all humans have physical form, even the most wise do not lack the mind of humans; and because all humans have this nature, even the most benighted must possess the mind of the way. If the two [aspects][146] become mixed up in one's heart/mind such that it does not know how to put them in proper order, then the precarious will grow ever more precarious and the subtle will grow ever more subtle, until finally the impartiality of heavenly pattern will no longer be able to overpower the selfishness of human desires. By being meticulous in distinguishing them, one will not intermix them; by being focused one will uphold the impartiality of one's inherent mind and not depart from it.

心之虛靈知覺，一而已矣，而以為有人心、道心之異者，則以其或生於形氣之私，或原於性命之正，而所以為知覺者不同，是以或危殆而不安，或微妙而難見耳。然人莫不有是形，故雖上智不能無人心，亦莫不有是性，故雖下愚不能無道心。二者雜於方寸之間，而不知所以治之，則危者愈危，微者愈微，而天理之公卒無以勝夫人欲之私矣。精則察夫二者之閒而不雜也，一則守其本心之正而不離也。[147]

Once again, the mind of the way is the actualization of the intrinsic nature of the mind and identified as where goodness comes from. Badness is a consequence of indulging in selfish desires. Our proclivity to do so is directly affected by the extent to which turbid *qi* obscures awareness of the normative patterns inherent in our nature. Badness is not generated by Taiji or by patterns. It becomes real when the mind of the way is ignored

---

[145] *Zhu Xi ji*, juan 32, 1375.
[146] The mind of the way and the mind of humans.
[147] Zhu Xi, "*Zhongyong* zhangju xu" 中庸章句序 (Preface to the Section and Sentence Commentaries on the *Doctrine of the Mean*), 14, *Sishu zhangju jizhu* 四書章句集注 (Section and Sentence Commentaries and Collected Annotations on the Four Books) (Beijing: Zhonghua shuju, 1983).

and the mind of humans is given free rein.[148] For Zhu Xi, the mind is an affective and cognitive capacity that enables us to discern the nature. The relationship between the mind of the way and the human mind is a *ti-yong* relationship.[149] It is only through dealing with the human mind, controlling the human mind, ensuring that it does not succumb to selfish desires, that the mind of the way is encountered.

Zhu's "mind of the way"-"mind of humans" distinction is isomorphic with the "awakening mind"-"nonawakening mind" distinction of the *Dasheng qixin lun* (see figs. 5.5 and 5.6), again suggesting the broader context of a shared body of discourse in which prominent paradigms became a resource for intellectuals over the course of centuries.[150] Just as the One Mind has two aspects or gateways, so too, the gateway of the mind of arising and ceasing—the *ālayavijñāna*—has two aspects: awakening and nonawakening:

> The arising and ceasing mind exists because of dependence on the *tathāgatagarbha*. That is to say, non-arising and non-ceasing combine with arising and ceasing: they are neither the same nor different. This is called the "*ālaya* consciousness." As the collector and producer of all dharmas, this consciousness has two senses. What are they? The first is awakening; the second is non-awakening. "Awakening" means that the intrinsic reality of the mind is free from conceiving. Being free from the characteristic of conceiving is identical to the realm of space: it is all-pervasive.

> 依如來藏故有生滅心，所謂不生不滅與生滅和合，非一非異，名為阿梨耶識。此識有二種義，能攝一切法、生一切法。云何為二？一者、覺義，二者、不覺義。所言覺義者，謂心體離念。離念相者，等虛空界無所不遍。[151]

---

[148] Even though the mind of the way is within "that which has form," as the analogue of the awoken or enlightened aspect of the mind of arising and ceasing, it is free of defilements caused by ignorance and so readily discerns the patterns inherent in the nature.

[149] Zhu is not explicit on this point, but his descriptions of their relationship conforms neatly with the *ti-yong* polarity construed as a relationship between the unconditioned and the conditioned, in which the former is wholly present in the latter. The closest explicit portrayal of the human mind and the mind of the way as a *ti-yong* relationship is the following passage at *Zhuzi yulei, juan* 62, 1488, where Zhu states: "If one achieves an understanding of the pattern of one's [heavenly-] ordained nature, then, even if it is the functioning of the human mind, it will be nothing other than the mind of the way. This is why Mencius pointed out that the 'the body and its appetites are the heavenly-endowed nature' [13.38]" (如其達性命之理，則雖人心之用，而無非道心，孟子所以指形色為天性者以此。). I am grateful to Anders Sydskjor for this reference.

[150] Peter N. Gregory, *Tsung-mi and the Sinification of Buddhism*, 311 is perhaps the first modern scholar to have written about this structural parallel.

[151] T32.1666, 576b8-13.

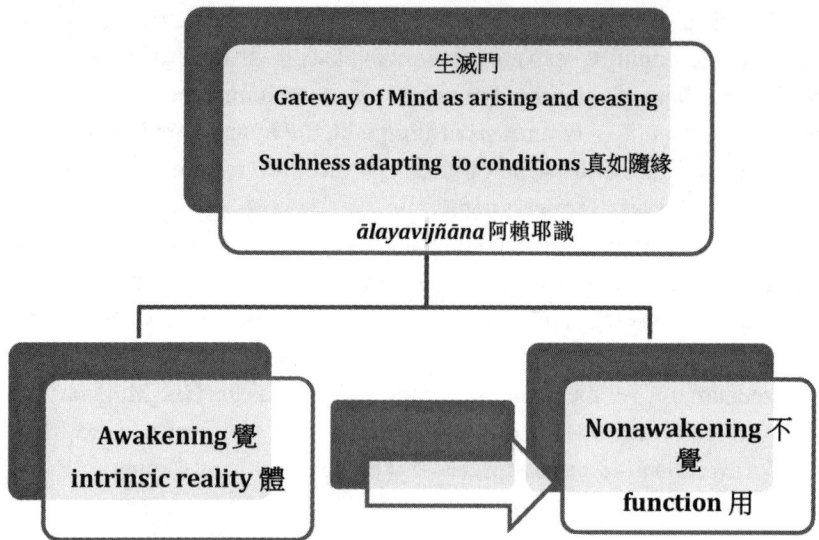

FIGURE 5.5 The *Dasheng qixin lun*'s "Awakening Mind"-"Nonawakening Mind" Model
CREDIT: This diagram was created by John Makeham.

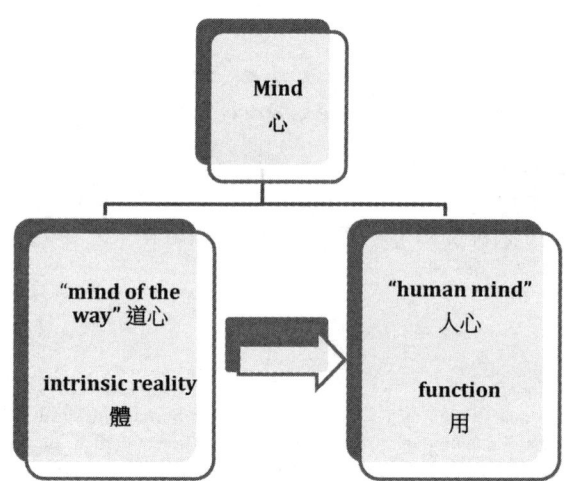

FIGURE 5.6 Zhu Xi's "Mind of the Way"-"Mind of Humans" Model
CREDIT: This diagram was created by John Makeham.

The intrinsic reality of the mind is suchness (*tathātā*), and suchness is reality as it is, without any conceptual overlay. Only ignorance prevents us from realizing the intrinsic reality of the mind. The distinction between awakening and nonawakening is a replication of the core thesis that the unconditioned—intrinsic reality, suchness—is not different from the conditioned and yet is not the same as the conditioned (*fei yi fei yi* 非一非異). This seemingly paradoxical formulation is used to convey the idea of immanent transcendence. Intriguingly, above we saw Zhu use this same idea to describe the relationship between the mind of the way and the mind of humans: "Even though the mind of humans is certainly different from the mind of way, nevertheless [the mind of humans and the mind of the way] cannot be regarded as two things nor sought in two different places."

There is only one mind but it has two aspects: discerning pattern or not discerning pattern. The mind of the way is replete with the myriad patterns, which are immediately accessible through their endowment as our human nature. The human mind, by contrast, is the failure to be aware of this. Correspondingly, in the *Dasheng qixin lun*, the gateway of the mind of arising and ceasing has two aspects: awakening and unawakening. And just as humans are inherently endowed with the mind of the way, even if they might fail to discern this, so too in the *Dasheng qixin lun*, sentient beings have never not been awoken—even if they might not realize this.

Above I argued that Zhu Xi's account of the relationship between "pattern and *qi*" and the *Dasheng qixin lun*'s account of the relationship between "the gateway of the mind as suchness, and the gateway of the mind as arising and ceasing" share a common structure. In both cases, the unconditioned (suchness, *tathāgatabarbha*, Taiji, Li, the "heaven-and-earth-bestowed nature" [天地之性], mind of the way) is somehow able to conjoin with the conditioned (the *ālayavijñāna*, qi, the psychophysical nature [氣質之性], mind of humans) yet simultaneously also extend beyond the conditioned; and the relation between the unconditioned and the conditioned is expressed in terms of the *ti-yong* polarity. I would further argue that the real significance of the intriguing isomorphism between Zhu's "mind of the way"-"mind of humans" distinction, and the *Dasheng qixin lun*'s "awakening mind"-"nonawakening mind" distinction, is that it replicates the common conceptual structure described in the previous sentence. This replication diminishes the possibility that this isomorphism is merely contingent.

5.4 Concluding Remarks

As with his Learning of the Way predecessors,[152] Zhu Xi was firmly committed to the belief that the cosmos is intrinsically morally-inflected,

---

[152] See the Introduction.

as evidenced by normative pattern (*yili* 義理, *tianli* 天理). The *Book of Change*, in particular, provided Song thinkers with much of the requisite metaphysical vocabulary and key cosmological models to secure new cosmological foundations and premises for moral philosophy, in response to the sustained stimulus of Buddhist philosophy, in particular. Despite this, the *Book of Change* provides a less than consoling rationale for why there should be badness at all. In stark contrast, Sinitic Buddhists had developed a sophisticated repository of resources to respond to this issue. By the Southern Song, these resources had become part of the intellectual heritage of Chinese literati, even if they were criticized by some as heterodox teachings. Ideas trump ideologies.

Zhu Xi addressed the issue of the origin of badness in order to provide a metaphysical defense of the inherent goodness of *xing* 性, a view consistent with a morally-inflected universe. To this end, he appropriated Zhou Dunyi's Taiji Diagram and its accompanying essay so as to provide a metaphysical framework to ground his concept of *xing*. It was in this connection that he developed his particular understanding of the relationship between *li* 理 and *qi* 氣. Zhu's understanding of the *li-qi* relationship is a further articulation of the rich and complex family of discourse that developed in the Tang and Northern Song about Li and phenomena. At the heart of this discourse is the attempt to reconcile the origin of badness with a monistic ontology, according to which the origin or cause of moral badness is to be explained as internal to or dependent on one fundamental basis. Zhu provided a new solution to the problem of how badness is possible, which avoided the radical proposals entailed in Buddhist attempts to deal with the issue for over half a millennium. Zhu's solution was to develop a monistic ontology in which the conditions that make badness possible are not associated with pattern but rather are associated with *qi*, but with the crucial stipulation that there can be no pattern without *qi*. Zhu's position draws on and extends styles of reasoning developed over centuries of Sinitic Buddhist discourse in response to the One Mind Two Gateways paradigm of the *Dasheng qixin lun*. In doing so, he also developed a view of immanent transcendence that sublates the two seemingly irreconcilable views animating key aspects of that discourse: the transcendence of exclusive non-dualism and the immanence of inclusive non-dualism.[153]

---

[153] In my essay, "Chinese Philosophy's Hybrid Identity," in *Why Traditional Chinese Philosophy Still Matters: The Relevance of Ancient Wisdom to the Global Age*, ed. Ming Dong Gu (London: Routledge, 2018), I argue Zhu Xi's "Taiji—pattern—*qi*" and the *Dasheng qixin lun*'s

Yet, even if we accept the premises Zhu was working with, is his solution to the problem of the origin of badness satisfactory? Does the mutual entailment of Zhu's *li-qi* monism, which provides that monism with a robust theoretical underpinning, also prove to be its Achilles' heel? Specifically, was his solution to the problem of the origin of badness secured at the expense of paying a costly theoretical price—that of having to accept a degree of moral determinism? Below, I will argue that it was not.[154]

Although, as we have seem, Zhu frequently cites Cheng Yi's dictum, "To discuss the nature without discussing *qi* is to be deficient; to discuss *qi* without discussing the nature is to be ignorant,"[155] his primary concern is with the first half of the dictum. For Zhu Xi, because Mencius lacked the concept of a psychophysical nature—crucial to which is the role of *qi*—he therefore failed to develop an account of the origin of badness.[156] Zhu's appeal to Cheng Yi, however, was more rhetorical than substantive in its import. Cheng Yi is able to deal with the origin of moral badness by presenting the relationship between pattern and *qi* as a dualism, in which the nature is inherently good and consists solely of pattern, and badness is associated solely with *qi*. For Cheng Yi, the psychophysical nature is not a fusion of *li* and *qi*:

> Someone asked, "If human nature is inherently bright, why is there delusion?"
>
> [Cheng Yi] replied, " . . . The nature is without badness; it is in the raw material (*cai* 才) that there is badness. The nature is nothing other than

---

"One Mind—the gateway of the mind as suchness—the gateway of the mind as arising and ceasing" should be understood as a homology. Unlike analogous structures, which are functionally similar but share no common ancestral character, homologous structures are modified descendants of a common ancestor. In that essay, I further argue that the "ancestor" component of this homology is a particular conception of the *ti-yong* polarity: one used to convey the relationship of the unconditioned to the conditioned as one of immanent transcendence. I conclude that this ancestor can be traced to developments in Southern Chinese Buddhist circles during the latter half of the fifth century.

[154] I do, however, note that despite being able to provide a new explanation for the origin of badness using his account of *li-qi* polar monism, Zhu did not explain why the conditions that make badness possible are associated exclusively with *qi* and not with *li*/Taiji. Zhu's polar monism explains how badness is able to occur in the phenomenal realm, the realm of human existence (*xing er xia* 形而下) due to *qi*, but does not explain why the ontological realm (*xing er shang* 形而上) of *li* or Taiji should have no role to play in the origin of badness. This presents a theoretical lacuna or deficiency in Zhu's account of the origin of badness. In a forthcoming essay, "Xiong Shili on the Nature, the Mind and the Origin of Badness as Evidenced in *Ming xin pian* 明心篇 (Explaining the Mind)," *Frontiers of Philosophy in China* 13.1 (2018), I argue that nearly seven centuries later, New Confucian philosopher Xiong Shili 熊十力 (1885–1968) was able to avoid the sort of theoretical deficiency evident in Zhu's account.

[155] Cheng Hao and Cheng Yi, *Er Cheng ji, Yi shu*, 81.

[156] See, for example, *Zhuzi yulei, juan* 4, 65, 70.

pattern, and from Yao and Shun to the person on the street, pattern is the same. Raw material is endowed in *qi*, and there is both pure and turbid *qi*. Those endowed with pure *qi* become worthies while those endowed with turbid *qi* become good-for-nothings."

問:「人性本明,因何有蔽?」曰:「...性無不善,而有不善者才也。性即是理,理則自堯、舜至於塗人,一也。才稟於氣,氣有清濁。稟其清者為賢,稟其濁者為愚。」157

[Someone asked,] "Are 'the innate is what is meant by the nature' and 'what is ordained by heaven is what is meant by the nature' the same?"

[Cheng Yi replied,] "The word 'nature' cannot be used with a single reference. 'The innate is what is meant by the nature' explains only what has been endowed [in *qi*]. 'What is ordained by heaven is what is meant by the nature' refers to patterns of the nature. Now, when people say that someone's nature is soft and slow, or tough and intense, these are all innate qualities and explain what has been endowed [in *qi*]. As for patterns of the nature, all are good. 'Heaven' means patterns as they inherently are."

「『生之謂性』與『天命之謂性』,同乎?」「性字不可一概論。『生之謂性』止訓所稟受也。『天命之謂性』,此言性之理也。今人言天性柔緩,天性剛急,俗言天成,皆生來如此,此訓所稟受也。若性之理也則無不善,曰天者,自然之理也。」158

Cheng Yi's solution to the problem of badness was not an option for Zhu Xi, given his monism. Although Zhu did appeal to naturalistic factors such as *ming* 命 to explain how individual endowments of *qi* (*qibing* 氣稟) account for differences in fortune, social rank, longevity, health and so forth,[159] such an appeal should have no purchase when it comes to matters concerning moral badness. Given the essential role that *qi* plays in the constitution of the mind, if moral badness were, even in part, to be determined by one's innate allotment of *qi*, would this not entail some kind of determinism that limits one's capacity to exercise control over moral decision-making?

Zhu was obviously aware of this, hence the attention he paid to the distinction between the mind of the way and the human mind. As passages such as the following make clear, however, a degree of slippage seems to

---

[157] Cheng Hao and Cheng Yi, *Er Cheng ji, Yi shu*, 18.
[158] Cheng Hao and Cheng Yi, *Er Cheng ji, Yi shu*, p. 313.
[159] See, for example, *Zhuzi yulei, juan* 4, p. 79.

appear when the focus shifts to the consequences of the human mind's being *qi* constituted:

> [Someone] asked: "The mind is something replete with the myriad patterns. The goodness that is developed certainly comes from the mind. As for all the badness that is developed, this is due to the *qi*-endowment and the selfishness that arises from the desires [stirred up] by things. Do these also come from the mind?"
>
> [Zhu] replied: "They are certainly not the intrinsic reality of the mind but they do also come from the mind."
>
> [This person] further asked: "Is this what is called the mind of humans?"
>
> [Zhu] replied: "Yes."
>
> Zisheng took the opportunity to ask: "Does the mind of humans also have both good and bad?"
>
> [Zhu] replied: "Yes."

> 問:「心之為物,眾理具足。所發之善,固出於心。至所發不善,皆氣稟物欲之私,亦出於心否?」曰:「固非心之本體,然亦是出於心也。」又問:「此所謂人心否?」曰:「是。」子升因問:「人心亦兼善惡否?」曰:「亦兼說。」[160]

> Someone asked: "Does the mind have goodness and badness?"
>
> [Zhu] replied: "As something active, of course the mind has goodness and badness. For example, compassion is goodness. If one saw a child about to fall into a well and had no mind of compassion, this would be badness. Absent goodness then it is badness. However, the intrinsic reality of the mind is never not good. By the same token, it cannot be said that badness has nothing at all to do with the mind. If not for the mind, how could it come about?"

> 或問:「心有善惡否?」曰:「心是動底物事,自然有善惡。且如惻隱是善也,見孺子入井而無惻隱之心,便是惡矣。離著善,便是惡。然心之本體未嘗不善,又卻不可說惡全不是心。若不是心,是甚麼做出來?」[161]

For Zhu, it is the mind that enables individuals to transform and purify their innate endowment of *qi* and so advance towards moral perfection. Is this vision compromised by the fact that the mind is *qi* constituted? Given

---

[160] *Zhuzi yulei*, juan 5, 86.
[161] *Zhuzi yulei*, juan 5, 86.

that the *qi* constitution of human beings renders them subject to the blind, natural determinism that results in individual differences in fortune, social rank, longevity, health, and so forth, does this same *qi* constitution similarly determine limits on the mind's cognitive, affective, and volitional awareness and hence its capacity to exercise appropriate control over its moral decision-making?[162]

I am not convinced that it does. Even though Zhu does not explicitly demonstrate why *qi* will *not* determine limits for the minds' capacity to be aware and to perceive—despite proclaiming that *qi* can determine fortune, social rank, and so forth—the charitable interpretation suggests his default position is that the mind's *qi* constitution will have a *constraining* effect on one's awareness/perception, rather than a determining effect. This does not, of course, mean that all people at all times are able to realize this capacity or are able to exercise it with the same facility. Importantly, however, over time and through practice, everyone has countless opportunities to learn how to develop and to apply this innate capacity[163]—hence the prominent role he accords to "investigating things" (*gewu* 格物) and "extending knowing" (*zhizhi* 致知), as well as his common refrain to "get it from/by/within oneself" (*zide* 自得).

Zhu developed the "mind of the way"-"human mind" distinction to avert moral determinism. After describing the dangers of not properly distinguishing the mind of the way and the human mind in his preface to *Zhongyong*, Zhu writes:

> By being meticulous in distinguishing them, they will not be intermixed (*za* 雜); by being focused, one will uphold the impartiality of one's inherent mind and not depart from it (*li* 離). Should one unceasingly apply oneself to this task, making sure that the mind of the way is constantly the ruler of one's body, and that the human mind always obeys its commands, then the precarious will become stable and the subtle will become manifest, such

---

[162] For a prosecution of the affirmative case for this line of argument, see Li Minghui 李明輝, "Zhuzi lun e de genyuan" 朱子論惡之根源 (The Roots of Zhu's Account of Badness), in *Guoji Zhuzixue huiyi lunwenji* 國際朱子學會議論文集 (Essays from the International Conference on Zhu Xi Studies), ed. Zhong Caijun 鍾彩鈞, 2 vols. (Zhonggyang yanjiuyuan Zhongguo wenzhe yanjiusuo choubeichu: Taipei, 1993), 551–589. I think Li downplays the role of the mind of the way. I am grateful to Professor Huang Yong 黃勇 for alerting me to this essay and also for generously providing a copy.

[163] For an instructive account of this sort of cultivation in relation to the development of character, see Joel J. Kupperman, *Character* (New York: Oxford University Press, 1991), especially chaps. 3 and 4. I am grateful to Steve Angle for referring me to this volume and also for challenging some of my earlier, more hastily conceived, assumptions.

that when active and at rest, in words and deeds, as a matter of course one will err neither in excess nor in deficiency.

精則察夫二者之間而不雜也，一則守其本心之正而不離也。從事於斯，無少閒斷，必使道心常為一身之主，而人心每聽命焉，則危者安、微者著，而動靜云為自無過不及之差矣。[164]

Although Zhu's prescription is abstract, elsewhere he provides a range of concrete examples to underscore that the opportunities to realize this goal are presented with ample frequency in the course of everyday life. Thus, whereas the desire to eat when hungry, or to wear more clothes when cold, is an expression of the human mind, determining under what conditions it is appropriate to do so,[165] is an expression of the mind of the way.[166]

Zhu's comment about the mind of the way and the human mind not being intermixed (*za* 雜), and not departing from (*li* 離) from one's inherent mind (= mind of the way), is significant.[167] It will be noted that the paired use of the terms "intermixed" (*za* 雜) and "depart from" (*li* 離) is a formula Zhu deploys in a variety of other passages, such as the following two already cited above:

> Although [Taiji] is the intrinsic reality by means of which there is *yang* in movement and *yin* in stillness, it is not possible for it to be separate from *yin* and *yang*. It is precisely in *yin* and *yang* that their intrinsic reality is pointed to. That is to say, their intrinsic reality is not intermixed with *yin* and *yang*.
>
> 所以動而陽、靜而陰之本體，然非有以離乎陰陽也。即陰陽而指其本體。不雜乎陰陽而為言耳。
>
> The nature as intrinsic reality [= the heaven-and-earth bestowed nature] is, however, never intermixed [with the psychophysical]. The key thing for people to understand here is that even though the nature as intrinsic reality

---

[164] *Sishu zhangju jizhu*, 14.
[165] Such as if the food or clothing is stolen, or someone else has a more urgent need for food or warmth, or if decorum warrants abstention, and so on.
[166] For example, *Zhuzi yulei*, juan 62, 1488; juan 78, 2011.
[167] Elsewhere he similarly writes: "The aim of being meticulous is so that [the human mind and the mind of the way] are not intermixed [and so confused with one another]; and the aim of being focused is so that [the mind of the way] is not departed from" (「惟精」是要別得不雜，「惟一」是要守得不離。) *Zhuzi yulei*, juan 78, 2013. I find no compelling textual evidence to dissuade me from the view that for Zhu Xi, *daoxin* and *benxin* are the same. The association provides a way to draw implicitly on Mencius' characterization of *benxin* and so bolster Zhu's characterization of *daoxin* in terms of innate moral purity.

is never apart from the [psychophysical] nature, it is never intermixed [with the psychophysical].

然性之本體，亦未嘗雜。要人就此上面見得其本體元未嘗離，亦未嘗雜耳。

In these passages, the mind of the way and the human mind; Taiji and *yin-yang*; and the heaven-and-earth bestowed nature and the psychophysical nature are each presented in a relationship of immanent transcendence of the *ti-yong* type. Each pair is used to affirm a consistent response to the following problem: "How can the unconditioned (the mind of the way, Taiji, the heaven-and-earth bestowed nature) be realized if our cognitive awareness is circumscribed by the conditioned nature of human existence?" Zhu's constant refrain that the unconditioned is never apart from the conditioned yet its unconditioned nature is not in any way compromised by that relationship, bears a distinct family resemblance to a cognate formulation in the *Dasheng qixin lun*, where the ocean water is never separated from the wind, but whether the wind blows or not, the wet nature of the water remains unchanged. For both Zhu Xi and the author of the *Dasheng qixin lun*, the key point is that the conditioned nature of human existence alone is the ground for practice and the locus for realizing the true nature of things. Because the unconditioned is never separate from conditioned existence, the promise is that one is always able to "get it from/by/within oneself," even though the conditions affecting individuals will vary.[168] As the *Dasheng qixin lun* insists, ignorance does not preclude awakening—rather it is the very condition for its possibility.

This chapter has argued that the *Dasheng qixin lun*'s One Mind Two Gateways paradigm was fundamental to Zhu Xi's metaphysics. Whether Zhu's understanding of "pattern" and "*qi*" and the *Dasheng qixin lun*'s account of "the gateway of the mind as suchness" and "the gateway of the mind as arising and ceasing" are not only isomorphic but can also be linked to more specific agencies of influence and appropriation is beyond the scope of this chapter. Of greater significance to our understanding of Zhu Xi's thought is that the research introduced in this chapter reveals the vital role that Buddhist resources played in Zhu Xi's philosophical repertoire.

---

[168] For Zhu Xi, the role of learning and the will play a key role here. See Huang Yong's discussion in "Evil in Neo-Confucianism," in *The History of Evil in the Medieval Age (450–1450)*, ed. Andrew Pinsent, vol. 2 of *The History Evil*, 6 volumes, eds. Charles Taliaferro and Chad Meister (forthcoming).